FBI Files on the LINDBERGH BABY KIDNAPPING

New Century Books

FBI Files on the LINDBERGH BABY KIDNAPPING

Thomas Fensch

Copyright © 2001 by Thomas Fensch.

Library of Congress Number: 2001116478
ISBN #:   Hardcover   0-930751-15-9
                 Softcover   0-930751-16-7

All photographs courtesy of the New Jersey State Police Museum.

Front cover: Bruno Richard Hauptmann, convicted of the kidnapping of Charles Lindbergh Jr.

All rights reserved. No part of this book may be reproduced or transmitted in any form or by any means, electronic or mechanical, including photocopying, recording, or by any information storage and retrieval system, without permission in writing from the copyright owner.

This book was printed in the United States of America.

New Century Books
P.O. Box 7113
The Woodlands, Texas, 77387-7113

Volumes in the Top Secret series by New Century Books:

World War Two:
U.S. Military Plans for the Invasion of Japan

The FBI Files on Elvis Presley

The Vietnam War:
Confidential Files on the Siege and Loss of Khe Sanh

CONTENTS

Introduction

The FBI Files:
The Kidnapping and Murder of Charles A. Lindbergh, Jr.

Index

New Jersey State Police photographs

The FBI Files:
The Arrest of Bruno Richard Hauptmann

Annotated Bibliography

Appendix

About the Editor

INTRODUCTION

Philip Graham, the late publisher of *The Washington Post* once said that daily journalism is "the first rough draft of history." He was not wrong; his own paper, *The Washington Post* and other newspapers, such as *The New York Times* offer major analyses and in-depth coverage of the issues of our day, which do, in turn, become "the first rough draft of history."

Yet there are other documents which are equally, "the first rough draft of history." They are formerly secret government documents, now de-classified and made available to the public.

The books in the Top Secret series published by New Century Books are such documents.

This volume, The FBI Files on the Lindbergh Baby Kidnaping is now the largest original record extant on the kidnaping of Charles Augustus Lindbergh Jr., the first son of aviator Charles Lindbergh.

The historic New York-to-Paris flight of Charles Lindbergh, which began at 7:51 a.m., May 20, 1927 near New York City, ended 33 and one-half hours later, at the Le Bourget airfield near Paris.

Charles Lindbergh had flown into immortality. And his flight galvanized the western world; he became an international celebrity. His life forever changed, in ways that few others have ever experienced since his time. As A. Scott Berg wrote, in *Lindbergh:*

Reporters stalked him constantly—almost fatally on several occasions—making him their first human quarry, stripping him of his rights to privacy as no public figure had ever been before. Over the century, others would reach this new stratum of celebrity.

The unwanted fame all but guaranteed an isolated adulthood. And, indeed, Lindbergh spent the rest of his life in flight, searching for islands of tranquility. Early on, he was lucky enough to meet Anne Morrow, Ambassador Dwight Morrow's shy daughter, who craved solitude as much as he did. They fell in love and married. Their "storybook romance," as the press always presented it, was, in fact, a complex case history of control and repression, filled with joy and passion and grief and rage. He scourged his wife into becoming an independent woman; and, in so doing, he helped create an important feminist voice—a popular diarist who also wrote one of the most beloved volumes of the century, and another that was one of the most despised.

The Lindberghs' love story had a tragic second act. His fame and wealth cost them their firstborn child. Under melodramatic conditions, Lindbergh authorized payment of a large ransom to a mysterious man in a graveyard; but he did not get his son in return. The subsequent investigation of the kidnaping uncovered only circumstantial evidence; and the man accused of killing "the Lindbergh Baby" never confessed—thus condemning the "Crime of the Century" to eternal debate. Because the victim's father was so celebrated, the case entered the annals of history, and laws were changed in Lindbergh's name. The media circus that accompanied what veteran court-watchers still refer to as the "Trial of the Century" forever affected trial coverage in the United States. The subsequent flood of sympathy for Lindbergh only enhanced his public profile, making him further prey for the media as well as other criminals and maniacs. In fear and disgust, he moved to Europe, where for a time he became one of America's most effective unofficial ambassadors. (pp. 7)

Charles Lindbergh and Anne Morrow were married May 27, 1929, in her family home in Englewood, New Jersey. As in every aspect of his life since his flight to Paris, Lindbergh—and the Morrow family—had to fight to keep his engagement and marriage secret from the press and the nation. Their honeymoon was planned ahead of time and was also secret. The press assumed that the newlywed Lindberghs would honeymoon via air; Charles and Anne managed a relatively quiet honeymoon via a yacht.

Charles Augustus Lindbergh Jr., their first son was born June 22, 1930, on his Mother's 24th birthday. The Lindberghs, fighting for their privacy, eventually found 425 acres for sale 10 miles north of Princeton, New Jersey. They eventually settled there and the property even had enough room for a landing field for Lindbergh's aircraft. It was there he taught Anne how to fly. The baby grew to be a charming, golden-haired child.

And then Charles Augustus Lindbergh Jr. was kidnaped.

Sometime in the night of March 1, 1932, someone leaned a ladder outside the Lindbergh home, climbed into the baby's second-floor bedroom and kidnaped the child. The Chronology in the first report offers a minute-by-minute resume of that day; investigations were immediately begun by local authorities, the New Jersey State Police and other government agencies.

Instrumental in the search, and a man Charles Lindbergh trusted, was H. Norman Schwarzkopf, Chief of the New Jersey State Police. Over 50 years later, his son, General Norman ("Stormin' Norman") Schwarzkopf, would distinguish himself as commander of the allied forces in Desert Storm, the Persian Gulf war, from Jan. 17, 1991 to March 3, 1991.

The kidnaping aroused as much anguish to the western world as Lindbergh's flight had generated euphoria; investigations dragged on for months with few solid leads and many, many false trails. Malcontents and outright lunatics claimed knowledge of the kidnaping; police had no real suspects, although go-betweens met with the alleged kidnapers to arrange ransom payments.

One of the most ingenious aspects of the case was the work of Arthur Koehler, who offered his services to the case. Koehler was a wood grain and fiber expert; there were no fingerprints on the ladder the kidnapers used to climb into the baby's window, but Koehler took samples of the wood and assured authorities that he could track down the origin of the ladder.

Koehler investigated 1,600 lumber wholesalers before establishing that the last dealer who sold the wood was the National Lumber and Millwork Company in the Bronx, New York. That lumberyard was the closest yard to the home of Bruno Richard Hauptmann. Authorities wouldn't arrest Hauptmann for a full year after Koehler found the National Lumber and Millwork Company.

Bruno Richard Hauptmann was finally arrested for the kidnaping after he bragged that he had some one hundred dollar gold certificates—money which was used to pay the ransom.

After he was arrested, much of the ransom money was found in or near his apartment; his handwriting matched the ransom note, in style, spelling and script; he knew the names of the go-betweens in the ransom and recovery attempts and, most telling, Arthur Koehler found that sections of the kidnap ladder matched perfectly sections of wood in Hauptmann's attic.

Bruno Richard Hauptmann was such a secretive person that his own wife didn't know his first name was Bruno until the middle of his trial for kidnaping.

Eventually the Lindbergh baby was found dead, in a make-shift grave only four miles from the Lindbergh home. Authorities believe that Hauptmann was able to climb his self-made ladder into the baby's bedroom, but the increased weight of Hauptmann climbing down with the baby apparently caused the ladder to break. The baby presumably fell from Hauptmann's arms and probably died when he hit the ground.

The trial of Bruno Richard Hauptmann was the biggest media circus in America until the O.J. Simpson trial Jan. 24, 1995 to Oct. 3, 1995.

Hauptmann's trial began Jan. 2, 1935, in Flemington, New Jersey. He was represented by Edward J. Reilly, who, unknown to neither Hauptmann nor his family, was alcoholic and had syphilis.

The trial flooded Flemington with media stars, such as Walter Winchell, Damon Runyon, Dorothy Kilgallen, Arthur Brisbane, of *The New York Times*, Adela Rogers St. John, chief reporter for the Hearst newspapers, and many others. All major media organizations were represented; the Associated Press had four teletype lines leading away from the courthouse and estimates were that well over four million words poured forth about the trial daily. Movies were even filmed inside the courtroom briefly until the judge, Thomas W. Trenchard discovered it and banished cameras from the courtroom. Over sixty years later, cameras are still banned from major courtrooms throughout the country.

Bruno Richard Hauptmann was never really able to explain away why he had much of the Lindbergh baby ransom money—in traceable gold certificates, nor why he knew the names of the random go-betweens or why the wood from the ladder matched the wood in his attic.

Charles Lindbergh announced from the witness chair that he recognized Hauptmann's voice as being that of a mysterious man who early met him and a go-between in a dark cemetery and demanded the ransom money. For many, when Lindbergh identified Hauptmann clearly and unequivocally, the trial was over. Hauptmann was guilty.

Bruno Richard Hauptmann died in the electric chair April 3, 1936, in the New Jersey State prison in Trenton, New Jersey.

He never confessed to the crime.

To this day, the Lindbergh baby kidnaping case remains one of the most fascinating cases in the country. Did someone else kidnap the Lindbergh baby? Or did Hauptmann have accomplices? Did he build the ladder himself? Did he drop the baby when he was climbing down the ladder? Was the trial fair? Would Hauptmann's fate been different if he hadn't been represented by Reilly? These questions will remain forever unanswered.

The significance of the following volume is simply this: this is *history laid bare*. These pages are mesmerizing and have the quality of the most dramatic nonfiction.

In fact, the second major report, the arrest of Bruno Richard Hauptmann end with the word PENDING as the case was still in progress. This is time figuratively stopped in 1934.

In the case of many formerly secret government files, words, sentences, paragraphs and whole pages of have been *redacted*, blacked-out, edited prior to release as public documents. In the case of these two major FBI reports, no such redactions appear. The reports, however, have been photocopied from the original pages in FBI files, then retyped for publication via electronic book production by computer. While every effort has been made to guarantee the accuracy of these pages, some are faint and numbers, especially, cannot be guaranteed. The only major change we have made was to omit the Index for the major FBI file, the Kidnaping of Charles A. Lindbergh Jr. as the pagination for this book has changed. We have added a new Index, based on these pages. The original FBI file on the Arrest of Bruno Richard Hauptmann contained no Index.

Samples of the pages appear in the Appendix.

Variations in spellings in the original have been retained.

In the words of Philip Graham, these files are surely "the first rough draft of history."

—Thomas Fensch

THE FBI FILES:
*The Kidnaping
and Murder of
Charles A. Lindbergh Jr.*

DIVISION OF INVESTIGATION

This case originated at NEW YORK, N.Y. N.Y. File No. 62-3057

Report made at NEW YORK CITY. Date when made 2/16/34. Report made by T.H. SISK
Period for which made March 1, 1932—February 1, 1934.

Title: Character of case:
   UNKNOWN PERSONS
   KIDNAPPING AND MURDER OF
      CHARLES A. LINDBERGH, JR.

Summary Report

This report was prepared jointly by Special Agents W. F. Seery, J. E. Seykore, T. H. Sisk and former Special Agent J. J. Manning.

It represents a compilation of all material information presently contained in the files of the New York Office. This information has been drawn from numerous sources including investigations conducted by the Division, by other authorities and, in some instances, where no other information was available, from published accounts, the purpose of the report being to present as complete a picture as possible on the basis of available information. All uncompleted matters mentioned in the report are receiving the further attention of this office. Other field offices of the Division will later be advised specifically of leads requiring attention in their respective districts.

The Division has designed "CALNAP" as the code word to be used in referring to this investigation in telegrams.

Approved and Forwarded

F. X. Fay, SAC

Copies of this report furnished to:
3 Division
4 New York

SUMMARY REPORT
In reply to: Unknown Subjects

Kidnaping and Murder of Charles A. Lindbergh, Jr. (N.Y. File 62-3057).

New York, N. Y., February 16, 1934.

Contacts

PREFACE

CHRONOLOGY

NARRATIVE

LINDBERGH HOME (LOCALITY AND DESCRIPTION)

LINDBERGH HOUSEHOLD AND EMPLOYEES:

Charles A. Lindbergh, Jr.
Aloysius Whately
Mrs. Aloysius Whately
Betty Gow
Dog (Trixie)
Betty Sheetz
Marie Cummings

MORROW HOUSEHOLD:
Morrow Family
Violet Sharpe (Mrs. George Payne)
Edna Sharpe
Septimus Banks
Charles Henry Ellerson
Mrs. Johannes Junge
John Saunders
Arthur Springer
Mrs. Roderick Cecil Henry Grime Graeme

PHYSICAL EVIDENCE:
Ladder
Chisel
Footprints
Fingerprints
Discovery of body of Charles A. Lindbergh, Jr.

CIRCUMSTANTIAL INFORMATION:
Questionable automobiles and persons observed
Stolen Automobiles
Local Cabins
Curtains and telephone lines
Men employed in construction of Lindbergh home
Search of roads and countryside
Babies mistakenly reported as Lindbergh child

FBI FILES ON THE LINDBERGH BABY KIDNAPPING

RANSOM NOTES

INTERMEDIARIES:
   Morris Rosner, Salvatore Spitale, Irving Bitz, et al
   Dr. John F. (Jafsie") Condon

RANSOM MONEY

SUBJECTS AND SUSPECTS:
   Unknown Person No. 1—"Man with ladder"
   Unknown Person No. 2—"John" (received ransom)
   Unknown Person No. 3—Suspect "lookout" at Woodlawn Cemetery
   Unknown Person No. 4—Suspect "lookout" at St. Raymonds Cemetery
   Unknown Person No. 5—alias "J. J. Faulkner, 537 W. 149th Street" (passed $2980 ransom gold certificates)
   Al Capone, Torrio, Nash, Bailey, Barry, Conroy, et al
   Purple Gang—Harry Fleisher, et al
   Finn Hendrik Johnson alias "Red" Johnson
   Peter J. Berritella, et al
   Enrico Gerardi, et al
   Jack Bennet, et al
   John Gorch and Walter Gray
   Gerald Bucholz
   John J. Baumeister
   Arthur Barry
   Lewis V. Cummings
   Nick DeAugustine, et al
   Sam Goldberg alias "Sam the Gas Man"
   Harry Meyers, et al
   William Patrick "Squawk" Reilly, et al
   Reo Verne Sankey, et al
   Garrett Schenck
   Charles W. Sellick, et al

Waslove Simek
Dean Preston Sutherland, with aliases
Unknown Suspect (Isadoro Ubaldi, informant)
J. Floyd Williams, et al

FRAUDS, HOAXES AND UNFOUNDED INFORMATION
John Hughes Curtis, et al
Arthur L. Hitner
Gaston B. Means, et al
James Oscar Farrell alias Jack Farrell
Miss Betty Jane Guthrie, re R.F.D. Lemon with aliases

INDEX

SUMMARY REPORT

In reply to: Unknown Subjects

Kidnaping and Murder of Charles A. Lindbergh, Jr. (N.Y. File 62-3057).

PREFACE

PREFACE

This is a joint report of Special Agents W.F. Seery, J.E. Sykora, T.H. Sisk, and former Special Agent J.J. Manning.

The prosecutive and investigative jurisdiction in this case lies primarily with Hunterdon and/or Mercer Counties, New Jersey, for the kidnaping and murder, and Bronx County, New York City, for the extortion of $50,000. ransom.

Colonel H. Norman Schwarzkopf, superintendent of the New Jersey State Police, has been in charge of the investigation for the State of New Jersey from the beginning. All original evidence is in his possession. During various periods, representatives of the Newark and Jersey City Police Departments worked on the investigation under the direction of Colonel Schwarzkopf to whose command they were assigned for that purpose.

The Police Department of New York City has conducted an independent investigation, in cooperation with other authorities, however, relative to the payment of the ransom and the subsequent passage of some of the currency in New York City.

The Federal government also has some jurisdiction in the matter, although to a much lesser degree, in relation to the misuse of the mails and the failure to pay income tax on the ransom money. As will be noted, however, the extent of the cooperation of the Federal Government with the State authorities has not in any way been restricted to the degree of its legal jurisdiction.

On March 2, 1932, the facilities and resources of the Division of Investigation were made available to the New Jersey State Police and the Police Department of New York City, and other State authorities. Thereafter the Division conducted numerous and extensive investigations as hereinafter indicated, reports of which were transmitted to the

New Jersey State Police. At no time, however, has the Division assumed co-jurisdictional authority with the New Jersey State Police. It has served as an auxiliary investigative service but has not been informed either in whole or in part of the scope or developments and results of the investigation conducted by the New Jersey State Police.

Shortly after the kidnaping occurred, an investigation was conducted by Immigration Inspectors of the U.S. Department of Labor relative to aliens residing in Hopewell, N.J. and vicinity. A copy of the report of this investigation was not available during the preparation of this report.

From March 18, 1932 until October 14, 1933, one or more representatives of the Intelligence Unit, Treasury Department, have been practically continuously assigned to this investigation working in very close association with the New Jersey State Police. Covering their investigation, the report of Special Agent Frank J. Wilson, Intelligence Unit, dated November 11, 1933, was received by the Division on November 15, 1933.

Extensive services in the investigation were also rendered by other government agencies including the United States Bureau of Standards, Department of Agriculture; Post Office Inspectors; Commissioner of Immigration, New York City; United States Coast Guard; State Department; Treasury Department and the Federal Reserve Bank in New York City.

The following is a chronological resume of the conduct of the investigation as pertaining to the Division:

On March 1, 1932, jurisdiction and responsibility for the investigation were assumed by New Jersey State Police.

On March 2, 1932, the facilities and resources of Division of Investigation made available to New Jersey State Police and Police Department, New York City.

ON March 5, 1932, a general police conference called

at Trenton, N.J. by Governor Moore, was attended by representatives of principal police departments, prosecuting authorities, and government investigative agencies.

On April 3, 1932, following negotiations for, and payment of the ransom money, and other developments in which the Division did not participate, the Division's activities were confined to specific requests from the New Jersey State Police and to receiving information from informants and correspondents for transmittal to State Police. In some instances, however, investigative activities were undertaken by the Division in order that an appropriate interpretation of all the facts in connection with some particular load or angle might be available to the New Jersey State Police in a comprehensive report.

On May 13, 1932, Presidential instructions were issued in effect that all government investigative agencies place themselves at the disposal of the State of New Jersey and that this Division serve as a clearing house and coordinating agency for all investigative activities conducted by the Federal investigative units in this case.

On May 17, 1932, a conference at Trenton, N.J. was attended by officials of the New Jersey State Police, Jersey City Police, prosecuting authorities, Intelligence Unit, and this Division.

Assistant Director Harold Nathan informed the conference of the Presidential instructions and outlined in detail the services which the Division and other governmental agencies were equipped to render, also suggesting that inasmuch as the Division was to act as a clearing house for all other departments, the more complete its stock of authoritative information was, the more complete service it could render and that consequently the Division would be glad to receive a report from the New Jersey State Police on the case up to that time.

Colonel Schwarzkopf suggested the appointment of a

Board of Strategy to conduct the investigation under his direction, the membership of the board to consist of himself and other representatives of the New Jersey State Police; representatives of the Newark and Jersey City Police Departments, prosecuting authorities of Hunterdon and Mercer Counties and the State of New Jersey, and representatives of the Intelligence Unit, and of this Division. Following this conference Special Agent in Charge F.X. Fay represented the Division as its liaison with the New Jersey State Police and remained at Trenton and Hopewell as long as appeared necessary.

On the following day, at a conference between interested government investigative agencies at Washington, D.C., the policy was adopted that actual direction of investigation was to continue in the hands of the New Jersey State authorities; that the Federal officials were to participate only to the extent of affording such assistance as might be required from time to time.

On July 21, 1933, the New York Office of the Division was instructed by the Director to procure all information available as to the status of the case with particular attention being given to the passage of the so-called ransom money and to effect arrangements so that the matter could be pursued without any investigative interruption. Pursuant to these instructions, information was procured from the Police Department of New York City covering all ransom money that had been discovered up to that time together with the results of the investigation thereof. Arrangements were effected so that investigation of all such ransom bills detected in the future would immediately be conducted jointly by a representative of the New Jersey State Police, the New York Police Department and this Division, which arrangement is in operation at the present time.

Under date of September 18, 1933, the Director brought

to the attention of the Superintendent of the New Jersey State Police that since the passage of the Federal Kidnaping Act in June 1932, the Division has exclusive jurisdiction for the Federal Government over all violations of that Act, in pursuance of which authority the Division has conducted many investigations since the enactment of that Act of kidnapers, extortioners, gangsters and racketeers; that much information concerning that particular group has been collected which so far as the Division knows has no connection directly or indirectly with the Lindbergh kidnaping case. Consequently the New Jersey State Police was invited to furnish the Division with a summary of the investigation made by the New Jersey State Police including the names of any persons suspected in connection with the case so that any circumstance or evidence discovered during the course of the Division's investigations which might check in any way with the circumstances or evidence present in the Lindbergh case, could be immediately made known to the New Jersey State Police. The information requested has not yet been received.

On October 19, 1933, it was officially announced that in order to coordinate all information and activities in the hands of the Federal government in connection with the investigation of the kidnaping of the Lindbergh baby, it had been decided with the approval of the Attorney General, that the Division of Investigation of the Department of Justice would henceforth have exclusive jurisdiction insofar as the Federal authorities are concerned in the handling of any investigative features of this case. Further, that the Division of Investigation would continue to cooperate with the New Jersey State authorities in this matter.

One of the by-products of the Lindbergh case was a mass of misinformation received from the well-meaning but uninformed, and a deluge of crank letters written by insane persons, nitwits, persons with a degraded sense of humor, and others with fraudulent intent.

Dr. Carl J. Warden, Professor of Psychology at Columbia University, regarding these letters, wrote "A great number of these letter writers are persons mentally unbalanced. They are border line case paranoiacs. By that I don't mean they are insane but they are filled with delusions of grandeur owing to the Lindbergh case. They believe that Lindbergh may send them an answer which they can show to their friends. It makes them look important. Some of the writers of these crank letters are monomaniacs, emotionally unbalanced. Some are evidently soaking publicity. If such letters could be stopped the real clue might be obtained."

Another writer states "The view that the crank letters were standing in the way of progress, by obstructing the mail and otherwise annoying everyone bent upon solving the crime was shared widely by educators; law makers; officials and other aids of the Lindberghs. Proposals went so far as to make 'crank letter writing' a crime thus establishing a hazard for the writers if they were located."

The unfortunate part of the matter is that in many cases, the crank letters could not immediately be distinguished beyond doubt from the important ones, with the result that much time has necessarily been wasted on false clues.

The Division has had its share of such investigations in this case and has also conducted numerous investigations of babies falsely reported to be the Lindbergh baby. It obviously would be impracticable to include such investigations in this report.

The New York Office of the Division has been designated the office of origin of this investigation, its files relating to the case have been sectionalized and there is maintained a full and complete card index of all names, organizations and other inferential data contained therein. It is, therefore, suggested that other Division offices before instituting any extensive investigation of information which appears to be unfounded, communicate with the New York office as such information may have already been investigated.

With reference to the taking up of currency used in payment of the ransom in this case, the Division has instructed that confidential blue slips may be used for the purpose of reimbursing the holders of any of these ransom bills, with an explanation as to what the expenditure represents. The bills as collected are to be maintained in a safe at the New York Office. The greatest of care should be exercised to see that these bills are maintained in safety and an accurate record kept concerning their serial numbers, and descriptions, as they will ultimately be returned to the United States Treasury.

As all offices have previously been advised, the Division has instructed that it be distinctly understood that no representative of the Division is to discuss with or give any information to the representatives of the press or any unauthorized person concerning any developments in the investigation of the Lindbergh kidnaping case; that any inquiry concerning this matter should be courteously referred to the headquarters of the Division at Washington.

Information will be submitted to the New Jersey State Police or other agencies only by the Division at Washington, D. C.

The field offices of the Division will be advised by letter as to undeveloped leads in their respective districts.

SUMMARY REPORT

In Re

Unknown Subjects

Kidnaping and Murder of Charles A. Lindbergh, Jr. (N.Y. File 62-3057).

CHRONOLOGY

CHRONOLOGY

Feb. 26, 1932—Colonel and Mrs. Lindbergh with Charles A., Jr., leave Englewood, N. J. to spend week-end at new home near Hopewell. Whately already there—Nurse Betty Gow left at Englewood.

Feb. 27,—Lindberghs and child at Hopewell.

Feb. 28,—Lindberghs and child at Hopewell.

Feb. 29,—9:00 A.M., Colonel Lindbergh leaves Hopewell and spends day in New York City. Sleeps this night at Englewood, Mrs. Lindbergh and child still at Hopewell.

March 1,—10:30 A.M., Mrs. Lindbergh extends usual week-end stay at Hopewell—telephones Morrow home and speaks to Violet Sharpe—leaves message for Nurse Betty Gow to proceed to Hopewell and advises family will remain at Hopewell due to baby's cold.

1 to 2:00 P.M., Betty Gow arrives in Morrow car driven by Chauffeur Ellerson.

5:00 P.M., Mrs. Lindbergh returns from walk. Nurse Gow sews flannel under shirt for baby to wear.

6:00 P.M., Sebastian B. Lupica observes man driving 1929 Dodge Sedan with ladders in it on highway near Lindbergh home.

7:30 P.M., Colonel Lindbergh telephones home—advises on way from New York. Mrs. Lindbergh and Nurse Gow prepare baby for bed.

8:00 P.M., Lindbergh baby asleep in nursery on second floor—last seen by Betty Gow. Colonel Breckinridge phones Lindbergh home relative to Colonel Lindbergh's absence from banquet.

8 to 10:00 P.M., Betty Gow in kitchen or west parlor on first floor. Whatelys in kitchen on first floor.

8:30 to 11:05 P.M., Violet Sharpe, Morrow waitress, with escort and another couple allegedly at "Peanut Grill" roadhouse in the Oranges, N. Y.

8:25 P.M., Lindbergh arrives home from New York in car alone—telephones New York explaining absence from New York University banquet engagement.

8:30—9:15 P.M., Dinner served to Lindberghs in dining room.

9:35 P.M., Henry "Red" Johnson telephones Betty Gow—informs her he is leaving for Hartford, Conn. And inquires about baby's health.

9:15—9:30 P.M. Lindberghs in parlor next to dining room.

9:45 P.M., Colonel and Mrs. Lindbergh hear noise apparently outside—resembling two boards striking—attribute it to natural causes.

9:50—10:00 P.M., Lindbergh in library under nursery.

10:00 P.M., Betty Gow discovers baby gone—informs Lindberghs. Colonel Lindbergh finds note on window sill of nursery demanding $50,000 ransom. Lindbergh and Whately search premises and immediate vicinity.

10:20 P.M., and shortly following, Lindbergh telephones Hopewell Deputy Police Chief Williamson, who calls for Chief Wolfe—they proceed to Lindbergh home—suggest notifying State Police.

Ladder and chisel apparently left by kidnapers found near house.

10:40 P.M., Lindbergh telephones New Jersey State Police Headquarters, Trenton—State Police assume charge of case.

10:50 P.M., News teletyped to police in New Jersey and neighboring states.

Traces of mud found on floor of nursery and footprints found on ground under nursery window.

12:00 P.M., No fingerprints found or developed, after expert search and examination.

March 2, 1932—Facilities and resources of Division of Investigation, United States Department of Justice, made available to New Jersey and New York authorities.

Colonel and Mrs. Lindbergh announce willingness to pay $50,000 ransom demanded in note left by kidnapers.

Morris Rosner contacts Colonel Breckinridge through Robert Thayer, attorney, associated with Colonel William J. Donovan, and proposed to contact underworld leaders.

Stolen Nash automobile abandoned by unknown person in front of 515 West 149th Street, New York City. (See reference to 537 West 149th Street on May 1, 1933 and August 20, 1933).

Extensive investigation instituted relative to Betty Gow and Henry ("Red") Johnson as well as other Morrow and Lindbergh servants and their connections.

Harold Fontaine alleged to have informed Robert J. Baird in Sandwich, Ontario Jail that Bill Bailey, Nash, Holden, Keating, et al, involved in kidnaping; subsequently investigated without material development.

Lindbergh designates Douglas G. Thomson, former Mayor of Englewood, and Arthur Springer, secretary of the late Dwight W. Morrow, to negotiate with the kidnapers. However, these men were never contacted by the kidnapers.

Investigation instituted relative to Charles Sellick, et al; upon conclusion developed no evidence of connection with Lindbergh case.

March 3,—Widespread radio appeal to kidnapers to start negotiations, pledging secrecy.

Henry ("Red") Johnson, sailor sweetheart of Betty Gow, arrested at Hartford, Conn.

Rosner given $2,500 by Colonel Breckinridge for purpose of contacting underworld leaders.

Rosner examines the original ransom note and is given copy of it made by Thayer.

Rosner contacts Owney Madden, racketeer.

March 4, 1932—Conference had between Colonel Lindbergh, Colonel Norman Schwarzkopf, Rosner, Thayer, et al, at Hopewell, N. J. Rosner given a clear untapped wire from Lindbergh house. Rosner indicates Madden has some definite information in regard to kidnapers.

Dudley Field Malone telephones that he had received a call from someone alleging to be the kidnaper. Malone visited by Colonel Breckinridge. No material developments.

Newspapers announce that Detroit Purple Gang sought by New Jersey State Police.

Gaston B. Means contacts Mrs. Evelyn Walsh McLean, Washington, D. C. informing her that he could secure return of the Lindbergh baby.

Investigation instituted relative to William P. "Squawk" Reilly (concluded without material result).

March 5, 1932—Second ransom note received by Colonel Lindbergh in envelope postmarked Brooklyn, N.Y. 9 P.M. March 4, 1932, mailed at Station near Borough Hall, Brooklyn, informing Colonel Lindbergh that he would have to take the consequences because of the publicity, and increasing the amount of ransom from $50,000 to $70,000.

General police conference at Trenton, N. J. by Governor Moore, attended by representatives of principal police departments; prosecuting authorities; and government investigative agencies.

Rosner reads second ransom note and proceeds to Malone's office to see Colonel Breckinridge. About midnight, Colonel Breckinridge and Rosner bring Salvatore Spitale and Irving Bitz, New York racketeers to Hopewell. "Owney" Madden telephones, is advised by Rosner of presence of Spitale and Bitz, Spitale talks with Madden. Spitale and Bitz named by Lindberghs to deal with underworld and act as intermediaries.

Informant at Detroit states certain members

of Purple Gang in New York at time of kidnaping.

Newspapers announce Betty Gow cleared of suspicion by New Jersey State Police.

March 6, 1932—Telegram received at Hopewell from Reverend Berritella instructing that he be communicated with regarding baby's whereabouts. Rosner telephones and invites Berritella to Hopewell. About 2 P.M. message received from Berritella then in Princeton, J. J. Colonel Breckinridge at Princeton interviews Peter J. Berritella and Mary Cirrito, who engage in spiritualistic séance relative to baby's whereabouts. (Developments indicate possible connection between Berritella, Mrs. Cirrito and kidnapers.)

Madden telephones Rosner apparently angry that Spitale and Bitz had been authorized to act as intermediaries, states he thinks kidnapers will be heard from the following Tuesday, March 8th.

Rosner privately informs Thayer that Galvin and Fogarty (investigators employed by Colonel Breckinridge) are in league with kidnapers, indicating to Thayer that Rosner is becoming mentally unbalanced or possibly has fraudulent intent.

March 7,—A prisoner, U. S. Penitentiary, Atlanta, (name on file Division and New York Office) furnishes statement alleging Al and Ralph Capone,

Holden, Keating, et al, planned some such move as the Lindbergh kidnaping for benefit of Al Capone.

Mrs. McLean delivers $100,000 as ransom money to Gaston B. Means on strength of his alleged contact with kidnapers.

March 8,—Third ransom note received postmarked New York City, Station "D" (132 Fourth Avenue) 1: P.M. March 7, 1932, addressed to Colonel Breckinridge, 25 Broadway, New York City, advising that the kidnapers would not accept any go-between appointed by the Lindberghs and that they would arrange this later, instructing that a short notice about the matter be inserted in the New York American. Advertisement inserted in the New York American by Colonel Lindbergh through Colonel Breckinridge as follows:
"Letter received at new address. Will follow your instructions. I also received letter mailed to me March 4 and was ready since then. Please hurry on account of mother. Address me to the address you mentioned in your letter. Father."

Dr. John F. Condon, elderly retired school principal, 2974 Decatur Avenue, Bronx, New York City, publishes announcement in the Home News for Bronx and Manhattan, offering to act as go-between and promising to pay $1,000 additional reward from his personal savings.

Thayer informs Colonel Lindbergh and Colonel Breckinridge of his opinion relative to Rosner but it is agreed that Rosner should stay on.

Owney Madden confers with Colonel Breckinridge and Colonel Lindbergh and Detective Fogarty at Hopewell.

March 9,—Advertisement signed "Father" reported in New York American.

Fourth ransom note received addressed to Dr. John Condon, 2974 Decatur Ave., New York City, postmarked New York, N. Y. Station "T" (165th Street and 3rd Ave., Bronx near Dr. Condon's home) 12 Noon, March 9, 1932, indicating Condon acceptable as go-between and instructing him to place advertisement in New York American.

A letter to Colonel Lindbergh is enclosed with letter to Dr. Condon advising that Dr. Condon may act as go-between.

Condon telephones Colonel Lindbergh and later same night, accompanied by two friends, Milton Gaglio and Rosonhain, delivers letter to Colonel Lindbergh at Hopewell, early morning of March 10th.

March 10,—Condon receives telephone message that he would receive another message Saturday night (March 12, 1932).

Robert Baird with aliases furnishes alleged information implicating Harold Fontaine, the latter's sister or sister-in-law Frances, Keating, Thomas Holden, Frank Nash, et al. Subsequently investigated with no material result.

About this date $70,000 in currency delivered to Dr. Condon with authority to pay as ransom.

March 11, 1932—Advertisement published by Dr. Condon in New York American and Bronx Home News as follows: "Money is ready. Jafsie."

Newspapers furnish offer of Al Capone to post bond up to $200,000 for his release to help search for baby.

Spitale, Bitz and twelve other arraigned in Federal Court, Brooklyn, N. Y. on prohibition case, later acquitted.

Circular issued by New Jersey State Police mailed by New York Office, Division of Investigation, to all police officers and certain other officials.

March 12, 1932—Dr. Condon's advertisement of March 11th repeated in New York American and Bronx Home News.

New Jersey State Police announce secrecy pledged to informants in Lindbergh kidnaping case.

Dr. Condon receives telephone message about 3 P.M. from unknown person said to be calling from Westchester Square, asking if he would be home between 6 and 10 P.M.

About 8:30 P.M. the fifth ransom note delivered to Dr. Condon by taxicab driver Joseph Perrone, who received message from unidentified stranger at Knox Place and Gun Hill Road, Bronx, New York City. Note informs Dr. Condon he would find another note underneath a stone on porch of vacant frankfurter stand 100 feet from last subway station on Jerome Avenue.

Sixth ransom note found by Dr. Condon as directed, instructing him to cross the street, follow the fence from the cemetery toward 233rd Street. At about 9:30 P.M. Condon meets an unidentified stranger giving the name of "John" at Woodlawn Cemetery near 233rd Street and Jerome Ave. and discusses payment of ransom. "John" agrees to furnish Dr. Condon a token of child's identity. Dr. Condon accompanied, except during contact with "John", by Al Reich, former pugilist and Condon's bodyguard. Both observe an unidentified man possibly a lookout for "John".

Rosner complained to Thayer that Colonel Lindbergh and Colonel Breckinridge had not taken him in their confidence regarding fourth ransom note.

Rosner, Spitale and Bitz in conference with

Thayer propose contacting Al Capone to enlist his aid; in return for consideration which they would try to arrange.

Rosner makes unauthorized statement to Associated Press that he has definite knowledge that the baby is safe and well and will be returned within a few days.

March 13, 1932—Dr. Condon publishes advertisement in the Bronx Home News reading as follows: "Baby alive and well. Money is ready. Call and see us. Jafsie."

Colonel Lindbergh, Mr. Thayer and Rosner confer at Hopewell. No further material developments through Rosner.

March 14,—Dr. Condon repeats his advertisement of March 11th in the New York American and publishes following advertisement in Bronx Home News: "Money is ready. No cops. No secret service. No press. I go alone like last time. Please call. Jafsie."

The New York Mirror publishes story that the Lindbergh baby held by the Purple Gang and that negotiations were being continued by Spitale and Bitz.

March 15,—Dr. Condon repeats his advertisement of March 14th in the Bronx Home News and his advertisement of March 11th in the New York American.

March 16,—Dr. Condon repeats his advertisement in the New York American of March 11th and publishes following advertisement in the Bronx Home News:

"I accept. Money is ready. You know they won't let me deliver without package. Please make some sort of C.O.D. transaction, you know you can trust Jafsie."

A freshly laundered Dr. Denton sleeping suit #2, purporting to be that of the Lindbergh baby received by Dr. Condon by mail in package postmarked Station "E", Brooklyn (2581 Atlar Avenue), N. Y.

Seventh ransom note received by Dr. Condon in package containing sleeping suit directing attention to the symbolic signature on the ransom letters and the sleeping suit as their identification, the kidnapers stating they would have to pay $3 for a new sleeping suit and insisting that $70,000 be paid without first seeing the baby.

March 17, 1932—Colonel Lindbergh arrives at Dr. Condon's home at 1:30 A.M. and is given the sleeping suit.

Dr. Condon's advertisement of March 16th in Bronx Home News published in New York American, and following published in Bronx Home News:

"Money is ready. No cops. No secret service. No press. I come like last time. Alone. Please call Jafsie."

Mr. Edwin H. Cassels, Chicago attorney, discusses case with Colonel Breckinridge and Special Agent in Charge Connelley, offering no new information but apparently interested in Al Capone and Harry Fleisher.

March 18—Dr. Condon's advertisement of March 17th repeated in New York American, and following published in Bronx Home News:
"I accept. Money is ready. John, your package is delivered and O. K. Direct me." (no signature).

Officials of Intelligence Unit, Internal Revenue Service, Treasury Department, confer with Colonel Lindbergh and Colonel Breckinridge and assume active share of investigation in close association with New Jersey State Police particularly relative to connection of Al Capone.

March 19, 1932—Dr. Condon's advertisement of March 18th reported in the Bronx Home News. His advertisement of March 17th reported in the New York American. Dr. Condon said to have received verbal instructions from unknown woman in charity Bazaar conducted by him at 394 East 200th Street in the Bronx, to meet him the following Wednesday, March 23, 1932 at Railway Station, Tuckahoe, N.Y.

Stolen 1929 Buick Sedan with motor removed found concealed in barn belonging to Casper Oliver about four miles from Lindbergh estate. Oliver and Sam Cucchiara arrested but not found to be connected with kidnaping.

March 20, 1932—Dr. Condon publishes following advertisement in Bronx Home News:
"Notify me how I can get my letter to you. Urgent. Jafsie."

March 21,—Dr. Condon's advertisement of March 20th published in New York American and repeated in Bronx Home News.

Eighth ransom letter received by Dr. Condon postmarked Station "N" (203 West 69th Street), New York, N.Y., 7:30 P.M. March 19, 1932, insisting on complete compliance with their program, advising that the kidnaping had been planned for a year and that the baby is well.

March 22,—Dr. Condon publishes the following advertisement in the Bronx Home News and the New York American:
"Thanks. That little package you sent was immediately delivered and accepted as the real article. See my position. Over 50 years in business, and can I pay without seeing goods? Common sense makes me trust you. Please understand my position."

John Hughes Curtis and Rev. H. Dobson-Peacock, and Admiral Guy Burrage of Norfolk, Va. Announce publicly that kidnapers have asked them to be intermediaries and thereafter continue their activities claiming contact with kidnapers. Their story, subsequent activities and alleged negotiations given much prominence in the press daily, until the baby's body was found on May 12, 1932.

Henry "Red" Johnson exonerated by New Jersey State Police.

March 23, 1932—Dr. Condon's advertisement of March 22nd repeated in Bronx Home News and New York American. Dr. Condon accompanied by Al Reich (former pugilist and alleged bodyguard of Dr. Condon) meets unknown woman at Tuckahoe, N.Y., is instructed by her to continue advertising.

Owney Madden, New York racketeer reported to have made several visits to Lindbergh estate.

H. W. Caldwell, former president, Chicago Board of education reported active at Hopewell and Washington, D. C. Apparently in connection with Al Capone.

March 24,—Dr. Condon's advertisement of March 22nd repeated in Bronx Home News and New York American.

New York Daily News announces that the New Jersey State Police were booking Abie Wagner, New York East Side gangster and Harry Fleisher of the Detroit Purple Gang.

March 25,—Dr. Condon's advertisement of March 22nd repeated in the Bronx Home News and New

York American. Publicity continued regarding Abie Wagner and Harry Fleisher.

Names and personal histories of members of Purple Gang received by New York Office from Detroit Office of Division of Investigation.

March 26,—Dr. Condon publishes following advertisement in Bronx Home News:
"Money is ready. Furnish simple code for us to follow in paper. Jafsie."

Additional publicity regarding Wagner and Fleisher. No material result.

March 27,—Dr. Condon's advertisement of March 26th repeated in the Bronx Home News.

March 28,—Dr. Condon's advertisement of March 26th repeated in the Bronx Home News and New York American.

March 29,—Dr. Condon's advertisement of March 26 repeated in the New York American.

Betty Gow finds thumb guard worn by baby at time of kidnaping in woods about half mile from Lindbergh house near entrance to estate.

March 30,—Dr. Condon's advertisement of March 26th repeated in the New York American.

Ninth ransom note received by Dr. Condon, postmarked Station "N" (203 West 69th Street)

New York, N.Y. 9: A.M., March 29, 1932 stating that if the matter was not closed by April 8th the ransom would be $100,000 also that they would give no code for use in the newspapers.

March 31,—Dr. Condon publishes following advertisement in the Bronx Home News and in the New York American:
"I hereby accept. Money is ready. Jafsie."

April 1,—Dr. Condon's advertisement of March 31st repeated in the Bronx Home News and New York American.

Tenth ransom note received by Dr. Condon, postmarked 9:30 A.M. April 1, 1932, Fordham Station (420 East 189th St.) Bronx, N. Y. (being the same station through which Dr. Condon received his mail). This note instructed him to have the money ready for Saturday night, April 2, 1932, and to inform by advertisement in the papers.

Dr. Condon published the following advertisement in the April 2nd issue of the New York American, which appeared on the street about 9:30 P.M. April 1st:
"Yes. Everything O.K. Jafsie."

Doherty, William Dooley, et al, attempt to interest Governor of Michigan in angle involving Harry Fleisher, Dooley and Harry Sitner. Dudley Field Malone and N. Y. Daily Mirror are interested; investigated by Michigan State Police without material result.

April 2,—Dr. Condon's advertisement in New York American of this date which was on street evening of April 1st, published in Bronx Home News, the latter being an afternoon paper.

Eleventh ransom note delivered to Dr. Condon at his home by unidentified taxi driver, who said he received it from unknown man at 188th Street and Marion Avenue.

Twelfth ransom note found by Dr. Condon underneath stone in front of Bergen's Greenhouse, 3225 East Tremont Ave., Bronx N. Y., in accordance with instructions in eleventh ransom note.

As directed in twelfth ransom note, Condon meets the representative of the kidnapers (whom Dr. Condon believed was "John" the man he had previously met in Woodlawn Cemetery), in St. Raymond's Cemetery near Whittemore Avenue and East Tremont Avenue, Bronx, N. Y. After persuading him to reduce the ransom to $50,000, give a receipt, Dr. Condon delivered to him a box containing $50,000 in currency, and in return was handed the thirteenth ransom note containing instructions where to find the Lindbergh baby on a boat near Martha's Vineyard, Mass. Colonel Lindbergh waits nearby in car and sees man possibly lookout for kidnaping.

Colonel Breckinridge, Al Reich and possibly others, waiting at Dr. Condon's home for return of Doctor and Colonel Lindbergh.

Arthur L. Hitner, known confidence man, injects himself into the investigation claiming to have information that Al Capone and the Purple gang including Fleisher and Wagner abducted baby.

April 3,—Colonel Lindbergh, Dr. Condon and party including representative of Intelligence Unit, conduct unsuccessful search for baby at Martha's Vineyard in accordance with directions in last transmittal letter.

Activities of Division of Investigation confined to specific requests from New Jersey State Police, and to receiving information from informants and correspondents for transmittal to State Police.

April 4,—Dr. Condon's advertisement of April 2nd repeated in the Bronx Home News and New York American.

Search in vicinity of Martha's Vineyard continues.

April 5,—The Norfolk negotiators, John Hughes Curtis, et al, publically announce their contact with kidnapers has convinced them child is well.

Police continue hunt for Harry Fleisher, wanted for questions.

$20. Ransom Bill—East River Savings Bank, 96th Street and Amsterdam Avenue, New York City.—(traced to David Mare 215 West 91st Street).

April 6,—Dr. Condon publishes advertisement in the Bronx Home News at New York American reading as follows:

"What is wrong? Have you crossed me? Please letter directions. Jafsie."

Edna Sharpe, sister of Violet Sharpe, Morrow waitress, returns to her home in England.

List of serial numbers of $50,000 in currency paid as ransom distributed by Treasury Department to banks in United States.

April 7,—Dr. Condon's advertisement of April 6th repeated in the Bronx Home News and New York American.

April 8,—Dr. Condon's advertisement of April 6th repeated in the Bronx Home News and New York American.

New Jersey State Police announce search for Fleisher continues.

April 9,—Colonel Lindbergh discloses publicly that ransom has been paid by him of $50,000 for regaining the child.

Treasury Department seeks bills used in payment.

April 10,—Dr. John F. Condon publicly revealed as "Jafsie" (name made up by him from his initials).

Serial numbers of $50,000 ransom money issued by Treasury Department published generally in all newspapers.

New York Police Department obtaining list of new renters of safe deposit boxes in New York State during March and April 1932.

April 11,—Henry ("Red") Johnson released by the New Jersey State Police to Immigration Service for deportation.

Bronx Home News publishes: "The True Story of Jafsie's Effort to Locate Stolen Lindbergh Baby", based on information obtained from Dr. Condon.

April 14,—$5 Ransom Bill—bank of Manhattan Co.—(traced to Frank G. Shattuck Co., proprietors of Schrafft's Candy Stores and restaurant's).

At request of State Police Division mails serial numbers of ransom bills to foreign countries.

April 20, —During this period the Norfolk negotiators continued making mysterious trips in yacht "Mercon" in attempt to contact the kidnapers at sea.

Lindbergh accompanied them on some voyages.

Arthur L. Hitner attempts to inject himself into Curtis, Dobson-Peacock, et al and Gaston B. Means angles, apparently with fraudulent intent.

May 1, —Norfolk negotiators publicly express belief their efforts nearing conclusion but developments failed to bear them out.

May 4, —Gaston B. Means arrested in Washington, D.C. charged with defrauding Mrs. Evelyn Walsh McLean out of $100,000 which she gave him to pay kidnapers.

May 6,—Public interest continue to center in Norfolk but results are negative.

May 7,—Hitner wrote to Mrs. Evelyn Walsh McLean, Washington, D.C. requesting certain information.

May 11,—Norfolk negotiators reported cruising off Block Island attempting to establish contact with kidnapers.

Gaston B. Means indicted U.S. District Court, Washington, D.C., Charged with larceny and embezzlement of $100,000 from Mrs. McLean.

May 12,—Body of Charles Augustus Lindbergh, Jr. accidentally found about four and one-half miles southeast of and within view of Lindbergh home, partially buried under dirt and leaves

> in woods, about seventy-five feet from Princeton-Hopewell Road near Mr. Rose, N.J. Body badly decomposed. Some members missing; head crushed and hole in skull, hole possibly made by bullet. Body identified by Colonel Lindbergh, Betty Gow and Dr. Van Ingen. Body found within few hundred feet of small house owned by Charles Schopfel which in summer of 1931 was occupied by Charles Moran, his demented mother and his stepfather Enrico Gerardi.

May 13,—Baby's body cremated at Trenton, N.J.

> Dr. John F. Condon and John Hughes Curtis questioned in detail by New Jersey State Police.

> Presidential instructions issued in effect that all government investigative agencies place themselves at the disposal of the State of New Jersey, and that the Bureau of Investigations serve as a clearing house and coordinating agency for all investigative activity conducted by Federal investigative units in this case.

May 14,—Statement made by Dr. Condon in office of Bronx County Attorney New York, N.Y.

May 17,—John Hughes Curtis formally confesses that his alleged contact and negotiations with kidnapers entirely fictitious. Curtis taken into custody by New Jersey State Police.

> Conference at Trenton, N.J. between officials

of New Jersey State Police, Intelligence Unit and Internal Revenue Service, Treasury Department, Prosecutive Authorities and Division of Investigation.

May 18,—Policy adopted that actual direction of case continue in hands of New Jersey State authorities. Federal officials to participate only to the extent of affording such assistance as might be required from time to time.

May 19,—$5 Ransom Bill—Central Hanover Bank & Trust Co.—(traced to Sinclair Oil Co., 52nd St. & Mill Ave., Brooklyn, N.Y.)

$5 Ransom Bill—Chase National Bank, 41st St. & 7th Ave., New York City—(traced to Bickford's Restaurant, 7th Avenue and 41st St., New York City).

Division's New York Office investigates report that George A. McManus has ransom money in safety deposit box, apparently unfounded.

May 20,—Bronx County Grand Jury investigates payment of $50,000 ransom; testimony given by Dr. Condon, Colonel Brickenridge, Max Rosenhain, Milton Gaglio, Al Reich and Joseph Perrone.

Investigation instituted relative Frank Cummings, gangster, alleged to have planned kidnaping, eventually concluded with no evidence developed indicating possible guilt.

May 21,—Circular containing specimens of handwriting

on ransom letters, issued by New Jersey State Police to all penal institutions, for comparison with prison records.

May 23,—$5. Ransom Bill—First National Bank, 52 Wall Street New York City—(traced to Max Gubenstein, Drygoods Store, 150 Orchard St., New York City).

New York Division Office circularizes banking institutions in Greater New York, advising of fact that Division is coordinating agency for all government activity in this case, and requesting close watch for ransom money.

May 24,—Assignment of Special Agent Frank J. Wilson, Intelligence Unit, continued as heretofore in close association with New Jersey State Police.

May 25,—Information furnished New York Division Office by Narcotic Agent that one John Baumeister might be implicated.

May 26,—New Jersey State Police circular announcing a reward of not exceeding $25,000 for information resulting in apprehension and conviction of kidnapers, distributed by New York Division Office to local enforcement officials and agencies.

May 28,—Reports of examination of handwriting experts indicate that ransom notes written by same person.

June 6,—$5. Ransom Bill—Chase National Bank—(traced to Brilliant Cafeteria, 151 Canal Street, New York City).

June 9,—Harry Fleisher voluntarily surrendered to Police Department, Detroit, Michigan, where he was wanted on murder charges. No evidence developed of his implication in this case.

June 10,—About to be questioned by New Jersey State Police, Violet Sharpe, Morrow waitress, commits suicide by swallowing cyanide of potassium.

Garrett Schenck abducted by private Detective J. J. Devine and others, near Hopewell, N. J., and held as alleged suspect in Lindbergh case until September 3, 1932. Devine and his associates subsequently arrested and charged with kidnaping by Pennsylvania authorities.

June 11,—Ernest Brinker alleged escort of Violet Sharpe questioned by New Jersey State Police. Subsequently exonerated.

June 15—Gaston B. Means sentenced to fifteen years imprisonment, having been convicted of defrauding Mrs. Evelyn Walsh McLean of $100,000.

June 16—$5. Ransom Bill—Drydock Savings Bank—(traced to Martha Sohn, 1025 East 167th Street, New York City).

June 17—Investigation instituted relative to Isidoro Ubaldi, alien, who offered to exchange information re kidnaping for cancellation of deportation order. (Not located).

June 24—Investigation instituted relative to John Condon, formerly of Newport, Ky., said to be connected with the Purple Gang. No evidence developed connecting him with Lindbergh case.

June 28,—Norman T. Whitaker, confederate of Gaston B. Means in swindling Mrs. Evelyn Walsh McLean, apprehended in New York City.

June 30,—$5 Ransom Bill—Mt. Vernon Trust Company—(traced to Post Office, Mt. Vernon, N. Y. and to Max Halperi, 25 Alamoda St., or E. A. Trotter, both Mt. Vernon, N. Y.)

July 11,—John Hughes Curtis sentenced to 1 year imprisonment and fined $1,000 being convicted of giving false information to authorities thereby obstructing arrest of kidnapers.

July 13,—$5 Ransom Bill—Chase National Bank, 18 Pine St., New York City—(traced to Federal Reserve Bank, New York City).

August 1—Rose Mary Sanborn and Robert Conroy, with aliases, found dead in apartment at 220 West 104th Street, named by several informants as possible suspects in instant matter.

August 2—$5 Ransom Bill—Manufacturers Trust Co., New York City—(traced to West End Avenue Corporation, 325 West 71st Street and 245 West 75th Street).

August 16—$5 Ransom Bill—Central Hanover Bank and Trust Company, 70 Broadway, New York City—(traced to Mrs. Albert Chamberlin, 1536 Bedford Avenue, Brooklyn or M. M. Babbitt, 387 Eastern Parkway, Brooklyn, N.Y.).

August 24—$5 Ransom Bill—1st National Bank—(traced to Consolidated Gas Co., 157 Hester St., New York City).

September 14—$5 Ransom Bill—Central Hanover Bank and Trust Co., 224 West 47th Street, New York City—(traced to Palace Café, 151 W. 46th Street).

October 6—$5 Ransom Bill—Chase National Bank, 75 Maiden Lane—(traced to David Bari; also spelled "Barry" and Joseph Korotsky, 1860 Broadway, New York City).

October 11—David Bari questioned re possession of $5 Ransom Bill.

October 14—Handwriting experts advise David Bari apparently did not write Lindbergh ransom notes.

October 15—$5 Ransom Bill—Federal Reserve Bank, New York City—(traced to Ernest and Emily Behrens, Irvington, N. J.)

October 22,—$10 Ransom Gold Certificate—Guaranty Trust Company—(traced to Adventurers Club, Hotel Astor, 44th Street and Broadway, New York City).

October 23—$5 Ransom Bill—Chase National Bank, 575 5th Ave., New York City—(traced to H. Levincat, Restaurant, 2nd Avenue and East 28th Street, New York City).

October 24—$5 Ransom Bill—Chase National Bank, (traced to Bronx Edison Company).

October 25—$5 Ransom Bill—(traced to Moe Levy, 1441 Broadway, New York City).

October 26—$20 Ransom Bill—Central Hanover Bank and Trust Company, 70 Broadway, New York City—(traced to Childs Restaurant, 570 Lexington Avenue).

October 28—$10 Ransom Bill—National City Bank, 55 Wall Street—(traced to Brooklyn Edison Co., 360 Pearl Street, Brooklyn, N. Y.)

October 29—$10 Ransom Gold Certificate—Guaranty Trust Co., (traced to United Cigar Store at 118-02 Jamaican Ave., Queens, New York City).

November 10,—$50 Ransom Bill—National City Bank, 5th Avenue and 23rd Street—(traced to H. Lambert Clothing Co., 254 5th Ave., New York City).

November 11—$5 Ransom Bill—Central Hanover Bank and Trust Company—(traced to Childs Restaurant, 570 Lexington Avenue, New York City).

December 6,—$5 Ransom Bill—Central Hanover Bank and Trust Company—(traced to Edward's Sport Shop, 111 Nassau Street).

December 22,—$10 Ransom Gold Certificate—Guaranty Trust Company—(traced to Whalan Drug Store, 1490 3rd Ave., New York City).

January 1, 1933—Investigation instituted relative to J. Floyd Williams, et al as possible suspects.

March 3,—$10 Ransom Gold Certificate—Guaranty Trust Co., 180 Broadway—(traced to United Cigar Stores, 504 3rd Ave., New York City).

April 5,—President orders all gold coin, bullion and gold certificates returned to Federal Reserve Banks or member banks, on or before May 1, 1933.

April 12,—$20 Ransom Bill—1st National Bank—(traced to Consolidated Gas Company, 14th Street and Irving Place, New York City).

April 13,—$10 Ransom Gold Certificate—Federal Reserve Bank—(traced to Public National Bank, Grand and Havemeyer Streets, Brooklyn, N.Y.).

April 14,—Circular letter issued to banking institutions by Treasury Department requesting careful search of gold certificates surrendered in accordance with the Presidential order.

$10 Ransom Gold Certificate—Federal Reserve Bank—(traced to Manufacturers Trust Co., Columbus Circle and 59th Street, New York City).

April 19,—$10 Ransom Gold Certificate—Federal Reserve Bank—(traced to Union Dime Savings Bank, 40th Street and 5th Avenue, New York City).

April 20,—Extensive investigation instituted relative to Dean Preston Sutherland, alleged extortioner of Indianapolis and elsewhere. (Developed no evidence of connection with instant matter).

April 22,—$10 Ransom Gold Certificate—Chemical Bank and Trust Company—(traced to J. H. Adams, Eagle Poultry Co., 2152 Broadway, New York City).

April 25,—Investigation instituted relative to Sam Goldberg alias "Sam the Gas Man", bootlegger—alleged suspect.

April 27,—$5 Ransom Bill—1st National Bank—(traced to Consolidated Gas Company thence to Paul Yakutis, 234 East 18th Street, rooming house proprietor).

April 28,—About this date State Police request New Jersey banks to be on lookout for gold certificates paid in ransom money.

April 29,—24—$10 Ransom Gold Certificates—Federal Reserve Bank, New York City—(traced to Chemical National Bank, Cortland St. and Broadway, New York City).

May 1,—30,000 circulars containing list of serial numbers of ransom bills offering rewards for locating the bills issued to police department, New York City, and distributed to banks and certain chain rental establishments, the latter with gold certificates omitted. Newspapers requested to refrain from publicity in connection with search for ransom money.

296—$10 Ransom Gold Certificates, and 1—$20 Ransom Gold Certificate—Federal Reserve Bank, New York City—Exchanged by unidentified person as "J. J. Faulkner, 537 W. 149th St., New York City".

26—$10 Ransom Gold Certificates—Federal Reserve Bank, New York City—(traced to Chemical National Bank, Cortland Street and Broadway, New York City).

May 2,—Investigation instituted relative to 537 W. 149th Street, Carl Oswin Giessler; Mrs. Carl Oswin Giessler nee Jane Emily Faulkner; H. C. Leipold; Duane Bacon, et al.

50—$10 ransom Gold Certificates—Federal Reserve Bank, New York City—(traced to Manufacturers Trust Co., 149 Broadway, New York City).

May 8,—$10 Ransom Gold Certificate—Federal Reserve Bank—(traced to Corn Exchange Bank, 85th Street and Lexington Avenue).

May 9,—$10 Ransom Gold Certificate—Federal Reserve Bank, New York City—(traced to Bank of the Manhattan Co., Union Square and 14th Street, New York City).

May 23,—Circular letter forwarded by New York office, Division of Investigation to banking institutions in New York City requesting them to notify this office of receipt of Lindbergh ransom bills.

May 26,—Norman T. Whitaker and Gaston B. Means sentenced to 2 years imprisonment each after being convicted of conspiring to obtain $35,000 additional from Mrs. McLean.

June 7,—$5 Ransom Bill—Chase National Bank, 7th Avenue and 41st Street, New York City. (traced to Albrecht and Co., 1372 Broadway, New York City).

June 10,—$10 Ransom Gold Certificate—Federal Reserve Bank, New York City—(traced to Irving Trust Co., East Fordham Road and Marion Ave., Bronx, New York City).

June 13,—$10 Ransom Gold Certificate—Federal Reserve Bank, New York City—(traced to National Central Bank of Cherry Valley, N. Y.)

June 18,—$10 Ransom Gold Certificate—Federal Reserve Bank, New York City—(traced to James A. Hoarn and Sons, drygoods, 20 West 144th Street, New York City).

July 20,—Investigation instituted regarding James Oscar Farrell, his alleged participation and that of others implicated by him.

July 21,—Arrangements made for procurement of information covering all ransom bills previously discovered; and so that investigation of all ransom bills detected in future will immediately be conducted jointly by a representative of the New Jersey State Police, the New York City Police Department, and this Division.

August 3,—Investigation instituted relative to Nick De Augustine et al.

August 20,—Henry Leipold, son-in-law of Carl Osborn Giessler, who in 1921 married Jane Emily Faulkner, former resident of 537 W. 149th Street committed suicide at Arthursburg, N. Y. shortly after he was questioned by Police Department and representative of Intelligence Unit.

October 1,—During October, New York Police again circularized chain retail establishments with serial numbers of ransom bills except gold certificates.

October 10,—John P. Pawelzycyk, prisoner, Joliet, Ill. Who designed and copyrighted symbols similar to symbolic signatures on ransom letters alleges Frank Nash told him kidnaping was perpetrated by Harvey Bailey, Frank Nash and Bob Berry alias Robert Conroy, etc. and instigated by Al Torrio for purpose of liberating Capone; that Nash was cheated out of the ransom money and was killed at Bailey's orders for fear that he would sell his story of the kidnaping.

October 19,—Officially announced that Division of Investigation, United States Department of Justice, would have exclusive jurisdiction in so far as the Federal Government is concerned in the handling of any investigative features of the Lindbergh case.

Confidential informant interviewed by Division Agents in Chicago, Ill. Alleges Lindbergh kidnaping done by Harry Meyers and Murray Moll; that former was killed about six weeks ago and the latter in June—1933 by orders of Chink Sherman, racketeer, also alleged to have been connected with Robert Conroy.

October 21,—John Gorch, with aliases, former resident, Hopewell, N. J. and Evelyn Klimasefska arrested at Boston, Mass. Gorch subsequently extradited by Philadelphia, Pa. Police on swindling charge together with Walter Gray, former associate of Gorch. Gorch received considerable publicity and investigative activity in Lindbergh kidnaping case.

October 22,—Arthur Barry, jewel thief, an escape from Auburn Prison, New York, apprehended in hideout near Nowtown, N. J. He received considerable publicy as possible suspect in Lindbergh kidnaping and murder.

November 13,—Investigation instituted relative to Lewis V. Cummings, with aliases, possible suspect, former employee of Epileptic Hospital, Skillman, N. J. near Hopewell, N. J. and known as erratic adventurer.

November 16,—Report of Special Agent Frank J. Wilson, Intelligence Unit, Internal Revenue Service, Treasury Department, received by Division of Investigation covering investigation conducted by him from March 18, 1933 to October 14, 1933.

Investigation instituted relative to R. F. D. Lamon, alleged suspect, without material result.

Gerald Buccholz with aliases opened account in Corn Exchange Bank, 525 Broadway, with large cash deposit, remarking to teller that he lived in back of Dr. Condon; further, that he had some $5 bills to deposit but changed his mind.

November 17,—Circular letter issued to banking institutions of New York City and Westchester County requesting that New York office of Division of Investigation be advised of the receipt of any ransom currency paid in the Lindbergh kidnaping case.

November 20—$5 Ransom Bill—First National Bank, New York City—(Traced to Public National Bank, Avenue C and 2nd St., New York City).

November 24,—$5 Ransom Bill—Corn Exchange Bank, 33rd Street and 7th Avenue, New York City—(Traced to Pennsylvania Railway Station).

November 27,—$5 Ransom Bill—Corn Exchange Bank, 59th Street and 7th Avenue—(Traced to Sheridan

Square Theatre, 8th Street and 7th Ave., New York City).

December 1,—Henry Logemann, alias John Damann, prisoner, United States Northeastern Penitentiary, Lewisburg, Pa. Admits signing bogus statement regarding Lindbergh case, upon request of Gaston B. Means also confined same penitentiary.

Also furnishes additional information concerning Jack and Robert B. Bennett, whiskey dealers, possible suspects.

Arthur L. Hitner repeats with variations his story concerning kidnaping, possibly with fraudulent intent at Green Bay, Wisconsin.

December 7,—$5 Ransom Bill—Corn Exchange Bank, 525 Broadway—(Traced to Banco di Napoli Trust Co., 526 Broadway, New York City).

December 8,—Investigation instituted regarding William Faulkner, Hollywood, Calif. Developed no evidence of connection with instant matter.

Investigation regarding Sam Cucchiara alias "Sam the Barber" developed no information evident of his implication in offense.

December 15—Information developed indicating Carl Oswin Giessler supplied nursery products to W. L. McKee, victim in pending extortion case—John Suddueth (former caretaker), subject.

December 18—$5 Ransom Bill—Corn Exchange Bank, 14th Street and 7th Avenue—(Traced to Gasoline Distributors in New York, Inc., 153 7th Ave., New York City).

> Investigation instituted regarding Mrs. James F. Berle nee Helen Faulkner convicted of the kidnaping of Billy Whitla, May 11, 1909.

December 20,—Arthur L. Hitner discredited intermeddler in Lindbergh case repeats his story, with variations, to Tilliam C. Merchant, attorney-at-law, Albany, N. Y. possibly with fraudulent intent.

December 27,—$10 Ransom Gold Certificate—Federal Reserve Bank, New York City—(Traced to Bank of New York and Trust Company, New York City, or Chartered Bank of India, Australia and China, New York City).

January 4, 1934—Investigation instituted relative to Eddie Sundelin and Laina Salo, alleged suspects.

> Verne Sankey, indicated as possible suspect upon publication of finding of file of Lindbergh case clippings in basement of his home. No further developments connecting him with instant matter.

January 5,—$10 Ransom Gold Certificate, Federal Reserve Bank, New York City—(Traced to Chase National Bank, Harlem Market Branch).

> $10 Ransom Gold Certificate—Federal Reserve

Bank, New York City—(Traced to Corn Exchange Bank and Trust Company, Fordham Road and Decatur Ave., Bronx, New York City).

January 6,—$10 Ransom Gold Certificate—Federal Reserve Bank, New York City—(Traced to United States Postoffice, Williamsbridge Branch, White Plains Road and Gun Hill Road, New York City).

January 9,—Enrico Gerardi, with aliases, possible suspect, arrested at Hackensack, N. J. charged with false imprisonment of his demented wife, the mother of Charles Maran. These three persons in summer of 1931 occupied small house located a few hundred feet from where Lindbergh baby's body was found.

January 16,—$10 Ransom Gold Certificate—Federal Reserve Bank, New York City—(Traced to Bank of Manhattan Co., Williamsbridge Branch, 220th Street and White Plains Road, Bronx, New York City).

January 17,—Circular letter issued by New York office, Division of Investigation to all banks and branches located in New York City requesting extremely close lookout for ransom gold certificates in view of Proclamation ordering all gold surrendered on that date which order was subsequently modified.

January 19,—$10 Ransom Gold Certificate—Federal Reserve Bank, New York City—(Traced to Bronx County Trust Co., 149th St. and 3rd Avenue, New York City).

February 1,—$5 Ransom bill—Corn Exchange Bank and Trust Co., 42nd Street and 8th Ave., New York City—(Traced to Globe Coat and Apron Supply Co., 526 W. 48th Street, New York City)—(Joseph Frederick Faulkner, employees, Cafeteria, DePinna Clothing Store, 52nd Street and 5th Ave., New York City).

February 16,—Division field offices furnished with supply of Division's revised pamphlet containing serials of ransom bills. New York Office distributing copies to each employee handling currency in banks, retail chain establishments, etc. in New York City and vicinity.

SUMMARY REPORT

In reply to: Unknown Subjects

Kidnaping and Murder of Charles A. Lindbergh, Jr. (N.Y. File 62-3057).

NARRATIVE

THOMAS FENSCH

NARRATIVE

On Tuesday night, March 1, 1932, between 6 P.M. and 10 P.M., Charles Augustus Lindbergh, Jr., 20 months old son of Colonel Charles A. Lindbergh and Anne Morrow Lindbergh, was kidnaped from his nursery on the second floor of the Lindbergh home, situated on a five hundred acre estate, which is partly in Mercer County and partly in Hunterdon County, New Jersey, the residence being in the latter county and three miles north of the nearest town, Hopewell, N. J. Betty Gow, the baby's nurse since shortly after his birth, was the person who discovered the baby was missing. She immediately notified Mrs. Lindbergh, then in the bathroom, and Colonel Lindbergh, who was downstairs in the library directly beneath the nursery. He came upstairs and with Mrs. Lindbergh and Betty Gow entered the baby's room where he observed a number of small particles of mud between the windows at the southeast corner of the room and the baby's crib, which was located in the far corner of the room away from the windows. An inspection of the room and the baby's bed by his parents indicated that the bed clothes were still pinned on the bed as Betty Gow had left them when she last saw the child, about 8 P.M.

On the window sill of the east window, Colonel Lindbergh found a note in a small, plain white envelope, which was unaddressed. The window was closed and the note had been placed on the window sill inside of the nursery. The note, very crudely written, read as follows:

"Mr. Col. Lindbergh
Hopewell, N. J.

Dear Sir:
    Have 50.000 $ redy 25 000 $ in 20$ bills 15 000 $ in

10$ bills and 10 000 $ in 5$ bills. After 2-4 days we will inform you were to deliver the money.

We worn you for making anyting public or for notify the Police. The child is in gut care. Indication for all letters are singature.

Ans. L 3 holes

This note bore a peculiar symbol signature. A photostatic copy of the ransom note, as well as other ransom notes received in this case, are attached to the instant report and will show clearly the nature of the symbol in question and the crudeness of the handwriting.

After the discovery of the ransom note, which was read by Colonel Lindbergh and his butler, Ollie Whately, Colonel Lindbergh and Whately immediately ran outside of the house and searched the grounds nearby, while Mrs. Lindbergh and Mrs. Whately peered out the nursery windows and heard a faint cry apparently coming from some distance. At approximately 10:20 P.M., Colonel Lindbergh, despite the warning in the ransom note, personally telephoned Deputy Chief of Police Charles E. Williamson, of Hopewell, and the New Jersey State Police. Since Lindbergh was able to put through those calls, the telephone wires leading to the Lindbergh estate had obviously not been cut. Williamson had retired for the night and there was some delay while he dressed, and there was further delay when he stopped to pick up Chief of Police Harry Wolf of Hopewell. These two officers arrived at the Lindbergh home at approximately 10:40 P.M. At 10:50 P.M. a flash on the kidnaping was teletyped throughout the East from police headquarters, Newark, N. J. Upon looking over the scene of the crime, the Hopewell officers suggested that Colonel Lindbergh get a fingerprint expert from Trenton to examine the ransom note and the nursery for fingerprints, and accordingly, Colonel Lindbergh called the State Police at Trenton and about midnight, State Trooper Frank Kelly, a fingerprint expert, arrived and powdered the ransom note and sections of the baby's nursery, but was unable to bring out any fingerprints whatsoever. Subsequently, efforts made by other experts were also unsuccessful.

The nursery window, through which it appeared the baby had been removed, is approximately fourteen feet from the ground. Inside the nursery, against the wall and just below the window in question, was a long, low cedar chest, on top of which was a large black suitcase, and on this was a child's "Tinker toy" on wheels. Betty Gow and Mrs. Lindbergh had observed the arrangement of these articles before and after the kidnaping, and stated there was no indication they had been disturbed. A close examination failed to reveal mud particles, footprints, or fingerprints on them. Experiments conducted by the New Jersey State Police showed that it was possible to hurdle those articles in affecting an entrance through the window if a certain amount of dexterity were used. However, it appeared to be a very difficult task for anyone to go out of the window with a thirty pound baby in his arms, without disturbing the objects at the window, or leaving a muddy footprint, mud particle or other telltale evidence on the objects. The walls of the Lindbergh house were about one and half feet thick; the window sills about one and a quarter feet thick.

Examination of the grounds outside the house resulted in the finding by police officers of a three section ladder, about fifty feet from the house in the direction of an abandoned road known as Featherbed Lane, about one hundred yards from the house. Two of the sections of this ladder were fastened together and the third section was found a few yards away. Of the two sections joined together, one was found to be split and broken on one side as though the ladder had collapsed. In the soft ground just outside of the library and directly below the nursery, New Jersey State Troopers found several rectangular impressions several inches deep, into which the base of the ladder fitted exactly. On the side of the house, at about the height of the second section of the ladder and directly above the rectangular impressions in the mud, some marks were found indicating the ladder had been rested against the side of the house. These marks were at the right of the east nursery window, resulting in the opinion by some of the officers that the kidnaper was left handed. Apparently only two sections of the ladder were used, as by placing the ladder in the rectangular impressions, the top of the second section would rest exactly over the marks under the nursery window. If the third section of the ladder had been used, the ladder would have reached almost to the top of the nursery window. Several feet below the marks in question were found other marks, resembling scratches on the side of the house, possibly indicating that the ladder had at least partially collapsed and struck the side of the house. Experts of the New Jersey State Police made a careful examination of the ladder, but no fingerprints were found on same. The New Jersey State Police conducted tests as a result of which it was determined that the ladder would not hold a weight of much over 125 lbs. In this connection, it should be considered that the baby alone weighed about 30 lbs. The details of the tests are not available. It was the consensus of opinion among investigating police officers that the ladder collapsed when the kidnaper descended it with the baby.

Although the night of the kidnaping was stormy and the ground was somewhat muddy, there was no evidence of footprints in the baby's nursery except the few particles of mud previously mentioned, nor were there any blood stains in or out of the nursery. Certain newspapers carried reports that blood stains were found on the window sill but the New Jersey State Police denied this. A small amount of yellow clay was found on the top edge of a lower window shutter, directly under the nursery window. Just outside of the nursery window, in the soft ground near the ladder impressions, were found indistinct outlines of footprints, incapable of measurement. An expert on trapping, as well as others qualified to render an opinion, decided that these impressions were made by someone with a small foot, possibly wearing moccasins, in stocking feet, or wearing socks or other cloth-covering over shoes. Apparently no plaster cast was ever made of same, though photographs of one or more are reported to be in the possession of the New Jersey State Police. A short distance from the house and east of the nursery window was found an old chisel, which was carefully examined but no fingerprints were found on same. If the chisel were brought by the kidnaper, he had no use for it, as the window through which entrance was apparently effected was already open.

The New Jersey State Police, upon arrival at the scene of the crime, took entire charge of the investigation; but so far as known, found no immediate clues other than those above mentioned.

For a number of months it had been the habit of Colonel Lindbergh and his wife, together with the baby, to leave the Morrow estate at Englewood, N. J. each week-end and spend Saturday and Sunday in their new home at Hopewell, usually returning thereafter on Monday to the Morrow estate at Englewood. On Friday night, February 26, 1932, in line with this custom, Colonel Lindbergh and his wife took the baby from the Morrow estate to the Hopewell home, which latter place was in charge at all times of Mr. and Mrs. Aloysius Ollie Whately, caretaker-butler and maid-cook respectively. The Whatelys lived over the garage annexed to the residence and remained on the estate continuously and were the only persons who continuously resided there. On the particular week-end in question, Mr. and Mrs. Ollie Whately were the only ones present at the Hopewell estate when Colonel Lindbergh, his wife and the baby arrived. Betty Gow, the child's nurse, remained at the Morrow estate in Englewood temporarily and did not arrive at the Hopewell residence until approximately 2:00 P.M. Tuesday, March 1, 1932, having been driven from the Morrow estate to the Lindbergh estate by the second Morrow chauffeur, Charles Henry Ellerson, upon telephonic instructions from Mrs. Lindbergh, who relayed the instructions through Violet Sharpe, Morrow maid, to whom she spoke over the telephone that morning at 10:30 o'clock.

The Lindbergh family was remaining at the Hopewell residence on this occasion longer than usual, due only to the illness of the child, who at that time was suffering from a chest cold, and Mrs. Lindbergh so told Violet Sharpe. Consequently, the Sharpe girl and probably other Morrow servants were aware of the plans to remain at Hopewell the night of March 1, 1932.

On Monday morning, February 29, 1932, about eight or nine o'clock, prior to the arrival of Betty Gow, the child's nurse, Colonel Lindbergh left the Hopewell estate for New York city where he spent the day. The Colonel spent that night at the Morrow estate in Englewood. He had a dinner speaking engagement for Tuesday night, March 1, 1932 in New York City, but forgot the engagement and returned to his family at Hopewell about 8:25 P.M. Tuesday, March 1, 1932. Previous to his arrival, about 7:30 P.M. he telephoned that he was on his way home. At 8:00 P.M. Colonel Breckinridge, Lindbergh's attorney, telephoned to inquire whether Colonel Lindbergh intended keeping his dinner engagement. The dinner Colonel Lindbergh was scheduled to attend that night at New York City was given by the Board of Regents of New York University. It appears that subsequent to the first trans-Atlantic flight of Colonel Lindbergh in 1926, he received an honorary degree from New York University, and since that had been receiving invitations from various members if the Board of Regents to attend the Board's dinners, but it appears that Colonel Lindbergh had not been in the habit of accepting these invitations. On the occasion in question, Chancellor Brown of this University, through his secretary, at the request of Mr. Barto, of the firm of J. Pierrepont Morgan & Company, extended an invitation to Colonel Lindbergh by letter to attend the dinner on the night of March 1, 1932. A Miss Betty Sheetz was then Colonel Lindbergh's secretary. Miss Sheetz upon the receipt of Chancellor Brown's letter made a proper notation on Colonel Lindbergh's engagement record that the dinner was scheduled to be held on the evening of March 1, 1932; in fact, such information was published by the various newspapers at New York City on that date. Subsequent thereto, a second letter was received from Chancellor Brown by Colonel Lindbergh and opened by his secretary, explaining to the Colonel that March 1st had been incorrectly designated in the previous letter as the time of the dinner and advising that the same was to be given a few days later. Accordingly, Miss Sheetz corrected the date on her engagement record. Apparently, however, Colonel Lindbergh was not informed of this change and remained under the constant impression that the dinner was scheduled for the evening of March 1st, which was, in fact, the correct date despite Chancellor Brown's second letter. News dispatches carried the story of Colonel Lindbergh's expected presence at the dinner in question on the evening of March 1, 1932.

Upon the arrival of Colonel Lindbergh at his Hopewell estate on the evening of March 1st at about 8:25 P.M., there were present at his home his wife and the baby, Betty Gow and Mr. and Mrs. Ollie Whately.

Lindbergh had driven in his car, alone, from New York

and upon his arrival at Hopewell was reminded by Mrs. Lindbergh of his failure to keep his dinner engagement and he then stopped to his telephone, Hopewell 303 at 8:30 and sent an apologetic telegram.

Due to the illness of the baby, he had remained in the nursery, in the southeast corner on the second floor of the residence, directly over the library, from approximately 7:00 P.M. to the time he was removed by the kidnaper. In the east end of the nursery are located two windows provided with shutters, which windows coincide with the two below in the east and of the library. On the night of the kidnaping, the east window of the nursery was left open and was, in fact, the only window in the nursery which was open. The windows in the nursery had two shutters, each of which was closed and fastened except one shutter on the east window, which was not fastened because of the fact that it was warped and could not be secured by the hooks. There were no curtains on any of the windows in the house; consequently anyone standing on one of the nearby knolls or hills could easily perceive the movements of those in the house. Thus, when the baby was put to bed and the lights extinguished, the kidnaper could have been aware of this fact.

It was a household rule at the Hopewell estate of the Lindberghs that no one, including Betty Gow, the child's nurse, was to disturb the child while it was sleeping between the hours of 8 and 10 P.M. About eight o'clock on the night of March 1, 1932 the baby was in his crib in the nursery, Mrs. Lindbergh having actually seen her child in the nursery at 7:45 o'clock on that night and having helped Betty Gow prepare it for bed at that time. Betty Gow states that at eight o'clock on the same evening, she returned to the nursery to observe the child and saw him in his crib at that hour, and it was she who fastened the shutters on the windows and left the east window open and the warped shutter unfastened. From the hour of 8:30 to 9:15 P.M. on that night, Colonel Lindbergh and his wife were at dinner in the dining room of the house on the first floor. The dining room is situated on the south side of the first floor, but separated from the library by a parlor. From approximately 9:15 to 9:30 P.M. Colonel Lindbergh and his wife stayed in the parlor next to the dining room, then Colonel Lindbergh went to the second floor for a few minutes without, however, entering the nursery, and returned again to the first floor. In the meantime, continuously from 8:00 P.M. to 10:00 P.M. Betty Gow was either in the kitchen, the west parlor on the first floor, or with Mrs. Whately in the latter's quarters, while Mrs. Whately was variously in the kitchen and in the Whately quarters. Ollio Whately was in the kitchen on the first floor during this period. At 8:35 P.M. Betty Gow received a telephone call from her sweetheart, Henry "Red" Johnson, who later was investigated as a suspect by the State Police and other authorities and exonerated.

At 9:45 P.M. Colonel and Mrs. Lindbergh heard a noise outside of the house resembling two boards striking together. They attributed this noise to natural causes. About 9:50 P.M. Colonel Lindbergh went into the library, situated immediately under the nursery, where he was reading when notified of the disappearance of the baby. Lindbergh proceeded promptly to the nursery and found the baby missing. He observed that the baby had been slipped from under the covers and removed clad only in a home made flannel shirt with slits down the side, two pairs of diapers, rubber pants and a brand new Dr. Denton #2 sleeping suit, in addition to two thumb guards tied around each wrist securely by a ribbon.

The flannel shirt had been made the evening of March 1st by Betty Gow, because of the baby's cold, and was stitched with blue silk thread. Mrs. Lindbergh observed this improvised shirt and helped Betty Gow put in on the baby.

Early in the morning of March 2nd, a local trapper and former Deputy Sheriff, Oscar Bush, was hired by Colonel Lindbergh to assist in the search of the immediate premises and of the surrounding countryside for the baby. Bush found tracks leading from under the nursery window to the spot where the ladder was found. This circumstance, together with others previously mentioned, strongly indicates that the ladder was used in the kidnaping. Bush traced the tracks, which he was inclined to believe were of two different persons, from the ladder through a field to Featherbed Lane, where they ended. Close to this point were marks in the bushes and in the grass which had apparently been made by an automobile. A woman's footprints were also found near the house but were apparently old impressions made by one of the household.

Featherbed Lane, which is an old abandoned country road, approximately parallel with the private road, runs from a point near the Lindbergh house, across the estate, to the Hopewell-Wertsville Road. The regular road used through the estate was constructed when the house was built. On March 29, 1932, Betty Gow discovered one of the thumb guards worth by the baby at the time of kidnaping, on the road at a point near the estate entrance.

The findings of Oscar Bush show, without much question, that the kidnapers used Featherbed Lane to effect their entrance to the estate, and their getaway. At each end of Featherbed Lane were posted notices—"Road Impassable—Drive at your own risk." Although this road was not actually impassable, it was in very poor condition and people living near it were surprised when about 6:30 P.M. the night of the kidnaping, they saw the lights of a car apparently on its way out of the Lane. Another resident of the neighborhood saw a car, in which were a number of ladders, at a point near Featherbed Lane, the evening of the kidnaping. With further reference to the findings of

Bush, it is stated that the trapper found indications that two cars were used in the kidnaping and that two individuals were present at the scene of the crime.

On March 2, 1932 Colonel Lindbergh designated Arthur W. Springer, secretary to the late Senator Dwight W. Morrow, and Douglas G. Thomson, former Mayor of Englewood, as intermediaries to make contact with the kidnapers, and it was publicly announced in all papers that the Lindberghs were willing to pay the ransom demanded for the return of their child. Meanwhile, the New Jersey State Police, commanded by Colonel H. Norman Schwarzkopf, were in charge of the case. The kidnapers had made a "clean getaway" and there were no clues except those previously mentioned. Likewise, there was no apparent motive for the crime except to obtain a ransom. Neither at the scene of the kidnaping nor from ransom notes subsequently received were latent fingerprints discovered.

A number of people residing near the Lindbergh estate had seen strange automobiles near the estate at different periods of time just prior to the kidnaping. Apparently the most important information along these lines concerned a 1929 Dodge Sedan bearing Mercer County, New Jersey license plates, which was seen on the highway near the estate about 6 P.M. This car was driven by a lone man, who was not recognized by the person who saw him as one of the local residents, but a good description of him was not obtained. In the car were a number of ladders similar to those found at the scene of the crime. This car was never located.

The New Jersey State Police had started an extensive investigation by stopping all cars and questioning their occupants. The territory for miles around was searched for days by the police, but no clues of value found. The twenty-nine servants of the Morrow household, and the few servants making up the Lindbergh household, were thoroughly questioned and statements taken from each. In addition, they were thoroughly investigated as to their past lives, associates and habits. Each of the servants apparently accounted for his or her activities during the period in which the crime occurred, except a maid in the Morrow employ, named Violet Sharpe. This girl when first questioned furnished an incorrect account of her activities and whereabouts the night of the kidnaping. It was she who received the telephone message from Mrs. Lindbergh at 10:30 A.M. the day of the crime, that the Lindberghs would extend their stay at Hopewell due to the baby's cold. Violet Sharpe had a sister, Edna, who frequently visited her at Englewood, and both of these girls had lived and worked in New York City and were fairly well acquainted there. The New Jersey State Police subsequently learned that Violet Sharpe had been out the night of the crime with Ernest Miller, Elmer Johnson of Closter, N. J. and Katherine Minners of Palisades Park, N. J., all subsequently exonerated. She originally made the acquaintance of Ernest Miller on the streets of Englewood, and together with him and the other couple, spent the evening in a roadhouse in the Oranges, N. J.

On March 2, 1932, an underworld character named Morris Rosner of New York City proposed himself and was introduced but not recommended by certain prominent New York people as an intermediary to contact the underworld. Rosner was allowed the free run of the Lindbergh home, and acted independently of the police. He was shown the first, second and third ransom notes and was given a sketch of the first note. On March 5, 1932 Rosner brought two other New York underworld characters, Salvatore Spitale and Irving Bitz, to Hopewell, and shortly thereafter these two were formally designated by Colonel Lindbergh as intermediaries to deal with the underworld. Although they received much publicity in connection with their efforts to contact the Purple Gang of Detroit and others, there ware no indications that they ever, at any time, established contact with the real kidnapers. Rosner was later discredited and withdrawn from the case.

The wide publicity given the kidnaping resulted in a deluge of letters from every direction, containing principally unfounded information. Many hoaxes and frauds were perpetrated by persons claiming to have contact with or information regarding the kidnapers, the most publicized of these being the $100,000 paid by Mrs. Evelyn Walsh McLean of Washington, D.C. to Gaston B. Moans, and the John Hughes Curtis fraud centering in the vicinity of Norfolk, Virginia. Alphonso Capone, who had been sentenced to a long term in a Federal Penitentiary for income tax violations, endeavored to secure his liberty by promising to bring about the safe return of the child.

On March 5, 1932 a second ransom note, bearing the same secret symbol used on the first note and postmarked Brooklyn, March 4th, was received by Colonel Lindbergh, informing him that he would have to take the consequences of the publicity and that the ransom was increased from $50,000 to $70,000. On the following day, one Peter J. Berritella, a self-styled spiritualist and "Reverend" and Mary Cirrito, his "medium", both of Harlem, New York City, communicated with the Lindbergh home by telegram and shortly thereafter were interviewed at Princeton, N. J. by Colonel Breckinridge. After engaging in a spiritualistic séance relative to the baby's whereabouts and making a number of remarks possibly indicating they had been sent by the kidnapers, they suggested that Colonel Breckinridge spend more time in his office, implying that he might receive word from the kidnapers.

On March 8, 1932 Colonel Breckinridge received the third ransom note at his office in New York City. The note, which had been mailed in New York City, the day previous, advised that the kidnapers would not accept any go-betweens appointed by the Lindberghs and instructed that an ad be placed in the New York American, stating whether the Lindberghs were "ready."

Also, on March 8th, an elderly, retired school teacher and principal, Dr. John F. Condon of the Bronx, New York City, offered through the Bronx Home News, to act as go-between in the case. Within twenty-four hours Dr. Condon received the fourth ransom note, bearing the secret symbol, and postmarked Bronx, New York City, March 9, 1932. The note stated that Condon was acceptable as go-between and instructed him to place an ad in the New York American. A note to Colonel Lindbergh advising of Condon's designation was enclosed. Late that night, Dr. Condon and two of his friends, Max Rosenhain, restaurant proprietor of the Bronx, and a young man named Milton Gaglio, proceeded to Hopewell and conferred with Colonel Lindbergh. On March 10, 1932 Condon received a telephone message to be at home the night of March 12th when he would receive further instructions. About this time $70,000 in old currency was delivered to Dr. Condon by Colonel Lindbergh, with authority to pay this sum as ransom.

On March 11th Dr. Condon placed the following ad in the New York American and Bronx Home News: "Money is ready. Jafsie." Dr. Condon assumed the pseudonym "Jafsie" so that his true identity would not be disclosed. On the day following the publication of the above ad, Dr. Condon received a telephone message from an unknown person instructing him to be at home that night. At 8:30 P.M. the fifth ransom note was delivered to Dr. Condon by a taxi driver named Joseph Perrone, who received the note from an unidentified man on a street corner near Woodlawn Cemetery in the Bronx. The note instructed Dr. Condon to proceed to a vacant frankfurter stand near Woodlawn Cemetery where he would find another note. Condon proceeded as directed, in company with his so-called bodyguard, Al Reich, and found the sixth note under a stone. Following directions contained in same, Dr. Condon crossed the street and followed the fence enclosing Woodlawn Cemetery, leaving Reich parked nearby in his car. An unknown individual, apparently an Italian, was observed to walk by with a handkerchief up to his face, and was possibly a "look-out." In the meanwhile, as Condon was walking alongside the cemetery fence, another man standing inside the cemetery, called out to him. They engaged in conversation for a few moments, when a cemetery guard approached, after which the unknown man climbed over the fence with agility and ran a short distance into Van Cortlandt Park. Dr. Condon ran after the stranger and persuaded him to stop and they then sat down together on a park bench and talked for about an hour. He stranger identified himself only as "John" and one of his first questions was whether Condon had the money. To this Dr. Condon replied that the money would not be paid without some token that "John" actually represented the kidnapers. "John" stated the baby's sleeping suit would be sent as "evidence". During the conversation "John" stated there were five persons involved in the kidnaping—three men and two women. At the conclusion of the conversation "John" disappeared into the wooded section of Van Cortlandt Park, walking in a northerly direction. Dr. Condon afterwards asserted that he could positively identify "John" if he ever saw him again. On the following day, and again on March 13, 14, 15, and 16th Condon inserted ads in the Bronx Home News and New York American that the money was ready and requesting that the kidnapers communicate with him. During this period Dr. Condon was in constant touch with Colonel Lindbergh; Colonel Breckinridge was continually at the Condon home.

Shortly before March 16th, exact date unknown, a young

Italian selling needles appeared at the Condon residence and sold some needles to Dr. Condon. After the Italian made his departure, Colonel Breckinridge and Dr. Condon observed that he walked off the block without stopping at the neighboring houses. About an hour later, another Italian of a similar description as the first and wearing gloves, appeared at the Condon residence with a scissors grinding apparatus and after sharpening some implements walked down the street like the first man without soliciting business at other houses. It appears possible that one or both of these Italians may have been emissaries of the kidnapers.

On March 16th Dr. Condon received a freshly laundered Dr. Denton #2 sleeping suit purporting to be the Lindbergh baby's. The package in which the suit was received was postmarked Brooklyn, New York, the same date, and contained, in addition to the suit, the seventh ransom note. This note directed attention to the symbolic signatures on the various notes and the sleeping suit, as the kidnapers' identification of themselves, and insisted that the ransom be paid prior to the return of the child. Colonel Lindbergh later identified the sleeping suit as identical with the one worn by his child when kidnaped.

From March 17th to 21st inclusive, Dr. Condon inserted ads in the Bronx Home News and New York American advising the money was ready and pleading with the kidnapers to get in touch with him. On March 19th an unknown woman approached Dr. Condon at a small charity bazaar conducted by him in the Bronx and requested him to meet her at the railroad station at Tuckahoe, New York on March 23rd. Dr. Condon kept this appointment accompanied by Al Reich, and was instructed by the woman to continue his advertising.

On March 21st the eighth ransom note, postmarked New York City, March 19th, was received by Dr. Condon, the note stating that the baby was well and insisting on complete compliance with all terms. On March 22nd Condon inserted an ad in the New York American that the package (meaning the sleeping suit) was received and "accepted as the real article." Between March 23rd and 30th inclusive, Dr. Condon published various ads in the New York American and Bronx Home News, requesting the kidnapers to get in touch with him and advising the money was ready. In some of those ads Condon requested that a simple code which could be followed in the newspapers be furnished by the kidnapers.

On March 29th Betty Gow, while walking near the entrance to the Lindbergh estate, found one of the thumb guards which the baby had on when kidnaped.

The ninth ransom note, postmarked New York City, March 29, 1932, was received by Dr. Condon on March 30th and advised that no code would be furnished for use in the papers, and further that if the matter was not closed by April 8th the ransom would be $100,000. On the following day Dr. Condon inserted an ad in the New York American and Bronx Home News "I hereby accept. Money is ready. Jafsie." This ad was repeated in both papers on the following day.

On April 1st, Dr. Condon received the tenth ransom note, postmarked Bronx, New York City, which instructed him to have the money ready for Saturday night, April 2, 1932, and to answer by an ad in the newspapers. Dr. Condon placed ads in the New York American and Bronx Home News of April 2nd that everything was ready. On this same date Dr. Condon received the eleventh ransom note, which was delivered at his home by a taxi driver who has never been identified. Following instructions contained in this note, Dr. Condon, taking the money with him and accompanied by Colonel Lindbergh, proceeded to Bergen's Greenhouse, across the street from St. Raymonds Cemetery in the Bronx, and there found the twelfth ransom note under a table. Colonel Lindbergh waited nearby in the car while Dr. Condon, following the directions in this note, entered the cemetery and there met "John" with whom he had previously conversed at Woodlawn Cemetery. "John" agreed to accept $50,000 ransom instead of $70,000 and after a trip back to the car to get the money, Dr. Condon handed the $50,000 to "John", who was standing behind a hedge in the shadows. At this time Dr. Condon observed another figure lurking in the background behind "John." The money when paid over was contained in a box which Dr. Condon had constructed according to directions contained in one of the ransom notes. "John handed Dr. Condon the thirteenth and last ransom note, which stated the baby would be found on a boat called "Nellie" off Martha's Vineyard, Elizabeth Islands, near Horseneck Beach. For the next few days Colonel Lindbergh and Dr. Condon, the United States Coast Guard, and others made a thorough search of the above vicinity, but were unable to find the baby. In the succeeding days Dr. Condon placed ads in the papers previously used requesting better directions. These ads were never answered and nothing more was heard from the kidnapers.

After Colonel Lindbergh's disappointment in the outcome of the negotiations, he was persuaded by John Hughes Curtis, shipbuilder of Norfolk, Virginia, to spend almost two weeks on a boat at sea off the Virginia Coast, trying to make contact with the kidnapers. Curtis finally confessed that the whole thing was a fraud and was convicted and sentenced to a year in jail.

In the meantime, on April 6, 1932, all banks throughout the country were furnished by the United States Treasury Department with the serial numbers of the ransom money and requested to keep a close lookout for the money. The first ransom bill in circulation was discovered on April 4, 1932 in New York City but the investigation concerning it developed no material results. Since that date ransom bills have been discovered in approximately fifty-five different places, in nearly every instance in Greater New York and its environs.

On May 12, 1932 the body of the Lindbergh child was accidentally discovered about four and a half miles southeast of the Lindbergh home, partially buried under dirt and leaves and in a badly decomposed condition. The spot where the corpse was found was about 75 feet from the Princeton-Hopewell road, near Mt. Rose, N.J. The body was subsequently identified by Colonel Lindbergh and Betty Gow and by a baby specialist who had examined the child shortly before the kidnaping. The coroner's examination showed that the child had probably been dead about two months and that death was caused by a sharp instrument of some kind or a bullet. The coroner found that the skull was crushed and that there was a hole in the skull. The body of the child was cremated on May 13, 1932.

During the entire period of the ransom negotiations above described, the case was receiving widespread investigative attention by the New Jersey State Police, who were supervising the investigation, and by the New York City police, and in a lesser degree by authorities in other parts of the country. Various government agencies offered their cooperation but were mainly used in an auxiliary capacity to interview the thousands of persons who claimed to have information of value.

On May 20, 1932 the Bronx County, New York Grand Jury conducted an investigation relative to the payment of the ransom money in this case, and Dr. Condon, Colonel Breckinridge, Joseph Perrone, Milton Gaglio, Max Rosenhain, and others were called as witnesses, but no indictments were returned.

On May 26, 1932 the New Jersey State Police issued a circular announcing that a reward of $25,000 would be paid by the State of New Jersey for information leading to the arrest and convictions of the guilty persons.

The New Jersey State Police had interviewed the Morrow servant, Violet Sharpe, a number of times and were about to question her again on June 10, 1932, when she committed suicide at the Morrow home, Engelwood, N. J. by taking poison. The motive for her suicide has never been learned. A search of her effects and belongings and an extensive investigation failed to develop anything incriminating.

An examination of the ransom notes by handwriting experts resulted in a unanimous opinion that all the notes, including the first or original, were written by the same person, and the further opinion that the writer was of German nationality, but had spent some years in America. Dr. Condon had described "John" as a Scandinavian. Unsuccessful efforts were made to trace the writing materials used.

After payment of the ransom money, the New Jersey State Police, the New York City Police, and the Intelligence Unit of the United States Treasury Department cooperated in an effort to apprehend the persons who were passing the ransom money in Greater New York. The $50,000 paid as ransom comprised $10,000 in $5 bills; $15,000 in $10 gold certificates, and $25,000 in $20 bills, of which $20,000 was gold certificates. All banking institutions and their branches and many of the large chain retail establishments in New York City were furnished with the serial numbers of the ransom bills and requested to cooperate. In addition, the New York police obtained the names of all persons who rented safety deposit boxes in the months of March and April, 1932, the names to be used in connection with the checking of suspects.

On April 5, 1933 the President issued an Executive Order to the effect that all gold, gold bullion and gold certificates under penalty of fine or imprisonment, should be turned in to the Federal Reserve Banks, branches or member banks on or before May 1, 1933. After the publication of this order the New York banks were again requested to be on the lookout for the ransom money, particularly, the gold certificates.

On May 1, 1933 an unknown person exchanged $2,980 of the Lindbergh ransom money, consisting of 296—$10 gold certificates and one $20 gold certificate at the Federal Reserve Bank of New York, New York City. The person who exchanged the above sum filled out a deposit ticket as was required in connection with the exchange of gold certificates and wrote thereon the name "J. J. Faulkner, 537 West 149." The teller who received this sum was unable to recall from whom he received it.

Immediately after the discovery of the $2,980 in gold certificates at the Federal Reserve Bank, an extensive investigation was instituted by the interested authorities and on a later date by the Division's New York office. The results to date are set forth in the body of this report.

Shortly after May 1, 1933 there were also discovered at the Federal Reserve Bank several other large sums of the ransom money, consisting of a package of ten dollar gold certificates amounting to $500, which was traced to the Manufacturers Trust Company, 149 Broadway, New York City and which had been exchanged in that bank between April 27 and 29, 1933. The other sums consisted of a package of twenty-four ten dollar gold certificates and another package containing twenty-six ten dollar gold certificates. Both packages were traced to the Chemical National Bank, Cortlandt Street and Broadway, New York city. The deposit slips covering the exchange of the ransom money in the Chemical National Bank and the Manufacturers Trust Company were not found.

The matters mentioned herein are covered in detail in the following sections of this report.

SUMMARY REPORT

In Re

Unknown Subjects

Kidnaping and Murder of Charles A. Lindbergh, Jr. (N.Y. File 62-3057).

LINDBERGH HOME

-o-

Locality and description

Thomas Fensch

THE LINDBERGH HOME
(LOCALITY AND DESCRIPTION)

Colonel Charles A. Lindbergh and Anne Morrow were married on May 27, 1929 at the Morrow home in Englewood, N. J. Charles A. Lindbergh, Jr. was born in the same house on June 22, 1930, and his first birthday was celebrated there. While Colonel and Mrs. Lindbergh were on their flying tour of the Orient in the summer of 1931, the child spent part of the season at the Morrow summer home in North Haven, Maine and later in the summer was back in Englewood, awaiting their return. In October, he again accompanied the Morrows to Maine. On October 17, 1931 the Lindberghs moved into the home of Harold L. Van Horn near Princeton, N. J. to stay there until the home they were building near Hopewell, N. J. should be completed.

It is said that the Lindberghs picked the site of their new home from the air as they were flying together over the Jersey forests seeking a suitable spot. It was selected for complete privacy. The only immediate neighbors are farmers who live a simple, rural existence, and there are only three other houses within a mile of the house.

The estate consists of several hundred acres of which only a small portion is cleared, lying partly in Hunterdon County and partly in Mercer County, the house being in Hunterdon County. The nucleus of the estate was purchased from Charles Rathousky, a farmer, and garage proprietor of Hopewell. The nearest traffic artery about one-half mile from the house, is the Hopewell-Wertsville Highway. It is located about three and one-quarter miles from Hopewell, N. J. Hopewell is ten miles northwest of Princeton, N. J.; twenty miles north of Trenton; about forty miles northeast of Philadelphia, and about fifty miles south of New York.

The Delaware River is fifteen miles to the west where it is bridged at Lambertville, N. J. The house stands in a secluded spot, on the summit of Sorrel Hill, in the Sourland Mountains, in a region sparsely inhabited, difficult of access, thickly wooded and clogged with underbrush, and was practically without organized police protection.

In back of the house are thick woods, which can be penetrated only by following long unused paths. In front and on both sides the country is more open. A quarter of a mile from the structure a meadow forms a natural landing field for airplanes, which it was planned to improve for this purpose.

The home was completed in December 1931 at a cost of approximately $50,000. It was built by the Conover Construction Company of Hopewell, which let out a number of sub-contracts. Lee Hurley of Hopewell was guard of the construction work during the building operations and left in December 1931. A list of the men employed in the construction work appears in the supplement of this report as Exhibit "I": The New Jersey State Police made a check of each of these employees but found nothing to implicate any of them. It is made of native field stone, covered with a white cement wash. It is a rambling two and half story structure of modified French provincial style of architecture and overlooks the town of Hopewell several miles away. On the ground floor are the living rooms connecting through French doors with a large porch, the dining room and the wing in which the kitchen and pantry are located. From the front door a small entrance leads into the living room which is the largest room in the house, with fireplaces at each end. French windows look out upon a stone paved terrace, beyond which the land extends away to the private landing field which was under construction. A three car garage is attached to the house, and at the other end of the building on this floor are two small chambers, used as a den and guest room. The stairway leading upstairs arises from the entrance hall to the family private chambers. Colonel and Mrs. Lindbergh's rooms are directly above the living room, with the baby's nursery adjoining. The servants' quarters are over the garage and the third floor consists of an unfinished attic. The windows of the house were equipped with shutters but were not furnished with either shades or curtains. The rear door opens on a paved parking space from which the private road extends to the highway.

Only three roads lead out of Hopewell, N. J. and it was along one of these that the kidnapers must have taken the Lindbergh baby; only a mile or two beyond Hopewell the roads branch out to meet other roads, intersecting roads that cross and recross to form a network of highways and by-paths over the entire state of New Jersey. It was reported that when only a mile or two out of Hopewell, the kidnapers had a choice of one hundred and eight different roads paved and unpaved. A few miles south Main Highways 29 and 31 cross and a few miles east is the main line road which connects New Brunswick and Princeton.

One road leads almost due south from Hopewell. It runs for six miles through Mount Rose (near where the baby's body was found on May 13, 1932) and Rosedale. It joins the Lincoln Highway just above Lawrenceville. If the kidnapers took this route and did not turn into any of the numerous side-roads that branch off of it they could have turned either north or south on the Lincoln Highway. Turning north they would have reached New Brunswick and there turning right they would have reached Newark and New York, or left, Easton, Pa. Turning south, they could have reached Trenton and Philadelphia.

Situated approximately three miles from the Lindbergh estate is New Jersey State Village for Epileptics. The New Jersey State Police conducted an investigation of the inmates and any who might have escaped, also of the employees, but found nothing to indicate complicity.

The Lindberghs' only contact with anyone in the vicinity of their home was with merchants in Hopewell in the purchase of groceries, meats, etc. However, even this contact was indirect as ordering and buying was usually done by servants over the telephone. The tradespeople and mountaineers repeatedly disliked the Lindberghs because of their aloofness, and natural dislike the natives had for strangers. It is known that the territory purchased by Colonel Lindbergh had been a favorite hunting ground for many of the natives. After this purchase of the estate Colonel Lindbergh barred everyone, which further added to the feeling against him. The Sourland Mountains are inhabited largely by uneducated people who keep much to themselves, many of them earn their livelihood by making applejack. According to news reports a number of stills were raided after the Lindberghs moved into their new home, and Lindbergh was blamed, this possibly furnishing a motive for the crime. The State Police, however, discounted these reports which apparently had no basis in fact.

SUMMARY REPORT

In re

Unknown Subjects

Kidnaping and Murder of Charles A. Lindbergh, Jr. (N.Y. File 62-3057).

LINDBERGH HOUSEHOLD AND EMPLOYEES

-o-

Charles A. Lindbergh, Jr.
Aloysius Whately
Mrs. Aloysius Whately
Betty Gow
Dog (Trixie)
Betty Sheetz
Marie Cummings.

LINDBERGH HOUSEHOLD & EMPLOYEES

The Lindbergh household was a comparatively small one and consisted of Colonel and Mrs. Charles A. Lindbergh, and their son Charles A. Lindbergh, Jr.; Bessie Mowat Gow (More commonly known as Betty Gow), nurse to Charles A. Lindbergh, Jr.; Aloysius Whately (also known as Olly Whately), butler-chauffeur and caretaker of the Hopewell estate, and the latter's wife, Phoebe Mary Whately, cook and maid at the Hopewell estate. The only other persons known to have been employed by the Lindberghs are Marie Cummings, a registered nurse, who attended Charles A. Lindbergh, Jr. at birth and for the onsuing six weeks, at the end of which time Nurse Gow was employed and Nurse Cummings departed, returning at a later unknown date, remained several weeks and was discharged; Elizabeth Sheetz of Montclair, N. J. employed by Colonel Lindbergh as secretary, at the time of the kidnaping. The files contain a reference to another registered nurse who attended Mrs. Lindbergh during the period between Nurse Cummings' employments but do not list her name. The Lindberghs are reported to have employed a Mr. And Mrs. John Tyler, who entered the United States, March 1930, with Quota Visas, and departed August 29, 1931 with entry permits which were not used up to and including March 12, 1932 indicating they were still absent from the United States. A Mr. And Mrs. Clarence Dyson also reported to have been employed by the Lindberghs, first entered the United States in September 1927 and departed August 27, 1931 with reentry permits not used up to and including March 12, 1932. The files do not contain any additional information concerning these couples.

CHARLES A. LINDBERGH, JR.

Charles A. Lindbergh, Jr., the first child of Colonel and Mrs. Charles A. Lindbergh, was born June 22, 1930 at the home of Dwight W. Morrow at Englewood, N.J. Dr. Hawkes was the physician in attendance. At the time of the kidnaping, this baby was 20 months old, weight 27 to 30 lbs., height 29", hair blonde and curly, eyes dark blue, complexion light, deep dimple in center of chin. He was perfectly normal and healthy in every respect; the only physical deformities being in his toes, which overlapped each other, on both feet. The baby had a high forehead, and rather large head. On the night of March 1st he was suffering from a croupy cold and was dressed in a flannel shirt made by Betty Gow, over which was placed a small sleeveless shirt of silk and wool; he also wore two diapers, one pair rubber pants, and a Dr. Denton's No. 2 sleeping suit of gray woolen material, 24" long, having four buttons up the back in a straight line and two buttons on the flapover; and strings attached to the sleeves and to the neck-band. The suit also had a pocket on the front left-hand side and a small red label at the back of the neck band, which contained the name of the manufacturer. He also wore thumb guards, a wire contraption to prevent him from sucking his thumbs.

ALOYSIUS WHATELY, commonly referred to as OLLY WHATELY and WHATLEY

Butler, chauffeur and caretaker of the Lindbergh residence at Hopewell, N.J. He is a native of England, of Scotch descent. He applied for emigrant's visa at London, England, December 16, 1929 and arrived in the United States via port of New York, March 12, 1930, aboard the S. S.

"Scythia". On his application for emigrant visa he listed his occupation as engineer; his nearest relative as Mrs. Moore, sister, 30 Stanley Avenue, Birmingham, England; date of birth as June 24, 1884; residence 37 Stanley Avenue, Hagley, West, Birmingham, England; married; wife Phoebe Whately, same address; destination 71 Franklin Avenue, New Rochelle, N.Y. where he expected to visit a friend, Mr. Dyson.

Whately entered the employ of Colonel and Mrs. Charles A. Lindbergh October 15, 1930, and with his wife acted as caretaker of the Lindbergh estate at Hopewell, N.J. and resided there continuously after the house was completed. Frequently in the absence of the Lindberghs, he acted as guide to tourists and other curious visitors showing them through the house and about the adjoining grounds.

Whately last saw Charles A. Lindbergh, Jr. at 5:30 P.M. March 1, 1932, at which time both were in the pantry. Shortly thereafter a telephone call was received from Colonel Lindbergh, advising that the latter would be late for supper. Lindbergh arrived home at about 8:30 P.M. Whately served supper between 8:45 and 9: P.M. and after completing his duties, he returned to the sitting room, while Mrs. Whately and Betty Gow proceeded to the Whately quarters. At 10:00 P.M. he was informed by his wife that Colonel Lindbergh wanted to see him immediately; that the baby had disappeared. He joined Colonel Lindbergh and assisted in searching the inside and outside of the house. He saw the ransom note, reading it over Colonel Lindbergh's shoulder. He telephoned to the police upon instructions from Colonel Lindbergh.

Whately's fingerprints were forwarded to the Identification Unit of the Division and to Scotland Yard, but no previous criminal record was ascertained. He died in the Spring of 1933, while still in the employ of the Lindberghs. Whately was prominently mentioned in the press reports of the instant kidnaping as one of those referred to by D.N. Stuart as having associated with Frederick V. Short, at Vancouver, B.C. during the summer and fall of 1930. This was subsequently disproved.

His description as contained on his application for emigrant's visa is:

    Age: 45 years
    Height: 6'8"
    Hair: Dark
    Eyes: Gray
    Complexion: Medium.

He has one brother in the United States, Reginald Whately, 2950 Nebraska Avenue, Detroit, Mich., an American citizen; occupation, caretaker of apartment house.

MRS. ALOYSIUS (PHOEBE MARY) WHATELY,
More commonly known as
MRS. OLLY WHATELY, and WHATLEY

Cook and maid at the Lindbergh residence, Hopewell, N.J. Wife of Aloysius Whately, butler, chauffeur, same manage. She was born in Birmingham, England, November 2, 1884; applied for emigrant's visa at London, England, December 16, 1929. She accompanied her husband to the United States arriving at the port of New York, March 12, 1930, aboard the S.S. "Scythia". In her application for emigrant visa, she described herself as married; occupation housewife; and listed nearest kin as Emily Ward, sister, 233 Baldwin Road, Birmingham, England; and stated that she expected to visit a friend, Mr. Dyson, 71 Franklin Avenue in New Rochelle, N.Y.

With her husband she entered the employ of the Lindberghs October 15, 1930 and after the completion of the Lindberghs' Hopewell house, resided there continuously until the death of her husband during the spring of 1933. It is not definitely known whether she is still in the employ of the Lindberghs.

She last saw Charles A. Lindbergh, Jr. at 5:30 P.M., March 1, 1932, when Betty Gow took him to the nursery. She was in her quarters at the Hopewell residence of the Lindberghs at the time Betty Gow discovered the disappearance of the Lindbergh baby.

Her fingerprints were furnished the Identification Unit of this Division and to Scotland Yard but no criminal record was developed. The Whatelys are childless.

Her description as contained on her application for emigrant's visa follows:

Age:	45 years
Height:	5'2"
Hair:	Fair
Eyes:	Blue
Complexion:	Medium

Betty Gow

Betty Gow is the last known person to have seen Charles A. Lindbergh, Jr. alive. She was born in Glasgow, Scotland, February 12, 1904, the daughter of William Gordon Gow and Isobel McClagen Gow, the latter now Mrs. Taylor. Her father was born in the Orkney Islands. She has two brothers living, James, 29, and Alexander, 18 years, (1932). She has two sisters, Agnes, 25, and Isobella, 16 years, all residing in Glasgow, Scotland and have never visited the United States. One brother, William Gow, died in the United States, September 4, 1931. She has an aunt and uncle known as Mr. And Mrs. Alexander Thom, residing at 187 North First St., Rittman, Ohio. While in Glasgow she resided at 30 Nithsdale Street, and was employed by A.L. Scott & Son, shoe dealers. She immigrated to the United

States, April 28, 1929, arriving at the port of New York, May 4, 1929, via the S.S. "Cameronia" of the Anchor Line, travelling under immigration visa issued at Liverpool, England, February 5, 1929 to Betty Gow. She immediately took up her residence with her brother, William Gow, at 147 River Road, Bogota, N.J., and a few days later entered the employ of the Fred Gibbs family at 183 Kings Court, Teaneck, N.J., where she remained until about January 1930, then employed by F. C. Gibbs Sunset House, Teaneck, N.J., quitting in May 1939, at which time she proceeded to Detroit where she resided with the Adam Jackson family at 5212 Lakewood Street. Mrs. Jackson is the sister of the wife of William Gow, brother of Betty Gow. She remained in Detroit until October 1930, and while there was employed for a few days by the Ross family at the Parkstone Apartments, and after leaving this position was employed for the succeeding two weeks by the Moser family at Grose Point. She then secured a position as chambermaid at the New Whittier Apartments, Jefferson Avenue, Detroit, under Miss V. Middy, and retained this position until her departure from Detroit during October 1930.

During her residence in Detroit, she is only known to have associated with one man, William Couttos, a fellow townsman from Glasgow, Scotland then employed at the Ford Automobile Company. Upon leaving Detroit she returned to the home of her brother, William Gow at Bogota, N.J. and remained there one week. Through the Lydia Lonquist Employment Agency, she then secured a position with Mrs. Warren Sullivan, Glenwood Road, Englewood, N. J. where she remained approximately nine months, leaving to take the position as nurse to Charles A. Lindbergh, Jr. She is understood to have secured this latter position upon recommendations made to Miss Elizabeth Morrow by Mary Beattie then in the Morrow employ at Englewood, N.J. Miss Beattie is reported to be related to Betty Gow.

Investigation to date has established Betty Gow's reputation as quiet, conscientious, reliable, studious and ambitious. The Lindberghs had and apparently still have implicit confidence in her. She had charge of Charles A. Lindbergh, Jr., to whom she is reported to have been greatly attached, during the several months his parents were absent on their flight to the Orient, and had sole custody of this baby for a forty day period during the "Flu Epidemic". She is still in the employ of the Lindberghs as nurse to the Lindberghs' second son "Jon".

William Gow, brother of Betty, was the husband of Jean Farley, also of Glasgow. While employed by the Public Service Electric Company of New Jersey, September 4, 1931 he was accidentally electrocuted. His widow shortly thereafter returned to Scotland.

Subsequent to the discovery of the body of the Lindbergh baby, Betty Gow positively identified the body found as that of Charles A. Lindbergh, Jr.

Several months after the discovery of the body of Charles A. Lindbergh, Jr., Betty Gow made a short trip to Glasgow, Scotland, where she visited her mother, and upon her return immediately reentered the Lindbergh employ.

Due to the desire of Mrs. Charles A. Lindbergh to become better acquainted with her son, Betty Gow did not accompany the Lindberghs to their Hopewell estate the week-end immediately preceding the kidnaping. She remained at the Morrow estate over this week-end and under date of Sunday, February 28, 1932, she went out with Finn Henrik ("Red") Johnson in his automobile. They drove for a while, had dinner and returned to the servants' quarters at the Morrow estate where they played cards with several of the other servants. On Monday, February 29, 1932, she again dated with Johnson and with him again played cards with several of the other Morrow servants and made an appointment to see Johnson the following night (March 1, 1932).

At approximately 10:30 A.M., March 1, 1932, a telephone call was received at the Morrow estate from Mrs. C.A. Lindbergh at Hopewell, advising that she intended remaining at Hopewell that night instead of returning that afternoon as previously planned. She instructed that Betty Gow join her at Hopewell that afternoon. Subsequent to the receipt of these instructions and prior to her departure for Hopewell, Betty Gow telephoned Johnson's rooming house, 41 James Street, Englewood, N.J., and after being informed that he was absent, requested his landlady, Mrs. W.T. Sherman, to have Johnson call her at the Morrow residence when he returned. She did this to save Johnson the cost of a call to Hopewell, knowing that the other servants at the Morrow residence would inform him of the changed plans and of her whereabouts.

Betty Gow left the Morrow estate at Englewood, at approximately 12 M to 1: P.M., March 1, 1932, in one of the Morrow automobiles, driven by the Morrow's second chauffeur, Charles Henry Ellerson, and upon arrival at the Lindbergh estate at Hopewell entered upon her duties attending Charles A. Lindbergh, Jr. At approximately 7:30 P.M. she assisted Mrs. Lindbergh in preparing him for bed, and at 8: P.M. left him in his bed in the nursery, apparently asleep. At approximately 8:35 P.M., Betty Gow received a long distance telephone call from Finn Henrik Johnson, and then explained to him her inability to keep the appointment made the previous evening. She was advised by Johnson that he intended driving to the home of his brother, John, at West Hartford, Conn., the following day. After the receipt of this telephone call, she was engaged by other household affairs until 10: P.M., at which time she visited the nursery and discovered the absence of Charles A. Lindbergh, Jr., and immediately notified Mrs. Lindbergh.

Under date of March 29, 1932, while walking she discovered one of the thumb guards worn by the baby at the time of the kidnaping, observing it lying in the middle of the road at the entrance to the estate, approximately one half mile from the Lindbergh home.

During the negotiations between Dr. John F. Condon and "John", the representative of the kidnapers, and during their first meeting at Woodlawn Cemetery, March 12, 1932, "John" informed Condon that neither Betty Gow nor "Red" Johnson was in any way involved in the kidnaping and that both were innocent.

Considerable investigation has been conducted in and about Detroit, in connection with a rumor to the effect that Betty Gow is the sister of one "Scotty" Gow, a reputed gangster and member of the Detroit "Purple Gang". This rumor was discredited.

Further investigation at Detroit was made relative to the possible relationship existing between Betty Gow and one Mortimer Farley, Windsor, Canada, a police character. However, investigation did not develop any relationship or acquaintance between the two.

Considerable investigation was conducted by the Seattle and San Francisco Offices relative to the possible association of Betty Gow, Henry "Red" Johnson, Olly Whately, Dr. John F. Condon and Frederick V. Short at Vancouver, British Columbia, during the latter part of 1930, allegations to this effect having been made by one D.M. Stuart of Vancouver, B.C. Investigation disproved these allegations.

DOG

A black Scotch Terrier puppy, named "Trixie" was permitted the run of the Lindbergh house at Hopewell; she usually retired early, in the hall outside the door of the nursery; she usually barked loudly at strangers but is reported to have been silent when the kidnapers were in the nursery. Olly Whately is reported as having stated that on the night of the kidnaping, the dog was in the butler's pantry. Colonel Breckinridge has stated that the dog was not in the house at the time of the kidnaping.

ELIZABETH SHEETZ

Secretary to Colonel Charles A. Lindbergh, at his office, 39 Broadway, New York City, at the time of the kidnaping; is reputed to be of excellent character, and a Social Registerite, residing at Montclair, N.J.

On the night of March 1, 1932, Colonel Lindbergh was scheduled to attend a dinner given by the Board of Regents of New York University. Miss Sheetz made the necessary notation on his engagement record. Subsequently the dinner was postponed to a later date and Miss Sheetz corrected Lindbergh's engagement record. However, Colonel Lindbergh apparently was not cognizant of the correction and was under the impression that the dinner was to take place on March 1, 1932 according to schedule.

As will be noted, Miss Sheetz was one of those aware of the likelihood of Colonel Lindbergh's absence from his home, March 1, 1932, and the possibility that she may have discussed this matter with others or before servants has been suggested as worthy of further investigation. The files in this office do not reflect that Miss Sheetz has ever been interviewed.

MARIE CUMMINGS

Marie Cummings, a trained nurse, secured temporary employment with the Lindberghs about June 22, 1930 when the baby was born. She was brought to the Morrow estate in Englewood where the Lindberghs were then staying, by a Dr. Hawkes, who was attending Mrs. Lindbergh. She remained approximately six weeks until Mrs. Lindbergh was well. Thereafter a second nurse, name unknown, was hired and remained three months, after which she was discharged. Marie Cummings then returned and was with the family for several months when she was discharged for some unknown reason. Miss Cummings was questioned on March 4, 1932 by the New York Police at her residence, 124 West 85th Street, New York City, where she was sick in bed with a severe case of laryngitis. She was cleared of all suspicion by them and so far as known offered no information of any value.

Miss Cummings is 35 years of age, allegedly from Canada, and is said to have lived for a while in a small town in upstate New York, and in Brooklyn, N.Y. She took her nurse's training at the Flower Hospital, 450 East 64th Street, New York City, and at the City Hospital. In 1930, she worked at the Knickerbocker Hospital, 70 Convent Avenue, Bronx, N.Y.

It had been alleged by an individual believed unreliable, that Miss Cummings made a remark in January 1932 to another nurse by the name of Gladys Bottrell that she was going to kidnap the Lindbergh baby and "make some big money". Miss Bottrell upon interview denied that Miss Cummings made any such remark, and apparently there is no truth in the informant's allegations. From information available it does not appear that Marie Cummings is related to suspects Frank Cummings, Roy Cummings, or Lewis V. Cummings, who are mentioned in this report.

With reference to the discovery of the $2,980 of the ransom money, gold certificates, which is described in detail in another part of this report, it is pointed out that a woman by the name of Mary Cummings or Cummins lived with her husband, Michael Cummings or Cummins, in the apartment house at 537 West 149th Street, New York City, which was the address given by the unknown individual who, using the name of J.J. Faulkner, exchanged the $2,980 in ransom money gold certificates. Investigation has not as yet been conducted to determine whether Marie Cummings or Mary Cummings or Cummins is the same individual.

SUMMARY REPORT

In re

Unknown Subjects

Kidnaping and Murder of Charles A. Lindbergh, Jr. (N.Y. File 62-3057.

MORROW HOUSEHOLD

-o-

Morrow Family
Violet Sharpe (Mrs. George Payne)
Edna Sharpe
Septimus Banks
Charles Henry Ellerson
Mrs. Johannes Junge
John Saunders
Arthur Springer
Mrs. Rhoderick Cecil Henry Grime Craeme

MORROW HOUSEHOLD, ENGLEWOOD, N. J.

The Morrow estate, consisting of about 50 acres, is located in Englewood, N. J. with the main entrance on Lydeker Street, about one mile from the business center. It is the principal residence of the Morrow family. They also maintain a New York City residence at 2 East 72nd Street, consisting of an apartment in a cooperative apartment house, of which Robert Ortquist is superintendent, and a summer home on an island off North Haven, Maine.

Under date of March 1, 1932, the members of the Morrow family then residing at the Englewood residence, were Mrs. Dwight W. Morrow (wife of U. S. Senator Dwight W. Morrow, deceased), Dwight W. Morrow, Jr., son, and Miss Elizabeth R. Morrow, daughter. The files contain no mention of Mrs. Dwight W. Morrow that would be of interest to this investigation. Elizabeth R. Morrow, the oldest of the Morrow children, prior to her marriage, December 28, 1932, and at the time of the kidnaping, operated a kindergarten school at Englewood, N. J. Constance C. Morrow, the youngest Morrow child, at the time of instant kidnaping, was absent attending school in another city.

As a possible item of interest, it is believed advisable to mention here a previous attempt at extortion directed against a murder of the Morrow family. During 1929 while Constance C. Morrow, then 15 years of age, was attending Milton Academy, Milton, Mass. Her father, Dwight W. Morrow, received a letter from an unknown person, demanding $50,000 to prevent harm to Constance. The family immediately removed Constance to the Englewood estate and thence to the Morrow summer home near North Haven, Maine. A girl of about Constance's age was secretly substituted for her at school, and a package as demanded by the extortionist was placed as designated by him "over the wall of the General Clarence Edwards' estate" near the school. Police officers maintained surveillance near this point but the package was not called for and nothing further was heard from the unknown writer.

DWIGHT W. MORROW, JR.

Dwight W. Morrow, Jr. is the only son of the late Senator Dwight W. Morrow and is presently a law student at Amherst University, Northampton, Mass. Where he also received his academic education. Reputedly Morrow, Jr. was appointed assistant to the president of the University. Shortly after the kidnaping, Mrs. Dwight W. Morrow and Morrow, Jr. are said to have taken a trip to Europe; the purpose of this trip is not known. Morrow, Jr. was at one time in a sanitarium at Beacon, N. Y. although the exact illness from which he was suffering is unknown. There have been rumors to the effect that this son was left out of his father's will at the suggestion of Colonel Lindbergh and that there was "something behind" the trip to Europe right after the kidnaping. There were also rumors to the effect that Dwight W. Morrow had an illegitimate son cut off in his will; these rumors supposedly were investigated by the Department of Labor but nothing definite as to same appears in the New York Office file. However, it is known as a fact that certain county detectives in New Jersey performed considerable investigation relative to same. Captain Lamb, of the New Jersey State Police has advised that an investigation was conducted by the New Jersey State Police relative to Morrow, Jr. and that it does not appear he had any connection with this crime.

MORROW SERVANTS

No complete list of the Morrow servants is contained in the files in this matter. Newspaper reports indicate that the servants numbered 29 (including 3 secretaries) at the time of the kidnaping. Inspector Harry Walsh, of the Jersey City Police, stated at a conference of police and Federal Agents at Trenton, N. J. on May 18, 1932, that a check had been made of the Morrow servants and all had been questioned and statements taken from them, and everyone checked except Violet Sharpe, who did not properly account for her whereabouts the night of the crime.

Those listed in the file are as follows:
Arthur Springer, secretary to Dwight W. Morrow, Sr.
Charles Henry Ellerson, second chauffeur.
Septimus Banks, butler.
Violet Sharpe, waitress.
Thomas O'Shaugnessy, house man.
Mrs. Johannes Junge, nee Margaret Jantzen, occasional seamstress.
Mary Beattie, personal maid to Elizabeth Morrow.

Catherine Sullivan, assistant secretary.
Flora Hughes, assistant secretary.
Charles Roisor, intermittently employed as gateman.
John Saunders, gardener.
Mary Smith, dressmaker and traveling companion of Elizabeth Morrow.
Mrs. Rhoderick Cecil Henry Grimes-Graeme, social mentor and secretary to Mrs. Morrow, and in charge of the Morrow servants.
Ida (last name not ascertained), cook.
Bessie Binns, parlor maid.
Isabelle McDonald, personal maid to Mrs. D. W. Morrow.
Emily (last name not ascertained) chambermaid.
Margaret (last name not ascertained) pantry maid.
Sullivan, (first name not ascertained), night watchman.
Burke, (first name not ascertained), head chauffeur.

In addition to the above, there is a laundress, another secretary, and a kitchen maid, whose names are still to be ascertained, presently employed, who were so employed 3-1-32.

VIOLET SHARPE, true name, MRS. GEORGE PAYNE

She was born at Bradford, England, July 25, 1904; her mother, is Mrs. L. Sharpe, of Beenham, England; sister, Edna (Emily) Sharpe, Beenham, England; brother, Private Z. Sharpe, First Royal Berks Regiment, Syzabad, India. She married George Payne during the winter of 1929-30 in London, England. She entered the United States April 14, 1930 via Niagara Falls, N. Y. as a quota immigrant, visa #59279. She entered the employ of the Morrow family at Englewood, N. J. as a waitress May 13, 1930. She occasionally acted as personal maid to Miss Elizabeth Morrow.

At 10:30 A.M. March 1, 1932 she is reported as having received the telephone call from Mrs. Lindbergh instructing Betty Gow to proceed to Hopewell as the Lindberghs were staying over that night. Consequently, she and probably all the other Morrow servants were aware of the Lindberghs' intention to remain at Hopewell the night of March 1, 1932.

According to Inspector Harry W. Walsh, of the Jersey City Police Department, detailed to the New Jersey State Police for this investigation, Violet Sharpe was interviewed on four separate occasions by representatives of the New Jersey State Police. She apparently was first interviewed by Lieutenant Arthur Keaton of the New Jersey State Police, and again by Lieutenant Keaton, and Inspector Harry W. Walsh. Under date of May 21, 1932 she was interviewed by Lieutenant Keaton and Walsh in the presence of Assistant Director Harold Nathan and Special Agent in

Charge E. J. Connolley of this Division. Walsh and Keaton on this occasion first outlined the substance of previous interviews with Violet Sharpe which had elicited from her information to the effect that some time prior to March 1, 1932 she and her sister, Edna, met a man in an automobile, as they were proceeding downtown from the Morrow home; that this man gave them a lift downtown; that as she left the car he took her name, address and telephone number, advising that he would call her in the future; that thereafter he did call her and made an engagement to take her out at 8:30 P.M. March 1, 1932; that during this telephone call he stated he would meet her at the same place they originally met; that she was delayed in serving dinner on this date and was unable to get to the point indicated at 8:30 P.M.; that shortly after 8:30 P.M. she looked out of the window and observed this party whom she knew by no other name than "Ernie" outside in his car. She motioned to him that she would be right down, and immediately secured her wraps and joined him at the automobile. That upon entering the car, he having driven up to the pantry door of the Morrow home, she met another girl and a man who were with Ernie; that this couple were introduced to her but that she cannot recall their names. That the four then proceeded to a picture show in Englewood, N. J., attended same and that she returned home at about 10:55 P.M. March 1, 1932.

In a subsequent interview with Lieutenant Keaton, she admitted that she had not told the truth during the previous interview; that instead of attending a picture show with Ernie and his companions, they had driven to a roadhouse in The Oranges, where they had a few drinks, danced a couple of times and then returned home, she arriving home about 11:05 P.M. March 1, 1932. She amplified this story to the effect that the name of the roadhouse visited was the "Peanut Grille" and that "Ernie" apparently was acquainted with the proprietor as he invited the latter to have a drink. She stated that she did not drink any liquor, taking only coffee. She described the place by stating that there was an Italian singer, and the dancing was to music by radio.

During the interview of May 21, 1932 Violet Sharpe stated that she did not know the identity of her three companions referred to above; that she could not recall their names nor where the lived nor could she suggest any means by which they could be located. She did state that the girl probably worked in New York City. During this interview she stated that since her previous interview with Lieutenant Keaton, Ernie had called her on the telephone again and endeavored to take her out, but that she declined the invitation. She offered no explanation as to why she had not tried to obtain Ernie's name and address though explicitly requested to do so by Lieutenant Keaton at a previous interview. During this interview she became highly nervous and further questioning was suspended for the purpose of obtaining a doctor before continuing with the inquiry. During the above interview, Violet Sharpe admitted that she knew of the call at 10:30 A.M. March 1, 1932 instructing Betty Gow to proceed to the Hopewell residence of the Lindberghs, and that she was aware that the Lindbergh family intended remaining at the Hopewell residence the night of March 1, 1932. She also stated that her sister, Edna, who was present when she first met "Ernie" had returned to Beeham, England under date of April 6, 1932; that she (Violet) would have returned to England also if the instant matter had not arisen.

Under direct questioning she indicated that she had never had a boy friend prior to this date with Ernie, however, when asked directly if she had not been friendly with a newspaper reporter or photographer by the name of McKelvie employed by the Daily News, New York City, she admitted that she had been out several times with McKelvie. (According to Inspector Walsh, McKelvie had made the statement that Violet Sharpe furnished him the first information from the Morrow home as to the scene of the Lindbergh baby then all newspapers were clamoring for this information, and that this tip from Violet enabled McKelvie to score a beat in that he furnished the desired information to his paper five hours before any of the other newspapers but that same could not be used for the reason that the information reached the paper too far in advance of its going to press to permit a "scoop").

Violet Sharpe would not answer questions as to whether she had furnished McKelvie the above information. She stated that she did not know how to get in touch with McKelvie. She did admit, however, that McKelvie called her during April and informed her that he would have called her earlier if it was not for the trouble and grief experienced by the Morrow household as a result of the instant kidnaping. During this interview of May 21, 1932 most of the questions put to Violet Sharpe remained unanswered as she refused to reply to them. At this time the New Jersey State Police indicated they intended requestioning her in the immediate future.

Examination of the effects found in the room occupied by Violet Sharpe at the Morrow residence, Englewood, N. J. disclosed addresses, telephone numbers and other memoranda as follows:

Bank Book indicating that Violet Sharpe had an account at the United States Savings Bank, Madison Avenue and 56th Street, New York City, under the name Violet Sharpe, account no. 177653.

Inquiry at the above named bank established that Savings Account No. 177653 was opened October 22, 1930 with a deposit of $260 in currency; that the balance as of

May 23, 1932 amounted to $1,632.91. The various deposit as indicated by dates appeared to consist almost entirely of savings from salary. (Violet Sharpe received $100 per month, room and board and had few, if any, expenses).

Receipt from Richard T. Hutchison, Bureau of Domestic Help, 506 Madison Ave., New York City, dated 5/13/30, indicating Violet Sharpe was referred to Mrs. Dwight Morrow as parlor maid.

Names and Addresses Found in Note Book

Mrs. Bond Buscot, or Bascot, Edith	Farrington, Berks, England. 24 Hans Court, Hans Road, London, Northwest.
Betty Smith	37 Walmer or Watmer Road, Toronto, Ont. Canada.
Annie or Ammie Dawson	146 Crescent Road, Rosedale, Toronto, Canada.
Mrs. Bull	24 or 44 Grove End, St. Johns Wood, London, Northwest.
Mrs. Perryman	7 Belfont Place, Park Lane, London.
Edna Sharpe	34 Edgar Ave., Toronto, Canada.
Private Z. Sharpe	First Royal Berks Regiment, Kandabar Barracks, Syzabad, India.
Mrs. Jennings	Fairview Island, Port Carling, Muskoka, Ontario.
Miss Z. Walter	Ashfield Hall, Neston, Birtenhead, Cheshire.
Margaret Hodges	707 or 207 Davenport Road, Toronto, Ontario, Canada.
Mrs. G. Payne	care of Mr. Albert, 37th Street, Martins Lane, London, England.

Other addresses and memoranda as follows:

<u>Alice Wilding</u>	care of Mrs. Anthony Gardner, Ocean Mound Cottage, Watch Hill, R. I.
<u>Alice Wilding</u>	care of Mrs. Buhl, 1116 Iroquois Ave., Detroit, Michigan.
<u>Mrs. A. Wilding</u>	151 Lake Shore Drive, Grosse Point, Detroit, Michigan.
<u>Jeane Drinnings</u>	The Barkigool, corner of Lexington Ave. and 53rd St., and care of Mrs. Elliot, 24 West 59th Street.

Investigation failed to develop any residence or apartment hotel or other structure at or near the corner of 63rd and Lexington Ave., New York City, designated as the Barkigool; however, the Barbizon Hotel is located at this point (140 East 63rd Street). Inquiry at said hotel developed that Jeane Drinnings was unknown there. Miss Rebekah Ward Elliot, representative of the Italian Grand Hotels Company, occupying Apartment 21 at 24 West 59th St., telephone Plaza 3-1131, advised that she was without knowledge of anyone bearing the name of Jeane Drinnings although a person named Jeane Jennings formerly a resident of the Barbizon Hotel was an intimate friend of hers (Miss Eliot) advising that Jeane Jennings is from Toronto, Ont. And visited New York for a short time, returning to Canada, and it was rumored that she had committed suicide. Miss Elliot was entirely unfamiliar with the names Edna or Violet Sharpe.

<u>Private Waiters Association</u>   120 East 59th Street.

Inquiry at the Private Waiters Association, Inc., telephone, Murray Hill, 2-8648, Room 201, 120 East 39th St., developed that neither Violet nor Edna Sharpe was known to the person apparently in charge whose first name was "John", last name not secured. John described the association as a semi-social club, possessing something of a fraternal character having approximately thirty active members, engaged principally in serving at dinners, banquets, etc. The association has furnished such service at various points in New Jersey and on one particular occasion during the time the late Senator Dwight Morrow was conducting his campaign for the United States Senate, the Private Waiters Association rendered service at one or more dinners given by Senator Morrow at his Englewood, N. J. estate.

<u>Mr. O'Brien</u>   326 East 155th Street, Bronx, N. Y.

Investigation: See interview under William J. O'Brien.

<u>Miss E. Marshall</u>   723 East 163rd Street and care of Mrs. E. Redmond, 640 Park Ave., corner of 66th Street.

Miss Edith Marshall who resides at 723 East 163rd Street and is employed at 66th and Park Avenue, New York City, advised that she met Violet Sharpe while both were in the employ of Robert K. Hass at Scarsdale, N. Y. by whom Violet Sharpe was employed immediately prior to entering the Morrow service. She stated that Violet had visited here several times since the Spring of 1930 and on two occasions since March 1, 1932. That on one of the latter two visits Violet was accompanied by her sister Edna, who was about to return to England. Miss Marshall stated that at no time since the instant kidnaping had Violet made any remarks concerning the Lindbergh baby with the exception of stating that all employees of the Morrow home in Englewood and of the Lindberghs' at Hopewell, N. J. were doing everything possible to assist the State Troopers.

At 640 Park Ave. it was ascertained that Miss E.

Marshall was at one time employed as secretary to Mrs. E. Redmond, a widow, residing at said address.

Edna M.,   Tall Pines, Old Fargo, N.Y.

Edna   430 East 86th Street and 333 East 70th Street.

Inquiry at the above address developed that same is an apartment house, officially opened September 15, 1931. Otto Eller, superintendent, was unfamiliar with the names of either Violet or Edna Sharpe and he displayed photographs of same to the other employees of the building, questioning them but none could furnish any information concerning their knowledge of either Violet or Edna Sharpe.

At 335 East 70th St., J. Nemecek, apartment #4, the caretaker of the premises located at 333 East 70th St., was interviewed but was without any information concerning Violet or Edna Sharpe other than to suggest the possibility that a person of similar name might have been employed by Mrs. William I. Crane at the latter address.

Repeated efforts to contact Mrs. Crane were unsuccessful. Several of the other residents at this address were interviewed without any information being secured concerning Edna or Violet Sharpe.

Anna Delmarter

Mrs. Catherine Cornelis   47 East Broad St., Bogota, N. J.

Ticket   bearing prescription No. 65255 of C. and R. Timmermann's Drug Store, 868 Lexington Ave., New York City, N. Y.

Investigation developed that Prescription No. 65255 issued by C. and R. Timmermann's Drug Store was based on a prescription issued by Dr. Dudly D. Stetson to a person named Sharpe Feb. 19, 1931, and consisted of a preparation for the treatment of the scalp.

<u>Dan Daly, Atw.</u>   (probably Atwater) 9-2420

<u>Dudly Stetson</u> 614 Park Ave., Rhi. (probably Rhinelander) 6339.

Investigation developed that Dudly Stetson is a physician with offices at 614 Park Ave., New York City. That Violet Sharpe, of Englewood, N. J. was his patient, receiving treatment for her scalp. Dr. Stetson had no definite recollection of Miss Sharpe. Recalled nothing of her personal history other than that a Mrs. Graham, a wealthy woman, had apparently referred Violet Sharpe to him.

<u>435 East 57th Street</u> Wickersham 2-0722.

Investigation of 435 East 57th Street developed that this address is that of a large apartment house. The superintendent is one Paul McMahon. His son, Edward McMahon, elevator operator at the apartment house, whose telephone number is Eldcrado 5-9298 advised that he is acquainted with Edna Sharpe, formerly employed by a Mrs. McDowell who died shortly after Christmas, 1931; that Edna Sharpe's employment terminated upon the death of Mrs. McDowell. McMahon stated that his cousin, Tom Batchelor, and he drove to the Morrow home at Englewood, N. J. during November, 1931, calling there for Edna Sharpe for the purpose of driving her back to 435 East 57th Street she having gone to the Morrow home to visit her sister, Violet.

That Ruby Smith was a close friend of Edna Sharpe;

that Ruby Smith resided at 72nd Street and Park Ave., telephone, Rhinelander 4-9221, and had relatives who resided at 163rd or 164th Street near St. Nicholas Ave., whose telephone number was Billings 5-9603.

McMahon stated that approximately a week after instant kidnaping, at the request of Edna Sharpe, he removed from the cellar of this apartment house two trunks which she had stored there, at the termination of her employment by Mrs. McDowell. That he transported those trunks in his automobile to Englewood, N. J. where they were transferred to a taxicab to be conveyed to the Morrow residence; that the reason for the transfer was due to New Jersey ordinances relating to the carrying of baggage on the sides of automobiles which prescribed such transportation of baggage by any motor vehicle other than taxicabs.

McMahon stated that on this occasion he was accompanied by Edna Sharpe and Ruby Smith both of them returned to New York with him without visiting Violet Sharpe at the Morrow home. McMahon stated that some time prior to her departure for England, Edna Sharpe informed him of her intention to visit her home in England and advised that she expected to return to the United States after a visit of several months. McMahon further advised that Edna Sharpe had never discussed instant kidnaping or related matters with him.

Edna 241 East 54th Street.

Inquiry at the above address (241 East 54th St.) developed that Edna Sharpe resided here for a short period with one Miss Ida Hagg. The latter stated that she became acquainted with Edna Sharpe while Edna was employed by J. G. Ryker as kitchen maid during May or June, 1931. Edna Sharpe was also employed by the Rykers at their summer residence, Little Moose, in the Adirondack Mountains; left their employ in October, 1931 and then entered the employ of Mrs. McDowell; that between these positions Edna Sharpe resided with her (Miss Hagg) for a period of two or three weeks. She described Edna Sharpe as of quiet demeanor and stated that Edna Sharpe did not convey to her any information concerning the activities or conversations of the employees of the Morrow household. She also stated that Edna Sharpe resided at the Morrow home with her sister, Violet, prior to her departure for England during the first part of April, 1932.

Address 2 East 72nd St. Investigation developed that this is the residence address of the Morrow family, the building being a cooperative apartment house of which Robert Ortquist, is superintendent.

Business card bearing inscription Earl L. D. Hester, D.D.S. Englewood, N. J.

Business card Mangol's, 734 Lexington Ave., New York City.

Business card Post Road Taxi, 50 East Post Road, White Plains, N. Y. telephone, White Plains 725.

Investigation in connection with the above established that the Post Road Taxi Company discontinued during the fall of 1931; that it was owned and operated by one Ernest Brinkert.

At the Bureau of Motor Vehicles, after considerable investigation, Ernest Brinkert, was located at 1073 North Ave., New Rochelle, N. Y. where he was employed by H. J. Southwell, as a chauffeur and butler. He denied that he was acquainted with any girl named Violet Sharpe or that he knew any person residing in Englewood, N. J. and denied that he had ever been in Englewood, N. J. at any time. He stated that on March 1, 1932 and at the time immediately preceding and following that date he was on the C. W. Moody estate at Rouken Glen, N. Y. where he was employed as a chauffeur. He exhibited his 1931-1932 chauffeur's license which contained his photograph and was entirely willing that said photograph be submitted to any girl for the purpose of identifying him. He also volunteered to proceed in his automobile to any place which this Division might designate so as to assist in any identification. Brinkert was subsequently questioned by the New Jersey State Police and was exonerated from suspicion in this connection.

Telephone No. At. 8613   (Probably Atwater 9-8613)

Located in the establishment of one Jeremia Shea of 1269 Lexington Ave., New York City. Shea operated a "soft drink" establishment at this address. He stated that he was acquainted with one John Banks, employed as butler in the Morrow home, Englewood, N.J. That he has known Banks for the past five or six years; that Banks visits Shea's establishment occasionally; the last visit being approximately May 10, 1932, said visit being Banks' first visit for a period of several months; that until this particular visit Banks had not been at Shea's establishment since some time prior to March 1, 1932; that during this last visit Banks did not discuss the instant kidnaping but advised that he was in town for the purpose of obtaining dental treatment. According to Mr. Shea the names Violet and Edna Sharpe were unfamiliar to him. He advised that he does not permit women in his establishment. He stated that to the best of his recollection, Banks at one time was employed by the Vanderbilts.

<u>Telephone No. 328R</u> No exchange; probably rural location.

<u>Admission card</u> New York Orthopedic Dispensary and Hospital, 420 East 59th Street, #136869, dated 3/7/31.

<u>Immigration Identification card</u> United States Department of Labor, to Violet Sharpe, bearing #640448.

<u>Business card</u> William J. O'Brien, Melrose 4643-W, 326 E. 155th St.

Investigation in connection with the above established that William O'Brien resides in Apartment 4B, 326 East 55th Street, New York City. When interviewed, Mr. O'Brien stated in the spring of 1930, he was manager of the drug store operated under the name of Willner Dr. Co. at 331 Lexington Ave., New York City; that during the course of his duties he became acquainted with one Violet Sharpe who at that time was living at the Tatham House (Y.W.C.A.) 138 East 38th St., New York City. That two or three weeks later Miss Sharpe obtained employment at the Morrow home, Englewood, N.J. and that he occasionally saw her at that place on Sunday afternoons or on her day off (usually Thursday); that in the summer of 1930 she accompanied the Morrow family to North Haven, Me. And corresponded with him from that point. That he has not seen her since the summer of 1930 and has not corresponded with her or heard from her during the past one and one-half years.

<u>Tel. No. Sac. 2-9565</u> (Probably Sacramento 2-9565—since discontinued.)

This telephone was listed to one Vernon Monroe, 1172 Park Ave., New York city.

Tel. No. E 34844 (Probably Englewood 3-4844)

Listed to Dr. Margaret N. Wuits, 39 Park Place, Englewood, N.J.

Recently, information has been received from an informant presently in the employ of the Morrow family at Englewood, N.J. to the effect that it is common talk among the Morrow servants that the cards, addresses and other memoranda found in Violet Sharpe's room belonged to her sister, Edna Sharpe, who resided with Violet for several weeks prior to her departure for her home in England.

The photograph of Ernest Brinkert was displayed to Violet Sharpe and she identified it as a likeness of the "Ernest" with whom she visited the Peanut Grille the night of March 1, 1932.

Under date of June 10, 1932 it was decided to requestion Violet Sharpe and she was instructed to prepare herself to accompany officers to Hopewell, N.J. Shortly after receiving these instructions and prior to the arrival of the officers, she retired to her room and committed suicide by swallowing cyanide of potassium.

Violet Sharpe was suspected by the New Jersey State Police, investigators, as being an informant of the kidnapers, due to her apparent agitation under questioning and because it appeared probable that the kidnapers had been forewarned of the intention of the Lindberghs to remain at Hopewell over the night of March 1, 1932, their previous intention having been to return to the Morrow residence in Englewood early March 1, 1932.

Her reason for identifying the photograph of Ernest Brinkert has never been ascertained. Subsequent to her suicide, Ernest Miller, Elmer Johnson and Katherine Minners came forward and identified themselves as the companions of Violet Sharpe the night of March 1, 1932.

Ernest Miller and Elmer Johnson are residents of Closter, Bergen County, N.J. Katherine Minners resides at 417 Grand Ave., Palisades Park, N.J. They were investigated by the New Jersey State Police and Frank J. Wilson, Special Agent, Intelligence Unit, Bureau of Internal Revenue and exonerated of any direct or indirect connection with this case.

According to an informant, presently employed at the Englewood residence of the Morrow family, Violet Sharpe spent a great deal of her time in the company of Septimus Banks, the Morrow butler; they appeared to be in love with each other and several months prior to the kidnaping Violet Sharpe underwent an abortion operation necessitated by her intimacy with Banks.

EDNA (EMILY) SHARPE

Edna (Emily) Sharpe is a sister of Violet Sharpe. She had been in the United States, employed as a domestic for several years prior to the kidnaping. She resided with Violet at the Morrow home at Englewood for several weeks prior to April 6, 1932 on which date she returned to England. She was not employed at the Morrow residence, and the actual dates of her residence there are being ascertained.

The files in this matter do not reflect any investigation concerning her activities or associates other than she appeared to have occasionally dated with one McMahon, who may be communicated with via telephone, number Eldorado 5-9298. Newspaper articles published shortly after the suicide of Violet Sharpe reflect that Scotland Yard had been requested by the New Jersey State Police to conduct investigation in England relative to the associations, activities, etc. of Violet and Edna Sharpe. The Division has been requested to secure report on said investigation, if possible.

At the United States Savings Bank, Madison Avenue at 58th Street, New York City, it was ascertained that Edna Sharpe maintained a savings account #177652; that this account was opened October 22, 1930 with an initial deposit of $300 in currency; that small additional deposits were made from time to time totaling $678.80; under date of 3/4/32 she withdrew $142.50 and under date of 5/23/32 had a balance of $201.75.

SEPTIMUS BANKS

Septimus Banks, butler, is reputed to be a heavy drinker. He is reported to have entered a sanitarium, Central Park West, near 66th Street, and to have remained there two weeks during August, 1932. Rumor prevalent among the Morrow servants is to the effect that the death of Violet Sharpe completely unnerved him. He is reported to have again spent some time in this sanitarium just prior to Christmas, 1932, as a result of overindulgence in alcoholic stimulants. Banks is reported to have kept "steady company" with Violet Sharpe prior to her death. Reported to frequent speakeasy or night club, 86th Street and Lexington Avenue. Is reported well acquainted with one Alferi, operator of the B. and M. Taxicab Co., Englewood, N.J., whose taxicabs are most frequently patronized by the Morrow servants.

CHARLES HENRY ELLERSON, true name reported to be EILERSON

He entered the Morrow service in the summer of 1931 as a gardener being hired by Mr. Arthur Springer. In the Fall of the same year he was made second chauffeur to the family, and in such capacity often drove Mrs. Lindbergh and the baby around Englewood and also to Hopewell, N.J. Shortly before the kidnaping Ellerson often drove the baby to a kindergarten school in Englewood which had been established by Miss Elizabeth Morrow. Ellerson has been in trouble several times for excessive drinking as a result of which he has been on the verge of being discharged. He is presently employed as a gateman at the Morrow estate. Ellerson is 29 years of age and was born and raised in Jersey City, N.J. His parents, however, were born in Denmark.

Ellerson is married and has two children, his wife being Polish. Prior to entering the Morrow employ he worked successively for the Bergen [text garbled] Bank as bookkeeper; Armour and Co., Jersey City, as order clerk [text garbled] (Duane Bacon, former superintendent of the Plymouth Apartments, [text garbled] 149th Street, also worked for Armour and Company, as a chauffeur [text garbled] year 1924); Western Electric Co. and Bell Telephone Company, New York City, as a clerk; as garage man in Little Ferry, N.J.; chauffeur for a woman in Ridgefield Park, N.J.; chauffeur for William H. Irving, retired banker, Leonia, N.J.; as truck driver for the Consolidated Film Industry, Fort Lee, N.J. For a period of time prior to entering the employ of the Morrow family, Ellerson was financially destitute and received city unemployment relief. His father is deceased and his mother operated a ladies hat store in Englewood. He has a close friend, one Hans Peterson, a German, who is a dancing instructor in Jersey City, and another friend by the name of Thomas Prennan, a taxi driver for the B. and M. Taxi Co., Englewood, which handles all of the Morrow business. Ellerson is said to be very friendly with a Polish maid, name unknown, in the employ of the broker, W. H. Irving. Ellerson is said to spend considerable time around Fort Lee, N.J. where he frequents the speakeasy operated by one [text garbled] who is a well known sports promoter and is on the State Boxing Commission. Ellerson has the following known relatives:

Mrs. Elizabeth Eilerson, mother, and Edna [text garbled] both of Norwood, N.J., the latter is divorced from her husband [text garbled] of Bound Brook, N.J.; Mrs. A. Bird of Jersey City, N.J., [text garbled] Frank Eilerson, uncle, Norwood.

On the night of the kidnaping, Eilerson, accompanied by a man named O'Shaughnessy, employed as a houseman at the Morrow residence, came into the Sha-Tee speakeasy on the outskirts of Englewood, N.J. between 8:00 and 9:00 P.M. Ellerson had apparently been drinking before he entered this place. A short time later, Banks, the butler, at the Morrow residence also entered the Sha-Tee accompanied by the taxi driver Thomas Brennan. According to information furnished the New York office, Brennan was complaining that he had been driving all night without any supper whereupon Banks gave him $20 and told him to get something to eat. Later in the evening, the exact hour is not known, someone came into the speakeasy and informed those present of the kidnaping after which all of the Morrow servants left. At 12:30 A.M. March 2, 1932 Ellerson telephoned Mr. Arthur Springer, the Morrow secretary, and told him he had heard about the kidnaping and asked if there was anything he could do. Further information is to the effect that Ellerson flashed large sums of money in the Sha-Tee speakeasy on a number of occasions prior and subsequent to the kidnaping. (This has been denied by the proprietor of the Sha-Tee). His explanation as to this was that he had been receiving "hot tips" on horse races. Further information is to the effect that at about 12:15 P.M. March 1, 1932 Ellerson drove Betty Gow from the Morrow residence in Englewood to the Lindbergh estate in Hopewell. According to information in the files of the New York office, there is some question as to the whereabouts of Ellerson after he left Hopewell. However, he was questioned by the New Jersey State Police, and apparently accounted for his movements. According to a confidential informant of the New York Office, one of the most trusted Morrow servants, who has been with the family twenty-five years remarked that in her opinion Ellerson had some connection with the kidnaping. Although Ellerson spends much of his time in Fort Lee, N.J. it is not known whether he is acquainted with Ralph Hacker, Dr. Condon's son-in-law. It is stated that in May, 1932, Ellerson wrecked his green Ford Sedan on a hill at Fort Lee, N.J. and the same was completely burned. Prior to the kidnaping he lived at 26 West St., Englewood, N.J. Since that time he has moved to 96-Engle St., where Mr. and Mrs. Junge also lived.

MRS. JOHANNES JUNGE
(see MARGARET JANTZEN)

Mrs. Johannes Junge (see Margaret Jantzen) is of German descent, and has been employed by the Morrows for several years as a dressmaker and seamstress. Some of here family are from Rutherford, N.J. and she has the following known relatives:

William and Juliette Ausborn, brother and sister-in-law, Auburndale, L.I.
Virginia Juntzen, sister, employed as governess by Mrs. James Warburg, of 36 East 70th Street, New York City;

John J. Jantzen, Mrs. Junge's father, was European agent for Lovell's Manufacturing Company of Erie, Pa. And was stationed at Hamburg, Germany, his native city, where he died in 1924.

Miss Margaret Jantzen married to George Johannes Junge in Hamburg, Germany, in the year 1923. The Junge family of Hamburg is reputed to be very wealthy and Johannes Junge is said to be well educated and to have served in the German Army. He entered the United States through New York Harbor on December 3, 1931 as a non-quota alien and took up his residence with his wife at 96 Engle St., Englewood, N.J. at which address there also resided for a time Henry "Red" Johnson and Charles Henry Ellerson, second chauffeur for the Morrow family.

According to an informant of the New York office, the fact that Margaret Jantzen was married did not come out until after the kidnaping. The investigation also developed that "Red" Johnson and Mr. and Mrs. Junge claimed to have been out for an automobile ride on the night of the kidnaping. All of these parties were subsequently cleared of suspicion by the New Jersey State Police. Mr. Junge is not known to have been employed since he entered the United States. Recently Mrs. Junge was discharged by the Morrows for stealing foodstuffs and is presently in the employ of a wealthy woman in the Waldorf Astoria Towers, New York City. So far as is known neither of the Junges has a criminal record.

JOHN SAUNDERS

This individual was employed at the Morrow estate in the year 1931-32 as a gardener. Not much is known about him except that he is Scotch while his wife, Anna, is Swedish. Both are from the state of Connecticut. In 1932 Saunders owned a Chrysler Sedan and lived at 266 Garden Street, Englewood, N.J. He is presently employed in a ship building plant in Hoboken, N.J. His handwriting has been found to have no resemblance to the documents in this case.

ARTHUR SPRINGER

Mr. Springer was secretary to the late Dwight W. Morrow for many years. After the Senator's death, he was retained in the family employ as a family secretary and handles most of the family's financial affairs including the estate of Senator Morrow. The latter left Mr. Springer a bequest of $25,000 in his will. The Springer family reside in Tenafly, N.J. they sometimes spend their summers in Oak Bluffs, Martha's Vineyard, Mass. Which latter locality was mentioned in the last ransom note. Mr. Springer, it appears, was quite active in the early stages of the investigation but after the baby's body was found he withdrew from active participation. When the kidnaping occurred Mr. Springer was at home with his family; shortly before midnight after learning of the crime he proceeded to the Morrow estate at Englewood and made himself available for any assistance he might be able to render.

MRS. RHODERICK CECIL HENRY GRIMES-GRAEME

This woman was social secretary to Mrs. and Senator Dwight W. Morrow for many years prior to the Senator's death, and at present is in charge of all Morrow servants. She has two sons, Arthur David Grimes-Graeme, age 23, and Rhoderick Cecil Grimes-Graeme, age 28. The youngest boy was born in Transvaal, South Africa, and the oldest in England. Both are attending McGill University in Montreal, Canada, and reside at 2020 Victoria Street, that city. The oldest boy is stated to have been out of school for a while working for a contractor. The whereabouts of these individuals at the time of the kidnapping is not known although one of them is alleged to have been on sick leave about that time. According to information emanating from a trusted Morrow employee, Mrs. Graeme receives a check of $350 per month from the Morrows and in addition the Morrow estate pays the rent of her New York City apartment, 155 East 73rd Street (formerly 4 East 66th St., New York City), which amounts to about $125 monthly. Also there is information to the effect that the Morrow estate pays the tuition of Mrs. Graeme's sons at McGill University. When Senator Morrow died he did not leave this woman or her sons a bequest in his will. Some of the Morrow servants dislike and distrust Mrs. Graeme and she is characterized by them as a "high flyer." Occasionally when she is in New York Constance Morrow spends the night in Mrs. Graeme's apartment.

Mrs. Graeme has a friend by the name of Mrs. W. Lillian Chignault, who lives in Hartford, Conn. But who has a summer place or camp at Lagoon Heights, Oak Bluffs, Mass. Which is part of Martha's Vineyard and close to Horseneck Beach, Gay Head and Elizabeth Islands. Mrs. Graeme and her sons are known to have visited this camp on several occasions; the last known visit was in August or September, 1932. The camp is said to be in an unsettled section and to have no light or water facilities. Specimens of Mrs. Chignault's handwriting are in the possession of the New York Office and will be submitted to the Division laboratory for comparison with the writings in the instant case. Specimens of the handwriting of the Graeme family have not yet been obtained. Efforts were made by an informant of the New York Office to obtain the handwriting of the oldest Graeme boy by writing to him under a pretext. The letter was answered but the reply, including the signature, was typed. An effort was also made by the informant in question to engage one of the Graeme boys in conversation under the pretext used by the informant that he was an insurance man. The Graeme boy was found to be very reticent and informed the interviewer that he had instructions to answer no questions without the presence of the British Consul. It appears that both Mrs. Graeme and her sons are British subjects.

Information is to the effect that the sons since the year 1932 have been heavily in debt in Montreal to various fellow students and others. The husband of this woman has apparently been dead for many years. From available information it appears he was with the British Civil Service in Africa. Various newspaper reports indicate that the Graemes, mother and sons, sometimes attend social functions at the Morrow home.

The New York office files do not contain descriptions of the various Morrow servants or of Edna Sharpe.

SUMMARY REPORT

In Re

Unknown Subjects

Kidnaping and Murder of Charles A. Lindbergh, Jr. (N.Y. File 62-3057).

PHYSICAL EVIDENCE

-o-

Ladder
Chisel
Footprints
Fingerprints
Discovery of body of Charles A. Lindbergh, Jr.

PHYSICAL EVIDENCE

LADDER

Immediately after the discovery of the kidnaping, police searchers located a ladder at a point approximately fifty feet east from the east side of the Lindbergh residence. Footprints led from the nursery window located on the east side of the house, second floor, directly to the abandoned ladder, the tracks continuing across the fields in an east by northeast direction apparently terminating at the road known as Featherbed Lane.

When found it was observed that the ladder in question was extensive in construction but that the upper section was not attached and probably had not been used; the two lower sections were still together and what appeared to be the middle section had split, apparently causing the ladder to jam against the building, as a well defined mark was left on the house to the right of the window directly under the nursery at about the eight of the lower section of the ladder.

Colonel Lindbergh informed State Police investigators that shortly after 9:30 P.M., March 1, 1932, while seated in the living room with Mrs. Lindbergh, they heard a noise resembling two boards striking together but hearing no further noise, attributed it to the wind or other natural causes.

The ladder was inspected by the New Jersey State Police for latent prints but none was developed. Tests were conducted by the New Jersey State Police to determine what weight the ladder would hold, and the consensus of opinion among a number of the officers present at the test, was that the ladder would not hold a weight much over one hundred and twenty-five pounds.

It was later brought to Washington, D.C. where it was

subjected to laboratory examination by experts of the Bureau of Standards, Department of Commerce; Bureau of Chemistry and Soils, and Forest Service, Department of Agriculture. Reports of these experts as submitted to the Division June 1st and June 4th, 1932 are in substance as follows:

The ladder was so made that the three sections nesting together could be carried in an automobile.

Dimensions determined as:
Lower section, uprights 6'8-3/4" long; 3-5/8" wide by 3/4" thick; steps 14-1/8" long, 2-3/4" wide; 3/4" thick. Center section, uprights 6'8-5/8" long; 3-5/8" wide by 3/4" thick; steps 12-1/2" long; 2-3/4" wide; 3/4" thick. Top section, uprights 6'8-3/4" long; 3-5/8" wide; 3/4" thick with steps 11" by 2-3/4" by 3/4" (top step 10-7/8" by 2-7/8" by 3/4.

The steps of the centre and top sections were nailed in flush, whereas those of lower section were nailed on the uprights; three sections were joined by round pins 3/4" in diameter.

The sides and steps were identified as Ponderosa pine, Southern yellow pine, (square edged stock not tongue and groove type) and Douglas fir. The two pins were identified as birch, probably paper birch, used in the manufacture of handles, such as broom and mop handles.

The construction of the ladder is very crude although displaying some knowledge of carpentry and use of carpenter tools. Some of the materials used appear at some time to have been used in low grade construction work, as from some old building. The sides of the top section contained nail holes made by old fashioned cut nails.

The raised ring of the wood was found to contain what appeared to be textile fibers, brown, white and black. The brown appeared to be dyed wool and the white and black to be cotton and/or linen.

The consensus of opinion of the experts is that the ladder was constructed from a miscellaneous accumulation of pieces some of which had been under cover for some time as the moisture content reflected by test was very low.

Analysis of a streak of paint found on the ladder indicated that the paint might have been a barn or roofing paint. Analysis is of two other marks found on the ladder developed that one is a deep pencil mark and the other was the result of an excess of silver nitrate used in attempting to develop latent prints. Analysis of the dirt scraped from various parts of the ladder and of the soil from the yard of the Lindbergh estate, developed that samples from the lower end of the ladder uprights in general checked with the soil sample from the yard; that the sample from the upper end of the left upright also checked with soil sample. The report also indicates that part of the ladder had been in contact with a soil of much more quartzose nature. The sample from the upper end of right upright upon analysis was found to differ markedly from other samples and indicated that this end had been in contact with a much more sandy soil having the general character of sandy loam.

L. Johnson, New Jersey State Wood Expert, expressed the opinion that the wood making up the ladder is of pine excepting the dowels which are maple, and that it is composed of ex-crating material; that some of the nail marks appeared to him to have been made by a nailing machine.

Nails used in constructing this ladder have been identified as a product of the Pittsburgh Steel Co., Pittsburgh, Pa., designated as #8 Common Fence Nail. It was ascertained that this is the largest selling nail manufactured by this company and that it was impossible to identify the nails as to date of manufacture, as the grip marks are the same as on nails manufactured during 1931 -32 -33. It was further ascertained that as this brand of nails is shipped to practically all jobbers and dealers throughout the United States, it would be practically impossible to determine the ultimate purchaser of the nails used in constructing the ladder. Colonel Lindbergh stated that the ladder was without identifying marks.

Frank W. Kelley, a house wrecker, residing in Ewing Township near Trenton, N.J., after examining the ladder expressed the opinion that it had been constructed from materials from a house in Pennington, N. J. demolished by him several weeks earlier, stating that it was composed of the same yellow pine with part of the paint peeled off as was considerable of the lumber recovered by demolishing the aforementioned house. He furnished the New Jersey State Police, the names of more than a score of persons to whom he had sold lumber from the wrecked house. The New Jersey State Police checked this information and apparently discredited it though the files at this office do not reflect results of said investigation. Inspector Walsh who assisted the State Police in the investigation of this case, stated that in his opinion the wood used in constructing the ladder was of the type generally used to crate furniture.

Marks on the Lindbergh house and on the ground adjacent, indicated that the ladder rested to the right of the nursery window entered by the kidnapers, the bottom shafts leaving impressions 1 1/2" deep, about 3 ft. out from building. The location of these marks suggests the possibility that the kidnaper might have been left-handed.

Sebastian Benjamin Lupica, residing R.F.D. #1, Hopewell, N. J. located near Buttonwood Corner, one-half mile from the Lindbergh estate, stated that at about 6: P.M., March 1,

1932, while returning home from Princeton and while nearing the first house on the right hand side of the road after passing the entrance to the Lindbergh estate, he passed a 1929 Dodge Sedan automobile bearing New Jersey license plates and containing several board like unpainted ladders piled one on another; that there were at least two and possibly three ladders so piled, laid horizontally, extending from the top of the rear seat to the right of the driver in the front seat; that the driver was the only person in the automobile observed by him. Lupica stated that he subsequently examined the ladders found abandoned at the Lindbergh estate, and that they closely resemble the ladder observed by him in the Dodge Sedan.

Further particulars as to the driver, automobile and ladder observed by Lupica are set out in the section entitled "Circumstantial Information—Questionable Automobiles and Persons Observed."

Photostatic pictures of this ladder will be found in the supplement to this report as Exhibits "C-1, 2 and 3", pages 39 and 40. Copies of the laboratory reports are set out therein as Exhibit "D-1 to D-6" inclusive, pages 43 to 55 inclusive.

CHISEL

During the search for physical evidence inaugurated by the State Police immediately after they were called to the Lindbergh residence, a chisel was discovered in the grass a few yards east of the widow through which the kidnaper apparently gained entry to the nursery. As it happened, the chisel was not needed as neither the nursery window nor shutter was locked. This chisel, one foot in length with wood handle bearing hammer marks, had a three-quarter inch blade of cast steel and was manufactured by Buck Brothers at factory near Worcester, Mass.

in 1892. The chisel does not bear serial number or other identifying features by which it might be traced.

The file reflects that all hardware stores in a radius of twenty miles of the Lindbergh home, were canvassed by the State Police with a view to having the chisel identified, without result.

An analysis of a scraping from the handle of the chisel developed an abundance of calcium carbonate in very small crystals which closely resembled those found in lime which has been exposed to air such as plaster, etc. indicating the chisel at some recent date had been used in construction work.

A photostatic picture of this chisel appears in the supplement to this report as Exhibit "C-4" page 41. Laboratory examination of the chisel is mentioned in Exhibit "D-1" page 44, and Exhibit "D-6" page 55 of the supplement.

FOOTPRINTS

Immediately after receiving notice of the kidnaping, Harry Wolfe, Chief of Police, Hopewell, N. J., and Charles E. Williamson, Deputy Police Chief, the first police officers notified, proceeded to the Lindbergh residence and upon examining the ground about the residence located footprints leading from the nursery window to a nearby field. They followed these impressions for several yards and decided that they indicated the person having made same was heading for Featherbed Lane which runs east and west approximately one-half mile south of the Lindbergh house.

According to newspaper reports at that time, the impression found in the clay under the nursery window appeared to have been made by a foot without a shoe or by a shoe enclosed in a cloth wrapping much as if a sock had been pulled over the shoe.

Muddy traces were found on the ladder used in reaching the nursery window, also on the window sill, and inside the nursery on the floor just under the sill.

According to John Brant and Edith Renard in the book "True Story of the Lindbergh Kidnaping", an unnamed expert, who had spent more than thirty-five years studying the human foot and making footwear of all descriptions to fit it, examined the photograph of the footprint found beneath the nursery window the morning after the kidnaping, and expressed the opinion that same was made by a bowlegged person as the impression is decidedly deeper along the outer lines of the foot print. The opinion has also been advanced that the footprint might have been made by a person who was lame. The expert is quoted as having added, that the owner of the footprint wore deeply ribbed stockings of the golf hose type but discredited the theory that they were worn over shoes or that moccasins, rubber soled shoes or galoshes were worn instead. The expert claimed that only a deeply ribbed stocking would make the clear straight vertical lines that were seen in the footprint.

Some of the newspaper reports current at the time were to the effect that "subsequent and more careful scrutiny convinced officials that the footprints found were from two different pairs of shoes."

Oscar Bush, former Deputy Sheriff, and trapper, residing near Hopewell, N.J., was called in by Colonel Lindbergh to assist. His examination of the footprints convinced him (Bush) according to a published article that "They were the foot prints of a smallish man with a crooked small toe on right foot, one that rested on top of another; that the imprints led from one hundred feet away, to the nursery window then back and across a grass field to the edge of Featherbed Lane; that the print did not cross the lane but probably continued along it and could not be followed further because of the loose gravel."

No plaster casts of the footprints observed at the Lindbergh estate have been made, according to Corporal William Horn of the New Jersey State Police; however, photographs of several footprint impressions were made and are in possession of the New Jersey State Police.

Subsequent to the payment of the ransom at St. Raymond's Cemetery, Colonel Breckinridge and officers from the New Jersey State Police returned to the cemetery and Condon there indicated to them the approximate point at which "John" was standing at the time of the ransom payment. A footprint was discernible near a new grave at this approximate point and a plaster cast was made of same by Colonel Breckinridge and is now in possession of the New Jersey State Police. With respect to this particular footprint, Corporal William Horn advised former Special Agent J. J. Manning, that the plaster cast of this print was of little value inasmuch as the ground in which the impression was imbedded was so soft that it spread under the mold; on the other hand, Colonel Breckinridge and corporal Horn on a previous occasion advised that the closest approximation indicates the footprint was about a size eight, although this is merely their opinion.

Search of the ground near the point where the baby's body was discovered failed to locate any footprints. As far as the New York office knows, there was no effort made to locate footprints at the Woodlawn Cemetery.

FINGERPRINTS

The newspaper stories published shortly after the kidnaping was announced, contained items to the effect that two sets of fingerprints were found on the nursery window through which the kidnaper was alleged to have entered; that each of the prints was sufficiently clear to classify. Corporal William Horn of the New Jersey State Police informed former Special Agent J. J. Manning that positively no slightest fragment of a fingerprint impression, susceptible to classification, was found at the scene of the crime, in the nursery, on the windows, ladder, chisel, or other likely object. The same negative results were realized from examination of the ransom letter.

The Lindbergh baby had never been fingerprinted but latent prints were obtained from his toys and other objects frequently handled by him.

DISCOVERY OF THE BODY OF CHARLES AUGUSTUS LINDBERGH, JR.

The body was discovered May 12, 1932, 3:15 P.M., by William Allen (colored), assistant on the truck driven by Orville Wilson, both Allen and Wilson being employed by Williams S. Titus, a nurseryman of Hopewell, N. J. Immediately after the discovery, Wilson notified Chief of Police Harry Wolfe of Hopewell, N. J.

The body was discovered approximately forty-five feet off the Hopewell-Mt. Rose Highway. It was discovered in thick brush near Mt. Rose Hill which is located two miles southeast of Hopewell, N. J. and approximately four and one-half miles southeast by air line from the Lindbergh residence. (See Exhibits "B-15" to "B-18" inclusive in supplement hereto).

The point at which the body was discovered, is on the land owned by one Robert Buffett, who with his housekeeper, Mrs. Lillian LaRue, resided nearby. The point of discovery is also approximately five hundred feet from the stone quarry owned by one C. Andrew, and within a few hundred feet of the house owned by Charles Schopfel, which was occupied during the Summer of 1931 by Charles Maran, his demented mother Sophie Gerardi, and his stepfather Enrico Gerardi with aliases, all of whom presently reside at 585 Teanock Road, Ridgefield Park, N. J. Under date of January 9, 1934, Gerardi and one Mary Griffin alias Mary Wilson were arrested by the Hackensack, N. J. Police, charged with false imprisonment of Mrs. Geradi, who was found insane and unclothed in one of the rooms. The possible participation of this group is presently receiving appropriate investigative attention as will be set out further in this report in the section entitled "Subjects and Suspects."

The body was cremated at Trenton, J. J. May 13, 1932.

The road opposite the point at which the body was found commands a clear view of the Lindbergh residence.

The point at which the baby's body was discovered is situated in Mercer County, N.J. whereas the Lindbergh residence from which the baby was kidnaped is situated in Hunterdon County.

When found the body of the baby was badly decomposed. It was found lying face downward. The left leg from the knee down and left arm below the elbow were missing. Newspapers and interested police officials attributed this dismemberment to prowling animals.

Newspaper reports state that close to the road, directly opposite the point at which the body was found, a somewhat shredded weather-stained burlap bag was discovered and that said bag appeared to be blood stained.

The autopsy developed that the body had been dead apparently since the date of the kidnaping. Mercer County, N.J. Coroner's Physician Charles H. Mitchell, following a post mortem at the Swayze Morgerum Morgue, Trenton, N.J., advised that he had never seen the Lindbergh child prior to its disappearance and hence could not positively identify the body as that of the body of Charles A. Lindbergh, Jr. A copy of the autopsy report made by Coroner Swayze was secured and is presently in the files of the New York Division Office. This report reads as follows:

Lindbergh, Charles.
Coroner Swayze, Swayze Morgue.
Body found near Hopewell, New Jersey.

May 12, 1932 and removed to morgue. Post mortem examination at 7:30 P.M. on May 12, 1932. Found a badly decomposed body of an infant, left leg from knee down gone, left arm below elbow gone, most of abdominal organs gone, muscles of limbs and abdomen gone, facial expression still sufficient to make a possible recognition of identity. Found the following marks peculiar to the Lindbergh baby, namely, 16 teeth, well developed upper incisors, overlapping of toes on right foot, first toe overrides the large toe, second toe partially overrides the large toe, fontanelle not closed, measurements show opening three-quarters of an inch in diameter, length of body overall 33 1/2", contour of cranium shows a head larger than normal in child of twenty months, forehead prominent.

These peculiar characteristics conform with a record made on February 14, 1932 by Dr. Van Ingen of New York.

Autopsy:

On removal of scalp I found a marked fracture of the left parietal and occipital bones, the fracture extended from the fontanelle across the left side of the head slightly posterior to a point posterior to left ear, then it divided a break going forward and one backward on the skull.

There was also a suspicious opening at a point about one inch posterior to the right ear, the opening was about one-half inch in diameter, somewhat rounded and resembled a bullet wound but, on examination of the cranial vault, I could not locate a bullet but the fracture of the skull was directly opposite this opening and could have been done by a bullet entering the right side of the skull, striking the inner table of the skull and the bullet could have been lost in transportation of the body as the brains were exuding from the fontanelle and from the opening on the right side of the skull. The marked decomposition of the tissues would indicate in a person exposed to the elements that the child had been killed and left at the point where it was found for a period of from seven to ten weeks.

Dr. Mitchell is quoted in newspaper reports published at the time of the post mortem as having advised reporters that the several holes found in the skull of the body located as described above, were similar to those made by bullets, but that both the fracture and the holes could also have been caused by the skull being hit by an automobile, banged against a tree or hit by a club or other heavy instrument.

IDENTIFICATION

Dr. Philip Van Ingen, baby specialist, attended the Lindbergh baby just prior to the kidnaping, and at that time made a number of measurements of the baby in connection with treatment for rickets. After the finding of the body, Dr. Van Ingen identified the toes, skull and the teeth of the corpse as identical with those of the Lindbergh baby, and found that the measurements of the corpse agreed almost exactly with those he had taken of the Lindbergh child. Curly blond hair found at the point where the body was discovered and samples of the hair of the Lindbergh baby were analyzed by chemists (identity not shown in New York Office files), and found to be identical. When found the corpse was clothed in two shirts which were identified as a small sleeveless shirt and the improvised shirt made by Betty Gow. The two diapers, rubber pants, both thumb guards and the sleeping suit which the baby was wearing at the time it was kidnaped, were missing.

The body was identified by Colonel Lindbergh as that of his son, Charles A. Lindbergh, Jr. It was not viewed by Mrs. Lindbergh. Betty Gow, the child's nurse, also identified the body as that of her former charge. In addition to the actual identification of the body there was further convincing proof of the identity. As shown in the section of this report entitled "Lindbergh Household and Employees", the baby had on, the night of the kidnaping, an improvised home-made flannel shirt made by Betty Gow from a petticoat and was stitched with blue silk thread. The shirt found on the body was examined by Betty Gow who stated positively that it was the home-made shirt, blue thread and all, which she had made for the baby. In addition, the shirt found on the body was unseamed on the left shoulder, which was the case with regard to the shirt made by Betty Gow, who left the left shoulder unseamed to facilitate placing the shirt on the baby. Further, remnants of the flannel petticoat from which the garment was made, were found to compare exactly with the material of the shirt found on the body.

Colonel Henry Breckinridge, Lindbergh's attorney, in testifying before the Bronx County Grand Jury, stated the baby's sleeping suit was not found on the body; however, that "the home-made improvised undershirt, which had been placed on the baby to keep the medicinal lotion on its chest because of a slight congestion, was still on the body when it was found, and was identified beyond peradventure."

SUMMERY REPORT

In Re

Unknown Subjects

Kidnaping and Murder of Charles A. Lindbergh, Jr. (N.Y. File 62-3057).

CIRCUMSTANTIAL INFORMATION

-o-

Questionable automobiles and persons observed
Stolen Automobiles
Local Cabins
Curtains and telephone lines
Men employed in construction of Lindbergh home
Search of roads and countryside
Babies mistakenly reported as Lindbergh child

CIRCUMSTANTIAL INFORMATION

Numerous circumstantial leads arose immediately after the kidnaping consisting mostly of automobiles seen in the vicinity under suspicious circumstances and other observations of local residents. Leads were immediately investigated by the New Jersey State Police, and the interested Police Departments without material result. The New York Office does not have official reports of the investigation of these leads, and the following information was obtained, except as otherwise stated, from published accounts of the investigation.

QUESTIONABLE AUTOMOBILES
AND PERSONS OBSERVED

According to newspaper reports published shortly after the kidnaping, Sebastian Benjamin Lupica, Princeton University student, residing approximately one mile from the Lindbergh estate, at about 6 P.M. on March 1, 1932 observed an automobile on a road near the Lindbergh estate, on the night of the kidnaping, with two sections of a ladder resting across the seat. Upon observing the ladder, apparently left by the kidnapers, he stated that it resembled the ladder he had seen in the automobile.

Lupica was recently interviewed by a Special Agent of the Division relative to his observation, and he stated that he is 21 years of age; that he is a Sophomore student at Princeton University, Princeton, N.J.; that his father, Charles Lupica, address R.F.D. 1, Hopewell, N.J. has a small farm near Buttonwood Corner, where his family has lived for about 15 years, his house being about one-half mile to one mile from the Lindbergh estate; that while in attendance at the Princeton University Preparatory School, during 1931-1932 Lupica lived at his parents' home and each day drove to the school in the morning and back to his home at night; that to reach his parents' home from Princeton, he drove through and about four miles beyond Hopewell; that after leaving Hopewell the road passed by the Lindbergh estate. After passing the road leading to the Lindbergh house, known as Lindbergh Lane, he continued to a second cross road and turned right, his parents' home being the first house on the right.

He further stated as follows:

"On the afternoon of March 1, 1932, I left Princeton, N.J. around 5:00 P.M. This was later than I usually remained at Princeton while attending Princeton Preparatory School, but I recall that I had been practicing some form of athletics, either baseball or track, and for that reason did not get started homeward until around 5:00 P.M. The drive from Princeton, N.J. to my parents home ordinarily occupies around forty-five minutes. The distance is approximately twelve miles, but part of the road was in poor condition in March, 1932, and therefore I did not drive at a very rapid rate of speed.

On March 1, 1932 I had proceeded beyond Hopewell, N.J. without event, and had passed Lindbergh Lane. It was then around 6:00 P.M. and dusk was coming on although it was still light enough so that the lights were not required and I could see about three hundred yards ahead. I was near the first house on the right side of the road after passing Lindbergh Lane, this house being about three hundred yards beyond Lindbergh Lane. As I recall, some Polish people with a name something similar to Kirstofer lived in the house referred to at that time. Just previously, I had stopped at a letter box located near the place where Lindbergh Lane runs into the highway and had gotten some mail. I drove along slowly, possibly eight to ten miles per hour, attempting to drive and read a letter at the same time. Looking up I saw a car approaching and coming toward me.

It was about one hundred and fifty yards away when I noticed it. When it was about one hundred yards away, I pulled the car I was driving a little to the right and stopped. When I first saw it, it was about in the middle of the road, and after it pulled over it was partially off the road on the left side for the direction it had been travelling. There was no apparent necessity for the car to stop as there was room enough in the highway for two or three cars to pass at this point. When the car that had been approaching stopped it was about thirty yards from the house in which the Polish family lived, between that house and Lindbergh Lane. When it stopped, I started and drove slowly past, and continued home.

I particularly noticed the radiator of the car as I drove past, and could tell from the winged emblem that it was a Dodge automobile. It had a rather high radiator with nickel shell. The emblem consisted of a center portion which was apparently of blue enamel, from which the nickel wings spread. From observation later made by me of other Dodge automobiles, I have ascertained to my absolute satisfaction that the car was a 1929 model Dodge. There had been a change in the type of radiator from previous models of Dodge automobiles, and it struck my notice as I had not at that time seen many Dodges with the new type radiator. I noticed no other insignia or peculiarities of the front of the radiator, and although I recall seeing the front license plate of the automobile, I cannot remember that it covered any part of the radiator. It seems to me it was in the middle, but lower down.

With reference to the license plate, I am positive that it was a New Jersey plate, although I do not now remember exactly what combination of colors it was. However, I was driving a car with New Jersey plates and the plate on the Dodge automobile referred to was similar to the plates on my car. It is my best impression that there were about five numbers on the plate. I believe that if there had been only three numbers on it, or even four, I would have noticed that it was not a "full" plate. I do not believe that it could possibly have had as little as three numbers on it, and that four numbers seems too few also. I am satisfied that the license plate had an "L" on it for I remember thinking after I had passed the Dodge, "What would a person from Hopewell want with ladders here in the mountains at this year of year?" I knew at the time that the letter "L" appeared on New Jersey plates which were issued for Mercer County, New Jersey. The only thing which could have suggested to me that the Dodge was from Hopewell, which is in Mercer County, is that it had an "L" on the license plate. If the license plate had not had an "L" on it, I do not see how the thought could have occurred to me. From the thought referred to, I am satisfied in my own mind that I definitely concluded when passing the Dodge that it was from Mercer County, and I assumed, Hopewell.

The appearance of the car was black, or possibly dark blue, at any rate it was dark in color. I am satisfied that it had spoke wheels. If they had been disc wheels I would have noticed it. I believe they were wooden and their color was dark and not in contrast with the color of the body of the car. After I passed the car, I glanced backward, and noticed that it had a spare tire without a wheel, but also without a tire cover. I did not notice the rear license plate but this can possibly be explained by the fact that it might have been on the far side from me.

The car appeared to be well-kept and in good condition insofar as I could tell from observation merely in passing it. I noticed definitely that the car was a Sedan. I saw three side glasses so it must have been a four door Sedan. The further fact that I noticed several ladders extending apparently from the top of the back seat to the right of the driver, lengthwise with the car, would indicate that it was a Sedan.

I think the car had Cowl lights but I am not positive in my recollection. I do not remember what type wind-shield it had or whether it had a windshield wiper. I do not remember any partitions in the windshield, but I do recall that I could see through it distinctly as well as through the side windows. I am sure the car had a nickel bumper of some width and not of the "bar" type as I recall the effect of space up and down in the bumper. It may have been more than one piece. The above refers to the front bumper. In the rear the car had separate bumpers or bumperettes. I do not remember anything about the door handles of the car or what sort of upholstery it had. I did not notice any mud on the car or any special peculiarities.

With further reference to the ladders in the car, they extended lengthwise in the car to the right of the driver and were horizontal, or nearly so, and one on top of another. I should say they were approximately seven feet long. I inspected the ladders at the Lindbergh home the following night and they resembled the ones I had seen in the Dodge car and I so stated at the time. They were board-like in structure and unpainted. My best recollection and judgment is that the ladders I saw in the Dodge car could have been the same ladders found at the Lindbergh home, but I could not say positively that they were actually the same ladders. I cannot say there were three ladders in the car, only that there were more than one, one on top of another. I saw only one man in the Dodge automobile. If any other persons had been visible from a passing car I would have seen them. While the ladder partially obscured my view of the rear seat, I could see through and into the car and unless someone would have been crouched down low I would have seen him. I remember looking at the face of the driver of the Dodge automobile and that I did not recognize him as being anyone that I knew. I had already noticed the "L" license and therefore my curiosity was casually directed to the drive as being someone from Hopewell, N.J. that I might possibly have known. I am satisfied that the driver was a stranger to me. I noticed that he had a thin face and long features. However, this impression may have been caused by the shadows. He had on a dark hat and a dark overcoat. I do not remember the color more definitely but I could say that neither the hat nor the overcoat were, for example, brown or grey.

I do not remember whether the driver wore gloves but I am sure he did not wear glasses and that he did not have a mustache or beard. He was not a boy or a young man, but fully mature, and I would guess his age as between thirty-five and forty years, although this is purely a guess. I can say however, that he looked considerably older than a college student usually looks. His complexion must have been abut medium or average. I wold say that he looked like a native (an American) as opposed to a foreigner. I do not remember the color of his eyes. He appeared to be cleanly dressed and after the manner of a resident in a city. He did not impress me as looking "tough." He did not speak or nod to me and I did not notice anything unusual about his manner. I saw nothing to indicate that he was excited or anything except matter-of-fact. He made no attempt to hide his face. I do not think I would recognize him if I were to see him again.

After passing the Dodge automobile I continued home, arriving when it was beginning to be slightly dark, about ten minutes after I passed the Dodge automobile. My father and sister were there. My father, as I recall it, was milking his cows. I fixed supper, and after supper stayed around the house. I went to bed around 10:00 or 10:30 P.M. We had no radio and I did not learn of the kidnaping of the Lindbergh baby until the following day.

On the morning of March 2, 1932, I arose around 6:45 A.M. and left home in my father's automobile around 7:00

A.M. I passed by the home of Nelson Wycoff, who has the same mailing address as my father, and who lives about a half mile or a little more from my parents' home and on the way to Hopewell. Mr. Wycoff is a man of about sixty years of age. I often picked him up in the car and took him to town with me. This morning he was standing in front of his house when I drove by, and I stopped and offered him a ride. He got in the car and as I drove along he asked me whether I had seen a car the previous night in driving from Hopewell up to my parents' home. I told him that I had seen one with some ladders in it, and he then informed me of the kidnaping and said that I should see the State Police. At the time I told him about seeing the ladders I did not know there had been a kidnaping. The State Police were on duty at Lindbergh Lane and I stopped the car there and Mr. Wycoff called an officer over who I believe was named Sullivan, although I am not positive of this. I told this officer about the car I had seen on March 1st, and after asking me a few questions, he left me continue to the Princeton Preparatory School. I left school about 2:30 P.M. or 3:00 P.M. that afternoon and on my way home I stopped at the home of Mr. Andrew Hausenbauer which is on the highway just before you reach Lindbergh Lane.

Hausenbauer's wife was there and also someone connected with the Associated Press and several reporters. The Associated Press man suggested that I go up to the Lindbergh house and look at the ladders which I did. The State Policeman I had seen in the morning was there and a number of other officials and plainclothesmen. However, the police had taken the ladder off temporarily and I was told to return later that night to inspect it. After being questioned again, I left and went home for supper. That night, I came back around 7:00 P.M. and looked at the ladders, and told the officers that they resembled the ones I had seen. Members of the State Police and plainclothesmen then took me out to various garages in Hopewell and Princeton, principally Princeton. We also went to some private homes checking on automobiles, but without result, as far as I know.

It was about 4:00 on the morning of March 3, 1933 when I got back home. I got up again at 7:30 A.M. and went to school. At about 10:30 A.M. some officers came to the Princeton Preparatory School for me. They had a list of a number of cars in the Princeton neighborhood but we checked on only a part of the cars on this list.

About two months ago I was called in by the State Police to make a signed statement which I did. This was done at the State Police Training School, near Washington Crossing and Captain Lamb was in charge. . . ."

In addition to the above statement, Lupica furnished the following general information. He stated that from talking to various residents and neighbors of Hopewell, and vicinity, he had learned that the Lindberghs' neighbors did not know that the family was staying at the Hopewell estate when the kidnaping occurred, but it was the general impression among the people in the vicinity that the Lindberghs were living in Englewood and had not as yet moved into their new home. Further that he had been around Hopewell approximately 12 years and feels that he knows the faces of all the natives; that he was positive that the man he saw driving the car was not one of the local element; that he has never been shown any photographs and feels that it would be a waste of time for him to attempt to identify anyone as he did not observe the unknown driver of the car closely enough to warrant the identification, but that he might be able to tell, by looking at a photograph or an individual, whether or not that person resembled the driver of the car.

The New Jersey State Police conducted experiments to determine whether or not the ladders abandoned by the kidnapers would fit into a 1929 Dodge Sedan in the manner in which Lupica claims he saw them, and Lupica stated that these experiments were conducted in his presence, and he observed that the ladders actually would fit in this type of car very conveniently.

Inquiry by the Division of the Dodge dealers in New York City developed that the description of the car as given by Lupica would be a 1929 Dodge with an outside possibility that it might be a 1928 Dodge.

With further respect to the Dodge car observed by Lupica, it is interesting to note that Dr. John F. Condon("Jafsie"), recently informed an agent of the Division that on the occasion of his first meeting with "John", at the Woodlawn Cemetery, he observed an old Dodge car believed to be a Sedan, parked at the Jerome Avenue entrance to the cemetery. Dr. Condon does not know whether or not "John" owned or used the said car. He does not recall seeing the Dodge car on his subsequent meetings with "John" at St. Raymond's Cemetery.

Mrs. Henry Wendling, who lived in a farmhouse on the Zion-Wortsville road, possibly saw the same car as Lupica, for she described it as he did, and said she had seen it between 5 and 6 o'clock on March 1st. It was bound west and would have entered the Hopewell-Wortsville road where Lupica was bound later. However, Mrs. Wendling was unable to describe the man in the car. The information presently available does not indicate whether she saw a ladder in the car.

Between 6:30 and 6:45 P.M. on March 1, 1932 Henry Conover and other members of the family residing at R.F.D. #1, near Hopewell, on the main road a short distance from where Featherbed Lane intersects the main road, saw the lights of an automobile about three hundred yards distant, the car being faced toward the main road as though on its way out of Featherbed Lane. When first noticed, the car was moving, then the lights went out. The members of the family were uncertain whether the car was still moving when the lights were extinguished, or whether it had come to a stop. They were surprised to see the car lights inasmuch as at that time there were notices posted on each end of Featherbed Lane reading "road impassable—drive at your own risk." It was the belief of the members of the Conover family that the driver of the automobile extinguished his lights when, and because, he saw the lights of the Conover house, as it appears that the lights of the car were extinguished when the lights in the house were turned on. The Conover house is within view of the Lindbergh house. The Conovers received some attention in the early stages of the investigation and were subsequently interviewed by agents of the Division.

Two sedans entered the Hopewell-Wortsville road leading to the Lindberghs at about 7:40 P.M. on the night the child was stolen, according to Archie Adam, Office Manager of the State Village for Epileptics at Skillman. Adam was headed towards Hopewell at the time he saw the two cars and they were coming from the village. He remembered the automobiles because he nearly ran into one of them and had to swerve to avoid a collision. He could not describe the occupants of the first car but was sure that there were two men in the second.

Dorothy Walker, waitress in the restaurant of Abraham Nimot, Pennington, N.J. stated that three men stopped in the restaurant on the Friday before the kidnaping and again during the evening on the night of the kidnaping and both times asked directions to the Lindbergh home.

At about 2:30 P.M. on February 28, 1932 John Donnelson Guinness, R.F.D. #1, Hopewell, who operates a gasoline filling station near Hopewell, and who was interviewed by a Special Agent of the Division, observed a man and a woman in a five passenger touring car which he believes was a Willys-Knight; Buick or Packard, about 1926 or 1927 model, bearing upstate New Jersey license, driving near the Lindbergh estate, and their actions were peculiar in that they drove off of the Rileyville road into a side road which became impassable after several hundred yards, turned back on to the Rileyville road and subsequently again reversed his direction and drove in an upstate direction toward Van Lues Corners. Guinness particularly observed the driver, and is quite certain that he would be able to recognize him; describing him as being in his 40's; average height; chunky build; possibly weighing 170 pounds; fairly light complexion; clean shaven; bluish gray eyes; possibly thin shell rimmed glasses; eye sockets appeared to be set out instead of being set in; he was definitely pop-eyed. His face was jowl-like and his chin was not prominent.

A blue green sedan with New York license plates was seen in the vicinity of the Lindbergh home several times before the kidnaping. It was said to have carried three men. The first recollection of the car was that of Theresa Dorsi, a music student, 19 years of age, residing near Featherbed Lane, near Hopewell. She said she had seen the car on February 22nd with three men in it, and that they had asked her the way to the Lindbergh home.

Alfred Hammond, a watchman at the Skillman Railroad Crossing, told of having seen the car which seemed just like the car described by Miss Dorsi, five or six days before the abduction. The car passed between 8 and 9 o'clock in the morning, Hammond said.

John Dougherty, a telephone line man, went further in bearing out this story. He was on the road to the Lindbergh home when he saw the automobile. Still nearer it was seen by Jay Moore, a farmer's son. Miss Dorsi was nearest to the Lindbergh home to see the auto.

Miss Rebecca Bush of Zion, reported having seen the

car east of the local post office, indicating that it may have returned by the north route to Zion. Apparently the car was never seen after March 1, the day before the kidnaping.

The following is a complete list of automobiles stolen in New Jersey during the twenty-four hours preceding 10 P.M. March 1, 1932.

Chrysler sedan, License No. E-70-70 1, reported stolen from Newark.
Chevrolet sedan, License No. H-5866, reported stolen from Camden.
Graham Paige sedan, License No. C-21917, reported stolen from Camden.
Buick sedan, License No. E-24-437, reported stolen from Camden.
Franklin sedan, License No. U-60940, reported stolen from Irvington.
Willys Knight sedan, License No. 1-E-8361, reported stolen from Newark.
Chevrolet sedan, License No. E-71624, reported stolen from Belleville.
Buick sedan, License No. E-13-640, reported stolen from Newark.
Hudson sedan, License No. 1-E-54006, reported stolen from Newark.
Buick coupe, License No. K-34-607, reported stolen from Newark.
Buick sedan, License No. ON-6009, reported stolen from Lakewood.
Pontiac sedan, License No. Z-12852, reported stolen from Swedesboro.
Ford coach, License No. C-25377, reported stolen from Camden.
Buick sedan, License No. C-22899, reported stolen from Camden.

Auburn sedan, License No. C-24837, reported stolen from Hammonton.

On March 19, 1932 a search for stolen automobiles resulted in finding a stolen Buick from which the motor had been removed, hidden under a ton of hay in the barn of Casper Oliver, about two miles from the Lindbergh estate. Oliver was arrested in this connection, together with Sam Cuchiara, a barber of Hopewell, who is known as "Sam the Barber." The police later announced that investigation of this matter developed no connection with the Lindbergh kidnaping. Subsequent investigation by Special Agents of the Division as to Cuchiara developed no evidence to connect him with the crime.

The New York office of the Division obtained from the Automobile Underwriters Detective Bureau, #1 Liberty St., a list of all 1928 and 1929 Dodge sedans reported stolen to that agency, for a period of two months preceding the Lindbergh kidnaping in the states of New York, New Jersey, Pennsylvania, West Virginia, Maryland, Delaware and District of Columbia and all of the New England states. A good many of the cars reported stolen were recovered prior to the kidnaping. The Automobile Underwriters Detective Bureau is endeavoring to obtain complete information relative to the names and addresses of owners, and details as to the recovery of the cars up to the present time.

The following listed cars had not been recovered at the time of the kidnaping.

Dodge sedan—(year unknown); motor B742358, New York 1932 license 8K7656.
Dodge sedan—(year unknown); motor B750968, New York 1932 license 4U4618.
Dodge sedan—(1929 model); motor 50929; stolen 1/22/

32 from 7 West 24th St., New York City; owner, Morris Schwab, 1709 St. John's place, Brooklyn; insured by British General Insurance Co., #1 Park Ave., New York City, under policy #5114.

Said car was recovered on 5/13/32. Details concerning the recovery not yet determined.

In the section of this report entitled Suspects and subjects on page reference is made to a stolen automobile which was found abandoned in front of 515 West 149th Street, near 537 West 149th Street which was the address given by the person who signed his name as J. J. Faulkner at the time of surrendering $2,980 in ransom gold certificates at the Federal Reserve Bank on May 1, 1933.

This office has ascertained from the New York Police Department that this automobile was a Buick 1926 model Brougham and was recovered in front of the address mentioned by Detectives Genet and Oak of the Automobile Squad on March 2, 1932, the day following the kidnaping. The police report shows that the car bore Motor #1583836; serial #155422 (apparently original and unchanged number) and New York 1932 license plates #6V2456. The car was stolen from its owner, Benjamin Schindelar of the Pines Hotel, Lakewood, N. J. January 28, 1932 from a parking place in front of the above hotel between the hours of 9 P.M. and 11 P.M. When stolen, the car bore 1932 license plates ON4904. The owner's plates so far as is known have not been recovered.

The police report further indicates that the car was unlocked when recovered, the battery was dead, and the keys missing. In the rear of the car were two old robes, and a milk bottle with a long rubber tube, was lying in front in the driver's seat. The milk bottle had an oily smell and possibly the tube and bottle had been used in syphoning gasoline. Also found in the car was a knife, of the type generally used for preparing grape fruit; also a book of matches with the following addresses:

West 147th Street Garage and 518 West 147th Street.

When the car was recovered, the inside lights were burning. Although the police reports are not clear in this respect, it is indicated that the robes and other articles found in the car were turned over to the New Jersey State Police who felt that the car in question might have been used in the kidnaping. The police reports do not reflect that any bloodstains were found in the car or on any of the articles mentioned or that there was anything suspicious other than as above mentioned.

After recovery the car was placed in the Police Department, Property Clerk's Garage, at 152nd Street and Amsterdam Ave. and subsequently, returned to its owner who personally called for the car and signed a receipt for it.

The police report further indicates that the police interviewed Mrs. Dorothy Stevens who lives at 515 West 149th Street, and she stated she observed the car being driven from Amsterdam Ave., west, and parked in front of her house. She noticed a man get out of the car and lock the outside door and then walk back toward Amsterdam Ave. She described him as being about 30 years old; 5'9" tall; of slender build; clean shaven; dark complexion; well dressed; wearing dark, soft hat. She was unable to identify any of the photographs in the criminal Identification Bureau of the Police Department as being a likeness of the man she saw leaving the car.

It appears from the police reports that the car in question was first observed by Patrolman Thomas Rossiter, shield #3410, and Joseph Doyle, shield [number garbled] both attached to the 30th Precinct and being suspicious of same, these officers communicated with the Auto Squad, after which Detectives Genet and Oak were assigned to the case and conducted the investigation. In connection with further investigation of the above car, it is stated that the following officers conduct same and should be interviewed:

Patrolmen Thomas Rossiter and Joseph Doyle, 30th Precinct.
Detectives Genet and Oak, Auto Squad.
Inspector Lyons, New York Police Headquarters.
Sergeant Stewart, Yonkers Police Department.
Captain Ford, Yonkers, New York Police Department.
Detectives Dunn and Sergeant Haussling, New Jersey State Police.
Detective Harrison, 30th Squad, New York Police Department.
Chief of Police, Lakewood, N. J.
Lt. Edward Dillon, New York Auto Squad.

In order to eliminate possible confusion concerning the recovery of the car, it is stated that the report of Frank Wilson of the United States Treasury Department, dated November 11, 1933, copy of which was furnished the Division, reflects that the car recovered in front of 515 W. 149th Street was a Nash. However, it is stated that the police reports clearly show the car was a Buick brougham. Copies of New York Police reports relative to the Buick brougham recovered in front of 515 West 149th Street, New York City, on March 2, 1932 are attached to and made part of the New York file.

The Automobile Underwriter's Detective Bureau have advised that their operator, Charles Black, who works the New Jersey territory checked a number of Dodge cars for the New Jersey State Police and can be of great assistance in checking any Dodge cars in that state. The New York office of the Division will give close attention to the phase of the investigation relative to the possible connection of stolen automobiles with the kidnaping.

LOCAL CABINS

Antonia Chowlewsky, known as the "Pig Woman", who resided near Zion and whose occupation was the rendering of pigs, and who also owned several small cabins in the vicinity, stated that on the night of the kidnaping someone had broken into a locked summer cottage that she owned.

A woman and several men left muddy tracks on the floor, she said. Major Schoeffel of the New Jersey State Police called her statement highly significant. It was later contended that the "muddy tracks" might have been made there by investigators after the crime or by persons who had broken into the place, for any reason, some period before the crime. It was reported that this woman was of the opinion that local folks had kidnaped the baby.

On another occasion during the investigation, a baby's diaper was found in one of her abandoned huts, however, it was later announced that examination enveloped that it had been there at least several months.

With further reference to Antonia Chowlewsky, a published account states that she was of the view that local folks had kidnaped the baby and further in this respect, as follows:

"A stranger moved into a house up the road from her in July, 1931, she said. The man came over one day and, after guarded hints, informed her that someone who "didn't like the Lindberghs" might be "paid well" for their views.

The man came from Brooklyn and was accompanied by another man and two women, the pig woman said.

Antonia said she was afraid to talk too much—afraid

of the mountain folks, she added. Her occupation as a "pig renderer" gave her opportunity to know the neighboring folks whom she apparently did not get along with, very well. Her job was slaughtering pigs and she did the smoking of ham and bacon, as well. Her job, she indicated wasn't conducive to warm friendships in the region.

Since no curtains hung in the Lindbergh home, she said, their business, despite their ideas of isolation and their love of it, was as open as "a goldfish bowl."

Antonia looked upon the kidnaping as a job of vengeance by a Brooklyn racketeer bent upon fastening the blame on a rival. The man had gotten local folks to do the kidnaping, the pig woman said. Although her theories were somewhat fantastic, her facts were not. She pointed out, for instance, that the supposed "racketeer" whom she had not seen since the summer before, appeared suddenly on the Zion road, in an automobile, the day before the kidnaping. He drove off without speaking to her.

Edward Kutchera, a New York cabinet maker, owned a small farm and house near Noshanic, N. J. in the Sourland country. Although questioned in the case, no suspicion of any sort was attached to him but it was thought that someone might have used his property during his absence as he only came to the place over weekends, and there were some evidences that the house had been broken into. State Troopers located wood on the farm which was said to bear some general resemblance to the lumber used in the ladder left by the kidnapers. A small stream runs through Kutchera's land over which he constructed a crude bridge. He stated that he had completely demounted the bridge just before he left for New York on the Saturday night preceding the kidnaping; that when he returned on the following weekend, he found it thrown back again; reinforced with some boards, hown with an ax, and that there were automobile tracks leading over it from the lane tat led down to the Neshanic Road.

CURTAINS AND TELEPHONE LINES

Much publicity was given to the theory that the baby had been kidnaped via the "inside tip." However, another theory was also seriously advanced that no "inside tip" was necessary; that the Lindberghs had no drawn curtains over their windows and at night, when the lights were turned on, in any of the rooms, it would have been a simple matter to stand on a near by hill and with the aid of binoculars look down into the room and see all that went on there.

The telephone lines at the Lindbergh home are buried underground for several hundred feet in a lead conduit.

According to newspaper reports published shortly after the kidnaping evidences were found by the New Jersey State Police of the apparent tapping of telephone wires at a point near Hopewell, probably by agents of the kidnapers seeking to keep informed of the progress of the hunt for the kidnapers.

MEN EMPLOYED IN CONSTRUCTOIN
OF THE LINDBERGH HOME

During the investigation, the New Jersey State Police announced that a careful and thorough check had been made on more than one hundred former employees hired to assist in the construction of the Lindbergh residence and that nothing of any kind was found to link them with the crime. A list of the names and addresses of these men is included in the supplement to this report as Exhibit "I."

Lee Hurley; a resident of Hopewell, was employed as a watchman during the construction of the Lindbergh home but was not retained after it was completed.

SEARCH OF ROADS AND COUNTRYSIDE

Immediately after the news of the kidnaping had been flashed by police teletype through New Jersey and adjacent states, all available state troopers were sent through the region in search of the missing child; police began holding automobiles for scrutiny; guards were posted along all the main arteries of traffic leading from New Jersey into New York and Pennsylvania; a close check was made of the occupants of all automobiles leaving the state as well as all cars along highways in the vicinity of the Lindbergh home. City and town police cooperated with the State Troopers in their search. As far north as the Canadian Border, every traffic lane; state road and highway was watched for persons traveling with the Lindbergh baby. In the next twenty-four hours all automobiles had been halted and the occupants obliged to give an accounting of themselves often at the local police station. Busses, bridges and ferry boats—all were searched.

The New Jersey State Police further announced that a thorough search of the countryside in the vicinity of the Lindbergh home was instituted immediately but was not productive of results.

BABIES MISTAKENLY REPROTED AS LINDBERGH CHILD

Numerous reports were received and investigated in all sections of the country, of babies seen and believed to be the Lindbergh baby which reports continued to crop up long after the kidnaping and even after the body was found, and are still being received. It obviously would be impracticable to include in this report the many investigations conducted by the Division in this respect.

SUMMARY REPORT

In Re

Unknown Subjects

Kidnaping and Murder of
Charles A. Lindbergh, Jr.
(N.Y. File 62-3057).

RANSOM NOTES

-o-

Thomas Fensch

RANSOM NOTES

The thirteen communications which apparently emanated from the kidnapers and led to the payment of $50,000 ransom on April 2, 1932, are referred to herein as the ransom notes. Photostatic copies reproduced from photographs of the notes, and the envelopes, and a composite set of specimens of the symbol signatures are included in the Supplement hereto as Exhibits "A-1" to "A-14" inclusive. The originals are in the possession of the New Jersey State Police. The text of the notes, the postmarks, etc. are clearly shown in the photostatic copies and therefore are not reported herein.

The ransom notes were submitted by the New Jersey State Police to handwriting experts Albert S. Osborn, Albert D. Osborn and Elbridge W. Stein for examination. Copies of their reports are included in the Supplement as Exhibits "E-1," "E-2" and "E-3" respectively. Composite specimens of the letters, words and sentences taken from the ransom notes are reproduced in Exhibits "F-1," "F-2" and "F-3". The notes were also examined at the request of Intelligence Unit agents, by Dr. Dudley D. Schoenfeld, psychiatrist. A copy of his report relative to the mentality and character of the writer of the notes is included in the Supplement as Exhibit "H".

Exhibit "G" is a suggested paragraph to be written by suspected persons, concerning which more is stated later in this section.

The Division's Laboratory at Washington, D. C. has conducted numerous examinations of suspected handwriting in this investigation. When such action is indicated, the respective field offices should obtain and transmit any suspected handwriting in this case to the Division for attention of the Laboratory for expert examination, directing a copy of the letter of transmittal to the New York office.

The reports of the handwriting experts previously mentioned are summarized as to finding and opinions as follows:

<u>ALBERT S. OSBORN, 233 Broadway, New York City</u>, (report dated 5-27-32):
Mr. Osborn concluded that all of the so-called ransom notes were written by one writer. The paper and envelopes used have distinct significance in connecting the letters with each other. The sheet of paper upon which letter #2 is written is the opposite half of the sheet upon which the first ransom note was written. This originally was a folded sheet of linen-finish paper, and, according to Mr. Osborn, was torn apart, one half being used to write the first ransom note and the other half used to write the second note. When the torn edges of these papers are placed together, it may be seen that the figure work in the paper as examined by transmitted light, indicates that the two edges were originally attached. In addition to this, numerous other points are indicated by Albert S. Osborn to show that the paper and envelopes used in writing the ransom letters have a significance in connecting the letters with each other. The letter of March 4, 1932, for instance, was mailed in an envelope with the script water mark "Fifth Avenue linen" which is exactly the same water mark as the blank envelope in which ransom letter #1 was found. This water mark is the property of the F. W. Woolworth Company 5¢ and 10¢ Stores and the paper is sold in their stores. Certain of the other letters are also written on the same type of paper.

The ingenious device which serves as a signature on these various letters in Albert S. Osborn's opinion, definitely connects these ransom letters with each other. A careful examination of these various letters, containing this so-called symbol signature, ten in all, indicates that they were all made at the same time, or from each other, and that they are practically duplicates of each other. The holes appearing in this so-called symbol signature were apparently made with a blunt pointed nail punched into the papers after which a circular bottle cover or similar device was inked with blue ink, and two intersecting circles about the size of a half dollar made. In the intervening space between the circles was a smaller circle about the size of a dime, probably made by an ink cork dipped in red ink.

The blue ink and the red ink used in making the symbol signatures are the same in all the letters. An examination of the writing of all the letters on which this symbol signature appears discloses that the devise was on the sheet when the writing was placed upon it. This, for example, is shown in letter #7, where the writing at the left avoids the device, although one line goes through the top of it. This avoiding of the punch hole appearing in the symbol signature seems perfectly obvious on the second page of letter #3, where the written line is made only half length, so that it will not run into the holes. Throughout the series of the ransom notes, several references in the letters are made to this means of identifying the notes as having come from the right source. For example, letter #2 has placed at the bottom the words "signature on all letters" with an arrow pointing to the device. In a like manner on letter #3 the word "signature" appears. Again on letter #8 it is written "how can Mr. Lindbergh follow so many false clues. He knows we are the right party. Our signature is still the same as in the ransom note."

In the opinion of Albert S. Osborn, the ink used in writing the ransom letters is a negrocine ink and easily smudged when water is applied. The ink used for the device or symbol signature on letter #1 seemed to Albert S. Osborn to be lighter than the ink in the body of the document but exactly like the ink of all the other symbols. The ink on letter #1 in the opinion of Albert S. Osborn has a very distinct secondary color; for instance, when looked at from an angle this ink appears red, and when looked at directly it appears blue or blue black. The ink of all the other letters is of a distinct blue color and shows the secondary color to a certain extent but not in so pronounced a way as letter 31. All of the letters except #1 appear to be written with the same ink, and with a broad pointed pen, which makes a broad stroke without leaving any nib marks, or very few if any. In Albert S. Osborn's opinion, the ink employed in all the letters is of the same class as in letter #1, although the writing instrument may have been different.

The writing in the first letter is, in the opinion of Albert S. Osborn, unmistakably unskilled and partially disguised in certain ways. Although it is possible that some part of this first ransom letter may have been written with the left hand by a right handed person, Albert S. Osborn is inclined to doubt this. He states that it is easier to disguise writing when writing with the right hand by a right handed person than to disguise it when written with the left hand. Although the particular writing in this letter is not so freely written as the writing in the following letters, in Mr. Osborn's opinion, the writing is by the same hand. There is the possibility that the first note may have been written in an automobile or under circumstances where it was difficult to write. The letters beginning with #2 display very little, if any, disguise, although some of the notes appear to have been written more rapidly and carelessly than others.

The original ransom letter and the various other letters, in Mr. Albert S. Osborn's opinion, unquestionably have certain national characteristics in style of handwriting and in language. In his opinion the letters show various delicate national characteristics and certain qualities in composition which can hardly be interpreted as unnatural disguise. A number of the words employed throughout the series of the ransom letters, such as "gut" (good); "haus" (house); "cansell" (cancel); "ouer" (our); "note" (not); "frankfurther" (frankfurter); "dank" (thank), and possibly others, appear to be distinct German words. While the use of these words might be a part of the disguise, Albert S. Osborn is inclined to the belief that they are the natural expressions of the writer of the ransom notes who did not feel that it was necessary in these notes to disguise his handwriting or his language. Various words and forms point toward the German language and German handwriting, but this does not necessarily indicate that the writer was a German but rather was one who wrote the German language. It is the statement of Albert S. Osborn that there are citizens even in France, Belgium, Sweden and Switzerland who write German as a native language, and that many individuals in other neighboring countries write German as well.

Certain forms in the ransom letters, such as the small "a", small "g", small "w", and capital "W", capital "I", small "t", small "I", small "x", in addition to the small "y", for examples, are stated to be definitely Continental European and characteristics of German writing. There are numerous expressions throughout the notes which seem to indicate the German influence. In addition to that, the writing appearing in the series of ransom notes shows a frequent misuse of prepositions and adverbs, which, in the opinion of Albert S. Osborn, is another German characteristic.

The two most significant German characteristics which, in the opinion of Albert S. Osborn, were unconsciously placed in the ransom letters are, firstly, the double German hyphen inclined upwards, on letter #5, in the middle of the word "frankfurter." Mr. Osborn states that this is an inconspicuous and delicate German characteristic and that thousands of German writers who write English do not know that it differs from the hyphen as employed in the English language. The second distinctive characteristic is the use of the exclamation point after the salutation, as it appears in the first letter. It is a peculiar use of the punctuation mark and its appearance on letter #1, is Mr. Osborn's opinion, is particularly significant. None of the other ransom letters appears to show it and several of them indicate the colon used as in English writing by many writers. Mr. Osborn is quite sure that numerous of these distinctive characteristics, the double hyphen, the exclamation point, in addition to the manner of writing the interlineation throughout the notes, are unconscious characteristics and particularly a significant as pointing to the nationality of the writer or his writing.

It will be noted from a reading of the ransom notes that these letters in their handwriting and in their language are somewhat inconsistent. In the opinion of Mr. Osborn, this inconsistency may be due to deliberate effort to disguise, to unconscious caution, or disturbing influence arising from the nature of the letters, and also to a mixture of foreign habits of composition and later acquired habits in a different language. For instance, letter #8, although containing numerous errors in spelling, is in composition and excellent piece of work, in the opinion of Mr. Osborn, and indicates to him that the writer of these letters has purposely used clumsy language. Throughout the series there may be found sentences and expressions which might be said to be good examples of the cruel deception employed by the author. When some of this clumsy language is slightly reconstructed or corrected to a small degree, the expressions would seem to point away from an illiterate writer. In the opinion of Mr. Osborn, numerous illustrations might be found throughout the various ransom notes which may be said to be examples of the deception and a condition of the criminal mind of the writer that is almost fiendish.

Mr. Osborn invites attention to the drawing of the box in letter #4-A, with the dotted line indicating the side and corner of the same. To him this is an example of the work of one who is not inexperienced but who understands some of the principles of drawing. From letter #2, in a like manner, in Mr. Osborn's opinion, there is some evidence that the person who wrote the letter indicated experience in matters of this kind, as there are many people who do not understand the significance of "serial numbers" on currency bills. Mr. Osborn feels that the series of letters in this case are connected with each other in other ways than by the handwriting. They seem to be connected by the composition and the errors which appear. The word "money" for instance, in letter #1, is spelled "mony" and this spelling appears elsewhere and once correctly throughout the notes. There is an incorrect use of the word "for" in the first letter, instead of "of" in addition to many other errors of a similar nature.

The letters and the contents thereof, in addition to the use of the device for the so called symbol signature, in Mr. Osborn's opinion, point to an experienced performer in matters of communicating with those who are being blackmailed or who have been the victims of kidnapers. The handwriting and the language employed throughout the notes indicate to Mr. Osborn that the writer has been in America for a considerable period of time. The writer has at least written for sometime in another language or style than the language he learned. In numerous particulars, this writing differs from ordinary German handwriting. The Germans handwriting is distinctly angular and is inclined to be condensed and long letters are much higher than short letters. The writing in the ransom notes further differs in these ways from German writing, especially in certain of the letters. This combination of characteristics and variation in handwriting indicates a mixture of habits to Mr. Osborn and it is his inference that the writer of these ransom notes if he were a German has been out of Germany a number of years.

As to the writings, circumstances and developments being indicative of the number of persons engaged in perpetrating this kidnaping and extortion, Mr. Osborn states that "It has been assumed that this performance was the work of several people, a 'band' or 'gang' working together, and the letters themselves suggest that more than one individual was involved, but in view of the developments in the case, the finding of the body of the dead child, the reference, even in the first letter, No. 2, to the baby as safe, all, in my opinion, point to one performer only in this crime. It is easy to understand the danger involved if 'two ladies' were taking care of the child. It is evident that this was a mercenary performance for the purpose of securing $50,000 and it is not at all, in my opinion, unlikely that murder was planned from the beginning, and if so, then there would be no necessity for any second party or assistant in the performance and the crime would be much safer."

ALBERT D. OSBORN, 233 Broadway, New York City (Report dated 5/31/32):

Dr. Albert D. Osborn examined the letters first to determine if possible whether the letters following the one left in the Lindbergh home had come from the same source as that letter, so as to dispel any doubt that the letters all came from the actual kidnapers. He, like Albert S. Osborn, was of the opinion, upon his examination of the ransom letters, that the writer thereof originally learned to write German. In his report, Albert D. Osborn states that he is convinced that the first ransom note and the subsequent ransom letters came from the same source for the following three reasons; firstly, that the writing in the first note is the same as the writing in the subsequent letters; secondly, that the design or symbol signature on the first letter is the same as that in subsequent letters, and the holes in this symbol, especially, are in the same position in each case, in relation to the bottom of the sheet; thirdly, there is some evidence that the first and second letters are the two halves of the same double sheet of writing paper.

The Division concurs with Mr. Albert D. Osborn in his belief that there will undoubtedly be many suspected writers of the Lindbergh ransom notes and that if the following paragraph was dictated to and written by such suspected writer about three times, it is probable, in Albert D. Osborn's opinion, that if such suspect actually wrote these letters, some of the characteristics appearing in the ransom notes themselves would undoubtedly become evident:

"We are not near Smith Hall where the robbery took place between 6 and 12 by our time. During all the time I was out of the house but later came home. Did you not write letters to New York sending back anything that was stolen from Mr. Conway? Police keep those letters and papers; they will be good for something later maybe. One of the letters said: 'Dear Sir: Thank you for the bills and for your money. We will send back the bills later perhaps, where shall we send them, the address we lost. Be at home every night so you will hear from us, you cannot tell when it will be.'"

Albert D. Osborn states that it is important to have the suspect write the above quoted paragraph about three times, taking each sheet away from such suspect as the writing is finished, for in this way if a disguise is being attempted, the first and the last specimens made probably will be quite different. It is difficult for any writer to remember how he has disguised a piece of writing even when it has just been written, while if a suspect is writing naturally, the three specimens will all look very much alike. The writing also of any suspect should be done with a fountain pen, the nibs of which are tight together, so that they show no nib marks in the paper. It might be well also to have the second specimen written with a stylographic pen, for it is possible that the ransom letters were written with such a pen, as the traces of nib marks in the paper are apparently entirely lacking in these communications. In addition to this, it might also be well to hand a suspect a different pen in a further effort to determine whether that particular suspect is making any effort to disguise his writing.

ELBRIDGE WALTER STEIN, 15 Park Row, New York City (report dated 6/24/32):

By comparing Mr. Stein's report with that of the findings of the handwriting experts mentioned above, it is noted that these experts agree on numerous points relating to the series of ransom letters. It was Mr. Stein's findings that all of the ransom letters were written by the same person; that ordinary domestic writing inks appear to have been used; that the letters were quite probably written by a German, a Continental European, or some individual who had learned to write German. It is his further finding that the handwriting in the letters was not effectively disguised and that the writing in the last few notes was disguised very little, if at all. In Mr. Stein's opinion, the notes were written by a person of rather keen intelligence even though he may not have had much education.

There will be found in the supplement to this report a copy of the sheet on which appear the certain form and characteristics employed throughout the series of the Lindbergh ransom notes. Attention is invited to this particular reference, in order that the field offices may have ready access to the comparative analysis in picture form of the numerous writings of various forms by the author of the Lindbergh ransom notes.

On November 1, 1932, Dudley D. Shoenfeld, M.D., New York City, N.Y., after having completed his examination of the Lindbergh ransom notes, submitted a report, copy of which will be found in the supplement hereto, in which is outlined his impressions and interpretations. These impressions, he states, were drawn from his experience as a psychiatrist, particularly interested in the functioning of the subconscious mind. He states that he did not read these various ransom letters from the standpoint of a criminologist or as a graphologist. It is interesting to note that Shoenfeld, like the above mentioned handwriting experts, upon a reading of the Lindbergh ransom letters, was immediately struck by the Germanic phraseology appearing thereon. According to Shoenfeld, in this phraseology whole sentences and phrases at times appear to be confused, one immediately corrects this when thinking of the sentences and phrases as a literal German translation. As a result of Shoenfeld's study of all of the ransom notes examined by him, he was of the opinion that the individual involved in this crime is a case of dementic praecox with intelligence apparently intact.

SUMMARY REPORT

In Re

Unknown Subjects

Kidnaping and Murder of Charles A. Lindbergh, Jr. (N.Y. File 62-3057)

INTERMEDIARIES

Morris Rosner
Salvatore Spitale
Irving Bitz, et al.
Dr. John F. ("Jafsie") Condon

Thomas Fensch

MORRIS ROSNER; SALVATORE SPITALE; IRVING BITZ

Morris Rosner, alias Morris Roesner, alias Moritz Rosner, alias Mickey Rosner, was a subject of much newspaper publicity in the early days following the kidnaping, as the mysterious investigator engaged in contacting the underworld. He was responsible for the entrance into the case of Salvatore Spitale and Irving Bitz, New York racketeers, who on March 5, 1932 were publicly authorized by the Lindberghs to deal with the underworld and act as their intermediaries.

Rosner is characterized by police officials as a "rather clever individual" who has contacts with the underworld. On March 25, 1925 after having been convicted in Federal Court, Eastern District of New York, of the charge of attempting to obstruct justice, wherein it was indicated that he obtained $450 from a Prohibition defendant upon the promise of fixing his case, Rosner was sentenced to one year imprisonment and fined $1,000. He appealed this sentence and on March 6, 1926 the United States Circuit Court of Appeals, Second Circuit, reversed the decision and he was discharged.

On October 5, 1931 Rosner was arrested; New York City Police Department Gallery #96987, charged with grand larceny in connection with alleged misrepresentation in the sale of supposed Treasury stock of the National Land Value Refunding Company on which charge he was indicted and released in bail of $20,000. This indictment against Rosner was dismissed by Judge Allen in the Court of General Sessions, New York, N. Y. on April 6, 1933. At the time of his arrest, he resided at 130 East 39th Street, New York, N. Y.

Salvatore Spitale, alias Salvy, is said to be a Brooklyn producer who has worked his way up until he occupies a place just below that of the more important racketeers. He started in the Williamburg Dance Halls as a "bouncer" and graduated to the gang that operated around Grand Street. Informants have stated that he was the first man to realize the possibilities of the Green and Sullivan County beer rackets which led him into inevitable conflict with the late Jack (Legs) Diamond. Spitale was sought for questioning when Diamond was shot. He resides in an expensive apartment at 241 Central Park West and is reported to own or have an interest in several cafes and restaurants. His police record shows a number of arrests but no convictions; on one occasion he was arrested for selling cocaine but was discharged.

The importance of Bitz in the underworld, according to informants, hinges entirely upon his association with Spitale. The files of the Division of Investigation show that on September 30, 1926 Bitz was received at the United States Penitentiary, Atlanta, Ga. As #23032, from New York, N. Y.—crime, conspiracy to violate Drug Act—sentence, one year and one day; discharged June 28, 1927. Further, that as Morris Grossman, he was arrested by the police Department, New York, N. Y. July 26, 1931 charged with felonious assault; disposition not given. The Police Department records indicate that Bitz was acquitted on this charge.

On March 11, 1932 Spitale, Bitz and twelve others were arraigned in Federal Court, Brooklyn, N. Y. on Prohibition charges and on March 12, 1932 were acquitted on that charge by the jury.

Concerning Rosner's entry into the Lindbergh case, in a conference at Trenton, N. J. on May 18, 1932 attended by representatives of this Division, the Intelligence Unit and other officials, Colonel H. Norman Schwarzkopf, superintendent, New Jersey State Police, stated in part as follows:

"The baby was kidnaped on a Tuesday night. On Wednesday, Ruth Pratt, Congresswoman, got in touch with Colonel Bill Donovan and said, 'You must put Morris Rosner on that case.' She recommended it to Bill Donovan and Bill Donovan then recommended the induction of Mr. Rosner and Rosner was brought down by Mr. Thayer. Rosner was vouched for by two United States Senators and was supposed to have done some undercover work for the Department of Justice for two years and was supposed to have been a very reputable man. He never double-crossed either the underworld or the overworld, as it were, and was a man that could be depended upon. He was to be the contact man. Subsequently it was decided in private conference by the family in which the police was not included. We did not know him except that Colonel Lindbergh told us Rosner was all right. He looked at him and thought maybe he was a gangster. We were told no, that he was vouched for. He was always in the inner circle of the family; knew the early developments of the case and saw the first and second and third letters, at one time taking either the first or the second letter to New York with one of two troopers in an automobile. . . .

Rosner had a copy of the note and he delivered that to Colonel Breckinridge who showed it to Owney Madden, Spitale, and Bitz all but the Condon letter. It was on this occasion Maddan advised Breckinridge not to show any more notes to anyone, including himself."

Further, with reference to Rosner's entry into the case, on November 15, 1932, the Jersey Journal, Jersey City, N. J., in a copyrighted series of interviews with Inspector Harry Walsh of the Jersey City Police Department, reviewing the investigation of the kidnaping and murder, quoted Inspector Walsh as follows:

"That Colonel Henry Breckinridge, close friend of Lindbergh, telephoned Edgar Hoover, Chief Agent of the Department of Justice, a few hours after the kidnaping and was told 'the best informer at his command' would be sent to the Lindbergh home; the following morning, one Morris Rosner, a common character in police circles . . . arrived."

Immediately after this publication, it was officially announced that at no time throughout the investigation of the Lindbergh case did Colonel Breckinridge call the Director on the Telephone and that the Director's contact and the Division's contact with the Lindbergh inquiry at all times was solely through Colonel Schwarzkopf, superintendent of the New Jersey State Police. Further, that neither he nor any official of the Division identified in any way with the Lindbergh investigation had anything whatever to do with the employment of Morris Rosner in connection with the Lindbergh inquiry. Further, that Morris Rosner has not at anytime been employed in any capacity by the Division, or as it was then named, the United States Bureau of Investigation.

On January 17, 1934 Dr. Robert Thayer, attorney-at-law, associated with Colonel William J. Donovan, New York City, furnished a memorandum to representatives of the interested police departments and this office, relative to the entry and activities of Rosner in the case, in substance, together with information from other sources as indicated, as follows:

That on Wednesday, March 2, Rosner approached Mr. Thayer who asked him if he could do anything in the Lindbergh case, reminding Thayer that he once said that if Thayer had any friends involved in a kidnaping case he should get in touch with him, because he knew how to handle this type of case, and had ways of getting in touch with the right people immediately. Rosner had always boasted to Thayer of his various contacts with underworld leaders including "Legs" Diamond; Owney Madden; Waxey Gordon, and others. Rosner further indicated that he personally had experience in kidnaping cases although he did not mention the name of any particular case. About an hour later, Rosner called Thayer and told him that he had received very important information, the nature of which he declined to state but insisted that Thayer communicate with the Lindberghs at once. Mr. Thayer discussed the matter with Colonel Donovan who advised him to do nothing unless Rosner was more explicit. At about four o'clock that afternoon, after having telephoned every half hour, Rosner called upon Thayer and told him that he had been informed that a certain man, well known in the underworld, had disappeared the day of the Lindbergh kidnaping; that this man had a kidnaping record and that all the underworld was convinced he had something to do with it and if authorized by the Lindbergh family would do everything they could. He also said he was a great personal friend of the chief of the Unione Sicilione who could have his whole organization out looking for the kidnapers and getting information.

Colonel Donovan was unwilling to make any recommendation about Rosner since he had never trusted him but thought that Colonel Breckinridge should be advised of what Rosner had said and use his own judgment as to whether he wished to employ Rosner. Col. Donovan then called Col. Breckinridge who said he would be willing to hear Rosner's proposition.

During the negotiations which followed Rosner told Thayer that he would require $2500 which he stated would be used by him to send emissaries to the various gang leaders throughout the country, including Spitale; Owney Madden; Waxey Gordon; the Purple Gang in Detroit; Bobo

Hoff in Philadelphia; the successor to Al Capone in Chicago, and others, and that each emissary would have to be given $250.

Mr. Thayer advised Colonel Breckinridge that neither he nor Col. Donovan could recommend Rosner because he was connected with the underworld and not to be trusted. Colonel Breckinridge replied that the plan was to get all the help possible, from any quarters, because they were absolutely in the dark, and would go to any length to get the proper information. After hearing Rosner's proposition Colonel Breckinridge stated that he was willing to go ahead with it. Colonel Breckinridge was accompanied at this meeting, which occurred in Mr. Thayer's home, by Captain William E. Galvin, a private citizen residing in Washington, D. C. and a close personal friend whom Colonel Breckinridge brought into the case to assist him in keeping track of its many angles. Thayer went upstairs with Galvin and the latter, at Colonel Breckinridge's request, produced $2500 in cash which Thayer carried into the living room, then called Rosner into the room and told him to carry out the plan he had proposed.

Rosner stated he would undertake the task under the following conditions:

That he should not be followed or interfered with by the police, and that the family should insist that the United States Secret Service be kept out because the underworld feared the Secret Service.

Rosner then went to the telephone and called several numbers; shortly thereafter two men appeared and were shown to another room. Rosner peeled off approximately $500 from the $2500 and put it into each trouser pocket and went into the other room with the two men. Thayer later learned that the name of one of the two individuals who came in was Sally, a thin, Italian looking individual who worked for Spitale. (Spitale later told Thayer that Sally had been given $20 by Rosner to go to see Spitale). Rosner told Thayer that those men were going to Chicago, Ill. that night.

Rosner, Breckinridge and Thayer then went to Hopewell, N. J. where they spoke to Colonel Lindbergh and the various servants in the house. While they were downstairs in the kitchen, Rosner asked to see the note, "the one that was left in the crib." This refers to the first ransom note, which, according to the accepted version, was left by the kidnapers on the window sill of the nursery. A photostatic copy of this note is included in the supplement hereto as Exhibit "A-1."

At about 6 P.M. Thursday, March 3, 1932 Rosner called at Mr. Thayer's home and indicated that he had an unpleasant experience with someone whose name he did not mention but who Thayer later learned was Owney Madden. He claimed that Madden suspected him of being in league with Federal men and stated that the Lindbergh family must make very plain that the Federal authorities would not be called in on the case. He expected to have a date later in the evening with Madden.

At about 11 P.M. Rosner and Thayer went by automobile to Broadway and 47th Street where Rosner went into a building, after instructing Thayer that if he did not come out in an hour, he should get help and come into the building because he would be in serious trouble. About an hour later he came out and seemed very agitated. After asking for Colonel Donovan who was in Albany, Rosner requested Thayer to get Colonel Breckinridge on the telephone right away because he had made the proper contact. Rosner told Thayer later that he had seen Owney Madden and had gathered from the way he talked that he knew something definite about the kidnapers. Mr. Thayer called Colonel Breckinridge and arranged to meet him at the lunchroom in Princeton, N. J.

Rosner and Thayer reached Princeton at about 4 A.M.

and there met Colonel Breckinridge. Rosner explained that he had talked to someone who he was positive had definite information; that this person had imposed two definite conditions:

1. That the Lindberghs must exonerate the kidnapers upon the safe return of the child, and

2. Rosner must be given a clear, untapped wire from the Lindbergh home so that this person could be reached without fear of Federal or local police interference.

They then went to Hopewell where they had a long conference with Colonel Lindbergh and Colonel Schwarzkopf relative to the conditions to which Colonel Schwarzkopf finally agreed. Captain Galvin drew up a form of statement to be issued by Colonel and Mrs. Lindbergh and arrangements were made for a clear wire for Rosner.

On Friday afternoon or evening, March 4, 1932 Rosner stationed himself at the telephone and every once in a while would call a number and say, "This is X. Have you any news for me?" he reply would invariably come back that someone was out and had not reported in. That evening Dudley Field Malone telephoned and stated that he had received a call from someone alleging to be the kidnapers. Col. Breckinridge went into Mr. Malone's office while Rosner and Thayer stayed on the telephone all night answering incoming calls.

On Saturday morning, March 5, 1932 when the mail came in, Col. Lindbergh and Thayer went over it hastily, searching for a possible second note. Colonel Lindbergh picked it out from the pile of mail, opened it and the state trooper in charge of the mail, read the note out loud.

This note was mailed in a post office station near Borough Hall, Brooklyn, N. Y. postmarked 9 P.M. March 4, 1932 and informed Colonel Lindbergh in substance that he would have to take the consequences because of the newspaper publicity in the case, and because he had notified the police. A photostatic copy of the note and its envelope are included in the supplement hereto as "Exhibit A-2."

Colonel Lindbergh took the note into the living room and Rosner suddenly appeared and saw Galvin reading the note. According to Mr. Thayer, Rosner "turned very white and was trembling all over." He turned to Colonel Lindbergh and asked him to get a car and some state Troopers because he said he had to go to town. This was arranged and it is understood that Rosner went directly to Dudley Field Malone's office and saw Colonel Breckinridge.

Rosner is said to have taken the second note with him on this trip to New York. The available information does not indicate whether he had an opportunity to reproduce it, although it appears that he was accompanied by one or more members of the New Jersey State Police. The reason why he took it at all is not indicated unless it was to show it to Colonel Breckinridge. The possibilities in this respect will be further developed by this office.

At about midnight, Colonel Breckinridge returned to the Lindbergh home with Rosner, also bringing Salvatore Spitale, Irving Bitz and Mr. Berto, the last named being a member of the firm of J. P. Morgan and Company. A long conference was held and a statement was issued by Colonel and Mrs. Lindbergh authorizing Spitale and Bitz to act. This statement was published in the papers on Sunday, March 6, 1932 reading as follows:

"If the kidnapers of our child are unwilling to deal directly, we fully authorize "Salvy" Spitale and Irving Bitz to act as our go-betweens. We will also follow any other method suggested by the kidnapers that we can be sure will bring the return of our child."

While Spitale and Bitz were at the Lindbergh home that night, Owney Madden called Rosner on the telephone.

Rosner told him that Spitale and Bitz were there. Spitale went to the phone and said a few words to Madden. After Spitale and Bitz left Rosner, Breckinridge, Colonel Lindbergh and Thayer had a conference in which Rosner stated that Spitale and Bitz were at the head of a large gang of Italians and Jews who could be put to work at once to comb the underworld for evidence of those involved in the kidnaping.

Rosner and Thayer answered the telephone all that night and on the following morning, March 6, 1932 a telegram was received, reading as follows:

"Communicate with me at once regarding your boy's whereabouts for further particulars telephone Harlem 7-1147

Signed Rev. Berritella"

When Rosner was shown the telegram he put in a telephone call and spoke to the person who answered and asked him to come right down to Hopewell. About two o'clock in the afternoon a message was received from Berritella who was in Princeton. Rosner and Colonel Breckinridge left in the car to interview him. Upon meeting him they found that he was accompanied by Mary Cirrito who he stated was a medium. He party then proceeded to a room in the Princeton Inn where Berritella conducted a séance with Mary Cirrito as the medium. She stated in substance that the baby was in a house 4 1/2 miles northwest of the Lindbergh house (more than two months later the baby's body was found about four and one-half miles southeast of the Lindbergh house). The medium asked if any message had been received. Although actually the second ransom note had been received, Colonel Breckinridge replied negatively. The medium then stated that Colonel Breckinridge should not remain in Hopewell but should be at his office in New York City at 9 o'clock every morning. On the following day the third ransom note, later mentioned in more detail, was mailed enclosed in an envelope addressed to Col. Breckinridge stating, in part, ". . . . we know police interfere with your private mail. . ."

(This note was mailed from New York City).

After concluding the séance, Berritella and Mary Cirrito with Breckinridge and Rosner proceeded to the Princeton Railroad Station. During the conversation there, Berritella stated twice "They bought us roundtrip tickets to Princeton Junction."

The possible significance of the Berritella and Cirrito incident is obvious and is treated in more detail in the section entitled "Subjects and Suspects." It is mentioned here because it was Rosner who telephoned Berritella and arranged for an appointment after Berritella's telegram was received at Lindbergh's home, and there is, of course, a possibility that Rosner may have had more to do with this contact than appears on the surface.

On the evening of March 6, 1932 Owney Madden called Rosner and Thayer listened in on the other wire. Madden was very angry that Rosner had called Spitale and Bitz to help and said that he could not see that they could do any good. Rosner pacified him slightly and he talked about the case. Madden said he thought the Lindberghs would hear from the kidnapers again on Tuesday although his conversation did not indicate to Thayer that he had the slightest clue as to who the kidnapers were. Madden requested Rosner to call him every hour. At the conclusion of this conversation, Mr. Thayer stated to Colonel Lindbergh and Colonel Breckinridge, John Fogarty and Captain Galvin that had said he thought they would hear from the kidnapers the following Tuesday. According to Mr. Thayer, Rosner became very angry at this and said that Madden had said no such thing and that he should not interpret Madden's language because he could not understand it. Later Rosner took Thayer aside and told him that he must be very careful because he had received word that the kidnapers had someone in collaboration with those in the Lindbergh house and that when Colonel Breckinridge had gone to Princeton they had searched Captain Fogarty's and Galvin's room and discovered evidence which proved that Galvin and Fogarty were in league with the kidnapers.

Captain Galvin has already been introduced in this section. John Fogarty had for some time been employed as a confidential investigator on various matters by Colonel Breckinridge's law firm and was well known to Colonel Breckinridge. Mr. Fogarty died in the summer of 1932. On Monday, March 7th Rosner and Thayer answered the telephone all day with constant calls from freaks and others.

On Tuesday morning, March 8, 1932 the third ransom note (see Exhibit "A-3" in Supplement was received in an envelope postmarked New York, N. Y. Station D, (134-4th Avenue), 1:00 P.M. March 7, 1932 addressed to Col. Breckinridge, 25 Broadway, New York, N. Y.

This note in substance advised that the kidnapers would not accept any "go-between" appointed by the Lindberghs but would, themselves, arrange for one later. As previously related it also contained the possible significant remark ". . . we know police interfere with your privat mail . . . ." The note also contained instructions for Lindbergh to confirm it's receipt in the New York American.

Mr. James M. Phelan, an office associate of Colonel Breckinridge immediately telephoned Colonel Breckinridge at Hopewell and delivered the note to him at Princeton Junction, N. J. Colonel Breckinridge was accompanied by Rosner, who observed the note and examined the contents. Colonel Breckinridge and Rosner then returned to Hopewell with the ransom note."

Thayer had been following Rosner very closely and suddenly Rosner came to him and told him that he ought to go into a room in the house and dictate a detailed report of what had happened to date. Thayer felt that Rosner's object was to get him out of the way so he could not follow him, and later explained to Colonel Breckinridge and Colonel Lindbergh what he believed Rosner was doing; however, it was agreed that Rosner should stay on.

On the night of March 8th Owney Madden came to the Lindbergh house and had a long conference with Colonel Lindbergh, Colonel Breckinridge and John Fogarty. At the end of the conference several of them expressed to Mr. Thayer that they thought that Madden did know something but that it was all very vague.

On Tuesday, March 8th, 1932, Colonel Breckinridge and Rosner went to New York City and Rosner upon authority of Colonel Breckinridge and Colonel Lindbergh had an advertisement published in the New York American, reading as follows:

"Letter received at new address. Will follow your instructions. I also received letter mailed to me March 4th and was ready since then. Please hurry on account of mother. Address me to the address you mentioned in your letter. Father."

The New York Daily Mirror on March 9, 1932 published a story that "Al Capone was the direct source of the order carried to New York racket powers that Salvatore Spitale and Irving Bitz seek appointment as agents between the underworld and Colonel Charles A. Lindbergh. Al Capone is said to have underwritten all expenses incurred by Spitale and Bitz including payment to the original kidnapers of the Lindbergh baby of any ransom money they expected to recovery."

On March 10, 1932 the New York Daily News revealed that Madden was brought into the case by Morris Rosner, and characterized the letter as "the mysterious investigator with far reaching underworld connection who was stationed in the Lindbergh home."

At about 9:30 P.M. March 10, Dr. John F. Condon telephoned the Lindbergh home and spoke with Mr. Thayer. Dr. Condon informed Mr. Thayer of the letter addressed to him which had apparently come from the kidnapers and bore the same symbol signature. Further details relative to receipt of this letter and Dr. Condon's connection therewith are set out in the section pertaining to him. Rosner returned to the Lindbergh home later that night but was not informed of the call from Dr. Condon or the existence of the latest ransom note. Dr. Condon later arrived at the Lindbergh home and remained over night. On the following day, Friday, March 11, 1932, Condon, under the name of "Dr. Stice" was introduced to Rosner. Rosner later informed Mr. Thayer that due to the seriousness of this case it had been necessary for him to work more or less alone, not confiding in anyone; that shortly after Rosner came into the case, he, Rosner, got in communication with the kidnapers by means of newspapers and the kidnapers replied to him by means of notes 2, 3, and 4. However, for reasons unknown to him, Colonel Breckinridge and Colonel Lindbergh refused to take him into their confidence upon receipt of note 4. That upon the receipt of the 3rd ransom note which called for an advertisement in the New York American, Colonel Breckinridge directed Rosner to insert the advertisement in his own way; that upon receipt of the 4th ransom note, since they had not taken Rosner into their confidence, they attempted to publish the advertisement called for by themselves; that Colonel Breckinridge sent his secretary, Miss Latimer, to the New York American and the New York American refused to publish it unless the identity of the person inserting it was revealed; that as a result Colonel Breckinridge had to call Victor

Watson and acknowledge it as his, and when Miss Latimer went back with it, she was forced to sign it. That upon Colonel Breckinridge's acknowledgment it became news and the fact of the insertion by Colonel Breckinridge was published in the news columns of the American and other papers; that the kidnapers becoming aware of this were furious, almost indefinitely postponing everything and threatened to kill the child. That he, Rosner, by working very hard, was able to explain everything and believed that negotiations would continue and that the child would be delivered within the next twenty-four hours or so.

Rosner further explained to Thayer that the 4th ransom note had come through a "Dr. Stacey" connected with Fordham University, and he asked Thayer to obtain the doctor's true name and his address. He stated that he had confronted Colonel Breckinridge and Colonel Lindbergh with the fact that serious consequences had almost resulted from their failure to show him the 4th letter and he said that when they found he knew about it they were astonished; that he must be the one who was in communication with the kidnapers; that he nevertheless believed that they were attempting to get back the child without his knowledge.

On the morning of March 12th, Rosner, Spitale and Bitz conferred with Colonel Breckinridge and Colonel Lindbergh for several hours. After this conference at which Mr. Thayer was not present, Spitale, Bitz and Rosner inquired of Thayer as to what favor he could procure from the government for Al Capone if he should bring about the return of the child. They did not say that Capone had the child or know of its whereabouts, but stated that his power was so great; he would shortly find it, if he once started to put his forces into action; that he would also upon finding the child furnish the necessary ransom money; in return, however, he would demand a favor with reference to the 11 year sentence which had then been imposed upon him. Thayer stated that the only possible favors in this connection could be (1) a pardon; (2) a commutation of sentence or parole. The pardon, they suggested, could be in the form of granting his appeal which Thayer pointed out would not be possible because it would simply result in a new trial. Thayer informed them that he was not at all sure of his success in this line but before trying he would have to consult Colonel Breckinridge and Colonel Lindbergh. Rosner replied that Colonel Breckinridge and Colonel Lindbergh had already been consulted and had refused to permit anything to be done in this respect; but that they, Thayer and Rosner, must work independently as to this. Spitale and Bitz thereupon stated that Thayer would have to try. Thayer agreed to make an attempt but said he could not commit himself. Rosner explained that he was getting Spitale and Bitz to approach Al Capone in this connection, as his ace in the hole, if the kidnapers refused to continue negotiations as a result of the mistake caused by Colonel Breckinridge's refusal to take Rosner into his confidence in regard to the 4th ransom letter.

On March 12, 1932 the New York Daily News published an announcement made by Colonel H. Norman Schwarzkopf, superintendent of the New jersey State Police, in a general statement made in response to a question concerning Salvatore Spitale, Al Capone and other underworld leaders as follows:

"The Police have not issued any request for the assistance of any of the characters mentioned. In the honest desire, however, to accomplish the return of the baby the police will welcome information of any kind leading to its recovery regardless of the source."

"The identity of all people disclosing information leading to the recovery of the baby, whether the information be valuable or not, will be treated with confidence. . . ."

"This confidence is guaranteed in this circular and we will adhere strictly to it."

In the same issue of the Daily News was published a report that Spitale and Bitz were about to start for Detroit as a "hot tip"; that their attorney, Abraham Kesselman scoffed at the idea of the trip. However, that Isiah Leebove, another New York lawyer, who said he "represented Spitale and Bitz declared at Clarke, Michigan, that he expected the two emissaries would join him soon."

On March 12th Colonel Breckinridge went to town with Dr. Condon, and Rosner went to town by himself. Mr. Thayer stayed on the telephone at the Lindbergh home all day.

During the day, Joseph Fishman, Deputy Commissioner of Corrections, telephoned. Rosner called later and Thayer told him about Mr. Fishman's call. Later that afternoon Fishman appeared at Hopewell with Rosner and Owney Madden and a man who claimed to have some information but who proved to be a "fake." Rosner and the others went back to town that day.

At about 6 P.M. on Saturday afternoon, a representative of the United Press telephoned the Lindbergh home and informed Mr. Thayer that the Associated Press was printing the fact that Morris Rosner had made a statement that he had definite knowledge that the baby was safe and well, and would be returned to his parents in a few days. Mr. Thayer stated that in view of the agreement existing between Colonel Lindbergh, Colonel Breckinridge, and the press, that no statements of any kind or information would be given out except through the office of Governor Moore of New Jersey at Trenton, this report placed Colonel Lindbergh in an extremely embarrassing position. The Press insisted that the A. P. reporter who obtained the interview with Rosner was to be relied upon, and that by reason of the statement the agreement had been violated.

Colonel Lindbergh replied that no statement by anyone, except through Trenton, had been permitted or authorized by him, and that no statement except through those channels was authentic.

However, Rosner's statement was given wide publicity in the press.

Rosner's explanation of his alleged statement was that the Associated Press reporter gained admission to his apartment under subterfuge and at the conclusion of a conversation, asked Rosner, "Do you think the baby is still alive?" and that he, Rosner, was shocked at the question and said, "Of course; we have always hoped that the baby was alive and well."

Later, Colonel Schwarzkopf examined the reporter of the Associated Press who had interviewed Rosner, and this reporter stated positively that he had taken down word for word the remarks that Rosner had made. Early on Sunday morning, March 13th, Rosner in a long discussion with Thayer admitted that Owney Madden, Spitale and Bitz had failed to date to locate who had the child but said they might yet succeed.

Later, on the same day, Thayer and Colonel Lindbergh reviewed the entire situation relative to Rosner, Spitale and Bitz. Rosner was then called into the conference and repeated in substance what he had told Thayer but denied that he had admitted that Spitale, Bitz and Madden had failed to locate who had the child, stating that he had simply said they had never told him so, but that they might have contact and yet deny it. It was concluded that although the gangs had not been successful in locating the child, Rosner had, by dropping a word here and there, left the impression that they were in contact in order to leave the way open to claim the credit even if the child were returned through channels other than the underworld. It was brought out that Rosner had told Colonel Breckinridge from the start that if an organized gang had the child, the underworld would produce it and no ransom would be paid but if the child was not held by the underworld, this could be found out and at least many possibilities would be eliminated.

ON March 14th the New York Mirror published a story that the Lindbergh baby was held by the Purple Gang, and that negotiations were being continued by Spitale and Bitz. On March 15th the Mirror reported that the underworld conference was called by Spitale and Bitz to which emissaries of the Purple Gang of Detroit had been summoned. On March 17th the Mirror published a story that Morris Rosner "man of super mystery in the shadowy group which includes Spitale and Bitz was definitely informed at Hopewell, N. J. by a spokesman for Lindbergh that he could consider his official relations with the search for the Lindbergh baby at an end."

Subsequently, according to Mr. Thayer, Rosner spent his entire time in town. Mr. Thayer communicated very rarely with him and saw very little of him except on one occasion which was about March 20, 1932. On or about that date Thayer accompanied Rosner at the latter's request to Newark, N. J. and contacted a woman who gave her name as "Elsie." This woman had previously informed Dudley Field Malone, Police Commissioner Mulrooney and the New Jersey State Police that she had been engaged, under suspicious circumstances as governess for a child which turned out to be the "Lindbergh baby." Allegedly, the child was kept in an old house with boarded up windows on Long Island near Corona, but "Elsie" refused to give the exact location of the house or lend any one to it. She accompanied Rosner and Thayer to the latter's home at 124 East 64th Street, New York City, where she was interviewed by Rosner alone. Later Rosner informed Thayer that Elsie admitted her previous stories were untrue in certain parts, and that she herself was in on the kidnaping. That he, Rosner, then offered her $20,000 to return the child but she said all she wanted was a ticket in her pocket that would take her three thousand miles away and then she would show where the house was. Rosner informed Thayer that he was certain she was a fake. However, on the following morning, Colonel Breckinridge told Thayer that Rosner had informed him in this connection that Elsie had asked for $20,000 and said for this sum she would return the baby, but that "Rosner had refused on the ground that the Lindberghs would not double cross the others." That Elsie replied that she was satisfied, and had only suggested it to test the Lindberghs as to whether they would double cross.

On March 23, 1932 the newspapers announced that Owney Madden was reported to have made several visits to the Lindbergh estate. On this same day, the New York Times published a story that H. Wallace Caldwell, former President of the Chicago board of Education, reputed to be interested in the possibility of enlisting Al Capone's aid in the search, attempted to contact Spitale and Bitz. Also, that Morris Rosner had not been seen in Hopewell the last few days.

According to the New York Daily News of April 17, 1932, Spitale made the statement that he believed the real kidnapers received the $50,000 ransom payment and were only waiting for the publicity to die down before returning the child.

On March 13, 1932 after the baby's body was found, Rosner announced publicly, in the New York Journal, that he still believed the kidnaping was the work of a professional gang.

On May 24, 1932 according to the New York Daily News, Morris Rosner testified before the Bronx County Grand Jury which investigated the payment of the $50,000 ransom. The files of this office contain no information as to Rosner's testimony at that time.

The New York newspapers of January 23 and January 24, 1934, published items indicating that Morris Rosner's wife, Mrs. Ethel Rosner, is suing him for divorce before Supreme Court Justice Louis A. Valente and that she alleged through her attorney, Irving Lifschitz, that Rosner received a ten thousand dollar retainer and twenty five hundred dollars expenses from Colonel Lindbergh in the kidnaping case and that he owned $75,000 in Long Beach real estate and has plenty of money in safety deposit vaults. Rosner's attorney, Jacob Sobell, admitted the $2500 payment but denied the other allegations. During this proceeding Rosner testified that he was ill and penniless.

In December, 1933 Irving Bitz forfeited $2500 bail posted in New York City by failing to appear for trial on a Sullivan Law charge (possession firearms). Bitz finally surrendered and was again indicted for jumping his bail and on the new charge was release from the Tombs January 8, 1934 in $30,000.00 bail.

With reference to the surrender of $2,980 in gold certificates (which were part of the $50,000 ransom payment at the Federal Reserve Bank in New York City, on 5/1/33 by a person who signed the name "J. J. Faulkner, 537 West 149th Street" it is noted that one Rose Rosner, formerly resided at 546 West 149th Street, and moved from that address to 530 West 144th Street on 5/17/30. No information is available in the files of this office as to whether this Rose Rosner is related to Morris Rosner.

Specimens of the handwriting of Morris Rosner were obtained and submitted to the Division laboratory for comparison with the Lindbergh ransom letters. On December 26, 1933 the laboratory reported as follows:

"There are similarities between the writing of Rosner

and the extortion letters, but there are more distinctive differences such as in the small "c". For instance, Rosner writes a hand which is far superior to the extortion letters and it is not believed that if he disguised his handwriting it would appear like those letters."

DR. JOHN F. CONDON ("Jafsie")

It was a relatively obscure story in the Home News, Bronx and Manhattan, N. Y. on March 8, 1932 that brought the name Dr. John F. Condon ("Jafsie") into the case. In the article which appeared in the edition of that paper on the above date, Dr. Condon offered himself as a "go-between" in possible negotiations for the return of the Lindbergh child. He made the offer through the columns of the Bronx Home News, as it is generally referred to, and even pledged himself to add one thousand dollars which he had saved from his salary to the suggested ransom of $50,000 which had been demanded of Colonel Lindbergh in the note left in the child's nursery by the departing kidnapers. His motive in utilizing the home News as the medium for his offer was stated by him to have been the friendship which he has entertained over a period of many years for those concerned with its publication.

The Home News, a publication having a daily circulation of approximately 150,000 copies through the Bronx and Manhattan, N.Y., on March 8, 1932 printed the following story that established contact in this case under the caption:

"DR. JOHN F. CONDON OFFERS TO ADD ONE THOUSAND DOLLARS OF HIS SAVINGS RANSOM LINDBERGH CHILD."

"An offer to act as 'go-between' in negotiations for the return of 20-months old Charles Augustus Lindbergh, Jr.

with the promise of absolute secrecy as to the identity of the kidnapers and an additional $1,000 to any ransom which may be arranged by Colonel Charles A. Lindbergh, was made today by Dr. John F. Condon, 2974 Decatur Ave., near 201st St., educator, author and lecturer.

The added ransom represents the major portion of Dr. Condon's savings, yet he asserted that he is willing to part with it in order to restore the child to his anguished parents.

In his appeal to the abductors, Dr. Condon said, 'I offer all that I can scrape together so that a loving mother may again have her child and that Colonel Lindbergh may know that the American people are grateful for the honor that he bestowed upon them by his pluck and daring.

Let the kidnapers know that no testimony of mine or information coming from me will be used against them.

I offer $1,000 which I have saved from my salary as additional to the suggested ransom of $50,000 which is said to have been demanded of Colonel Lindbergh.

I stand ready at my own expense to go anywhere, alone, to give the kidnaper the extra money and promise never to utter his name to any person.

If this is not agreeable then I ask the kidnapers to go to any Catholic priest and return the child unharmed, with the knowledge that any priest must hold inviolate any statement which may be made by the kidnapers.'

Dr. Condon is one of the best known educators of the Bronx. He retired in 1930 after serving for 46 years as a school teacher and principal and since than has devoted much of his time to giving lectures at Fordham University. In offering to act as 'go-between' for the return of the Lindbergh baby, Dr. Condon said that he was doing so on his own initiative and would be responsible to no person for information which he might obtain from the abductors."

Condon's associates in this enterprise were few in number. They included no member of any police force, nor any of the professional investigators. They were Colonel and Mrs. Lindbergh, Colonel Henry Breckinridge, and Al Reich, a former Metropolitan New York star heavyweight prize fighter and confidante of Dr. Condon, and to a lesser extent Milton Gaglio and Max Rosenhain, as will be shown.

Dr. John F. Condon presently resides with his wife, Myra, in a modest dwelling located at 2974 Decatur Avenue, Bronx, N.Y. He has resided in the Bronx all his life and at that particular address for the past fourteen years. In his immediate family there are three children, namely, a daughter Myra, and two sons Lawrence and John, all of whom are married and reside in their own respective homes. The daughter, Myra, a former school teacher, within the past several years married a young architect named Ralph Hacker, of alleged German extraction, who came to New York from northern Montana, Backer and his wife, Myra, presently reside in what is reputed to be their own home at West Englewood, N. J., while Hacker's place of business is situated at Fort Lee, N. J. a few miles north. Lawrence and John Condon, both of whom are lawyers, practice their respective professions at and reside within the confines of New York City. Dr. Condon has a brother, Joseph F. Condon, a practicing lawyer in the Bronx, N.Y., and it is understood that he has a sister who is reputedly Mother Superior of a Catholic educational institution known as New Rochelle College at New Rochelle, N. Y. Practically all members of the Condon family have devoted their lives to the field of education, and it is stated that Mrs. John F. Condon during her younger days was a teacher in the New York City Public Schools.

The Condon family has always enjoyed in the Bronx, the reputation of being respectable, home loving and substantial citizens. None of their number as far as known has been involved in a matter of a criminal nature. While rumors which have reached the New York City Police Department have had it that Dr. Condon himself during his past life has been involved in shady real estate transactions in the Bronx and City Island, N.Y. and that on August 14, 1888 he misappropriated a purse containing $300 belonging to a passenger on board a boat sailing between New York and Vancouver, B.C., nothing tangible has been developed to date upon which to predicate the statement that Dr. Condon has or has had criminal tendencies.

Inquiry concerning Al Reich, who has been popularly characterized in this case as "Condon's bodyguard", has failed to find him involved in any criminal enterprise. Lizzie Hartigan, the Hungarian maid stated by Mrs. John F. Condon to have been employed at the Condon house on Decatur Avenue for the past nine years off and on, is not known at this writing to be other than an honest individual. She is a person in whom Mrs. Condon has always reposed implicit faith.

While Dr. John F. Condon is by no means a wealthy man, he frequently discusses his many real estate holdings in the Bronx, City Island and Dobbs Ferry, N. Y., and speaks of such holdings as "frozen assets." At various intervals during the summer months with his wife and friends he occupies one of his small houses and adjacent to the water at City Island and there makes use of his small boat, the description of which is presently unknown. With further regard to his real estate ventures, it is believed that at one time Condon engaged in real estate transactions in the State of New Jersey, although at this writing nothing is known by this office of the details concerning them. It is also his statement that in the past several years he has engaged with Al Reich in a joint real estate venture at City Island, N. Y., the result of which netted both a small profit.

The fact that Dr. John F. Condon was selected by the alleged kidnapers to act as their intermediary, furnished the basis of directing some degree of suspicion toward him. Subsequent to the discovery of the Lindbergh baby's body near Hopewell, N.J., May 12, 1932, Condon visited the New Jersey State Police Barracks at Alpine, N. J. and there explained his activities in a statement made by him to Inspector Harry Walsh of the Jersey City Police Department, and Lieutenant Arthur Keaton of the New Jersey State Police. This statement is on file with the New Jersey State Police at Trenton, N. J. Al Reich was likewise interviewed by Lieutenant Arthur Keaton and various members of the New Jersey State Police, and his statement is on file with the New Jersey State Police at Trenton, N. J.

Dr. Condon for an approximate period of twenty-five years occupied the position of principal of various New York City Public Schools in the Bronx. Lieutenant Arthur Keaton, New Jersey State Police, and Special Agent Frank J. Wilson, Intelligence Unit, Bureau of Internal Revenue, United States Treasury Department, during the course of their investigation of this case called upon the Superintendent of Schools at New York City and obtained his permission to secure a list of the names of boys who had attended the schools of which Dr. Condon was principal. Pursuant thereto a card index of fifty thousand pupils who had attended these schools, was turned over to Special Agent Wilson and Lieutenant Keaton. It was the thought then as well as a suspicion that one of the kidnapers in this case may have known Dr. Condon personally and possibly may have attended his school, in view of which it was considered advisable to check the list of former students of these schools in search of criminal records relating to any of their number. Consequently this list was furnished to, and checked by the Identification Unit of this Division, the Identification Bureau of New York City Police

Department, and Identification Bureau of the New Jersey State Police, and it was found that some of the boys did have criminal records. The Division has been requested to furnish the New York Office with their names, photographs and criminal records. Where available, the pictures of the students were submitted to Dr. Condon by the New Jersey State Police, for possible identification. Condon failed to identify any of those pictures as the man who called himself "John", and to whom he paid the ransom money.

It is stated that since the inception of this case, Dr. Condon has tentatively identified the photographs of at least six men as a likeness of the man to whom he paid the ransom money. However, investigation by the New Jersey State Police and New York City Police Department developed that none of these six men had anything whatsoever to do with the crime. Information as to the names of these men is not presently available but will be obtained.

Subsequent to his retirement from the New York Public School System in 1930, Dr. Condon became identified with Fordham University at New York, as a lecturer on the institution's courses of "Inter-relation of principles and methods in Elementary Education" and "Drafting and Manual Work applied to elementary subjects". His work with the university continued from about the middle of 1930 until the latter part of March or the beginning of April 1932, when the name of "Jafsie" of the newspaper advertisements was revealed as Dr. John F. Condon. Within a short time after that discovery, Dr. Condon severed his connection with the university. He gave as his reason therefor that his connection with this case, since it was interpreted by many in the light of unfavorable publicity for the university, furnished the basis upon which the authorities of Fordham predicated their request that Condon resign.

Dr. Condon's work with Fordham University was somewhat restricted in that it consisted of only two lectures a week on subjects, which as previously mentioned, were identified with elementary education. While Dr. Condon even today seems to retain the urge for recognized prominence, it is interesting to note that the Registrar of the Fordham University Graduate School with which Condon was connected on March 21, 1932, expressed his opinion to an Agent of this Division to the effect that "Professor Condon might possibly be inclined to seek publicity if given an opportunity and that he possessed a like inclination to identify himself with civic movements, concerning himself with the social and athletic activities of young men and boys." He is known to have been an ardent devotee of their participation of the game of baseball and attempted to organize a baseball team among some of the younger students at that branch of the university maintained at the Woolworth Building in lower Manhattan. This branch of the university takes no direct part in the athletics of the school itself, and same being confined to undergraduate students at the main buildings of Fordham University at East Fordham Road and Third Avenue, in the Bronx, New York City.

It was also the knowledge of the Registrar of Fordham University Graduate School that prior to March 8, 1932 Professor Condon's name had been identified with the "Bronx Home News" either directly or as a contributor of special articles to this paper. In a telephone conversation held by the Registrar above mentioned with Professor Condon, about March 14, 1932, the latter stated in substance: "You will be interested in knowing perhaps that I have taken a personal interest in this Lindbergh case and that I am personally offering a reward of one thousand dollars for the safe return of the Lindbergh baby." The Registrar at the time was inclined to doubt the effectiveness of any effort which Professor Condon might put forth in this regard, due principally to his advanced age and the further fact that his particular training had not exactly fitted him for participation in efforts among individuals who would more properly come under the notice of the Police Department.

Dr. Condon was reported to have formerly served as the coach or assistant coach of the prisoners' baseball teams at Sing Sing Prison. Information as to the period and duration of this activity is not presently available but will be obtained. Aside from this, there is nothing in his known history which would indicate the possibility that professional criminals would select him as their intermediary.

His standing and popularity are principally local and confined to his bailiwick, Bronx County, where he is known as an altruistic and honorable educator, having a great interest in children, and as a devotee of sports, amateur as well as professional. On the other hand he also has the reputation for being somewhat of an eccentric, some persons even going so far as to state that he is a "nut".

Dr. Condon has stated repeatedly that on each night of the school year he made it a practice to remain at his home devoting certain time to his studies in preparation for the classes that would come on the day following. After finishing this work on each of these nights, Condon states that he was in the habit of taking a walk, stopping on the way at restaurants in the neighborhood and there partaking of a small repast a cup of coffee or the like. Condon explains that the restaurant most frequented by him on these occasions was that operated by Max Rosenhain located at 3469 Grand Concourse near Fordham Road, in the Bronx, New York City, but that he also sometimes would drop in Bickford's Restaurant located at East Fordham Road near Webster Avenue. As is the custom in any neighborhood, explains Condon, there is a certain group of individuals who hang out at Rosenhain's and Bickford's restaurants, which is quite similar to any group which frequently hangs out at the neighborhood poolroom and is popularly characterized as the "Poolroom Crowd". It was in such an atmosphere, states Condon, on the night of March 7, 1932 that he found the inducement to offer his services as an intermediary in connection with this case. While at Max Rosenhain's restaurant, about 10: or 11: o'clock on this night, Condon states that several individuals, whose names or identities he does not now recall, were discussing the Lindbergh kidnaping case in general terms, arriving apparently at the conclusion that this country was a terrible place in which to live and that the Lindbergh kidnaping case would probably never have happened in any country other than the United States. Condon states that after listening to these individuals criticize the country he gave them a lecture on patriotism and proceeded to his home sometime near midnight of March 7th and there sat down by himself writing an open letter to the Bronx Home News, in which he offered himself as a "go-between" in this case and further offering a reward of $1,000 in addition to the $50,000 which was suggested as the ransom demanded by the kidnapers of the Lindbergh baby, as previously mentioned.

Since the time of the above explained incident, Dr. Condon pursued an active interest in connection with the negotiations that were to follow. His explanations, of which there are many, are now a matter of record. On May 14, 1932, he appeared at the Bronx County District Attorney's office and there made a statement concerning his connection with this case in the presence of Assistant District Attorney Edward F. Breslin, Inspector Henry Bickman, Acting Lieutenant James A. Dinan and Detective Charles G. Winterhalter, New York City Police Department, and Thomas J. Riordan, court stenographer. On May 20, 1932,

Condon appeared before the Bronx County Grand Jury and on that date gave further testimony concerning his connection with and participation in this case.

Since that date he has been consulted on numerous occasions by the New Jersey State Police, particularly, the New York City Police Department as well as this Division. At the Bronx County District Attorney's office Condon explains his entry into this case in substance as follows:

While in Max Rosenhain's restaurant on the night of March 7, 1932, he heard many people, most of whom had decided foreign accents, state that such an outrage as the Lindbergh kidnaping case would not occur in any other country in the world. His American spirit was then aroused. He was urged forward by the distress of the Lindbergh family, Colonel Lindbergh being one of the greatest patriots of all times. His patriotic spirit as an American urged him on and greater than that was his hope that he might have the joy of seeing the baby back in its mother's arms and the baby's arms around its mother's neck and have her enjoy those moments of maternal bliss. Condon began to plan as to how he should proceed to do something himself as it might be a rebuke to those who were talking about our country and the individuals who would not do anything to help the Lone Eagle. Condon then conceived the idea of writing an article to the Bronx Home News offering $1,000 to the one who would be instrumental in carrying out that idea of restoring the baby to its mother's arms. He took $1,000 because it was all he had available at the time. All this, of course, on Condon's part was done without first consulting the Lindbergh family.

It will be noted that Dr. Condon in his above remarks, stated that it was in Max Rosenhain's restaurant on the night of March 7, 1932 when he heard a number of individuals remark that such an outrage could not occur in any country other than the United States. Since the time of that statement, Condon has frequently stated that he was "in Bickford's restaurant on East Fordham Road and Decatur Avenue in the Bronx" when he heard such individuals make the remarks which he attributes to them.

Although Condon's statements concerning the place in which he was allegedly present on the night of March 7, 1932 when he heard the country being "run down" are, to a slight extent in contradiction, it is believed that he was in Max Rosenhain's restaurant rather than Bickford's restaurant, for the reason that he was known to have patronized Rosenhain's quite regularly in the course of his nightly strolls.

Dr. Condon is an extremely difficult person to interview, especially when the topic of conversation relates to this case. He gives the impression, presently, at least of being somewhat of an eccentric individual and seems careful to avoid a discussion relating to what he terms the "delicate" angle of this case. A reading of his statement made in the Bronx County District Attorney's office on May 24, 1932, and of his testimony before the Bronx County Grand Jury at New York City on May 20, 1932, readily indicates that his explanations of his activities in the course of the ransom negotiations are rather incoherent. For this reason and to render it possible for the various field offices to have a clear picture of what activity Condon performed in this case subsequent to the publication in the Bronx Home News at New York City on March 8, 1932 of his "go-between" offer, the following narrative is set forth; this narrative is based principally upon Condon's testimony and statements at various intervals, corroborated in some instances, by physical evidences and in addition by statements of other individuals believed qualified to testify relative thereto.

Before returning to Dr. Condon's entry in the case, it is believed desirable to briefly summarize the material events prior thereto.

As related earlier in this report, the first ransom note in the case was found in the baby's nursery on the second floor of the Lindbergh estate at Hopewell, N.J., at about 10:45 o'clock on the night of March 1, 1932, shortly after it was discovered that the baby had been kidnaped. In compliance with the demand of the kidnapers in that note for a $50,000 ransom, Mr. and Mrs. Charles A. Lindbergh, on March 2, 1932, publicly announced their willingness to pay over that sum. During the course of the next few days further word was awaited from the kidnapers, but to no avail. In the meantime, however, numerous inquiries were made in New York, New Jersey and elsewhere concerning possible suspects in the case, while law enforcement officials conferred at Hopewell in addition to various other points throughout the country with special reference to the case. The newspapers generally throughout the nation continued their wide publicity unabated.

On March 5, 1932, the second ransom note in this case was delivered. It was received by Colonel Lindbergh at Hopewell, N.J. in an envelope postmarked Brooklyn, N.Y. 9: P.M. March 4, 1932, and had been mailed at the United States Post Office Station near Borough Hall in Brooklyn. The contents of this note in substance increased the amount of ransom from $50,000 to $70,000 and informed Colonel Lindbergh that he would have to take the consequences because of the newspaper publicity concerning the case and because he notified the police.

Nothing further was heard from the kidnapers and no additional communication received from them until March 8, 1932. On this date the third ransom note was delivered. It was addressed to Colonel Henry Breckinridge, 25 Broadway, New York City, and received there by attorney, James M. Phelan, an associate in this law office. As Colonel Breckinridge was at the particular time in Hopewell, N.J., attorney James W. Phelan communicated with him by phone, and by the first train from New York thereafter, Mr. Phelan proceeded to Princeton Junction, N.J. where he was met by Colonel Breckinridge and to him delivered the third ransom note. As has been shown Rosner, who accompanied Colonel Breckinridge to Princeton Junction on this occasion, observed the third ransom note and examined its contents. The third ransom note was postmarked New York City, Station "D", (132 Fourth Avenue), 1:00 P.M. March 7, 1932, and in substance, advised that the kidnapers would not accept any "go-between" appointed by the Lindberghs, and that they (the kidnapers) would arrange this latter. Lindbergh was instructed in this ransom note, to insert a short notice in the New York American concerning the receipt of this letter. Subsequent thereto, the following advertisement was inserted in the New York American of March 8, 1932, by Colonel Lindbergh, through Colonel Breckinridge:

"Letter received at new address. Will follow your instructions. I also received letter mailed to me March 4 and was ready since then. Please hurry on account of mother. Address me to the address you mentioned in your letter. Father."

This advertisement was repeated in the same paper by Colonel Lindbergh on the day following.

Within twenty-four hours subsequent to the publication of Condon's "go-between offer" in the Bronx Home News on March 8, 1932, he received a reply from the alleged kidnapers. At 12: o'clock noon on March 9, 1932 a letter postmarked New York, N.Y., Station "T" (165th Street and 3rd Avenue, Bronx, near Dr. Condon's home), March 9, 1932, and addressed to Dr. John Condon, 2974 Decatur Ave., New York City, was received by Condon, at his home. This communication was the fourth ransom note received in the Lindbergh case although it was the first letter received by Condon. It indicated that the kidnapers would accept Condon as their "go0-between" and instructed him to place an advertisement in the New York American. Enclosed in Condon's letter was also a letter in a separate envelope intended for Colonel Lindbergh advising the Colonel that Dr. Condon was authorized to act as the kidnapers' "go between". Condon was instructed in this communication to tell no one about this message and the kidnapers in substance threatened to cancel everything in the event the press or the police was notified. The letter further instructed that after Condon had received "the money" from Lindbergh he was to put the following three words in the New York American "Money is ready", and Condon was further advised that he would receive additional instructions subsequent to the publication of this advertisement and further informed that he should not be afraid since the kidnapers were not out for the $1,000 which he had offered as a reward.

In the enclosure with Condon's letter for Colonel Lindbergh in which the Colonel was advised that Condon was authorized to act as "go-between", it was stated by the kidnapers that the $70,000 ransom demanded was to be placed in a packet, the size of which was designated as 6" by 7" by 14".

Upon Condon's receipt of the above letter through the mails and after his opening and examining same during which he noted the peculiar symbol signature inscribed on the communication, he states that at first he thought that this message was more or less of a "crank" letter and for a moment or so dismissed it from his mind. Later in the evening, however, he decided to take a walk in the vicinity of his home as was his usual practice to get a cup of coffee. The thought then occurred to him that he would show this letter to one or two of his friends and thereby determine just what they thought about it. On that evening, Condon did take his walk for his usual cup of coffee and adjourned for the purpose to Max Rosenhain's restaurant on Grand Concourse near Fordham Road in the Bronx, New York City. There he met two of his friends, Milton Gaglio and Max Rosenhain, the proprietor of the restaurant, and to whom he spoke freely concerning the message which he had received. To each of these individuals, Condon exhibited the letter and they examined it carefully. Considerable discussion followed, the net result of which convince Condon that he "ought to call" Colonel Lindbergh. Thereupon, from the telephone in Rosenhain's restaurant, Condon called Colonel Lindbergh's estate at Hopewell, N.J., was connected with somebody at the Hopewell, N. J. estate, whose name Condon did not then know, but he has since learned was Robert Thayer. Mr. Thayer is a lawyer, very friendly with Colonel Lindbergh and has been for the past several years, an associate of Colonel William J. Donovan, Broad Street, New York City. During the course of Condon's conversation with Thayer which took place about midnight, March 9, 1932, Condon described the message which he had received and gave a brief outline of the symbol inscribed thereon. Mr. Thayer, after hearing the above, requested Condon to come to Hopewell immediately, bringing the above mentioned communication with him. After finishing this telephone conversation, Condon went back to his table in Rosenhain's restaurant and in the course of a moment or so Gaglio and Rosenhain came over and sat down at his table with him. Gaglio then remarked, "I have a nice car and I will be glad to drive you over." Condon replied, "I don't think I ought to go down,", but finally, however, both Gaglio and Rosenhain persuaded him to make the trip. Condon then advised Gaglio that he was willing to have him drive down to Hopewell and for his service in connection with the trip Condon would pay him; although Condon states he did not then know the location of the Lindbergh estate. About midnight, March 9, 1932 in company with Gaglio and Max Rosenhain, in Gaglio's car, Condon started off from Rosenhain's restaurant enroute to Hopewell, N.J. taking with him the message received by him through the mails on March 9th bearing the peculiar symbol signature. Early in the morning of March 10, 1932 while enroute to Hopewell, Condon, Gaglio and Rosenhaim stopped at the Baltimore Lunch in Princeton, N.J. for a cup of coffee. After leaving the lunch room Condon talked with a policeman in uniform whose name he believed to be Murray, who directed him over the road leading from Princeton to Colonel Lindbergh's estate. Before leaving Princeton, however, Condon called Hopewell from a telephone in the Baltimore Lunch talking in this instance with Colonel Henry Breckinridge, who was then at the Lindbergh estate. Condon continued his journey in company with Gaglio and Rosenhain in the direction of Hopewell when he was met a short while later by Colonel Breckinridge who had come down the road for some distance to meet Condon. Upon Condon's arrival at the Lindbergh home which was about 3: A.M., March 10, 1932, Condon immediately explained to Colonel Lindbergh and Colonel Breckinridge that Rosenhain and Gaglio, who were waiting outside, were respectively, a proprietor of a restaurant in the Bronx and a clother in the same vicinity. Upon Condon's entering the Lindbergh residence he went first to Lindbergh's room and there he discussed his experiences in this case up to that time with both Lindbergh and Breckinridge. Thereafter, Colonel Lindbergh took out one of the ransom letters which he had previously received and compared it with the missive received in the mails by Condon. These letters compared, were superimposed one upon the other, and it was observed that the holes which were part of the symbol signature concided, and for this reason in addition to many others it was the opinion of all concerned then and there that Condon's communication had been received from the persons who had previously written to both Colonel Breckinridge and Colonel Lindbergh. Condon stated that he had interpreted this signature in various ways with the assistance of one of his Italian friends, although he did not give his name.

After some discussion concerning this case among Colonel Lindbergh, Colonel Breckinridge and Dr. Condon, the latter was invited to remain in the Lindbergh home over night. It was then suggested that in view of Condon's staying over, in order to conceal his identity, Condon would have to be referred to by some other name. Pursuant to this suggestion, Condon stated that at one time he used to work for a local paper in the Bronx, in the course of which he used the name "J.F.C." which, Condon stated, if pronounced fast—, gave the sound of "Jafsie". Condon further remarked in the same connection that in many instances in the past when it became necessary for him to write and answer many letters he used the name of J. U. Stice, which if carefully observed and spelled out is "Justice". When mention is made of this, it is also stated that Condon in discussing this case with former Special Agent J.J. Manning, has also indicated that in many of his stories and special articles which he has heretofore written for the Bronx newspaper he employed the name P.A. Triot, which if spelled out is "Patriot."

The above name "Jafsie" is the pseudonym with Condon utilized in this case in his newspaper advertisement and concerning which additional comment will be made further in this report.

In the continuation of his conversation at the Lindbergh household on the early morning of March 10, 1932, states Condon, it was at Colonel Lindbergh's suggestion that Condon assumed the pseudonym of "Jafsie" in continuing negotiations with the kidnapers and in placing advertisements in the New York newspapers in an effort to establish contact. Condon remained all night at the Lindbergh home and slept in the improvised bed on the floor in the nursery room from which the Lindbergh baby had been kidnaped. On that night Lindbergh did not exhibit to Dr. Condon any of the clothing similar to that worn by the Lindbergh child prior to its being kidnaped. However, Condon in making examination of the room from which the baby had been taken, measured roughly the distance from the crib to the window and examined it very carefully observing on the outside wall a spot where the ladder had been placed against the building, after which he returned to the baby's empty crib. Condon thereafter knelt down and prayed and took an oath on the baby's crib determining to leave no stone unturned in his effort to locate the child and the kidnapers until "the Lindbergh baby was restored and its arms around its mother's neck." During Condon's further discussion of his experiences in the case with Colonel Lindbergh and Colonel Breckinridge on that night, Condon asked Colonel Lindbergh to pick out a toy that the Lindbergh baby could recognize or say something about. Condon wanted the toy which the Lindbergh baby "loved best". Lindbergh advised Condon then that the baby could say "lion" and liked that toy very much. Lindbergh also told him that the baby had a particular liking for the toy "elephant" and that the child likewise was very fond of the toy "camel." Condon, with Lindbergh's permission took these three mentioned toys and placed them in his pocket. Lindbergh, however, did not give Condon any of the child's garments to compare with what the child wore at the time of its being kidnaped. Condon spoke further with Colonel Lindbergh and asked him whether he might take the two safety pins for use in further negotiations with the alleged kidnapers. These two safety pins fixed the crib blankets around the baby after it had been placed in the crib on the evening of March 1, 1932 by its nurse, Betty Gow. Condon thereafter with Lindbergh's permission took both of these small pins with him.

At about 2: o'clock in the afternoon of March 10, 1932, Condon left the Lindbergh estate accompanied by Colonel Breckinridge, going directly to Breckinridge's law offices at 25 Broadway, New York City. Max Rosenhain and Milton Gaglio had departed Hopewell, N.J. for New York City earlier in the day. Breckinridge remained at his office for a while and Dr. Condon continued from there to his home at 2974 Decatur Ave., Bronx, Condon did not insert the advertisement requested by the alleged kidnapers in the New York papers on that date because it was then too late to include the same in the last edition of the paper.

Shortly after his arrival at his home, Condon received a telephone message from an unknown man advising him that he would receive another message on Saturday night, March 12, 1932.

On March 11, 1932, Condon placed the following advertisement in the New York American and in the Bronx Home News:

"Money is ready. Jafsie."

On March 12, 1932, this advertisement was repeated in the New York American as well as the Bronx Home News. At about 3: P.M. on this day Condon received a telephone message from an unknown man inquiring if he would be home between the hours of 6: o'clock and 10: o'clock on that night. Condon stated that he would. Although the person calling did not furnish sufficient information in his conversation to indicate his possible identity he did advise Condon that he was then calling from

Westchester Square, Bronx, New York City, where Condon is known.

At about 8:30 P.M. on the night of March 12th, the fifth ransom note in this case was delivered to Dr. Condon at his home, 2974 Decatur Avenue, by a taxicab driver whose identity was learned to be Joseph Perrone. Shortly prior thereto Perrone had received the message from an unidentified man at the corner of Knox Place and Gun Hill Road, in the Bronx. This communication informed Dr. Condon that he would find another note underneath a stone on the porch of a vacant frankfurter stand, 100 feet from the last subway station, on Jerome Avenue in the Bronx, New York City. Colonel Lindbergh at the time of the receipt of this note was personally present at Dr. Condon's home. Immediately after the receipt of the message which Perrone had delivered, Dr. Condon proceeded to the frankfurter stand on Jerome Avenue, accompanied by Al Reich in the latter car. Condon went to the stone on the porch of the frankfurter stand as directed and there found another note which instructed him to cross the street and follow the fence from the cemetery to 233rd Street.

After having examined the note and read its directions, Condon crossed the street from the frankfurter stand to the southwestern entrance of Woodlawn Cemetery and Jerome Avenue, looked around for a moment, and saw no one with the exception of a man who was walking slowly past holding a handkerchief to his face. It is inferred that he was there for the purpose of observing Condon find the note and subsequently follow its directions, and to see that no police were near. Condon stated that the man was wearing a brown fedora hat and a brown overcoat; that the man passed him walking in a southerly direction while he, Condon, walked north on Jerome Avenue on the sidewalk outside of Woodlawn Cemetery. Reich, who remained in the car, has stated that he also saw this man and that he appeared to be an Italian.

Approximately five minutes later, Condon saw a man inside of Woodlawn Cemetery, shake his handkerchief between the iron bars of the fence. Condon called "I see you. It is all right." Then Condon walked over near the cemetery fence at the spot where he believed he had seen the handkerchief. Al Reich did not leave his car during this time but remained in the vehicle while it was parked close by the vacant frankfurter stand on Jerome Avenue near the Woodlawn Cemetery. The time was then about 9:15 or 9:20 on the night of March 12, 1932. Condon continued his walk on Jerome Avenue in the direction of 233rd Street, and approached the northwestern entrance to Woodlawn Cemetery. He looked around for a while but was unable to find anyone in that vicinity. At the expiration of a few minutes he saw a man again waving a handkerchief through the large iron bars of the gate at the northwestern entrance of the Woodlawn Cemetery. This man was then on the inside of the cemetery and had apparently walked up to this point on the inside of the cemetery while Condon was walking up Jerome Avenue. The large gate of the cemetery at 233rd Street and Jerome Avenue was then fastened as it seemed to Condon. Condon went over to the gate and there began a conversation with the man on the inside of the fence who seemed to know Condon, by name or reputation. Condon had been speaking with this unidentified man for only a few minutes when a uniformed cemetery guard made his appearance on the inside of the cemetery about twenty-five feet away. The unknown man talking to Condon, turning around saw this cemetery guard approach and immediately, as Condon describes it, with the agility of an athlete, lifted himself over the eight foot Woodlawn Cemetery gate, and after reaching the outside of the fence, ran in a northerly direction across 233rd Street into Van Cortlandt Park. The cemetery guard thereupon came over to Condon and said, "What is the matter with that fellow?" To which Condon replied "He was a little frightened, I guess, with an officer near." Condon held no other conversation with the guard, and walked thereafter a short distance from East 233rd Street near Jerome Avenue with the hope of again finding the unknown man to whom he had talked at the cemetery gate.

Up to this point, states Condon, the unknown man with whom he talked at the cemetery gate, held his coat up well over his face with one hand and kept the other, his right hand, in his pocket. Condon, in the course of the next succeeding minutes, saw this man cross East 233rd Street and enter Van Cortlandt Park, and walked in that direction toward him. He called to this unknown man to come back since he was Condon's "guest" and that nobody would touch or harm him. Then, states Condon, this unknown man turned and walked slowly back in the direction of Condon and at the latter's request sat down with Condon on a park bench located a short distance from East 233rd Street across from Woodlawn Cemetery in Van Cortlandt Park. The bench upon which Condon and the unknown man were seated was situated in front of a small building that might properly be termed a tool house. While seated on this bench Condon states that he held his "guest" in conversation for a period of time variously estimated but stated by Condon to be one hour and fifteen or twenty minutes. There was much conversation between Condon and his "guest" at this time, during the course of which the unknown man asked Condon to call him "John" and informed him that he came from Boston. Among "John's" first inquiries of Condon was "Have you got the money?" To this Condon replied "No; I could not bring that up here without some evidence that you had the child." "John" is alleged then to have said that the gang would not stand for any such thing as producing the child or even letting them see the child. Condon them remarked "Well, I could not bring the money up here. I will go and get it if you will take me to the child as hostage." Condon has a vague recollection that these remarks were passed in the conversation which took place at the northwestern entrance to Woodlawn Cemetery prior to the appearance of the cemetery guard as well as on the park bench in front of the tool house in Van Cortlandt Park. Condon stated that while seated with "John" in Van Cortlandt Park he spoke with him in very friendly terms; assured him that he was unarmed and that Al Reich who was then parked in a car near the frankfurther stand on Jerome Avenue near the southwestern entrance to Woodlawn Cemetery, was a friend of Condon's, whom he had brought with him for the reason that Condon himself could not drive a car. Condon assured "John" that Reich was all right and there was no occasion to have any fear. "John" then is alleged to have told Condon that there were five people involved in this case, three men and two women, and that the extra money demanded as ransom was for an additional woman who had to be called to take care of the baby; that previously one woman had been engaged, taking care of the baby, with the assurance that she would not have to remain more than one week, further that she did however, become discontented and restless which required another woman to be engaged and that these two women each spent twelve hours of the day looking after the child. "John" further advised Condon that he was to receive only $10,000 and that each of the women would receive $10,000; that No. 1 and No. 2, who were men were to receive $20,000 apiece. "John" stated that No. 2 knew Dr. Condon and in the discussion that followed, Condon stated that he argued with "John" on the injustice of raising the ransom from $50,000 to $70,000. "John" further advised Condon that "Red" Johnson had nothing to do with the case nor did the unnamed woman mentioned in the press in connection with "Red" Johnson have anything to do with it. In the course of the conversation that followed, Condon informed "John" that he had visited the vicinity of Boston and that he had made a trip up to Newport on the Enterprise and that everybody in that vicinity, in Condon's opinion, was of Scandinavian extraction. On this meeting of Condon's with "John", the latter was clad in a regular spring overcoat, light in fabric and dark in color. "John" put his right hand in his pocket and used his left hand in holding his collar close up to and around his face. In one instance during the conversation Condon says that he commanded, "Take that collar down and be a man. You needn't be afraid of me." Complying with this, Condon explains, that "John" immediately brought down his collar from his face and coughed, in the course of which Condon caught a glimpse of him just for a moment. It was then that "John" told Condon that one of the men who was to get $20,000 was "in the government." Condon saw no revolver on "John" during this conversation although he assumed that "John" was armed and that he had a gun in the right hand pocket of his overcoat, since "John" at no time removed his right hand from this pocket other than at the brief time required for "John" to use "both hands with dexterity" in climbing over the Woodlawn Cemetery fence. In "John's" further conversation with Condon on the park bench, he advised him that the three men and two women involved in the case were then stationed on a boat in waters quite distant. That when the time came "John" would signal from a point on the shore which would advise these two women and three men of the action which they were to take from time to time. No particular names or locations of boats or waters were mentioned. Condon states that he then inquired of "John" if he ever thought of his mother. To this Condon states "John" replied "yes" and a tear came to "John's" eye which Condon saw. Condon then said, "Give me back the baby and it will be all right with the Colonel." "John's" answer to this was "Well, we have to get a lot of money because if any of us get in trouble they will have to have money to get us out." "John" went on to relate that the baby was safe, well and happy, and that it was getting more to eat than it had been previously. Condon says that "John" further advised that he was reading the newspapers very carefully and had noted the published instructions of Mrs. Charles A. Lindbergh requesting that the kidnapers of her baby to give him the proper food. "John" reiterated to Condon that the baby was "on a boat" and that the parties holding it would not be caught since "John" would transmit to them a proper signal from a point on the shore which other people would not understand. In explaining the hiding place of the baby, "John" is further alleged to have stated that if Condon would get him the money demanded as ransom he would signal from this particular point on the shore subsequent to which Colonel Lindbergh could take his plane and drop down on the spot where the baby was held, and there reclaim it. "John" explained that the baby was kept in a place six or eight hours away from the Bronx by airplane travel. "John" further remarked that the kidnapers had to act quickly since the baby was being relayed "from one boat to another". On the next succeeding days, according to Condon, he made a trip by boat to the Narrows, Hart's Island, Fort Schuyler, and from there to Morris Cove, in search of a boat on which he believed the Lindbergh baby might be held. Condon's efforts were unproductive of results in that he was unable to find any information concerning the hiding place of the Lindbergh child.

It is stated above that "John" for a moment took down his coat from his face and coughed. Immediately prior to this, when Condon commanded him to take down his coat,

"John" replied, "No, I couldn't, I got a cold." Condon then offered to get some medicine that would possibly benefit "John's" cold but this request "John" is alleged to have refused. "John" then said that something happened. One of the men had gotten in trouble and another man had to be taken in. Condon states that "John" was quite surprised that Condon did not have the money with him on that particular night. In answer to "John's" question as to why Condon did not have the money, Condon said "No, I couldn't bring it without evidence." "John" then said, "I will give you the evidence." Condon said "How?" To this Condon states that "John" replied "I will send the baby's sleeping suit." No further conversation was held concerning the sleeping suit, states Condon. In the course of the conversation which followed, "John" advised Condon that he was Scandinavian. To this Condon replied "Lindbergh is Scandinavian too" and for that reason "John" should not have anything against him. "John's" answer to this statement was that he had been brought in on this case for the reason that they had something on him. Condon claims that "John" told him that he did not want to come in on the case and he "wished he was out." In "John's" further remarks Condon claims that he stated that they did not think the case would last a week and since it had been delayed and continued the Colonel would now have to pay $70,000. Condon replied to "John" that they had made a bargain with Lindbergh for $50,000 and ought to abide by it. It was here that "John" remarked "There is a very high man involved in this case," and that "it was planned for a year before it was actually performed." The "highman" mentioned by "John," was said to be smart, and in fact, "one of the smartest men." John departed from the park bench into the roads in a northerly direction disappearing in the darkness in Van Cortlandt Park.

After the above conversation with "John," Condon returned to the parked car of Al Reich's on Jerome Avenue near the frankfurter stand and Al was there waiting for him. Al Reich was then of the opinion that the medium sized Italian man who passed Condon while he was walking on Jerome Avenue in the direction of East 233rd Street prior to his meeting "John" was one of the confederates of the kidnapers and was employed for the purpose of observing Condon remove the note from under the stone on the porch of the frankfurter stand and that when Condon did so, this medium sized Italian gave to "John" the signal verifying Dr. Condon's identity. In company with Al Reich, Condon thereupon drove to his home on Decatur Avenue in the Bronx where Colonel Breckinridge was waiting for him. It was about 11:45 o'clock on the night of March 12th when he returned home. Condon then stated that he could identify "John" positively if he saw him again and related to Colonel Breckinridge in detail the events which had transpired on Condon's visit with "John" shortly prior thereto.

On March 13, 1932, Dr. Condon published an advertisement in the Bronx Home News, reading as follows:

"Baby alive and well. Money is ready. Call and see us. Jafsie"

During this time it is stated, Dr. Condon was in almost constant touch with Colonel Breckinridge, Lindbergh's adviser, who had spent most of the time between March 10, and April 2, 1932 at Dr. Condon's home in the Bronx. On March 14, 1932, Dr. Condon repeated his advertisement of March 11th in the New York American, and published the following advertisement in the Bronx Home News:

"Money is ready. No cops. No Secret Service. No press. I go alone like last time. Please call. Jafsie."

On March 15, 1932, Dr. Condon repeated his advertisement of March 14th in the Bronx Home News and his advertisement of March 11th in the New York American. On March 16, 1932, Condon repeated his advertisement of March 11th in the New York American and published the following advertisement in the Bronx Home News:

"I accept. Money is ready. You know they won't let me deliver without package. Please make some sort of C.O.D. transaction, you know that you can trust Jafsie."

About this time, exact date unknown, an incident occurred at the home of Dr. Condon which might have some bearing on this case. Colonel Henry Breckinridge and Dr. Condon were at the latter's home awaiting further word from the kidnapers, when a young Italian about 25 years of age, height 5'7", dark complexion, came to the house and stated he was selling needles. Both Dr. Condon and Colonel Breckinridge went to the door and Dr. Condon purchased some of the needles. The Italian then departed, and as far as Colonel Breckinridge could see, he walked off the block entirely without making any effort to sell needles at neighboring houses.

About an hour after the above incident, another Italian individual, of a similar description to the first, called at Dr. Condon's house with a scissors grinding apparatus. According to Colonel Breckinridge, this person looked the part of a scissors grinder and Colonel Breckinridge gave him a knife to sharpen, also Dr. Condon gave him a few implements to sharpen, and upon completion of the job, the Doctor handed him a quarter. Colonel Breckinridge advised that the scissors grinder was wearing gloves and fumbled in his vest pocket to make change. Thereafter the scissors grinder took his departure and, as in the case of the first

Italian, walked off the block without making an effort to solicit business elsewhere in the neighborhood.

Colonel Breckinridge expressed an opinion that either the needle vendor or the scissors grinder or both were emissaries of the kidnapers employed for the purpose of visiting Dr. Condon's house to determine whether there was a "plant" in the house and to determine accurately just how well the police were guarding the house. It appears possible that either one or both of these persons may be identical with one or the other of the "lookouts" observed at Woodlawn and St. Raymond Cemeteries, as set out in this report under Sections entitled "Unknown Person #3" and "Unknown Person #4".

On March 16, 1932, shortly after the above incidents, a freshly laundered Dr. Denton Sleeping Suit #2, purporting to be that of the Lindbergh baby, was received by Dr. Condon through the mails in a package wrapped in brown paper, postmarked Station "E", Brooklyn, N.Y. (2581 Atlantic Avenue). Enclosed within this package, together with the sleeping suit, was a communication, the seventh ransom note, addressed to Dr. Condon, directing attention to the symbol signatures on the previous ransom letters and inviting further attention to the fact that the sleeping suit was further identification. This letter further set out that they would have to pay $3.00 for a new sleeping suit and insisted that $70,000 be paid without first seeing the baby. Condon immediately advised Colonel Breckinridge of the receipt of the above, and shortly after, Lindbergh himself was notified. On March 17, 1932, Colonel Lindbergh arrived at Dr. Condon's home at 1:30 o'clock in the morning and there viewed the sleeping suit which Dr. Condon had received on the day previous. Condon states that the sleeping suit was then placed on the piano in Condon's parlor and after Lindbergh had examined it closely he remarked "It looks like my son's garment." On this date also Dr.

Condon's advertisement of March 16th in the Bronx Home News was published in the New York American. In addition thereto, Condon also published an advertisement in the Bronx Home News reading as follows:

"Money is ready. No cops. No Secret Service. No press. I come like the last time. Alone. Please call. Jafsie."

On March 18, 1932, Dr. Condon's advertisement of the day previous was repeated in the New York American. He published the following advertisement also on that day in the Bronx Home News:

"I accept. Money is ready. John, your package is delivered and is O.K. Direct me." (no signature).

On March 19, 1932, Dr. Condon's advertisement of March 18th was repeated in the Bronx Home News and his advertisement of March 17th repeated in the New York American. On this date also, Dr. Condon found time to spend an hour or two at his Bazaar, which was then being conducted in a store located at 394 East 200th Street, Bronx, New York City, which is located close to Dr. Condon's home. In this store at the above address, Dr. Condon had been conducting a Bazaar for the benefit of a new chapel on Hart's Island in or near the Bronx. While he was in attendance in this store at the Bazaar, an unidentified woman is alleged to have entered, expressing shortly thereafter an interest in one of the several violins which were displayed by Condon for sale. It became evident that she was not particularly interested in Dr. Condon's description of the instrument, and then she made a remark that indicated her true purpose. She is alleged to have said "Nothing can be done until the excitement is over. There is too much publicity. Meet me at the depot at Tuckahoe on Wednesday at five o'clock. I will have a message for you." Condon states he then sought more information concerning the above but the woman made a hasty departure from the Bazaar rendering it impossible for Condon to elicit anything further.

On March 20, 1932, Dr. Condon published the following advertisement in the Bronx Home News:

"Notify me how I can get my letter to you. Urgent. Jafsie."

On the day following, March 31, 1932, Dr. Condon's advertisement of March 20th was published in the New York American and repeated in the Bronx Home News. On this date the eighth ransom letter of this case was received by Dr. Condon. This letter was postmarked Station "N" (203 West 69th Street, New York, N.Y.) 7:30 P.M. March 19, 1932. The contents of this communication in substance insisted on complete compliance with the kidnapers' program and advising that the kidnaping had been planned for a year and further that the baby was well. On March 22, 1932, Dr. Condon published the following advertisement in the Bronx Home News and the New York American.

"Thanks. That little package you sent was immediately delivered and accepted as the real article. See my position. Over fifty years in business and can I pay without seeing goods? Common sense makes me trust you. Please understand my position."

On the day following, March 23, 1932, Dr. Condon's advertisement of March 22nd was repeated in the Bronx Home News and the New York American. On that day, accompanied by Al Reich, his so-called bodyguard, Condon in Al Reich's car drove over from the Bronx to Tuckahoe,

N.Y. for the purpose of meeting the woman who is alleged to have visited Condon at the Bazaar at 394 East 200th Street, Bronx, N.Y. on March 19, 1932. On the evening of this date, March 23rd, Condon and Reich arrived at Tuckahoe, N.Y. and Condon went alone to the Tuckahoe depot of the New York Central Railroad to keep the appointment with the "violin prospect" of the Bazaar. In the early stages of this case and shortly after this date, Condon stated that the woman whom he had met previously, was waiting for him at the Tuckahoe depot, and that when Condon made his appearance there, she announced merely "You will get a message later. Keep advertising until you hear more." After that remark the woman is alleged to have again made a hasty departure. Condon states that no attempt was made to follow her, giving as his reason therefor that the safety of the child was the first consideration in his mind and that he did not wish to pursue any activity that would bear even the slightest possibility of arousing the distrust or suspicion of the kidnapers. Dr. Condon has made conflicting statements relative to the woman who contacted him in the Bazaar, and whom he later met at Tuckahoe. At one time he is said to have implied that he did not meet anyone at Tuckahoe connected with the case and that the purpose of his journey there was to see a relative of his.

On March 24, 1932, Dr. Condon's advertisement of March 22nd was repeated in the Bronx Home News and the New York American. On the day following, March 25, 1932, his advertisement of March 22nd was repeated in the Bronx Home News, and likewise, the New York American. On the day following, March 26, 1932, Condon published the following advertisement in the Bronx Home News:

"Money is ready. Furnish simple code for us to follow in paper. Jafsie."

On March 27, 1932, Condon's advertisement of March 26th was repeated in the Bronx Home News. On the following day, March 28, 1932, his advertisement of March 26th was likewise repeated in the Bronx Home News and in addition repeated in the New York American. On March 29th, his advertisement of March 26th was repeated in the New York American.

On March 29, 1932, Dr. Condon received the ninth ransom note. It was addressed to him at his home on Decatur Avenue, Bronx, N.Y., postmarked Station "N" (203 West 69th Street), New York, N.Y., 9: A.M., March 29, 1932. The substance of this letter indicated that if the matter was not closed by April 8th the ransom would be $100,000. The kidnapers further indicated that they would not comply with the request that they give a code for use in the newspapers.

On March 31, 1932, Dr. Condon published the following advertisement in the Bronx Home News and in the New York American:

"I hereby accept—money is ready. Jafsie."

On April 1, 1932, Dr. Condon's advertisement of March 31st was repeated in the Bronx Home News and the New York American. On this date, Dr. Condon received the tenth ransom note. It was addressed to him at his home on Decatur Avenue in the Bronx, postmarked 9:30 A.M. April 1, 1932, Fordham Station, New York (420 East 189th Street, Bronx, being the same station through which Dr. Condon received his regular mail). This communication instructed Condon to have the money ready for Saturday night, April 2, 1932, and to inform the kidnapers by an advertisement to that effect in the newspapers. Pursuant thereto, Dr. Condon this date published the following advertisement in the April 2nd issue of the New York American which appeared on the streets about 9:20 P.M. April 1, 1932:

"Yes. Everything O.K. Jafsie."

On April 2, 1932, Dr. Condon's advertisement in the New York American of this date was also published in the Bronx Home News which, it is stated, is an afternoon paper. During the course of that day, the eleventh ransom note of this case was delivered to Dr. Condon at his home on Decatur Avenue, allegedly by a taxicab driver. At the time of the delivery of this note Colonel Breckinridge was in a back room of Dr. Condon's house, and Colonel Lindbergh was also in the house, but neither saw the person who delivered the note. Dr. Condon is the only one who saw the man, and according to him, the man arrived driving a taxicab. Condon could give no description of either the man or the taxicab. This note instructed in substance that Condon, within a very short time after the receipt thereof, should proceed to Bergen's Flower Shop on East Tremont Avenue, Bronx, New York City, where from under a stone beneath a table in front of the establishment he would find a further note of direction. This flower shop is located immediately across the street from St. Raymond's Cemetery on East Tremont Avenue in the Bronx. It will be noted that previous negotiations had taken place at Woodlawn Cemetery, several miles distant.

It is stated at this point that subsequent to Dr. Condon's visit to Hopewell, N.J., $50,000 was delivered to his home in United States Currency by Colonel Breckinridge. This money, for a short period, was kept in Dr. Condon's home. Condon apparently became uneasy as to the security of these funds and after a few days removed the entire amount from his home to the Fordham branch of the Corn Exchange Bank Trust Company on Decatur Avenue and East

Fordham Road, the Bronx, for safekeeping, until such time as the currency was needed for delivery to the kidnapers. The money was not deposited in anyone's name, previous arrangements having been made with the president of this bank, by Mr. Barto, who is a partner in the firm of J. Pierpont Morgan & Company and who is likewise a close friend of Colonel Lindbergh and Colonel Breckinridge. Mr. Schneider, the manager of the Fordham branch of the Corn Exchange Bank, had been advised by the president of his institution that the $50,000 in currency had been placed with the bank for safekeeping subject to call at the order of Dr. John F. Condon. Within the course of the negotiations and prior to April 2, 1932, this money was removed from the Corn Exchange Bank by Colonel Breckinridge and taken to a downtown institution possibly the establishment of J. Pierpont Morgan. Condon since shortly after March 10, 1932 had full authorization from Colonel Lindbergh to deliver the above amount of money to whomsoever he believed to be the actual kidnapers of the Lindbergh child. During a considerable period over which these negotiations were being conducted, Max Rosenhain and Milton Gaglio were present in Dr. Condon's home on Decatur Avenue and were apprised of the events as they transpired. It became known that there was a newspaper "leak" somewhere in the house, concerning the negotiations, and Condon states that he then decided to keep Rosenhain and Gaglio on the outside. It appeared that a reporter by the name of Gregory Coleman, who is associated with the Bronx Home News, was "on the inside" up to and including April 2, 1932. Condon states, and the same is confirmed by Colonel Breckinridge, that his plan concerning the delivery of the cash to the kidnapers, was quite similar to the theory that "nobody buys goods unless he sees those goods." Condon was of the opinion that no ransom money should be paid in this case to anyone unless the child were actually produced. Colonel Lindbergh was hesitant, states Condon, to pay the ransom money before getting proof that the child was alive and well; apparently agreeing to make payment only after receipt by Condon on March 16, 1932 of what appeared to be the child's sleeping suit. Condon believed that it was the female members of the Lindbergh family who urged him to assent to paying the ransom, without first having the child produced.

At one time during the negotiations, states Condon, he was called to the Morrow town house, 2 East 72nd Street, New York City, for the purpose of attending a meeting of what he stated to be the Secret Service, the New Jersey State Police, and a representative of the New York Police Department. Condon attended and was then asked to listen to what those in attendance at the meeting had to say. It seemed to Condon that everybody present, with the exception of himself, was in favor of paying over the ransom money on the information available to that date without first having seen the Lindbergh baby.

It is Condon's statement that the communication received by him from an unidentified taxicab driver on April 2, 1932, was delivered to his home shortly after 8: o'clock on that evening although the surrounding circumstances relative to the delivery of this particular note are still in dispute. It is Dr. Condon's explanation that he went to the door upon the arrival of his taxicab driver and after receiving the note inquired from the taxicab driver as to the place where he had received the message. Condon states that he then said "I came from 188th Street and Marion Avenue with this note for Dr. Condon." Condon further states that he then asked the taxi driver what kind of a man delivered the note to him, whereupon the taxi driver said "not richly dressed. Brown fedora." Personally, states dr. Condon, he did not get the taxi driver's name and made no attempt to do so because in his opinion at that time there was nothing involved except the communication from the kidnapers. Condon further adds that he believed someone then in the house attempted to get the name and address of this taxi driver but these efforts were without success although just why he did not know. In Condon's recollection, Gaglio was not present in Condon's home at the time of the delivery of this note. Condon has said that he cannot identify this taxi driver of April 2nd, nor does he think he could identify or recognize him if he saw him again, giving as his reason therefor that at the time of the appearance of the taxi driver, Condon was interested only in the note from the kidnapers and was not careful to note the description of this man, or of his taxi.

Shortly after Condon's receipt of the note in question directing him to proceed to Bergen's Flower Shop on East Tremont Avenue, the Bronx, in search of further directions, arrangements were immediately made to fulfill this part of the kidnapers' request. The $70,000 demanded by the kidnapers, had been delivered to Condon's home by Colonel Lindbergh and Colonel Breckinridge. This money was wrapped in two packages, one containing $50,000 in $5, $10, and $20 bills, and the other containing $20,000 in $50 bills. Before this money left the house, it was placed by Colonel Lindbergh in a box, 6" by 7" by 14", which had been provided by Dr. Condon, pursuant to instructions in the fourth letter. Further comment on this particular feature will be made further in this report. In placing the two packages of $50,000 and $20,000 in this box, Colonel Lindbergh in his attempt to close the top of the box, pressed it down so tightly that it cracked, rendering it impossible to lock the container. It was thereupon wrapped with paper and tied securely by cord. Specimens of the wrapping paper and the cord which enclosed the box are presently in possession of Mr. Barto at the establishment of J. Pierpont

Morgan and Co. The New York Office has been advised, although not informed officially, that representatives of the Intelligence Unit of the U.S. Treasury Department were among those present in Dr. Condon's home at this time.

After the $70,000 was securely placed in the box, Colonel Lindbergh placed the same under his arm and covered the box with his top coat. Taking Dr. Condon with him, he proceeded in Al Reich's car to the vicinity of Bergen's Flower Shop on East Tremont Avenue. After arriving there, Condon, as he had been advised, found a note beneath the table in front of Bergen's Flower Shop. The contents of this note gave instructions to proceed to the Whittemore Avenue entrance of St. Raymond's Cemetery. Dr. Condon following instructions, proceeded as directed but carried no money with him. Condon states that he had with him written authorization from Colonel Lindbergh under date of March 30, 1934 to pay the $70,000 to the alleged kidnapers.

Colonel Lindbergh and Condon arrived at Bergen's Flower Shop on the night of April 2, 1932 at exactly five minutes after 9: o'clock, which Condon states is accurate since he looked at his watch purposely on that night. After reading the instructions contained in the note found in front of Bergen's Flower Shop, Condon walked down to the corner of East Tremont Avenue to the Whittemore Avenue entrance of St. Raymond's Cemetery, where he saw a man and a little girl on the corner and from them he inquired as to whether they knew where Whittemore Avenue was. Condon states that in making this inquiry he had only one purpose in view and that being his effort to find out whether these individuals were any persons known to him. Condon states he cannot describe either the man or the girl from whom he made this inquiry, both being unknown to him. Up to that time Condon did not look at the street sign, it being assumed that because of his familiarity with that territory he knew the exact location of Whittemore Avenue. However, he states that after making inquiry of the above mentioned man and girl they advised him that they did not know the location of East Whittemore Avenue. Condon waited on the corner for a few minutes and in full view up to this time of Colonel Lindbergh. He walked back and forth at the entrance of St. Raymond's Cemetery on East Tremont Avenue during which time Lindbergh was stationed in Al Reich's car which was parked on the north side of Tremont Avenue facing west near Bergen's Flower Shop. Condon was now on the east side of the Whittemore Avenue entrance to St. Raymond's cemetery; as he turned around to walk in a westerly direction he heard a voice yell out "Hey, Doc". Upon hearing this voice, Condon looked around in search of the person calling to him and called out "Where are you?" Condon, receiving no answer, states that he thought since there were no lights in the cemetery the person calling out to him was possibly afraid of the dark. He then walked down the center of the comparatively rough road until he came to the entrance of the hedge in the cemetery on Whittemore Avenue. Condon walked in the direction of the hedge and then discovered that the man who had called out "Hey, Doc" was on the inside. As soon as Condon came closer he recognized the individual partly hidden behind the four or five foot fence as being the "John" with whom he had spoken on the night of March 12, 1932 in Van Cortlandt Park directly across East 233rd Street from Woodlawn Cemetery in the Bronx. Then Condon came within a few feet of "John" near the hedge in St. Raymond's Cemetery, "John" is alleged to have asked "Have you got the money?" Condon replied "No. I did not know whether you would have the baby or not. I could not give it to you." To this "John" then replied "Where is it?" Condon then stated "Up in the automobile." "John" then commanded "Get it." Condon replied "I can't get it without a receipt." "John" then said "Well, I didn't get a receipt but I could get that in two minutes." Condon replied "I see." Condon thereupon departed but before so doing he states that he engaged in a conversation with "John" during which he tried to impress upon him that it was a terrible thing; that in view of the hard times and depression, money was so hard to get, and that Condon did not think Colonel Lindbergh was in a position to pay $70,000 ransom without being hurt very much financially by it. Condon states that in answer to this, "John" said "Well, I suppose if we can't get $70,000 I will have to take $50,000." Thereupon Condon went back to the car in which Lindbergh was stationed and there discussed with Lindbergh the events which had taken place. In the course of this conversation Condon said, "Colonel, I tried to do you a little favor—I am told that your boy will be returned if I can give them $50,000." Lindbergh then untied the cord enclosing the box containing $70,000 and extracted the bundle of $20,000 which consisted of $50 bills therefrom. The box was retied and Condon took it with him, going down Whittemore Avenue to the cemetery hedge. Condon states that he could not get a good glimpse of "John" at first and because of that said to him "Stand up". "John" was then crouched down, says Condon, and when he did standup, Condon was completely satisfied that it was "John" whom he had previously met in the Woodlawn Cemetery. To make sure of this, however, Condon stated that he said to this individual, "I never saw you before, did I? Where did I ever see you before?" and "John" is alleged to have said "I am the one that spoke to you at the other cemetery." Condon states then that he said "Where?" "Well, I can't see you." "John" then said "Have you got the money?" and Condon said "Yes." Condon then said "Where is your receipt?" and explains that "John's" voice changed and his English became better. "John" is then alleged to have said "They have agreed to go through with this and your work is perfet. They are pleased." Whereupon Condon stated "Well, I kept my word—where is the note?" To this "John" replied "I got it right here." Whereupon, with his left hand and facing Condon he handed the note to him putting his coat up again however, over his face and further remarking to Condon "Everyone trusted and that one of them knew him". Again Condon states that "John" used the word "<u>perfet</u>."

"John" is alleged to have stated to Condon that <u>they</u> cannot double cross him. Upon receiving the note from John, states Condon, he handed to "John" the box containing $50,000 ransom. Condon tried to catch some German accent from "John" but was unable; however, in conversing with "John" further was satisfied that he was the so-called "Scandinavian," with whom he had previously spoken in the Woodlawn Cemetery. Condon remained on the Whittemore Avenue side of the hedge while "John" was on the opposite side in the cemetery. It was over this hedge separating the cemetery from Whittemore Avenue that Condon handed the $50,000 ransom to "John". When "John" received the money he stood up on both feet and after Condon glanced at him in this position he was satisfied beyond doubt that this "John" was the same person with whom he had spoken in Woodlawn Cemetery. As soon as "John" received the ransom money he left Dr. Condon and travelling on the inside of St. Raymond's Cemetery he made his departure walking in the direction of Westchester Creek. Condon went immediately back to Lindbergh with the note which he had received from "John", and remembering the instructions which he clamed that "John" had given to him to the effect that the note enclosed in the letter was not to be opened for at least two hours until "John" and the kidnaping gang had a chance to make their getaway, Condon got in the car with Lindbergh and drove over to Westchester Square stopping in front of what

Condon called Kiddy Corner, and explained by him to be the Edwin Gould Kiddy Corner which Condon claimed to have established years ago as a spot in which children could play. In fact, Condon claimed that he had charge of this reservation at one time. Here the note was opened and ready by Lindbergh and Condon. Its contents in substance informed that the baby was on board a boat called "Nellie", a 28 foot craft in Martha's Vineyard. Colonel Lindbergh and Condon returned to Condon's residence immediately thereafter with the $20,000. Arrangements were then made for the securing of an amphibian plane in which to proceed to the vicinity of Martha's Vineyard, Grayhead Island, Horse Neck Beach and Elizabeth Islands in search of the Lindbergh child. Condon then stated that before he left "John" in St. Raymond's Cemetery he shook hands with him and noted at the time that "John" on this occasion was not wearing gloves.

Early in the morning of April 3, 1932, Colonel Lindbergh, Colonel Breckinridge, Elmer Irey, Intelligence Unit, Internal Revenue, Washington, D. C. Dr. Condon and Al Reich motored to Bridgeport, Conn. At this place all of the above mentioned with the exception of Al Reich proceeded to an amphibian plane to search the waters in an endeavor to locate the boat which was supposed to have the child aboard in possession of two innocent persons. The futility of this journey is well known. On this date also Dr. Condon's advertisement of April 2nd was repeated in the Bronx Home News and the New York American. The search in the vicinity of Martha's Vineyard continued and during its progress Condon stated that he had not been up in that vicinity theretofore. The plane was lowered at a place in the Elizabeth Islands called Cutter Hunt where the searching party went into a restaurant or boardinghouse on the island and there had lunch.

A composite description of the man "John" as given by

Dr. John F. Condon on May 14, and 20, 1932 at the Bronx County District Attorney's office and since that time supplemented by him in interviews with an Agent of the Division's New York Office, follows:

Name:	"John"
Height:	5'8" to 5'10"
Age:	30 to 32
Weight:	158 to 165 pounds
Build:	Well, and similar to "middle weight boxer".
Complexion:	Fair, no blemishes.
Scars:	None apparent. No tattoos visible.
Eyes:	Bluish-Gray—wide—almond shaped—resembled those of a Chinaman or Japanese. Did not wear glasses.
Hair:	Medium chestnut approaching a dirty blond or sandy.
Teeth:	Fair and regular; no gold or fillings noticed
Facial features:	hatchet face appearance; straight nose; prominent forehead; eyebrows medium heavy and in straight line across forehead; clean shaven; prominent and high cheek bones running down to almost a pointed chin.
Ears:	Unusually large.
Hands:	Calloused; not noticed if any jewelry worn.
Neck:	Average medium slender, not short and fat.
Shoulders:	Inclined to droop but fairly straight; not quite a military carriage.
Peculiarities:	Could run fast and use hands with dexterity. Had unusually large muscular or

	fleshy development on inside thumb of left hand; did not wear gloves.
Occupation:	Mariner, carpenter or painter.
Marital status:	Stated to be married.
Residence:	Stated Boston, Mass.
Criminal record:	Unknown.
Color:	White
Nationality:	Said to be Scandinavian or German.
Handwriting specimen:	None, other than ransom notes possibly written by this person.
Speech:	Spoke with foreign accent; broken but fair English, presumably Scandinavian or possibly German; used expressions "Smack me out"; "Did you got our letter"; pronounced the word "perfect" as "perfet", the word "Colonel" as "kennel", and the word "five" as "fife".
Shoe:	Size not determined; color or style unknown.
Feet:	Normal, did not walk lame.
Clothing:	Gray trousers and black suit; coat heavier then alpaca but not as heavy as broadcloth; regular Spring overcoat worn loose, light in fabric, dark in color; one button used on overcoat; wore dark grayish brown fedora hat pulled well down over forehead.

Condon states that he had never seen one Morris Rosner prior to March 10, 1932 nor has he seen him since that time. Rosner at no time has visited Condon's home in the Bronx or elsewhere. Condon likewise did not know Irving Bitz or Salvatore Spitale. It is claimed by Condon, however, that Rosner had knowledge that Condon was negotiating with the alleged kidnapers. Although Condon does not know positively whether Rosner was shown the notes received by him in this case from the kidnapers, he was of the opinion that Rosner had some associates, possibly Bitz or Spitale, and that one of them is an architect or draftsman with ability to copy the symbol signatures from the notes which Rosner had seen and possibly possessed.

On April 6, 1932, Dr. Condon published an advertisement in the Bronx Home News and the New York American reading as follows:

"What is wrong? Have you crossed me? Please better directions. Jafsie."

On the following day, April 7, 1932, this advertisement of Condon's of April 6th was repeated in the Bronx Home News and the New York American. It was likewise repeated in both of these papers on April 8, 1932. On April 9, 1932, it was disclosed by the newspapers that Colonel Lindbergh had actually paid the $50,000 ransom in an effort to regain his child. On the day following, April 10, 1932, the newspapers carried a more or less full account of the most recent developments in the case up to that time and publicly revealed that the "Jafsie" of this case was Dr. John F. Condon, 2974 Decatur Avenue, Bronx, New York City. On the same date the newspapers generally published the serial numbers of the $50,000 ransom money paid in the St. Raymond's Cemetery to the kidnapers by Dr. Condon.

With particular reference to the box in which the ransom money was contained at the time of this payment by Dr. Condon to "John" in St. Raymond's Cemetery on April 2, 1932, further comment is offered here.

On September 8, 1933, former Special Agent J.J. Manning of the New York Office, discussed this angle with Dr. Condon at his home in the Bronx. It appears from Condon's explanations relating to this feature of the case that his son-in-law, Ralph Hacker, who is an architect with a business address at Fort Lee, N.J. actually saw the note sent by the kidnapers in which appeared a picture of the "box" together with its given dimensions in which it was designated that the ransom money should be placed. It further appears that Ralph Hacker, the son-in-law, who had married Condon's daughter, Myra, personally made a set of plans from which this packet or box, 6" by 7" by 14" was to be made. These plans, Condon now refers to as "my plans" and are stated by him to be presently in his possession at his home in the Bronx. Condon states that he shortly after the receipt of this ransom note, made it a point to get three pieces of wood from which the box should be made in strict compliance with the terms of the kidnapers. Although Condon does not explain the source from which he obtained this wood, he does state that he obtained a piece of white pine, a piece of poplar and a piece of boxwood or possibly mahogany and that he took them thereafter together with the plans to the business address of one of his friends. Condon at that particular instant could not recall the name of this friend but did state that he was quite certain that no one not even Lindbergh himself had any knowledge concerning the person by whom this particular box, nor about the place at which it was made. Condon related further that there was something peculiar about this box in that upon its completion $50,000 would just fit in and that the remaining $20,000 or a part of it had to be placed on top of the box and the box had to be tied by cord by Lindbergh on September 2, 1932; further, that in attempting to place all of this money in the packet in a compact manner, Lindbergh had split one side of the box. This box is further described by Condon as having had an ordinary cabinet lock placed thereon although at the time the money was paid over since the lock on the box could not bend down tightly because of the overstuffing of the currency therein, it was impossible to lock same; however, states Condon he still has the key together with the plans in his possession and presently kept at his home.

From Condon's statements to Agent Manning on September 8, 1933, it seems that the poplar, white pine and boxwood or mahogany were glued together by Condon's friend who was stated to be a cabinet maker and the box thereafter made from the combined material. This, Condon stated, he did only for the reason that in the event the box showed up at a later date he should be able to identify it. On the same date, Dr. Condon accompanied Agent Manning in the latter's car in a drive down Webster Avenue in the Bronx, and upon arrival at 2703 Webster Avenue, Condon requested Agent Manning to stop and upon so doing, Condon pointed to what was then a vacant store at 2703 Webster Avenue, stating that the "fellow by the name of Peretty" who used to have a cabinet making shop at this address, made the box. Condon referred to this cabinet maker as "Old Man Peretty" and one of his old friends and that after making this box Condon paid Peretty the sum of $3.25. Colonel Breckinridge was thereupon interviewed with reference to the box and he stated that he had never known where the particular box came from nor had he any knowledge concerning the person who made it.

In the course of the investigation which followed, it was determined as a fact that on June 1, 1931, Frank Pereni, Jr. of 2800 Pond Place, Brooklyn, N.Y. signed a lease for the premises at 2701-2703 Webster Ave., Bronx, N.Y. It was learned that Frank Pereni, Jr. in March 1932 engaged at this address with his father in the business of making furniture and cabinets, and following the carpentry business generally. Subsequent thereto certain inquiry concerning this box was conducted by Lieutenant James J.

Finn, main office division, New York City Police Department; Sergeant Andrew Zapulsky, Alpine Barracks, New Jersey State Police, in company with Agent J.J. Manning of the New York Office. Frank <u>Peremi</u> Jr., was finally located residing in Apartment 1-D, 414 East 204th Street, Bronx, New York City, and under suitable pretext he was interviewed on September 22, 1933. After a conversation under this pretext was had, Peremi was led into the conversation relating to the Lindbergh kidnaping during the course of which he remarked that "it was just about the time Condon paid the ransom money was it not?" Subsequent thereto it was learned from Peremi, Jr. that approximately ten days prior to the payment of the ransom in this case Dr. John F. Condon, accompanied by Al Reich, personally appeared at Peremi's carpentry shop at 2703 Webster Avenue, Bronx, N.Y. and inquired of Peremi as to whether he would make for Condon a small box 6" by 7" by 14" in dimension. Peremi stated that he advised Condon of his willingness to make the box providing, however, that Condon would pay him $3.50 for such service rendered in connection therewith. Condon seemed to think that $3.50 was too much money for such a job, thereupon he departed from Peremi's carpentry shop in company with Al Reich remarking that if he changes his mind in the matter he will probably return in about an hour. Peremi stated that Condon failed to return and that he had no idea where Condon may have gone alone or with Reich for the purpose of having this box made. Nothing was said by Condon or Reich in Peremi's shop which would suggest a reason for which the box was to be made. Frank Peremi, Jr. further advised that his father, Frank Peremi, while he lived was engaged also in the cabinet making and carpentry business with Frank, Jr. at 2703 Webster Avenue; however, the father, Frank Peremi died in October 1931, so that obviously it was quite impossible for the father to have made any box for Condon or any other person during February or March 1932.

William Bay, 306 Mosholu Parkway South, Bronx, New York City, and former partner of Frank Peremi, Jr., was present in the carpentry shop at 2703 Webster Avenue at the time of the visit by Condon and Reich and since he heard the entire conversation as outlined is in a position to testify to the above indicated circumstances. It would seem, therefore, from the foregoing that Condon's statements concerning the identity of the person alleged by him to have made the box in which was contained the ransom money paid "John" in St. Raymond's Cemetery on April 2, 1932 is apparently untruthful.

Further investigation concerning this angle is current at the New York Office and it has been stated by Colonel Breckinridge that on Colonel Lindbergh's next visit with Dr. Condon he will attempt to elicit from him the information concerning the person who made this particular box and the place in which it was made. It is stated that on November 31, 1933, Dr. Condon informed a Special Agent of the New York Division Office that the box was a "family heirloom", without, however, making any effort to reconcile his previous statement that the box was constructed by a friend.

The above narrative concerning Dr. Condon's experiences and his activities in connection with the Lindbergh ransom negotiations are stated by Colonel Breckinridge to be substantially correct. On May 17, 1932, Colonel Breckinridge appeared before the Bronx County Grand Jury and there gave certain testimony covering his connection and activities in the Lindbergh kidnaping case. Colonel Breckinridge presently resides at 455 East 57th Street, and maintains his law offices on the 30th floor of 39 Broadway, New York City. Colonel Breckinridge was first advised of the kidnaping of the Lindbergh baby at 11:15 P.M. on

March 1, 1932 when Colonel Lindbergh phoned him at his New York home. Immediately Breckinridge proceeded to the Lindbergh estate at Hopewell. Breckinridge is still of the opinion that the kidnaping occurred some time between the hours of 7:30 and 9:30 P.M. March 1, 1932. He indicates, however, that the exact hour of the kidnaping is unknown to anyone and the actual time is still undiscovered. Breckinridge related to the circumstances of the finding of the original ransom note demanding $50,000 from Colonel Lindbergh and warning against notifying the police or press. Breckinridge first knew of Dr. Condon's entry into this case when Condon called at Hopewell by telephone late on the night of March 9, 1932. Upon Condon's arrival at Hopewell on the early morning of March 10th and after Condon's trip from Hopewell to Colonel Breckinridge's law office later on the same date, Breckinridge began to question Condon as to who he was and the like. In this conversation Condon mentioned the name of Addison W. Kelly, who had been a classmate of Colonel Breckinridge's at school. Breckinridge had not seen Kelly for years, but did recall that he was the greatest halfback that Princeton University had ever produced. Kelly was in his class at Princeton with Breckinridge's brother, and the Colonel himself had last heard of Kelly from Chicago several years previously. In an effort to check, partially at least, the statements made by Condon, Breckinridge by long distance telephone to Chicago made inquiry concerning Kelly and was advised from that point that Kelly left Chicago in 1910. Breckinridge then found that Kelly was in New York and called him at the Princeton Club asking Kelly to meet him at Breckinridge's office. Kelly had not seen Condon for years, and when they both got together they fell on each other's neck at the joy of seeing each other. With particular reference to the sleeping garment received by Condon through the mails on March 16, 1932, Breckinridge states that he was in Condon's home on Decatur Avenue when the package was delivered; that special care was used in the opening of said package so that latent fingerprints could be obtained in the event any of them were susceptible to developing. Lindbergh was thereafter notified of its receipt. Breckinridge states that this sleeping garment was definitely identified as either the sleeping garment worn by the baby at the time of its being kidnaped or an exact duplicate. It was an exact counterpart, states Breckinridge, of the sleeping garment which the baby wore when taken including the mark of identification. Breckinridge would not think it impossible from any description of the garment that might have been disclosed in the newspapers for any person to purchase such a garment and send that in the mail to Dr. Condon. It was Breckinridge's further testimony relative to this case that throughout the entire negotiations in Breckinridge's opinion Dr. Condon was opposed to any plan of paying the ransom money without first seeing the baby. It was Breckinridge's further statement that Dr. Condon took with him a camel, lion and elephant, toys of the baby as a possible means of identifying the baby, and that Condon did go to Tuckahoe to fulfill the engagement there with a possible contact in this case but Breckinridge did not think that Condon met the woman there or any place else.

It was Colonel Breckinridge's recollection that the communication delivered by the unknown taxi driver to Dr. Condon at his home on Decatur Avenue, in the Bronx, arrived at Condon's home at 7:40 or 7:45 P.M. on that night. From carelessness no one in the house at the time secured any information from the taxi driver, the reason being given therefor was that they were apparently so excited about going through with the payment of the ransom that no one seemed to question the taxi driver nor did anyone get his name.

An important incident concerning the payment of the ransom on the night of April 2, 1932 is stated by Colonel Breckinridge as well as Colonel Lindbergh to Agents of the New York Office. While Colonel Lindbergh was parked in Al Reich's car near Bergen's Flower Shop on that night and while Dr. Condon was walking down East Tremont Avenue near Whittemore Avenue close to St. Raymond's cemetery, Colonel Lindbergh from the car observed a man with a handkerchief held to his face. This man blew his nose in a loud manner and then dropped the handkerchief. He was at the time on the street near St. Raymond's cemetery. It is the opinion of both Colonel Lindbergh and Colonel Breckinridge that this person who discarded the handkerchief was a confederate of the kidnapers and in dropping the handkerchief it was the signal to "John" or any of the other kidnapers concerning Dr. Condon's identity. In Colonel Breckinridge's recollection when Dr. Condon picked up the note in front of Bergen's Flower Shop on East Tremont Avenue both Condon and Colonel Lindbergh observed a man in the vicinity who was coughing obviously to attract Condon's attention. This man may have meant the cough as a signal of identification to "John."

With particular reference further to the payment of the ransom money, April 2, 1932, Colonel Breckinridge as well as Colonel Lindbergh, is still doubtful about one particular angle of Condon's conduct. On that night in St. Raymond's Cemetery when Condon first entered St. Raymond's Cemetery he walked to the entrance directly from Al Reich's car in which Lindbergh was parked; however, when Condon returned and advised Colonel Lindbergh that <u>they</u> had agreed to receive $50,000 and after Condon's obtaining this money he departed the parked car and again returned to the cemetery to recontact "John". On this return trip, however, instead of taking the first turn off East Tremont Avenue into St. Raymond's Cemetery, Condon passed the entrance and walked down another block, completely outside of the sight of Colonel Lindbergh, then Condon turned around, walked back and walked into the cemetery with box apparently under his arm. It is not known to Colonel Lindbergh or Colonel Breckinridge nor has Condon explained it satisfactorily just why he went one block further down the cemetery before he returned and entered it, to contact "John" the second time on the night of April 2nd. This particular angle has been discussed with Dr. Condon by Agent J. J. Manning of the New York Office during the course of which Condon has given at least three explanations of the above. Condon states that on his second trip back to the cemetery on the night of April 2nd in passing the entrance he thought he saw some shadows behind the tombstones and thinking possibly that someone had concealed himself there, he would "stick him up" and take the ransom money from him, he walked down another block to give this matter serious thought before he turned around and entered the cemetery. Condon's second explanation for his walking the extra block is that he did so to give him sufficient time in which to say a prayer. His third explanation is in substance that he was confused, and did not know exactly where he was going, since he may have been a little excited at the time.

Colonel Breckinridge in outlining the steps taken during his search of Martha's Vineyard, stated that on the morning of April 3, 1932, he arranged through the president of the National City Bank of New York, who was a classmate of Breckinridge's, for an Amphian Sikorsky plane. This plane was boarded at Bridgeport, Conn. By Colonel Lindbergh, Elmer Irey, Dr. Condon and Breckinridge on the morning of April 3, 1932. The party proceeded to the vicinity of Martha's Vineyard, made a thorough search of all boats but failed to find any answering the description of the boat "Nellie". On the following day, Lindbergh in company with Breckinridge made a further search, using in this instance a land plane, but the search was without avail. The coast guard stationed in that vicinity, states Breckinridge, reported having seen a boat called the "Nellie" which was a strange boat in these waters on the proceeding day (April 2, 1932). However, the coast guard's description of this boat was from 48' to 50' long. Several boats, called "Nellie," were thereafter found on the run in from Elizabeth Island and Martha's Vineyard, and since it was discovered that these boats were for the main part either fishing boats or bootlegging boats and that none of them had on board the kidnaped Lindbergh baby, the search was abandoned.

Colonel Breckinridge further related that shortly after the payment of the ransom in St. Raymond's cemetery he personally made a plaster cast of the footprint found on one of the graves in the cemetery which was thought to have been left by the departing "John" on April 2nd. The cast since the time of its construction has been in possession of the New Jersey State Police at Trenton, N. J. With reference to the discovery of the body of the Lindbergh baby on May 12, 1932, Colonel Breckinridge states that the sleeping suit was not found with it. However, that the home-made improvised under shirt, which had been placed on the baby to keep the medicinal lotion on its chest because of a slight congestion, was still on the body when it was found and was identified beyond peradventure. It is the opinion of Colonel Breckinridge that the man who received the ransom money in this case from Dr. Condon was unquestionably an accredited representative of the abductors. It is Breckinridge's further opinion that his man's authenticity had been established in a manner entirely satisfactory to all of those directly concerned with the search for the baby.

Max Rosenhain, who resides at 200 Grand Concourse,

and who conducts a restaurant at 2469 Grand Concourse, Bronx, New York City, was questioned by Assistant District Attorney, Bronx County District Attorney's office, Edward Breslin, on May 20, 1932, concerning his connection and experiences during the ransom negotiations. Max Rosenhain's restaurant is located one block immediately south of East Fordham Road. Max has been in business at that address for ten years. He has been a resident of the Bronx for thirty years and up to the time of the kidnaping had known Dr. Condon quite well for a period of five years or more. Max was also acquainted with Al Reich.

Max Rosenhain was injected into the case on March 9, 1932 when Condon came into his store on that night and displayed to him the letter which Condon had received on that date. Max then inquired from Condon as to how he received the letter and Condon replied that he had placed an announcement in the paper on the day previous. In fact, Condon showed to Max at that time the announcement in the Bronx Home News in which it was outlined that Condon offered $1,000 reward and offered himself as the "go-between" in this case. After a short discussion of the case including the receipt of the above letter, Max states that he suggested to Condon that he call Colonel Lindbergh. This Condon did a short while later. Max knew all about the contents of Condon's letter including the size of the packet which was to contain the ransom money and the amount of ransom demanded including the particular denominations of bills. The telephone call made from Rosenhain's restaurant to the Hopewell estate was put through between 11: and 12: o'clock on the night of March 9, 1932, Milton Gaglio, states Rosenhain, was not present while the call was being made but came into the restaurant just as Condon had completed his call. Max Rosenhain described the circles which were part of the symbol signature on the ransom letters received by Condon as "two circles interlocking each other, the circles being blue and the center of it was in red sort of forming a heart with a hole punched through the heart and a hole on either side about 1/4" on the outside of the circle."

Max Rosenhain saw all letters with the possible exception of one, which Condon received from the kidnapers. After Dr. Condon had finished his telephone conversation with the Hopewell estate on the night of March 9, 1932 he asked Max Rosenhain if he would not act in this case with him. Max states that his first reaction was that he would not have anything to do with the case but upon Condon's stating that he ought to, Max assented. Max then said to Condon, "Let's have a cup of coffee and we will go down to Hopewell." It was then that Gaglio came into Max Rosenhain's restaurant and upon hearing Max state that we were going to Hopewell, Gaglio remarked that he would be glad to drive them down. On the way down Gaglio said "We three started this thing together and we should go through with it." Max, however, was still of the opinion that the letter which Condon had received on March 9th was nothing more than a "crank" letter. He later, however, dismissed this thought from his mind. The party arrived at Hopewell around 3: o'clock in the morning on March 10th. Condon first entered the house and there conferred with Colonel Lindbergh and Colonel Breckinridge, after which Rosenhain and Gaglio were introduced to Colonel Lindbergh. Max Rosenhain knew that arrangement had been made to bring the ransom money to the Bronx on the following day. Rosenhain and Gaglio left Hopewell about 5: o'clock in the morning of March 10th while Condon stayed over. On the evening of March 10, 1932, Condon went back to Max Rosenhain and stated to him that Lindbergh had instructed Condon to return to the Bronx and place an advertisement in the paper pertaining to the kidnapers' letter to the effect that "Money is ready." Within a few days, states Max Rosenhain, Condon received a telephone call from the alleged kidnapers. Max was not present personally in Condon's house at the receipt of this call; however, Condon told him about it later and explained to him that it was a very strange message and that it came between 8: and 9: o'clock, in which Condon was advised that between 8: and 9: o'clock on the following night, March 12, 1932, Condon would receive a communication. Condon told Max at the time that it was a male voice which called.

Max attended many of the subsequent conferences held in Condon's house, the last conference being one during which a taxi driver delivered the letter, in which Condon was instructed to proceed to the empty frankfurter stand located about one hundred feet north of the subway station on Jerome Avenue. It was Max Rosenhain's recollection that on this night, Condon left his Decatur Avenue home in company with Al Reich about twenty minutes to nine.

On the following night, Sunday, March 13, 1932, Max Rosenhain was present in Condon's house. A general discussion was had of various angles of the case and numerous suggestions were offered as to the procedure which should be followed. Breckinridge took a short walk and came back when he stated that someone had "tipped off" the newspapers, and Breckinridge, in Max's opinion, was apparently quite peeved about it. Then Max decided that he had better go home, and said to Condon upon leaving "If you want me for anything meet me at the house because I don't want to be implicated in a tip off to newspapers." Max further told Condon at the time of his departure that Condon should not tell him anything that he did not want him to know.

Condon at no time in Max Rosenhain's recollection told him about his alleged meeting with the woman at the bazaar in the Bronx in the vicinity of Bedfort Park Boulevard, or in Tuckahoe, N.Y. Max further states that he was not at Condon's house when the ransom money was paid to the alleged kidnapers on April 2, 1932. He first learned about the delivery of this money when he read about it in the newspapers on April 4, or 5, 1932; in fact, states Max, Condon came to his restaurant about April 3, 1932 and asked Max whether he would turn the money over without first seeing the baby if he were in Condon's position. Max replied to this that "it would be better if Condon would make a C.O.D. transaction." Condon at no time related to Max what actually took place on April 2nd. Max stated that he did not know the second taxi driver who was alleged to have delivered a note to Dr. Condon at his Decatur Avenue home nor did he have any knowledge that the second taxi driver hacked around the vicinity of Rosenhain's restaurant on Grand Concourse in the Bronx.

Joseph Perrone, 2010 Powell Avenue, Bronx, New York City, age 35, a taxi driver by occupation, and who is employed by Samuel Diotz, 1940 Jerome Avenue, Bronx, New York City, was questioned at the office of the Bronx County District Attorney subsequent to the above. Perrone stated that on Saturday evening, March 12, 1932, his hack stand happened to be on Mosholu Parkway and Jerome Avenue. At about 7:45 to 8:30 P.M. on this date he received a note from an unknown man for delivery to Dr. Condon, 2974 Decatur Avenue, Bronx, New York City. Perrone had just discharged a passenger at 3440 Gates Place, just one block west of Knox Place and Gun Hill Road. Perrone came down Gun Hill Road, traveling east and when he arrived at Knox Place, an unknown man came running off the sidewalk in front of him waving his hand up to stop which Perrone did. This unknown man was standing on the street trying to open the front door of Perrone's taxicab and since it was a cool evening Perrone had the window all the way up. As

Perrone was opening the window he said "Wait a minute" and after the widow had been completely open, in an excited way the unknown man asked him if he knew the location of 2974 Decatur Avenue. To this Perrone replied "Yes". "I know where it is". The unknown man then said "Well that is around 201st Street isn't it?" and Perrone said "Yes, just about where that number is." With that the unknown man said, "How much would it be over there" and before Perrone could tell him the cost of the trip to that point, the unknown individual stated "It would only cost about fifty cents, wouldn't it?" and Perrone remarked that was about what the clock would register. With that Perrone remarked, the unknown man reached in his pocket and pulled out a letter saying "How would you like to deliver a letter for me for a dollar?" Perrone said "Yes" after which the party with whom he spoke gave him a letter. Perrone remembered the letter very well. The capital "R" appeared to him to be blurred and it seemed to Perrone that this capital "R" was written with ink that had later been blurred. After the unknown individual gave Perrone the dollar he walked in back of the taxicab very quickly and started looking at the license numbers. Perrone thought that this man took down the license numbers as he kept looking at them and then started backing up the street. Perrone did not realize what the letter was at the time and the thought of its importance did not occur to him until he traveled down Jerome Avenue when he happened to pass Mosholu Parkway and recalled that Dr. Condon is located near Mosholu Parkway South. When he passed the corner there appeared to be a fellow there by the name of James O'Brien and the traffic light being against him, he said to O'Brien, "I am making a delivery of a letter." O'Brien looked at the letter, saw the name on it and said to Perrone, "That is Dr. Condon, the man that is offering $1,000 in the kidnaping case." Perrone immediately went over to Dr. Condon's house, Decatur Avenue and 201st Street. He was not very sure whether the number was 2974 Decatur Avenue as it was pretty dark and Perrone just had a good idea where the number was actually located. The first house that Perrone located at was 2972 and he was quite sure that the next house was 2974. Arriving there he went in. It was rather dark, but looking at the number closely he observed the same to be 2974. Perrone rang the bell and Condon came to the door. However, he did not know Condon at that time. Condon inquired of him "Well, what is it, young man?" and Perrone said "I have a letter for Dr. Condon". Condon then asked Perrone to step inside and this Perrone did. Immediately Dr. Condon inquired of Perrone as to where he had received the letter, and Perrone explained that he had gotten the communication at Knox Place and Gun Hill Road. Condon thereafter questioned Perrone concerning the description of the man from whom he had received the money, the details of which are set forth further in this report. Perrone had not seen the man from whom he obtained the note prior to March 12, 1932 nor has he seen him since. He is quite sure, however, that if he sees him again he can identify him. As he was talking with Dr. Condon, Perrone states that a young man came running downstairs in Condon's house, and Perrone at the time thought it was Condon's son. Condon said at the time "Milton, take good care of this young man and give him something." Perrone alleged that Milton then said "Where did you get this note—Bainbridge and Gun Hill Road?" and Perrone replied "No, I got it at Knox Place and Gun Hill Road." Perrone left his name and address at Condon's house with Gaglio on that night, and left Condon's house. He later found out that the name of the young man with whom he spoke was Milton Gaglio. From Condon's house Perrone returned to his hack stand and there saw the O'Brien individual mentioned above. He said to him "That's funny; I never knew anything about that. My wife gets the Home News every day and I never seen anything about it." Perrone told O'Brien about the above incident and it happened to get around, according to Perrone, to a man by the name of "Al the Horseman". Perrone stated that "Al the Horseman" at different times used to come up to his hack stand and at other times he followed the Rosenhain line and is well acquainted with Dr. Condon, Milton Gaglio and Al Reich. It was Perrone's statement that "Al the Horseman" had been driving Gaglio, Condon and Reich home at all hours of the morning prior to the above date. It was Perrone's further statement that "Al the Horseman" happened to take Gaglio home one morning, mentioning Perrone's name to him saying that Perrone had been the one who delivered the note to Dr. Condon. Gaglio was then alleged to have said to Al "Do you know that fellow?" and Al said "Why certainly, he is working the same job with me now." Gaglio said "I thought he was a racketeer." In the course of the next few days, Perrone was seated in the restaurant right beside the hack stand on Mosholu Parkway North. "Al the Horseman" came in with Milton Gaglio and approached Perrone at the table. Shortly thereafter Perrone states that Gaglio said "Now listen, Inspector Bruckman will try to get in touch with you and we don't want them to bother you yet. Is there any possible way you could leave the house for three days?" Perrone looked at him but did not answer him. Gaglio left his number with Perrone stating that he would send him a number by telegraph, and when Perrone would receive it he should know that Gaglio sent it and that it would mean that Perrone should go right out of the house. The number was 2865W. Perrone states that "Al the Horseman" then took Gaglio away, but when Al returned, Al said to him "What does he mean" (meaning Gaglio), "to go away for three days?" and Perrone said "I can't understand him either. I can't go away for three days and leave my wife.

There is no reason for it. If the police want me they know where I am." A few days later Gaglio called at Perrone's house accompanied by a young lady driving from there to a place on Tremont Avenue, where a number of pictures were displayed to Perrone. Gaglio inquired as to whether any of these pictures exhibited to him resembled the man from whom he received the note. Perrone advised that none of these pictures was a favorable resemblance. It was Perrone's recollection that Gaglio showed to him photographs of Abie Agner and Harry Fleischer together with several others unknown to him.

A statement made by Perrone covering the circumstances of the receipt by him of the ransom letter for delivery to Dr. Condon including his experiences with Milton Gaglio, etc. is presently attached to the New York Office file relating to this case. A description of the individual from whom taxi driver Joseph Perrone between 7:45 and 8:30 Saturday evening, March 12, 1932 at the corner of Knox Place and Gun Hill Road, Bronx, New York City, received addressed ransom letter for delivery to Dr. John F. Condon, 2974 Decatur Avenue, Bronx, New York City, is set forth as follows:

Name:	Unknown.
Height:	About 5'9"
Age:	35
Weight:	180 pounds
Build:	Erect and of good build: appeared muscular.
Hair:	Dark blond.
Eyes:	Blue.
Facial features:	Full face, good-looking, clean shaven.
Occupation:	Believed carpenter or mechanic.
Teeth:	Unnoticed.
Eyebrows:	Heavy and same color as hair.

Scars:	No marks or scars apparent.
Ears:	Did not notice whether ears were large, small, or peculiar.
Nationality:	German or Scandinavian.
Speech:	Had German or Scandinavian accent, sounded more like German; pronounced the word "where" as "vere".
Peculiarities:	Appeared to be of a nervous type.
Clothing:	Fairly well dressed; wore a brown soft hat and brown overcoat; did not notice whether gloves were worn; soft hat which fitted nearly straight on head and pinched in front.

Mr. James J. O'Brien, 3190 Rochambeau Avenue, Apartment 58, Bronx, N.Y., on May 22, 1932, was questioned by Sergeant Andrew Zapulsky of the New Jersey State Police, Trenton, N.J., Detective James Fitzgerald of the Jersey City Police Department, together with an Agent of the New York Division Office. O'Brien stated that he is a taxi driver by occupation. He is married and has two children. He has been employed as a taxi driver for five years. According to his own statement he has no criminal record. O'Brien is 38 years of age. In stating his knowledge concerning Dr. Condon, O'Brien indicated that the only thing which he knew about Condon was what he had read in the Bronx Home News, March 8, 1932, to the effect that Condon had offered a reward of $1,000 for information concerning the kidnapers of the Lindbergh baby. This, stated O'Brien, he read about two days previous to the occasion when Joe Perrone received a letter from the kidnapers for delivery to Condon and that on the way over to Condon's house when he stopped his cab at Fordham Road, Mosholu Parkway at the hack stand, the light being against him. Perrone then held the note in his hand and in this position it could be seen by O'Brien. Perrone stated at the time of his holding the letter he said "Here's an easy buck". O'Brien looked at it. The address of Condon was printed in letters about a half inch in size. O'Brien asked Perrone where he had gotten the letter, and Perrone replied "I got it from a fellow around the corner, Knox Place and Gun Hill Road." O'Brien then said "Do you know that letter concerns the kidnaping?" Perrone replied "I did not know that." O'Brien then said "Didn't you ever read the papers lately?" Perrone replied "What papers?" To this O'Brien replied "The Home News." O'Brien did not know Condon or Gaglio nor had he ever had them as fares in his taxicab. Although O'Brien knew of a fellow by the name of "Al the Horseman" he did not know where Al lived nor had he any knowledge of the place where Al hacked his taxicab. He was described as a "drifter" by O'Brien, and was believed by O'Brien to be an Italian. O'Brien stated also that "Al the Horseman" is also known as "Al the Wop" and that he is described as 5'8"; weight 130 to 145 pounds; build thin; age 40 years; complexion dark; eyes dark; clean shaven. Other than the above nothing material could be learned from James J. O'Brien.

On May 22, 1932, Albert Santella, 229 East Kingsbridge Road, Bronx, New York City, employed as a taxi driver made a statement to Sergeant Andrew Zapulsky, Detective James Finn and Agents of the New York Division Office, in which he outlined his acquaintanceship with Dr. Condon. Santella stated that he had seen Dr. Condon around the Bronx for a period of a year or more although he had never taken Condon as a fare in his taxicab. Santella also knew Milton Gaglio and stated that he first met Gaglio and Condon around Max Rosenhain's restaurant in the Bronx. Joseph Perrone had related the circumstances of his receiving ransom note for Dr. Condon to Albert Santella and for this reason Santella was questioned relative thereto. Nothing in addition to information already developed could be obtained from him. Santella recalled that one night Gaglio came around to the restaurant near Fordham Road or Mosholu Parkway desiring to see Joe Perrone, Gaglio stating that he did not know Perrone's address. Santella stated to Gaglio that he thought he would be able to locate him since he knew that Perrone used to hack at Mosholu Parkway and Jerome Avenue. A short while later Santella observed Perrone's taxicab and pointed it out to Gaglio. In the conversation that followed between Gaglio and Perrone, whatever was said was unknown to Santella as he did not hear any part of it. Santella picked Gaglio up on that night at the corner of 188th Street and Grand Concourse. Gaglio spoke to Perrone about ten minutes on that night. It was around 12: or 12:30 o'clock in the morning, the exact date of which was unknown to Santella. This was previous to the time the money was paid in the Lindbergh case to Santella's recollection because on one night prior to April 2, 1932, there was a taxi driver on the corner of Fordham Road and Jerome Avenue whom Santella had never met before. This taxi driver said "I got a good call. I think I am going to Hopewell, N. J. with Dr. Condon." Dr. Condon at that time was in Max Rosenhain's restaurant on Grand Concourse, the exact date Santella could not remember. This cab had waited for Dr. Condon for about two hours; Dr. Condon came out of Rosenhain's and said to the taxi driver, "I am sorry; one of my friends has a car" and Gaglio's car according to Santella was the car in which Condon went to Hopewell, N.J. Other than recalling the incident of Condon's trip from Rosenhain's restaurant to Hopewell, and the circumstances of Perrone's receiving the ransom note from the unknown man at Knox Place and Gun Hill Road, as related by Perrone, Santella has offered no further material information in connection with this case.

On May 21, 1932, August Daniel Hognall, Bronx, New York City, made a statement in connection with this case to Detective Finn; Jersey City Police Department, and Sergeant Andrew Zapulsky of the New Jersey State Police, together with Agents of the New York Division Office. It appears that Hognall, then 44 years of age, was born in Bothenburg, Sweden. He is a citizen of the United States having been for a period of twenty years or more, and a carpenter by trade. At one time he was employed by the Burns Bros. Coal Company at New York City in the capacity of a carpenter. Hognall, a possible suspect, stated that on March 1, 1932 he was at his home in the Bronx. Hognall at one time held a membership in the Scandinavian Society called the "Scandia" which at one time held its meetings in Castle Hall on 149th Street and Mott Avenue, Bronx, New York City. Hognall denied being in the vicinity of Gun Hill Road about 8: o'clock in the evening of any night in March or April 1932, and further stated that he had not been at Gun Hill Road since he lived in Throggs Neck five years prior to May 1932. At one time Hognall resided in Ridgefield, N.J. possibly during the year 1930. During part of that time he was unemployed. While he last resided in New Jersey he came back to the employment of Burns Brothers, after which he moved to New York City when on or about June 1, 1931 he was discharged. Hognall was positive in his statement that no one ever turned over a note for him to deliver. Since it could not be established that Hognall had handled the note above mentioned as had been claimed by an anonymous person, and since no information could be developed to indicate that anyone had paid Hognall to deliver this note in this place, Hognall virtually dropped from the picture for the time being, at least.

On May 25, 1932, Milton Gaglio, 2685 Webb Avenue, Bronx, New York City, appeared at the New York Office of the Division and there made a statement concerning his connections and experiences with this case in the presence of Sergeant Andrew Zapulsky of the New Jersey State

Police; Detective James Finn of the New York City Police Department, as well as agents of this office.

A copy of this statement is presently attached to the New York Office file on this case. With reference to Gaglio's alleged statement to Joseph Perrone, the taxi driver, at the time Perrone deliverd a note to Dr. Condon at his home, 2974 Decatur Avenue, the Bronx, and especially as to Gaglio's supposedly asking Perrone if he had gotten this note at Bainbridge Road and Gun Hill Road, Gaglio stated that when Perrone called at the address Dr. Condon himself came to the door. Perrone then advised Condon that he had a letter for him and when Condon asked Perrone where he had gotten the note, Perrone explained that he had received the same from an unknown man at the corner of Knox Place and Gun Hill road. Gaglio states that Condon then asked Perrone to give him a good description of this man which Perrone complied with. As to this angle, Gaglio stated that he is not clear as to what he, Gaglio, said to Perrone on the above occasion, and Gaglio did not recall having asked Perrone if he had received a note at Bainbridge Avenue and Gun Hill Road. However, stated Gaglio if any such inquiry was made as is alleged by Perrone it was possibly the request by Gaglio for a verification of what he had possibly overheard Perrone state to Condon before he, Gaglio, was advised by Dr. Condon to take care of Perrone on the night of the delivery of this particular ransom letter. In connection with the conflicting statements between Gaglio and Perrone as to whether it was Bainbridge Ave. and Gun Hill Road or Knox Place and Gun Hill Road where Perrone met the unknown man from whom he received the letter, Gaglio has not been at all definite as to just what had been said. It seems possible, however, that Perrone intended the inference that Gaglio may have known where the unknown man who tendered Perrone the letter would contact with him although nothing has been determined to date from Gaglio or other sources which would bear out such an inference. In addition to Gaglio's outlining his experiences and activities in connection with this case together with certain other incidents relating to his personal history and the like, nothing further has been developed from or concerning him that would serve to place him in the picture of this case to the extent, at least, that further suspicion should be directed upon him.

SUMMARY REPORT

In Re

Unknown Subjects

Kidnaping and Murder of
Charles A. Lindbergh, Jr.
(N.Y. File 62-3057).

RANSOM MONEY

-o-

Thomas Fensch

RANSOM MONEY

The actual ransom paid in this case by Dr. John F. Condon amounted to $50,000, the bills comprising this sum numbering 2000 of the $5 denomination; 1500 of the $10 denomination; and 1250 of the $20 denomination. All bills are of the series of 1928. The serial numbers of the ransom bills, with the exception of those bills discovered up to and including January 6, 1934, are listed in the Division booklet recently published. This booklet is based on the United States Treasury Department publication of April 6, 1932, which is the official list of the serial numbers.

All $5 ransom bills included in the above sum are United States notes and bear red seals and red serial numbers. With the exception of eleven bills, whose serial numbers begin with an asterisk (*), the serial numbers of the $5 denomination begin with the letters "A" and "B", ranging in the "A" series from 78000000 to 99000000, and in the "B" series from C0621668 to 78000000. All serial numbers of the $5 denominations are followed by the letter "A".

All of the $10 ransom bills are United States gold certificates. The serial numbers of all certificates of this denomination are preceded by the letter "A", with the exception of two certificates whose serial numbers are preceded by the letter "B", and eighteen, which are preceded by an asterisk (*). Likewise, all serial numbers of the $10 denomination are followed by the letter "A".

The $20 bills in the ransom payment comprised 1000 United States Gold Certificates and 250 Federal Reserve notes. The serial numbers of the Federal Reserve notes are all preceded by the letter "B" and followed by the letter "A", with the exception of one bill, B 00015922*, which is followed by an asterisk (*). The serial numbers of the gold certificates of this denomination are preceded by the letter "A", with the exception of fifteen, whose serial numbers are preceded by an asterisk (*).

The letters "A" and "B", which precede and constitute a part of the serial numbers of the ransom bills, should not be confused with the plate letter appearing on the respective bills. In both the United States Treasury publication of April 6, 1932, and the Division booklet, the plate letters are listed in the extreme left. In making a check on suspected ransom bills, it is not necessary to take the plates letters into consideration.

The $50,000 ransom money paid in this case was prepared for Colonel Lindbergh by Mr. F. D. Barto, a partner in the firm of J. P. Morgan & Company, bankers, 23 Wall Street, New York City. Before turning the money over to Colonel Lindbergh, Mr. Barto obtained the serial numbers and a description of the money. Shortly after March 10, 1932 the ransom money was delivered to the home of Dr. Condon by Colonel Breckinridge. Subsequently, Dr. Condon removed the entire sum to the Fordham Branch of the Corn Exchange Bank & Trust Company for safe-keeping. Just prior to April 2, 1932 the money was again moved, this time to an institution in downtown New York designated by the Morgan firm. On April 2, 1932, the ransom money was again brought to Dr. Condon's home by Colonel Lindbergh and Colonel Breckinridge, and on the same date was brought to St. Raymond's Cemetery by Colonel Lindbergh and Dr. Condon and there paid to "John" by Dr. Condon, as described in another section of this report.

Under date of April 6, 1932, the United States Treasury Department transmitted to the various banking institutions throughout the United States a list of the serial numbers of the currency constituting the ransom payment, with the request that the Treasurer of the United States be notified by telegraph if any of the ransom money was discovered. An effort was made to keep confidential the fact that the authorities had in their possession the serial numbers of the ransom bills, and were endeavoring through the banking institutions to apprehend the guilty parties.

Under date of April 14, 1932, at the request of Colonel Schwarzkopf of the New Jersey State Police, the Division mailed copies of the Treasury Department's publication containing the serial numbers of the ransom bills to various foreign countries.

On April 10, 1932, as the result of a Newark, N. J. bank employee violating this confidence, the serial numbers of the ransom currency were published generally in newspapers throughout the United States, together with the exposure of the fact that all banking institutions were on the look-out for the money.

On May 23, 1932, after the designation of the United States Division of Investigation as the coordinating agency for all Government activity in this case, the New York office of the Division circularized all banking institutions and their branches in Greater New York, advised them of this fact, and requested a close search for the ransom money.

On May 24, 1932, Governor A. Harry Moore of New Jersey, issued a proclamation announcing a reward of $25,000 would be paid for information resulting in the apprehension and conviction of the kidnapers. Under date of May 26, 1932 circular letter announcing the proclamation and containing a description of the individual to whom the ransom money was paid, wee mailed by the Division to all law enforcement officials throughout the United States, at the request of Colonel H. Norman Schwarzkopf.

In June, 1932, the Intelligence Unit of the United States Treasury Department and the New Jersey State Police decided to broaden the search for the ransom money and 100,000 circulars were printed containing the serial numbers of the bills, and announced that the State of New

Jersey had offered a reward of $25,000 for information leading to the arrest and conviction of the guilty persons. Through arrangements with the Chief Post Office Inspector, Washington, D. C., 60,000 of the above circulars were distributed to post offices throughout the United States. The balance were distributed to banking institutions and gasoline filling stations throughout Greater New York. Circulars were also placed in the hands of pari-mutual departments of various race tracks for the purpose of checking funds wagered on horse races.

Subsequent to April 10, 1932, because of the widespread publicity accorded the serial numbers of the ransom money, it appeared possible that the money may have been cached in a safety deposit box. The New York Police Department obtained the names of all persons in New York State who rented safety deposit boxes in March and April, 1932, together with photostatic copies of their signatures, same to be checked against possible suspects.

Under date of April 5, 1933 the President directed by Executive Order that all gold and gold certificates in circulation be surrendered to a Federal Reserve Bank, branch, or member bank on or before May 1, 1933. Following this order, the United States Treasury Department, under date of April 14, 1933, circularized all banking institutions and requested that a close check be made of all gold certificates exchanged or deposited to determine whether they were part of the ransom money. Just prior to May 1, 1933, the New Jersey State Police requested all banks in the State of New Jersey to make a careful check of all gold certificates being surrendered. Likewise the New York City Police made similar arrangements with the Federal Reserve Bank of New York and all chain banking institutions.

Despite the above precautions, an aggregate sum of $3,980 of the ransom money, in gold certificates, was exchanged between April 27, 1933 and May 1, 1933, at three New York City banks, located in the downtown section, within a few blocks of each other. The discovery of this money and of other ransom bills is treated in a subsequent paragraph of this section.

On May 1, 1933 the New York City Police Department distributed 50,000 circulars containing the serial numbers of the ransom bills, with the exception of the gold certificates, to all chain retail establishments in New York City. In addition, a limited supply of small booklets containing the serial numbers was distributed to New York City banking institutions. The circulars announced that the finders of the first one hundred bills would receive rewards of ten dollars each, and the second one hundred bills five dollars each. The appropriation for which the rewards were being paid has recently run out due to the payment of rewards to bank employees. The New York police have advised that to date not a single retail establishment has reported the discovery of a ransom bill. At the present time none of the authorities engaged in the investigation of this case is paying rewards for the discovery of bills, although the $25,000 reward offered by the State of New Jersey is still outstanding.

In August, 1933, the New York Police made arrangements with the Consolidated Gas Company, electric companies, and the Sinclair Oil Company to be on the look-out for ransom bills.

In October, 1933 the New York Police circularized the larger chain retail establishments, including the United Cigar Stores, the Schulte Cigar Stores, Childs and other chain restaurants, retail chain grocery stores, etc., furnishing them with the serial numbers of the ransom bills, with the exception of the gold certificates, and requested a close look-out for the ransom money.

Under date of November 17, 1933 the New York Division office, in order to revive interest in the search for the ransom currency, again circularized all banking institutions and their branches in Greater New York, requesting a close search for the bills. As a result of this circular letter, a large number of banks communicated with the New York office and requested that they be furnished with the serial numbers of the ransom bills. The only lists of serial numbers available were the large 17 x 17 inch circulars in small type, prepared by the New Jersey State Police and these were furnished all banks which made a request. A survey of the situation revealed that the circulars in question were inconvenient for the use of bank tellers who have limited space in which to work. Further, it appeared that the booklets furnished the banks by the New York Police, although convenient in size, were limited as to number, with the result that in most cases a single copy only was available to each bank. Thus, it appears that each bank employee handling money has never been provided with a list of the serial numbers in handy form. Consequently, the Division has published a convenient booklet, which is being distributed to each employee handling money in the banks of Greater New York and Westchester County, which adjoins the upper Bronx. It is also planned to place the booklet in the principal chain retail establishments of Greater New York, and other appropriate places.

Copies of this new booklet are being furnished to each field office of the Division. For obvious reasons it is of extreme importance to keep strictly confidential all investigation concerning the ransom money in this case. The New York Division office has stressed the confidential nature of the matter in all circular letters sent to banks and others.

Instructions were received by all New York banks, pursuant to a Presidential Proclamation, that after midnight, January 17, 1934, gold certificates and gold coin could be accepted only for collection. There appeared to be a distinct possibility that the gold certificates paid as ransom money in this case might be surrendered at some of the New York banks within the time limit specified. Therefore, all banks in Greater New York and their branches were circularized and urged to maintain an extremely close lookout on January 17th for gold certificates which might be ransom bills. In addition to the circular letter, a personal watch was maintained throughout the day at the Federal Reserve Bank and a number of other banks in the Bronx, where it appeared most likely an effort would be made to exchange the ransom bills; however, nothing developed. Subsequently the Order was modified and banks were permitted to accept gold coin and gold certificates as before.

The United States Treasury Department, at the request of the Division, is making an appropriate search to determine whether any of the ransom money has been returned to the Treasury through the surrender of gold certificates and the retirement of worn out and mutilated currency.

All ransom money which has turned up to date in this case is in the custody of Mr. Hugh McQuillan, Special Agent in Charge, Bureau of Internal Revenue, United States Treasury Department, New York City. The practice of giving Mr. McQuillan custody of the money was established during the joint investigation conducted in the years 1932 and 1933 by the New York Police, the New Jersey State Police and the Intelligence Unit. The practice has been to redeem a ransom bill whenever discovered, with another bill of the same denomination.

For the information of all Division offices, the Division under date of December 15, 1933, advised the New York office that "confidential blue slips might be used for the purpose of reimbursing holders of any of the ransom notes, with an explanation as to what the expenditure represents. The notes, of course, as collected will be maintained in a safe at the New York office and the greatest of care should be exercised to see that they are maintained in safety and an accurate report kept concerning their serial numbers and descriptions as they will ultimately be returned to the United States Treasury."

Among the theories advanced in this case has been that of Lieutenant James Finn of the New York City Police, assigned to the case since its inception, to the effect that the unknown individual passing the ransom money usually carries only one bill at a time on his person, and that he keeps the bill folded three ways in his vest pocket. Lieutenant Finn has arrived at this opinion because of the fact, as he states it to be, that all of the individual ransom bills discovered bore creases indicating the three way fold. It appears, however, that most of the individual bills discovered were "floaters" and also that nearly every old bill has the same creases. The theory of Lieutenant Finn that the guilty person or persons are making the creases therefore appears to be largely speculation.

A number of the ransom bills which turned up in November and December, 1933, apparently bore grease marks or an oily substance of some nature. These bills were examined by Dr. Alexander O. Gettler, Chief Medical Examiner, Bellevue Hospital, New York City, who reported as follows:

"The chemical analysis of the stains removed from the three bills which you submitted to me indicate that the stains are mainly of animal or vegetable fat. The consistency of the purified material indicates that it is composed of glycerine asters of the saturated fatty acids."

It has also been reported by Lieutenant Finn that the large sums of the ransom money which turned up in April and May, 1933, bore a strong odor or stench, possibly indicating that the money had been buried in the ground. To date no effort has been made to determine the cause of this odor.

From time to time since the payment of the ransom, newspaper dispatches and unofficial reports have indicated that some of the ransom money had made its appearance in London, Paris, Berlin, Antwerp, Geneva, Montreal, and other foreign points, but official inquiry in each instance resulted in the finding that all news dispatches and similar reports were without foundation in fact. There have likewise been numerous unfounded reports concerning the appearance of the Lindbergh ransom money at New York City and vicinity. In this connection, on May 19, 1932 the New York office was advised by Colonel Lindbergh and Colonel Schwarzkopf to the effect that they had received a confidential report from a newspaper in New York City that George A. McManus, well known underworld character in New York, who was tried for the murder of Arnold Rothstein, a notorious gambler, had purchased $40,000 of the Lindbergh money for $16,000 and had the same in a safety deposit box in a bank believed to be the Harmon National Bank, 44th Street and Broadway, New York City; also, that he had a woman, Pauline Spruce alias Haddock alias Devoe at the Windsor or Queens Hotel in Montreal, Canada, passing some of the five dollar ransom bills. An investigation at New York City by the Division did not locate a safety deposit box in the name of George A. McManus, nor could his picture be identified at any of the banks in the vicinity of Times Square as a likeness of any person who then had a safety deposit box in any of the institutions. Investigation at Montreal likewise failed to disclose that the Spruce woman under that name or any other known alias, had registered in any of the Montreal hotels during April or May, 1932. She was unknown to the Montreal Police and no information in that vicinity could be obtained concerning her.

For the information of the various field offices of the Division and to prevent any possible error in the checking of the serial numbers of the ransom bills, it is stated that shortly after the payment of the ransom, a booklet was issued by the Charleston National Bank of Charleston, West Virginia, purporting to contain the serial numbers of the ransom notes used in the Lindbergh case,. A review of this booklet disclosed several errors in the serial numbers, and the distribution was stopped but not before a number of them had been distributed.

Two days after the payment of the ransom, one of the twenty dollar ransom bills was discovered at the East River Savings Bank at New York City in the regular course of the bank's daily business. From that time on until the present date, Lindbergh ransom bills of all denominations aggregating $4,390 have been discovered within the metropolitan area of New York City. These particular ransom bills have been discovered at approximately fifty-five different places within the city of New York and in but few instances in adjacent territory.

Listed herein below in chronological order is a resume of the known history of each ransom bill discovered, detailing the significant facts developed. In this connection, the information concerning ransom bills discovered prior to November, 1933 was obtained from the New York City Police Department. Thereafter joint investigations were conducted by representatives of the New York Police, the New Jersey State Police, and the New York Division office.

$20 Bill—Serial No. B04173050

This bill was received on Monday afternoon, April 4, 1932, or on the morning of April 5, 1932, by the East

River Savings Bank located at 95th Street and Amsterdam Ave., New York City. A list of the depositors of $20 currency notes in that bank for the dates mentioned was obtained, after which all such depositors were interviewed. In some cases satisfactory explanations were furnished by depositors as to the source of $20 bills, in other instances depositors had received the currency as salary on March 31, 1932 and April 4, 1932. No information of any material value has been developed by this Division to date concerning this particular bill.

$5 Bill—Serial No. B26909389

This bill was deposited at the Bank of the Manhattan Co., 40 Wall Street, New York City, by the F. G. Shattuck Company, owner of Schraffts Stores, New York City, on April 14, 1932 and was included in a consolidated deposit from five branch stores as follows: 31 Broadway—181 Broadway—281 Broadway—48 Broadway and 61 Maiden Lane, lower Manhattan, New York City, and was apparently received in the preceding day's business. Nothing further concerning the source of this bill is known.

$5 Bill—Serial No. A85819751

This bill was received at the Chase National Bank, 7th Avenue and 41st Street, New York City, in a deposit of the receipts of Bickford's Restaurant, 225 West 42nd Street, New York City, on May 19, 1932. It was apparently received at Bickford's between the hours of 2:30 P.M. May 18, 1932 and 6 A.M. May 19, 1932 and is believed to have been received by Peter Reilly, night cashier at Bickford's, about 3:00 A.M. May 19, 1932. Reilly did not receive any $5 bills during his period of duty until 3:00 A.M. on May 19, 1932, and between that time and 6:00 A.M. received approximately five bills of the $5 denomination.

The bill in question was possibly presented by an unknown man apparently of Irish, Italian, or possibly American extraction, about 30 years of age; 5'8" tall, weighing about 150 pounds; with dark brown hair and eyes, tall flabby face; dark complexion; mild manner; had appearance of taxi driver or chauffeur, dressed in shabby clothes, old grey cap and grey suit. This individual came into Bickford's Restaurant, purchased 15¢ worth of food, and presented his food check and a $5 bill to Cashier Reilly. This is the only instance during Reilly's period of duty as cashier on May 19, 1932 which aroused any attention on his part to a $5 bill received by him. Reilly thereafter viewed various photographs contained in the records of the Bureau of Identification, New York City Police Department, but he was unable to find any photograph there which resembled favorably the person who came into Bickford's restaurant during his period of duty, May 19, 1932 and gave to him during that period a $5 bill.

$5 Bill—serial No. B52611313

This bill was received at the Chase National Bank, 18 Pine St., New York City, on June 6, 1932. On that date one of the messengers of the Chase National Bank at the above address, presented a note for $25.11 which had been received for collection from the Ozone Park National Bank, Ozone Park, Long Island, N. Y. to the proprietor of the Brilliant Restaurant, 151 Canal St., New York City, at approximately 11:00 A.M. and received in payment therefor two $10 notes, one $5 note and 11¢ in change. When this money was turned into the Chase National Bank, one of its note tellers discovered this particular $5 ransom bill. The Brilliant Restaurant, located at the entrance to the Manhattan Bridge, at the corner of Canal Street and the Bowery, is quite a large restaurant and caters to a considerable transient trade. Between 7:00 A.M. and 11:00 A.M. on June 6, 1932, the cashier of the Brilliant Restaurant received six $5 bills; no attention was paid, however, to the persons passing any of these six bills. A description of the man "John" to whom the ransom was paid in this case, was given to the cashier of the Brilliant Cafeteria after which she advised that a man answering this description visited the Brilliant Restaurant every other day. That suspected person usually partook of some coffee and cakes but had not, to the knowledge of the cashier, previously given her a $5 bill in payment for same; he usually paying his meal checks with small change. On the day following, June 7, 1932, this man who was believed to answer the description of "John" appeared again at the Brilliant Restaurant. He was taken to New York City Police Headquarters and there questioned during the course of which he gave his name as William Heilewertz, 19 Orchard St., Brooklyn, N. Y.

He was then searched, and at the time had 7¢ on his person. After the investigation of this individual, the New York Police were satisfied that he was not the individual "John" and that he did not pass the bill in question whereupon he was released. Heilewertz is described as a person about 40 years of age, 5'6 1/2"; 145 pounds; high cheek bones; brown hair; Polish, and has no criminal record at New York City Police Headquarters. No other ransom bills have turned up at this restaurant since that time to the knowledge of the New York City Police Department or this Division.

$5 Bill—serial No. B48612232

This bill was discovered at the First National Bank, 52 Wall Street, New York City, on May 23, 1932. It was included in a deposit made on May 20, 1932 by the Consolidated Gas Co., which deposit represented the combined deposits of the Consolidated Gas Co., the Standard Gas Co., and the New Amsterdam Gas Co., all of New York City. The investigation developed that this ransom bill was accepted by one of 65 collectors employed by the Consolidated Gas Co., 157 Hester St., New York City, on May 19, 1932. Further inquiry revealed that the bill had been obtained from Harry Kushner, a gas consumer located at 150 Orchard Street, New York City, in payment of a gas bill amounting to $5.95 at 10:30 A.M. May 19, 1932. This bill was received by Kushner from Max Rubinstein, 20 Allen St., New York City, who conducts a drygoods store in the basement of 150 Orchard St. No further information could be developed concerning this bill or the possible source from which obtained.

$5 Bill—serial No. B-53222632

This bill was received at the Central Hanover Bank and Trust Company, Madison Avenue and 42nd Street, New York City, on May 19, 1932, in a deposit of the receipts of the Sinclair Refining Co., 42nd Street and Mill Ave., East New York, Brooklyn, N. Y. It was received with other moneys from various customers of the Sinclair Oil Refining Company at the Sinclair Station on 62nd Street and Mill Ave., Brooklyn, N. Y. on May 17, 1932. No information concerning the source from which obtained other than this has been developed.

$5 Bill—B50522787

This bill was placed on deposit with the Drydock Savings Bank, 341 Bowery, New York City, on June 16, 1932 by one Martha Sohn, 1025 East 167th Street, Bronx, New York City. It was included in a deposit of $110 in cash, a check for $10 together with an additional check of unknown amount, representing a dividend of the Gulf Sulphur Company. It was found that Martha Sohn is a person of good reputation and character and nothing could be obtained that she had any possible connection with this case in any manner. The only possible source from which this bill could have been obtained by Martha Sohn as stated by her was that she probably received it from J. Lynn and Company, 46 Bond Street, New York City, as salary for services rendered. Further inquiry at the offices of J. Lynn and Company indicate that the monies given to Martha Sohn as salary had been obtained by Lynn and Company from the National City Bank, Bowery and Bond Street, New York City. No further information concerning it could be developed.

$5 Bill—A44358167

On June 30, 1932 the Assistant Postmaster at Mt. Vernon, N. Y. advised the Mt. Vernon Police Department, that Postal Clerk F. W. Brown, Mt. Vernon, N. Y. in chare of C.O.D. parcel post department, reported the discovery of this bill in the collections of Gilbert R. Anderson, sub-letter-carrier, employed at the Mt. Vernon Post Office to deliver C.O.D. parcel post packages. This bill was received by Anderson from one of two persons, Max Halpern, 25 Alameda St., Mt. Vernon or Edward A. Trotter, 358 Onion Ave., Mt. Vernon, N. Y. On June 30, 1932, Max Halpern paid sub-letter carrier Anderson $24.90 which was due on a parcel post package delivered to him on that date and paid this amount to Anderson with a $20 bill and a $5 bill. The $5 bill he stated he obtained from his petty cash box which was in charge of Peter Odomrik, 23 years of age, of Yonkers, N. Y. who is employed by Halpern. Odomrik stated that he had had this $5 bill in his petty cash box for two or three weeks prior to June 30, 1932 and that it was probably received in payment of a check cashed at that time by the Mt. Vernon Trust Co. of Mt. Vernon, N. Y. The check cashed by Odomrik at that time was in the amount of $10 and in payment therefor Odomrik recalled having received two $5 bills. The $5 bill other than that included in the petty cash box in charge of Peter Odomrik, was given by Halpern to his wife, and upon inspection was found not to be one of the ransom bills of this case. Edward A. Trotter, Mt. Vernon, N. Y. recalled that he had given the postal carrier $5 in payment of a $1.69 charge due on a parcel post package delivered to and received by him on June 30, 1932, and stated that this particular bill had been received by him in payment of a salary check which was cashed at a bank, name not recalled, on Broadway, Yonkers, N. Y. shortly prior to June 30, 1932. He was, however, unable to state whether the $5 bill given by him to the postal carrier was the $5 bill in question.

$5 bill—No. B-55637129

This bill was received at the Manufacturers Trust Co., 8th Avenue and 34th Street, New York City, on August 2, 1932, and was contained in a deposit made with that bank on that date by the West End Avenue Corporation of 325 West 71st Street, New York City.

The West End Avenue Corporation operates the buildings at 245 East 75th Street and 325 West 71st Street, both of which are buildings containing furnished apartments. The deposit of the West End Avenue Corporation of August 2, 1932 was made by Joseph Reville of 325 West 71st Street who is employed by the corporation for the purpose of collecting the rents and managing both apartment houses for the company. Reville recalled that this deposit was made up of money collected by him as rents from various persons residing on both premises. A number of the tenants were thereafter interviewed concerning the possible source from which this bill had been obtained but further than recalling that they had given Reville one or more bills of $5 denomination, nothing could be added which would seem of material assistance in this investigation.

$5 Bill—No. B-38146929

This bill was received by the Chase National Bank, 18 Pine St., New York City on July 13, 1932 from Lapham, Potter and Holden, stock brokers, 44 Pine Street, New York City. It was included in a deposit of $500, made in the afternoon of that date by the above stock brokers. At Lapham, Potter and Holden, it was learned that each morning of their business day they receive $500 from the Chase National Bank, and deposit the remainder of it each evening with the same bank. On July 13, 1932, Lapham, Potter and Holden received $500 from the Chase National Bank and deposited the same $500 in the evening as no cash had been paid out on that particular day. On July 13, 1932 the Chase National Bank at the above address received over $1,000,000 in currency from the Federal Reserve Bank of New York and it was indicated that the above mentioned $5 ransom bill was apparently a part of that money. Other than this no information could be obtained as to the original source of this bill.

$5 Bill B-33379453

This bill was found in a deposit made by the Eastern Parkway Bedford Corporation of 387 Eastern Parkway, Brooklyn, N. Y. in the Central Hanover Bank and Trust Co., 70 Broadway, New York City, on August 16, 1932. An investigation at the office of the Eastern Parkway Bedford Corporation indicated that this particular bill which was the only $5 bill in the Eastern Parkway Bedford Corporation deposit of August 16, 1932 had been received a few days previously from Albert Chamberlain of 1536 Bedford Ave., Brooklyn, N. Y. Chamberlain who had shortly prior to August 16, 1932, paid his rent to the above corporation evidently included this $5 bill in the money paid by him. He conducts a candy store at 1536 Bedford Avenue, Brooklyn, N. Y. and when interviewed could not recall the source from which this ransom bill was obtained.

$5 Bill B-41589162

This bill was found in a deposit made at the First National Bank, 2 Wall Street, New York City, for the Consolidated Gas Co., 157 Hester St., New York City, on August 24, 1932. Investigation at the Consolidated Gas Company failed to reveal any information concerning this bill or the possible source from which it had been received.

$5 Bill—B-53198947

This bill was discovered at 12:30 P.M. September 14, 1932 at the Central Hanover Bank and Trust Co., 224 West 47th Street, New York City in a deposit made on that date with this bank by the Palace Café, 151 W. 46th Street, New York City. Investigation indicates that this bill was received at the Palace Café from a customer between the hours of 6 A.M. September 13 and 6 A.M. September 14, 1932. No further information could be developed to indicate the possible source from which this particular ransom bill was obtained. This particular café is patronized for the most part by theatrical people and the class of persons usually found in the mid-town section of New York City.

$5 Bill—B-37032270

This bill was received on October 6, 1932 by the Chase

National Bank, 75 Maiden Lane, New York City. It was a part of the cash deposit made by the Perrin Durbrow Life Associates, Inc., 75 Maiden Lane, New York City, on October 6, 1932 at about 2 P.M. This bill was traced to a cash deposit on a thrift account, made on October 4, 1932 to the Perrin Durbrow Life Associates, Inc., by one David Barry (also spelled Bari), 3975 Sedgwick Ave., Bronx, New York City. Barry, upon thorough questioning, advised that this bill had been given to him by Joseph Koretsky, his employer, 1860 Broadway, New York City, who later confirmed this allegation in a satisfactory manner. Both Barry and Koretsky denied any connection with the Lindbergh case and nothing was developed to implicate either of them. Koretsky stated that he withdrew $45 from the Public National Bank and Trust Co., New York City, on September 28, 1932, in which amount the $5 bill in question was included. Submission of numerous handwriting specimens of Barry to Albert D. Osborn and Albert S. Osborn, examiners of questioned documents, Woolworth Building, New York City, resulted in the expression of an opinion from each indicating that although Barry's handwriting bore marked resemblance to the handwriting appearing in the Lindbergh extortion letters, various dissimilarities were also apparent. In the opinion of the Messrs. Osborn, the comparison of the handwriting of Barry with the original ransom notes did not justify Barry's arrest. No further information could be developed concerning the previous source from which this bill was obtained.

$5 Bill—B-40970075

This bill was discovered October 15, 1932 at the Federal Reserve Bank of New York, Liberty and Nassau Streets, New York City. It had been received by the Federal Bank of New York from the Irvington National Bank and Trust Co., Irving-on-Hudson, N.Y. On August 13, 1932 this bill was received at the Irvington National Bank and Trust Co. in a deposit made by one Ernest Behrens of 106 Main St., Irvington, N. Y. a building contractor. The bill was deposited in the Irvington Bank on August 13, 1932 by Behrens with other currency, approximately $56 in cash, together with a check of $20. Ernest Behrens recalled that he received this bill from his sister, Emily Behrens of 104 Main Street, Irvington, prior to August 13, 1932. Emily had a recollection of receiving the bill from the Westchester Savings Bank at Tarrytown, N. Y., where she had an account, and from which institution she did on August 12, 1932 make a cash withdrawal, receiving four bills of $5 denomination. She remembered giving her brother, Ernest, one of these $5 bill in change for a $20 bill. After a careful study of the possible sources from which the bill in question could have been obtained, Miss Behrens was quite positive that the $5 ransom bill represented by the serial number listed above, was obtained by her from the Westchester Savings Bank, Tarrytown, N. Y. on August 12, 1932. Other than this no information could be obtained concerning the previous source from which the bill had been received.

$10 Bill—A74137326

This bill was discovered in the Guaranty Trust Company, Madison Avenue and 60th Street, New York City, on October 22, 1932. It was deposited with other funds on that date by the Adventurer's Club of New York City. Investigation developed that the Adventurer's Club on or above October 20, 1932 had given a dinner at the Hotel Aster, 44th Street and Broadway, and that this bill apparently had been tendered to the Adventurer Club by someone who purchased an admission to attend the dinner. Nothing further concerning it was developed that would serve to indicate source from which this note had been obtained.

Thomas Fensch

$5 Bill—B-48602813

This bill was found in a deposit made by Moe Levy and Son, clothiers, 4141 Broadway, New York City, with the Chase National Bank, 575 Fifth Ave., New York City, on October 23, 1932. This particular bill had certain pencil marks inscribed on one side thereof and it was learned that same were placed there by a collector of the Bronx Edison Co., 555 East Tremont Ave., Bronx, New York City. Investigation at the Bronx Edison Company disclosed that this ransom note had previously been tendered to it in payment of an electric light bill by H. Levincat, 1663 Washington Ave., Bronx, New York City, who when questioned stated that he had received it in payment for a meal purchased by a person, name or description unknown, at his restaurant located at Second Avenue and East Street, New York City. Other than this no further information could be developed to indicate the previous person who had handled this bill.

$20 Bill No. B04052604

This bill was discovered in the Central Hanover Bank and Trust Company, 70 Broadway, New York City, on October 26, 1932. It had been received in a deposit made on the previous date by Childs Restaurant, 570 Lexington Ave., New York City. Nothing has been developed to date to indicate the source from which this bill had previously been obtained. The only information at Childs Restaurant concerning it, is that it was apparently received from one of the many persons who patronized this restaurant on October 25, 1932.

$10 Bill—A73682326

This bill was discovered in the National City Bank,

main office, New York City, on October 28, 1932. It had been received in a deposit made on the previous date with this bank by the Brooklyn Edison Co., Brooklyn, N. Y. and had apparently been accepted by the Brooklyn Edison Company from one of its many sources of collection. No information had been received to date that would materially assist in tracing this bill further.

$10 Bill A-70412014

This bill was found at 10:15 A.M. October 29, 1932 in the Guaranty Trust Co., New York City, and had been received on that date in a deposit made by the United Cigar Stores Co., New York City. Further investigation developed only that this particular bill had been accepted from an unknown person who purchased a quantity of cigars in the United Cigar Store No. 1017, located at 118-02 Jamaica Ave., Queens, N. Y. on Thursday morning, October 27, 1932, between 7:00 A.M. and 12:00 Noon.

$5 Bill B-34534059

This bill was discovered at 10:00 A. M. November 11, 1932 in the Central Hanover Bank, 70 Broadway, New York City. It was found in a deposit made on that date by Childs Restaurant, 570 Lexington Ave., New York City. This bill, which is the second ransom note to make its appearance at this Childs Restaurant, was contained in a package containing $625, representing the receipts of this restaurant, from 8:00 A.M. November 10, 1932 to 1:30 P. M. November 10, 1932. This package was delivered to the Central Hanover Bank by the Armored Service and was intact at the time of its delivery. No information concerning the identity of the person who may have passed the bill could be secured from the different clerks on duty at this particular Childs Restaurant during the time in which this bill was accepted there.

$5 Bill—B-57929279

This bill was found at 3:10 P.M. November 10, 1932 in the Fifth Avenue Branch of the National City Bank, Fifth Avenue and 23rd Street, New York City. It was discovered among four $5 bills offered to a clerk at that bank for exchange by a woman named Anna Selman, Spring Valley, N. Y. who is a cashier employed by H. Lambert, 254 Fifth Ave., New York City.

Investigation in the store located at 254 Fifth Ave., New York City and interview with H. J. Cohen, the manager, and Miss Selman, developed no information concerning the identity of the salesman from whom Miss Selman received this particular bill although she was under the impression that between 11:00 A.M. and 2:15 P.M. November 10, 1932, which is the busiest time of Miss Selman's duty in the store, there was a hosiery sale in progress and that during this periods she received a number of $5 bills; other than this she could offer no further information concerning this particular ransom bill.

$5 Bill—B-35054555

This bill was found in the business of the Brooklyn Edison Company, Surf Avenue, Coney Island, Brooklyn, N. Y. on November 19, 1932 in a payment of an electric light bill for the premises located at 1967 East 92nd Street, Brooklyn, H. Y. Mr. Louis Alfenbein of these premises who tendered this bill advised that the same had been withdrawn by him from the Bowery Savings Bank, 42nd Street and Lexington Avenue, New York City, on October 28, 1932. Thereafter investigation was conducted at the Bowery Savings Bank at this address in New York City but nothing was learned concerning the source from which the bill had previously been secured.

$5 Bill—B52374914

This bill was discovered at 2:30 P. M. November 21, 1932 in the Times Square Branch of the Chase National Bank, 7th Avenue and 41st Street, New York City, in a deposit made on that date by the Great Western Beef Co., 591 Ninth Avenue, New York City, at 2:00 P.M. same date. The cashier of the Great Western Beef Company who made the deposit, recalled that the deposit consisted of $26 in currency which represented the sales of the beef company for Saturday, November 19, 1932 and $50 in currency received from the Sheridan Cafeteria, 223 West 36th Street, New York City, in payment of a worthless check. The proprietor of the above store advised that 1,100 customers came into his place of business on Saturday, November 19, 1932, and in view thereof he was unable to state the possible source from which the bill had been obtained. He also advised that he was unable to recall the source from which the bill may have been received by him except that it was apparently part of the receipts of Saturday, November 19, 1932.

$5 Bill—A-56258526

This bill was discovered in the Times Square Branch of the Chase National Bank, 7th Ave. and 41st St., New York City, on November 29. It was part of a $50 deposit made on this date with this bank by the Minsky Burlesque Theatre, West 42nd Street, New York City. The deposit consisted of three $5 bills and twenty five singles. Investigation developed that this deposit was part of the receipts of Friday, November 25, 1932, Saturday, November 26, 1932 and

Sunday, November 27, 1932 of the Republic Theatre, West 42nd Street, New York City, which is also owned by the Mirth Theatrical Company. Nothing has been developed to indicate the source from which this bill had previously been obtained. It appears likely that it was tendered by someone attending a burlesque show at the Republic Theatre on one of the above mentioned dates.

$5 Bill—No. B-50669762

This bill was found in the Central Hanover Bank and Trust Company, 70 Broadway, New York City, on December 6, 1932. It was contained in a deposit made by the Edwards Sport Shop, 111 Nassau Street, New York City, on December 5, 1932. This bill was among the cash receipts of the Edwards Sport Shop at the above address on the date previous. Investigation which followed thereafter at the Edwards Shop failed to develop any information which would throw light on the person who passed the particular ransom bill, nor could there be learned any indication of the source from which it had been obtained.

$10 Bill—No. A-45271903

This bill was discovered in the Guaranty Trust Co., 140 Broadway, New York City on December 22, 1932. It was contained in a deposit made by the Whelan Drug Store at 1490 Third Ave., corner 84th Street, New York City on the day previous. Investigation there developed that the bill had been received by the store, apparently from a customer. Nothing further concerning this bill could be learned.

$10 Bill—No. 13447722

This bill was found on March 3, 1933 in the Guaranty

Trust Co., 180 Broadway, New York City. It was contained in a $50 deposit made on that date with this bank by the United Cigar Store, #492, 504 Third Ave., New York City. Inquiry revealed that this bill had been received at the United Cigar Store on March 1, 1933 between the hours of 12:00 Noon and 1:00 P.M. It was learned from the manager, Philip Alsofrom, who was on duty during that period, that he received this particular bill from an unknown man whom he described as being about 6' tall, 40years of age, light complexion, long thin face, and who wore a soft hat and dark clothing. This man was not a regular customer, and in the recollection of the manager, had never been in the store before. He does not believe he would know the man if he saw him again.

$20 Bill—B-03525275

This bill was discovered in the First National Bank, 52 Wall Street, New York City, on April 12, 1933. It was contained in a deposit of $32,275 made with this bank on the above date by the Consolidated Gas Company, 157 Hester St., New York City, and more particularly, in a bundle of $350 which had been counted and strapped at the Consolidated Gas Company on April 11, 1933. Investigation developed that on April 11, 1933 the Consolidated Gas Company, received their payroll from the National City Bank, 137 East 14th St., New York City, out of which the various employees were paid. A number of these employees thereafter came to the Cashier of the Consolidated Gas Company for the purpose of having $20 bills changed. The payroll received from the National City Bank on the above date had been taken from accumulated money at the bank. Investigation concerning this bill failed to develop any information of value with respect to its source before reaching the bank.

$10 Bill A-27452504

This bill was discovered in the Federal Reserve Bank, New York City, on April 13, 1933. It was included in a deposit of $25,250, made on this date by the Public National Bank, Grand and Havemeyer Streets, Brooklyn, N. Y. Further inquiry revealed that this ransom bill had been contained in a $250 bundle of gold certificates included in the $25,250 deposit. The bills comprising the $250 bundle were an accumulation of gold certificates received by the Public National Bank between March 26, 1933 and April 11, 1933. No information of material value has been developed to date which would indicate in any way the identity of the previous holder of this ransom bill.

$10 Bill—A-72061393

This bill was discovered on April 14, 1933 in the Federal Reserve Bank of New York. It was included in a $4,000 deposit on this date by the Manufacturers Trust Co., branch office, Columbus Circle and 59th Street, New York City. Investigation indicated that this bill was among an accumulation of gold certificates deposited in the above branch of the Manufacturers Trust Company between the dates of April 4 and April 11, 1933. No information of any value other than this was obtained.

$10 Bill—A-68440693

This bill was found in the Federal Reserve Bank of New York, Liberty and Nassau Streets, New York City, on April 19, 1933. It was a part of a deposit made with this bank on April 13, 1933 by the Fifth Avenue branch of the Chase National Bank, 5th Avenue and 23rd Street, New York City. Inquiry concerning it indicated that the bill was included in a package of $500 in currency which had been counted, sorted and wrapped by the head receiving teller, Chase National Bank, on April 11, 1933, and which had been forwarded to the Federal Reserve on April 13, 1933. This amount represented a deposit made by the Union Dime Savings Bank, 6th Avenue and 40th Street, New York City. It was learned at the Union Dime Savings Bank that the bill in question was one of the gold certificates accumulated at this bank between April 4, and April 11, 1933, and further than this no information could be obtained, concerning the person who had previously held it.

$10 Bill—A-42040299

This bill was found in the Federal Reserve Bank of New York, New York City, on April 22, 1933. It was contained a deposit of $6,000 made with the Federal Reserve Bank on April 18, 1933 by the Chemical Bank and Trust Co., Broadway and 73rd Street, New York City. Inquiry indicated this bill had been received at the Chemical Bank about 2:00 P.M. April 18, 1933. A search of the deposit tickets was made at the chemical Bank, and the names of six depositors from one of whom it was thought this ransom bill was received, were obtained. Interview of the six depositors developed that on April 16, 1933, J. H. Adams, 2152 Broadway at 75th Street, a poultry and meat dealer, and one of the depositors in question, sent an employee, John Cooper of 259 West 234th Street to the Chemical Bank with the $150 deposit. It appeared, from the investigation of this angle, that Cooper had made the deposit in which the ransom bill was found.

Further inquiry disclosed that Miss Kay, 57 Wadsworth Terrace, Washington Heights, New York City, cashier in the employ of J. H. Adams, remembered receiving this bill on April 18, 1933 from an unknown woman, about 35 years of age, 5'6" tall, 135 pounds, medium dark complexion, who spoke with an accent which Miss Kay believed to be French. The woman left the store after having purchased a small quantity of meat; she wasn't seen at this place of business prior or subsequent to that date. Other than this no information was obtained.

$5 Bill—No. B-56667794-A

This bill was discovered in the First National Bank, main office, New York City on April 27, 1933. Investigation following its appearance there traced it into the possession of one Paul Yakutis (also spelled Youkutis), proprietor of a rooming house, where he also resides, at 234 East 18th Street, New York City. Investigation by representatives of the Intelligence Unit, and the New York City Police Department developed that Yakutis had made long distance telephone calls to a person named J. Fries at Youngsville, N. Y. It was ascertained from the Youngsville Postmaster that Fries had worked in that vicinity but was not well known. The investigation further developed that a person named J. Fries worked on the Lindbergh home as a steam fitter at which time he roomed with a farmer in Hopewell named Hurley, whose son also worked on the Lindbergh home as laborer and after the house was completed, he acted as caretaker for about a week while Whately, the butler, and his wife were at Englewood. It appears that the New Jersey State Police had been making efforts to check up on all persons employed in the construction of the Lindbergh house but Fries was not located. An undercover man was placed by the New York City Police Department in the Yakutis home and arrangements were made to observe all phone messages coming in or out of the house. Further efforts were made to trace the steam fitter, Fries, and through a labor union of which he was a member, he was located in Connecticut where he satisfactorily explained his activities to the police. After his activities had been observed by the police for a week, he was taken to Police Headquarters at New York City and questioned, as a result of which it is reported they were convinced he had no connection with the case and that the source of the $5 bill he tendered to the Gas Company could not be traced further.

Additional details of the investigation in this respect have not been received, and this matter will be given further attention.

(Approximately one page here is partially garbled and can not be fully deciphered. The text describes 50 $10. gold certificates apparently found at a Federal Reserve Bank. The depositor was the Manufacturers Hanover Bank and detailed investigations there could not determine how the Lindbergh ransom money was dposited there, then subsequently deposited at the Federal Reserve Bank.) and likewise failed to reveal which deposit slip of those received at the bank during the dates in question, was used to effect the exchange of the ransom money for other money. Recently, the New York Division Office obtained from the Manufacturers Trust Company a list of depositors who deposited amounts of $500 or more between the dates of April 21st and April 29, 1933, and an effort will be made to determine the identity of the person who passed the ransom bills and the name used on the deposit slip.

```
A 4822 0403 A    A 4810 2958 A
A 5233 8174 A    A 4656 9655 A
A 5697 5901 A    A 2188 1440 A
A 3802 8467 A    A 6842 6532 A
A 7421 3743 A    A 6412 4620 A
A 3432 4054 A    A 7782 1741 A
A 5828 4160 A    A 7207 3453 A
A 6930 5762 A    A 7711 0135 A
A 7716 7793 A    A 6189 9785 A
```

```
A 5888 2706 A    A 6850 0707 A
A 7355 9218 A    A 3766 9650 A
A 4459 4492 A    A 5585 0795 A
A 3021 3831 A    A 3259 9257 A
```

These bills were found on May 1, 1933 at the Federal Reserve Bank of New York, Liberty and Nassau Streets, New York City. Investigation developed that the above mentioned bills were included in a deposit of $113,350.00 received from the Chemical National Bank and Trust Company, main office, Broadway and Cortlandt Street, New York City, on April 29, 1933. The bills in question were apparently contained in a separate package of $50,000.00 in gold certificates, made up in the Chemical National Bank by Mr. Gilbert Yates. Each receiving teller at the Chemical National Bank was questioned with reference to the above bills but none could furnish any information concerning the person who deposited or exchanged the bills. The investigation by the New Jersey State Police and the Intelligence Unit developed that the ransom bills were probably received at the Chemical Bank on April 28, 1933, on which date there were 110 depositors. The investigation developed no information of material value and failed to disclose the name used on the deposit slip. It is the intention of the New York Division Office to make a further check as to these ransom bills.

On Saturday, April 29, 1935, twenty-four $10 Gold certificates of the Lindbergh ransom money were discovered by a counter at the Federal Reserve Bank of New York, Liberty and Nassau Streets, New York City. These bills had been included in a deposit of $153,500 made, by the Chemical National Bank and Trust Co., Cortlandt Street and Broadway, New York City, on April 28, 1933. Nothing was developed at the Chemical National Bank from any of the tellers, which would indicate the identity of the person who deposited or exchanged these bills. Investigation by the New York

Police developed that the ransom bills were probably received at the Chemical National Bank on April 27, 1933, on which date there were 41 depositors. The 24 ransom bills were wrapped as follows:

One package of $1,000 in which was contained a $10 ransom bill, No. A 7722 9167, with the initial "G" thereon. The teller at the bank who was represented by the initial "G" was thereafter questioned thoroughly but he could furnish no information relative to the depositor of this bill.

A second package of $1,000 containing seven ransom bills was wrapped by a teller having the initial "M." This teller likewise could impart no information which would be of assistance in determining the person who made the deposit. The numbers of the ransom bills contained in this package are as follows:

A 3431 0684 A   A 5549 8743 A
A 7774 0948 A   A 2018 7949 A
A 7588 5670 A   A 0111 4064 A
A 6952 6422 A

A third package of $1,000 contained 16 ransom bills, and was wrapped by a person having the initial "G" who, upon questioning, could furnish no information relative to the source from which same had been obtained. The following ransom bills were contained in this package:

A 1826 9432 A   A 5192 7257 A
A 4459 5644 A   A 6992 3957 A
A 7860 2221 A   A 7460 4907 A
A 6097 3801 A   A 7398 4627 A
A 7901 1582 A   A 3482 3304 A
A 7381 2241 A   A 5540 7650 A
A 0730 8597 A   A 5153 3325 A

A 5727 2301 A   A 7592 1021 A

It is the intention of the New York Division office to check further as to the above.

On May 2, 1933 there were discovered in the Federal Reserve Bank of New York, 296—$10 gold certificates, and one $20 gold certificate, all Lindbergh ransom notes. These bills are included among the currency received at the Federal Reserve Bank on May 1, 1933 and apparently had been made in one deposit. Immediately upon the discovery of these bills, deposit tickets at the Federal Reserve Bank for May 1, 1933 were examined. One was found bearing the name and address of "J. J. Faulkner, 537 West 149th Street" which had marked thereon "Gold Certificates" "$10 and $20" in the amount of $2,980. Receiving Teller, James P. Estey, of 92-St. Nicholas Ave., New York City, who received these bills examined the deposit ticket of J. J. Faulkner, and stated that he personally had placed the numerals "10 and 20" together with words "gold certificates" on the slip. He recalled having wrapped the bills and he remembered that he did not check them at the time. Although he gave careful study to deposits and exchanges received by him on May 1, 1933 he was unable to furnish any information concerning a description or the possible identity, other than the name appearing above, concerning the person who made the deposit. Estey recalled having received the currency from some unknown person, some time during May 1, 1933. After its receipt, Estey strapped the currency and forwarded some to the Money Department of the Federal Reserve for counting. The serial numbers of the 296-$10 gold certificates and the one $20 gold certificate are as follows:

A 0074 5214 A   A 5149 1045 A   A 0098 3568 A
A 5240 7603 A   A 1010 1997 A   A 5315 3540 A
A 1070 0210 A   A 5535 7248 A   A 1520 6556 A

A 5683 3070 A	A 5714 0329 A	A 1525 4981 A
A 7379 4987 A	A 1774 7568 A	A 7409 3726 A
A 1960 5653 A	A 7418 0074 A	A 2610 4642 A
A 7439 7192 A	A 2961 7269 A	A 7446 3294 A
A 3128 0395 A	A 7453 6606 A	A 3228 0973 A
A 7497 2436 A	A 3437 5616 A	A 7579 1084 A
A 3761 0166 A	A 7582 4312 A	A 4022 5011 A
A 4181 6472 A	A 7618 2635 A	A 4417 8773 A
A 7641 5256 A	A 4426 0463 A	A 7662 1113 A
A 4436 1730 A	A 7701 7916 A	A 4609 2673 A
A 4831 6400 A	A 7723 3219 A	A 4891 1894 A
A 7745 1361 A	A 4911 2607 A	A 7749 2616 A
A 4926 0411 A	A 7762 8941 A	A 5021 1347 A
A 7774 3254 A	A 5041 9555 A	A 7797 5255 A
A 5043 7803 A	A 7811 1593 A	A 5051 5461 A
A 7818 0766 A	A 5074 4245 A	A 7822 9518 A
A 5817 0760 A	A 7841 3093 A	A 6975 2884 A
A 5985 1005 A	A 7901 7136 A	A 6022 7228 A
A 7912 7369 A	A 6106 2922 A	A 7923 1393 A
A 6170 4266 A	A 8006 3692 A	A 6578 9176 A
A 8006 6450 A	A 6848 3986 A	A 8012 6526 A
A 6896 1055 A	A 8037 3165 A	A 6987 2500 A
A 9462 5105 A	A 7002 1786 A	A 3310 5945 A
A 7016 1660 A	A 5682 0311 A	A 7148 6032 A
A 5703 3047 A	A 7179 1384 A	A 5225 1543 A
A 7271 6954 A	A 5018 9491 A	A 7287 0700 A
A 6016 5033 A	A 7295 1259 A	A 2772 5584 A
A 7296 2112 A	A 6089 4108 A	A 7331 9156 A
A 3518 9042 A	A 7737 2384 A	A 0248 8125 A
A 7495 2099 A	A 7967 5552 A	A 2439 7028 A
A 4229 7940 A	A 7343 2848 A	A 7847 0736 A
A 7543 4336 A	A 6899 4126 A	A 1160 3969 A
A 3732 1167 A	A 2690 4993 A	A 5703 6715 A
A 2160 5839 A	A 6416 4748 A	A 6145 0422 A
A 5829 4152 A	A 4920 3298 A	A 6607 3082 A

A 5019 5412 A   A 2892 8826 A   A 7987 1602 A
A 2204 1967 A   A 3446 5746 A   A 4613 3623 A
A 7562 1046 A   A 7834 3247 A   A 3611 2681 A
A 6012 9373 A   A 2817 9971 A   A 5817 9864 A
A 6014 6719 A   A 6851 3853 A   A 5324 4691 A
A 7310 2904 A   A 3535 3132 A   A 7454 5057 A
A 6936 5635 A   A 7864 0556 A   A 5792 2663 A
A 4224 9451 A   A 5328 2521 A   A 2242 8404 A
A 3021 1325 A   A 4486 3837 A   A 2007 4137 A
A 7656 6829 A   A 6823 9511 A   A 3494 9038 A
A 7054 2601 A   A 6075 9048 A   A 2530 3419 A
A 7715 4989 A   A 1159 4811 A   A 0346 4675 A
A 6094 6515 A   A 3236 4559 A   A 7813 6709 A
A 6847 4507 A   A 7963 7232 A   A 7490 1477 A
A 1335 7881 A   A 2948 9796 A   A 7836 6742 A
A 6188 6008 A   A 2756 6868 A   A 5310 7316 A
A 7633 9845 A   A 4135 0108 A   A 6035 9613 A
A 0240 8689 A   A 4492 0823 A   A 7406 7207 A
A 7561 0086 A   A 7673 6191 A   A 7791 1474 A
A 1693 7807 A   A 2470 5754 A   A 7836 3297 A
A 5078 9113 A   A 2544 5459 A   A 1743 2368 A
A 4921 1496 A   A 5728 6024 A   A 7766 7043 A
A 0970 7654 A   A 0715 0111 A   A 7742 4606 A
A 4066 5582 A   A 7602 7618 A   A 6604 6522 A
A 5945 6073 A   A 7415 3934 A   A 1278 8456 A
A 6989 3954 A   A 7912 7114 A   A 5564 3361 A
A 7281 6663 A   A 5587 1477 A   A 7673 0490 A
A 3093 8353 A   A 7853 0740 A   A 5728 1267 A
A 7551 3861 A   A 7613 0893 A   A 3089 1968 A
A 9601 0618 A   A 2465 5047 A   A 4416 3814 A
A 7760 0550 A   A 2693 9378 A   A 1403 0957 A
A 0895 5578 A   A 7227 2783 A   A 6028 1917 A
A 3747 5973 A   A 2805 8389 A   A 7047 4673 A
A 5334 1864 A   A 5879 3545 A   A 4128 1487 A
A 7822 3785 A   A 6311 4275 A   A 5147 7630 A

A 7179 1372 A	A 7218 7206 A	A 7514 3234 A
A 5528 2526 A	A 7865 3351 A	A 3922 3051 A
A 7959 2707 A	A 7352 7793 A	A 1954 3100 A
A 5330 4852 A	A 7156 6221 A	A 5099 1864 A
A 1958 9775 A	A 7343 7955 A	A 7630 0934 A
A 1839 2019 A	A 2973 3483 A	A 6951 8549 A
A 0452 3922 A	A 0884 8695 A	A 3827 1290 A
A 1067 3449 A	A 3621 6609 A	A 3263 4509 A
A 4035 9570 A	A 3424 7883 A	A 7029 2021 A
A 7069 2236 A	A 7847 9047 A	A 3427 8321 A
A 4082 3554 A	A 3017 6447 A	A 3156 8006 A
A 6324 7794 A	A 7311 2386 A	A 7927 8644 A
A 6639 2964 A	A 4209 7894 A	A 7225 2470 A
A 3498 9947 A	A 2014 7593 A	A 1693 2732 A
A 7600 8064 A	A 7719 9207 A	A 4814 6994 A
A 7849 1851 A		
A 7993 0014 A	A 3618 3364 A	A 3266 5500 A
A 3089 1968 A	A 7767 7909 A	A 5826 0530 A
A 5586 6934 A	A 1518 9995 A	A 7125 7304 A
A 3320 2835 A	A 6012 3403 A	A 3093 2397 A
A 7766 5717 A	A 7706 2747 A	A 7065 8598 A
A 3800 7612 A	A 3280 6786 A	A 6916 2772 A
A 6001 2972 A	A 3246 8877 A	A 6926 3547 A
A 7189 0125 A	A 4952 6207 A	A 7447 6562 A
A 6406 2850 A	A 0387 6138A	A 5914 7286 A
A 7417 6145 A	A 7746 9078 A	A 6866 3651 A
A 4943 3868 A	A 4886 9912 A	A 6618 6861 A

<u>$20. Gold Certificate A 3934 1874 A</u>

The New York Police; the New Jersey State Police and the Intelligence Unit conducted a joint investigation at the address "537 West 149th Street", New York City but failed to find anyone at that address by the name of "J. J. Faulkner". Additional details as to this phase of the case are set forth in the section "Subjects and Suspects", sub-section "Unknown Person No. 5, J. J. Faulkner et al."

$10 Bill—A60846145

This bill was discovered on May 8, 1933 at the Federal Reserve Bank, New York City. It was included in a deposit of $970,876.00 made with this bank on May 7, 1933 by the Corn Exchange Bank, 86th Street and Lexington Ave., New York City. This deposit was made up at the Corn Exchange Bank on May 3, 1933. The bill itself was contained in a package of $500 bearing the notations "No. 34" and in pencil the initials "J L" indicating that head teller J. Lynch of the Corn Exchange Bank had prepared this package of $500. Investigation indicated that the ransom bill in question had been received at the Corn Exchange Bank prior to May 2, 1933, although nothing could be learned to indicate the possible source or person from which the same had been obtained.

$10 Bill—A-18300206

This bill was discovered on May 9, 1933 in the Federal Reserve Bank of New York, Liberty and Nassau Streets, New York City. It was included in a $31,400 deposit made by the Union Square branch of the bank of Manhattan, Union Square and 16th Street, on the same date. The bill, in a package of $1,000, representing an accumulation of currency received at the Union Square branch of the Bank of Manhattan during May 3, and 4, 1933. No information of value was obtained concerning the identity of the depositor or the source of this bill.

$5 Bill—B-15910798

This bill was discovered on June 7, 1933 at the Chase

National Bank, Times Square Branch, 7th Avenue and 41st Street, New York City. It was included in a night-box deposit made on that date by Albrecht and Co., dealers in ladies' novelties, 1375 Broadway, New York City. The deposit was made by Sidney Jacobson, Southern Boulevard, Bronx, New York City, who is employed as a salesman by Albrecht and Company. Jacobson recalled that about 3:00 P.M. on June 6, 1933 he received this bill in payment for a pair of ladies' cotton gloves valued at 59¢. Jacobson stated that he remembered receiving this bill because the woman who tendered same, looked at him in a very suspicious manner; however, Jacobson was unable to furnish a description of the woman and nothing further concerning her identity could be learned.

$10 Gold Certificate—A-35186638

This bill was discovered on June 10, 1933 at the Federal Reserve Bank, New York City. It was contained in a deposit made by the Irving Trust Company, Fordham Branch, East Fordham Road and Marion Ave., Bronx, New York City, on the day previous. An investigation conducted at the Fordham Branch of the Irving Trust Company failed to elicit any information that might indicate the source from which this bill had been obtained. An examination was made of all deposit tickets at this bank, during the period over which a number of gold certificates, including this bill could have accumulated but this failed to reveal the identity of the depositor.

$10 Gold Certificate—A-79742843

This bill was discovered on June 13, 1933 at the Federal Reserve Bank, New York City. It was included in a deposit made by the First National Bank of Cooperstown, N. Y. by registered mail under date of June 8, 1933, in a package containing $200 in old bills, characterized by the Federal Reserve as "rags", bearing a label marked 1733. The investigation developed that the Postmaster at Cherry Valley, N.Y. had included this bill in a deposit of $525 which he made at the First National Bank of Cooperstown on June 7, 1933. Inquiry at the post office Cherry Valley, N.Y. developed that this gold certificate was obtained from a Mr. E. C. Fonda of Cherry Valley, who on or about June 3, 1933 purchased a money order. Fonda stated that on June 3, 1933, a Mrs. John O'Neill, the wife of a farmer located on Sharon Road near East Springfield, N.Y. purchased a quantity of drygoods from him and in payment for same gave him the gold certificate in question. Mrs. O'Neill obtained the bill from her husband, John O'Neill, who advised that on or about the 19th of February, 1933, he obtained this particular ransom bill together with five other gold certificates from the National Central Bank of Cherry Valley, N.Y. This bank was closed on March 4, 1933, when it was placed under the supervision of a Conservator, J. S. Scott. Other than the above, nothing has been developed to indicate the identity of the previous holder of this ransom bill.

$10 Gold Certificate—A-12859632

This bill was discovered on June 18, 1933 at the Federal Reserve Bank of New York, New York City. It was included in a package of 100—$10 bills and deposited with the Federal Reserve to the account of James A. Hearn and Son, drygoods, 20 West 14th Street, New York City on May 29, 1933 at the Washington Square branch of the National City Bank, 13th Street and Fifth Avenue, New York City. No information has been developed to indicate the identity of the previous holder of this bill and it appears that the bill was accepted from one of the customers of

Hearn and Sons, drygoods store, in the regular course of their business prior to May 29, 1933.

$5 Bill—B-49005340

This bill was discovered in the First National Bank, 2 Wall Street, New York City, on November 20, 1933. It had been received by this bank in a deposit amounting to $3,043 made by the Consolidated Gas Company, New York City, on November 17, 1933. The bill was traced back to a Mrs. Rosa Fuhr, 230 East 7th Street, New York City, who had obtained the same as part of a cash withdrawal amounting to $30 made by her from the Public National Bank, Avenue C and 2nd Street, New York City on October 23, 1933. No further information could be obtained concerning the previous holder of this bill.

$5 Bill—B-26913067

This bill was discovered on November 24, 1933 at the Corn Exchange Bank, Pennsylvania Station Branch, 33rd Street and 7th Avenue, New York City. It had been placed with other currency as a deposit by the Pennsylvania Railroad on the date previous. Other that the finding that this bill had been accepted at the Pennsylvania Station in New York City from one of thousands of persons who purchase tickets at that station, nothing could be learned to indicate the actual person who had passed it or the possible source from which it had been obtained. During the investigation concerning this bill, Cashier James MacWhan, Pennsylvania Railroad employee, although he could not recall the source from which this particular bill had been obtained, related that on Tuesday evening, November 21, 1933 at about 10:00 P.M. while he was working Window No. 23 at the Pennsylvania Station, a male individual approached him apparently from the 33rd Street entrance to the Pennsylvania Station and inquired as to whether he, MacWhan, would exchange a number of $5 bills for other currency. This individual was described by MacWhan as being 5'5" tall; weight 145 pounds; dark complexion; no glasses; no scars; poorly dressed; wearing a soft, dirty, light brown hat; brown overcoat and being of Italian or Jewish extraction. He exhibited no bills and did not buy a ticket but merely inquired as to whether MacWhan would exchange some $5 bills for other currency. During the conversation the stranger stated that he had on his person about 100—$5 bills. MacWhan dismissed him with the comment that the cashier at the station could possibly exchange the bills for him if they were <u>good bills</u>. This individual did not thereafter go to the cashier's window as MacWhan observed him leave the Pennsylvania Station by the 33rd Street exit. He has not been seen since by MacWhan nor did MacWhan recall having seen him prior to the above occasion.

$5 Bill—B-35435796

This bill was discovered on November 27, 1933 at the Corn Exchange Bank and Trust Company, 7th Avenue and 14th Street, New York City. It was contained in a deposit of $3,022.23 made at this bank on the same date by the Sheridan Square Theatre, New York City, N.Y. The investigation developed that this bill was received at the Sheridan Square Theatre, 7th Avenue and 8th St., New York City, at approximately 9:30 P.M., Sunday, November 26, 1933 by one of the cashiers from an unknown man who attended the show alone at the Sheridan Square Theatre on that night. The cashier recalled the receipt of this bill only for the reason that the man virtually threw it, folded, through the ticket office window, causing her to look up at him in some anger. The picture which was being exhibited at that time was entitled "Broadway through a Keyhole" featuring Texas

Guinan. The cashier held no conversation with the man from whom she received the bill. The cashier described this man as being about 30 to 35 years of age; slender build; 5'8" or 9" tall; about 155 or 160 pounds; light complexion; thin face; light brown hair; smooth shaven; high cheek bones; broad shoulders; apparently American and wore at the time a dark soft hat with the front brim pulled down, dark suit and no overcoat. The cashier stated she had not seem him prior to November 26, 1933, nor has she seen him since, and believes that she can identify him if she sees him again.

$5 Bill—A-57865184

This bill was discovered on December 7, 1933 at the Broadway Branch of the Corn Exchange Bank and Trust Company, 525 Broadway, New York City. It was included in a currency exchange made at this Bank on that date by the Banco Di Napoli Trust Co., of New York, 526 Broadway, New York City, and apparently accepted by the latter from of approximately five hundred persons, chiefly Italians making foreign remittances from the Napoli Bank to points in Italy, on December 6, 1933. The identity of the person who may have presented this bill to the Napoli Bank is unknown.

$5 Bill—B-12695891

This bill was discovered on December 18, 1933 in the Corn Exchange Bank and Trust Company, 7th Avenue Branch, New York City, and was contained in a deposit of $251.34 made on the same date at this bank by the Gasoline Distributors of New York, Inc., 153 Seventh Ave., New York City. Investigation disclosed this bill was received by the gasoline station conducted by the gasoline distributors at the above address, between 7:00 A.M., December 16, 1933 and midnight December 17, 1933. There has not been developed to date any indication as to the source from which this bill was obtained by the gasoline station.

$10 Gold Certificate—A72984929

This bill was discovered at the Federal Reserve Bank of New York, Liberty and Nassau Streets, New York City, on December 27, 1933. It was contained in a deposit made at the Federal Reserve on the previous date by the Bank of New York and Trust Company, Wall and William Streets, New York City. The investigation to date has not developed the real source from which this bill was obtained. There is a possibility that it may have been included in a deposit made by the Hong Kong, China, branch of the Chartered Bank of India, Australia, and China, New York City, and there likewise exists a possibility that the bill itself may have been tendered by any of the individual depositors of the Bank of New York on December 26, 1933. The investigation of the particular bill is still pending.

$10 Gold Certificate—A-13727291

This bill was discovered on January 5, 1934 at the Federal Reserve Bank of New York. It was contained in a deposit of $26,067.00 made on December 28, 1933 by the Harlem Market Branch of the Chase National Bank of New York. It was learned at the later branch that the bill in question was received there from one of eight depositors between the date of December 23 and December 28, 1933. A further investigation, however, failed to develop any information which would indicate the identity of the previous holder of this bill.

$10 Gold Certificate—*01122111A

This bill was discovered on January 5, 1934 in the Federal Reserve Bank, New York City. It was included in a package of $500, which in turn was part of a total deposit of $56,971.00 made to the Federal Reserve Bank by the Corn Exchange Bank and Trust Company of New York on December 27, 1933. Further inquiry indicated that this bill came from the Fordham branch of the Corn Exchange bank and Trust Co., Fordham Road and Decatur Ave., Bronx, New York City. (The bank patronized by Dr. J. F. Condon) No information was developed at this bank indicating the previous holders of this bill. The investigation of this bill is still pending.

$10 Gold Certificate—A-76464756

This bill was discovered on January 6, 1934 at the Federal Reserve Bank of New York. It was included in a deposit of $18,500 made by the National City Bank of New York, Williamsbridge Branch, Bronx, on December 30, 1933. Investigation revealed that the Williamsbridge Branch of the U.S. Post office placed this bill, with other currency, on deposit with the National City Bank on December 30, 1933. Further inquiry revealed this bill was received at the Williamsbridge Post Office Station in the course of business during December 29, 1933 and probably represented some of the cash receipts of the Postal Savings and the Money Order Departments on Friday, December 29, 1933. The investigation of this bill is still pending.

$10 Gold Certificate—A-34408398

This bill was discovered on January 16, 1934 in the Federal Reserve Bank, New York City. It was contained in a deposit of $10,077.50 made with the Federal Reserve on January 12, 1934 by the Williamsbridge Branch of the Bank of the Manhattan, 220th Street and White Plains Road, Bronx,

New York City. No information has been developed at this Bank as to the source from which the bill was obtained other than statements that the bill was probably received from one of the many depositors at this bank between January 9th and 11th, 1934. The investigation of this bill is still pending.

$10 Gold Certificate—A-94624481

This bill was discovered on January 19, 1934 at the Federal Reserve Bank, New York City. It was received at 7:30 P.M. January 17, 1934 in a deposit of $19,820.00 made by the Bronx County Trust Co., 149th Street and 3rd Avenue, Bronx, New York City. Investigation conducted at the Bronx County rust Company other than indicating that the bill itself was received in the main office of the Bronx County rust Company or at one of its eight branches, between December 28, 1933 and January 17, 1934, failed to reflect any information which would indicate the real source from which this bill had been obtained.

$5. Bill—B48613534A

This bill was discovered on February 1, 1934 at the Corn Exchange Bank and Trust Company, 42nd Street and 8th Avenue, New York City. It was included in currency deposited at this bank by the Globe Coat and Apron Supply Co., of 526 West 48th Street, New York City. Investigation developed that John Haberlin of Astoria, Long Island, a driver of this company, apparently received the bill in question on January 31, 1934 from one Joseph Frederick Faulkner, employee of a cafeteria operated on the top floor of the De Pinna Clothing Store, 52nd Street and Fifth Avenue, New York City, for De Pinna employees. The cafeteria is managed by Mrs. Catherine Buckley, sister of Faulkner, who resides at 205 East 78th Street, New York City; her husband is deceased. Faulkner resides at 953 Amsterdam Avenue, New York City, with two elderly unmarried sisters, Elizabeth (Belle) Faulkner, a practical nurse, and Mary, who helps in the cafeteria. Their parents are said to be John Faulkner, born in England, and Margaret Donahue, born in Lawrence, Mass. Although the investigation as to this bill is not complete, it appears that the above individuals are not related to the Faulkner family of 537 West 149th Street.

Joseph Frederick Faulkner, Mrs. Buckley, and employees of the restaurant were thoroughly questioned regarding the source of the ransom bill but were unable to recall where they obtained it. Faulkner stated he was confident he took the bill from the cash register, and that it had been tendered on January 31, 1934 by one of the two hundred or more De Pinna employees who eat lunch daily in the cafeteria. Faulkner remembered distinctly that he gave the bill to the laundry driver, and claims he took it directly from the cash register. Both he and the driver agree that it was a common practice for the driver, who frequently eats in the restaurant to change bills for the cafeteria people. Faulkner and Mrs. Buckley are the only ones who have access to the cash register. The laundry driver had an impression that Faulkner took the bill in question from his wallet, rather than from the cash register, but this Faulkner denies. The investigation further developed that the cafeteria is not open to the general public, however that a number of employees of three firms in the building next to the De Pinna Store eat there daily.

On the back of the bill, written in pencil, are the initials "E.D.W." Investigation to date has not developed the identity of the individual who wrote the initials, nor the identity of the individual whose initials they are. Neither the De Pinna store, the cafeteria, the Globe Coat & Apron Supply Co., nor the Corn Exchange Bank has an employee bearing the initials in question. The investigation of this ransom bill has not yet been completed.

Thomas Fensch

RECAPITULATION OF RANSOM MONEY

Denomination	Date of Discovery	Discovered at
20	4-4 or 5-32	E. River Savings Bank 96th St. & Amsterdam Ave., New York City
5	4/14/32	Bank of Manhattan Co. 40 Wall St., N.Y.C.
5	5/19/32	Central Hanover Bank & Trust Co., Madison Ave. and 42nd St., N. Y. C.
5	5/19/32	Chase National Bank, 7th Avenue and 41st St., New York City
5	5/23/32	First National Bank 52 Wall Street, New York City.
5	6/6/32	Chase National Bank 18 Pine Street, New York City.
5	6/16/32	Drydock Savings Bank, 341 Bowery, New York City.

FBI Files on the Lindbergh Baby Kidnapping

Traced to	Date rec'd at Place Traced to
David Marcus, 215 West 91st Street, New York City	4/4 or 5/32
One of Schrafft's stores 31 Broadway; 48 Broadway, 181 Broadway; 281 Broadway; 61 Maiden Lane	4/13/32
Sinclair Oil Station, 62nd St. and Mill Ave., Brooklyn, N.Y.	5/17/32
Bickford's Restaurant, 7th Ave. and 41st St., New York City	5/18 or 19/32
Max Tubinstein, Dry Goods Store, 150 Orchard Street, New York City	About 5/18/32
Brilliant Cafeteria Canal St. and Bowery, New York City.	6/6/32
Martha Sohn, 1025 E. 167th St. (Nat'l City Bank, Bowery & Bond St., NYC)	6/16/32

Denomination	Date of Discovery	Discovered at
5	6/30/32	Post Office, Mt. Vernon, N. Y.
5	7/13/32	Chase National Bank 18 Pine St., N. Y. C.
5	8/2/32	Manufacturers Trust Co. 8th Ave. & 34th Street New York City
5	8/16/32	Central Hanover Bank & Trust Company, 70 Broadway, N. Y. C.
5	8/24/32	First National Bank 2 Wall Street, New York City
5	9/14/32	Central Hanover Bank and Trust Company, 224 West 47th Street, N.Y.C.

FBI Files on the Lindbergh Baby Kidnapping

Traced to	Date rec'd at Place Traced to
Max Halpern, 25 Alameda St., Mt. Vernon, N. Y. (Mt. Vernon Trust Co.) or Edw. A. Trotter, 358 Union Ave., Mt. Vernon (unknown bank, Yonkers, N. Y.)	Prior to
Federal Reserve Bank N. Y. (apparently)	7/13
West End Ave. Corp. 325 West 71st and 245 West 75th, New New York City	Prior to 8/2
Albert Chamberlain, candy store, 1536 Bedford Ave., Bklyn Or M. W. Babbitt, 387 Eastern Parkway, Brooklyn	Prior to 8/16
Consolidated Gas Co. 157 Hester Street, New York City	Prior to 8/24
Palace Café, 151 West 46th Street, N. Y. C.	9/13 9/14

Denomination	Date of Discovery	Discovered at
5	10/6/32	Chase National Bank, 75 Maiden Lane, N.Y.C.
5	10/15/32	Federal Reserve Bank Liberty & Nassau Streets, N.Y.C.
10*	10/22/32	Guaranty Trust Co. Madison Ave. & 60th St. N. Y. C.
5	10/23/32	Chase National Bank 575 Fifth Ave., N.Y.C.
20	10/26/32	Central Hanover Bank & Trust Co., 70 road way, N.Y.C.
10*	10/28/32	National City Bank 55 Wall Street, N.Y.C.
10*	10/29/32	Guaranty Trust Co. N. Y. C.

Traced to	Date rec'd at Place Traced to
David Bari (or Barry) & Joseph Koretsky, 1860 Broadway, N.Y.C. (Public National Bank & Trust Co., N.Y.C.)	9/22
Ernest & Emily Behrens, Irvington, N. Y. (Westchester Savings Bank, Tarrytown, N. Y.)	8/12
Adventurers Club (Hotel Astor, 44th St. & Broadway, N. Y. C.)	About 10/20/32
H. Levineat, Restaurant, 2nd Ave. & E. 28th St., N.Y.C.	Prior to 10/20/32
Child's Restaurant 570 Lexington Ave. N.Y.C.	10/25/32
Brooklyn Edison Co., 380 Pearl Street, Brooklyn, N. Y.	10/27/32
United Cigar Store, 118-02 Jamaica Ave. Queens, N. Y.	10/27/32

Denomination	Date of Discovery	Discovered at
5	11/10/32	National City Bank 5th Ave. and 23rd St. N. Y. C.
5	11/11/32	Central Hanover Bank 70 Broadway, N.Y.C.
5	11/19/32	Brooklyn Edison Co. Coney Island, Brooklyn, N. Y.
5	11/21/32	Chase National Bank 7th Ave. & 41st St. N.Y.C.
5	11/29/32	Chase National Bank 7th Ave. & 41st St. N. Y. C.
5	12/6/32	Central Hanover Bank & Trust Co., 70 Broadway N. Y. C.
10*	12/22/32	Guaranty Trust Co. 140 Broadway, N.Y.C.

FBI Files on the Lindbergh Baby Kidnapping

Traced to	Date rec'd at Place Traced to
H. Lambert, clothing store, 254 Fifth Ave., N. Y. C.	About 11/10/32
Child's Restaurant 570 Lexington Ave. N. Y. C.	11/9/32 11/10/32
Bewery Savings Bank 42nd St. & Lexington Avenue, N. Y. C.	10/28/32
Groat Western Beef Co. 591—9th Ave., N.Y.C. or Sheridan Cafeteria, 223 West 36th St. N.Y.C.	About 11/19
Republic Theatre, Minsky Burlesque Co., West 42nd St. & roadway, N.Y.C.	11/25 to 11/27
Edwards Sport Shop, 111 Nassau St., N.Y.C.	12/4
United Cigar Store Dept. of Whelan Drug Store at 1490 Third Ave. (corner 84th St., N. Y. C.)	12/21

Denomination	Date of Discovery	Discovered at
10*	3/3/33	Guaranty Trust Co. 180 Broadway, N.Y.C.
20	4/12/33	First National Bank 52 Wall St., N.Y.C.
10*	4/13/33	Federal Reserve Bank N. Y.C.
10*	4/14/33	Federal Reserve Bank, N. Y. C.
10*	4/19/33	Federal Reserve Bank of New York
10*	4/22/33	Federal Reserve Bank of New York.
5	4/27/33	First National Bank 2 Wall St., N.Y.C.

Traced to	Date rec'd at Place Traced to
United Cigar Store, 504 Third Ave. (corner 34th St.) (Unknown man).	3/1/33
National City Bank, 137 E. 14th St., N.Y.C. (Consolidated Gas Co., 180 Hester St., N.Y.C.)	Prior to 4/11/33
Public National Bank, Grand & Havermeyer Sts. Brooklyn, N. Y.	Between 3/28/33 and 4/11/33
Manufacturers Trust Co. Columbus Circle & 59th St., N. Y. C.	Between 4/4/33 and 4/11/33
Union Dime Savings Bank, 6th Ave. and 49th St., N.Y.C.	Between 4/4/33 and 4/11/33
J. H. Adams, Eagle Poultry & Meat Co. 2152 Broadway (corner 75th St. N.Y.C.)	4/12/33
Paul Yakutis (or Youkutis) Rooming house proprietor, 234 E. 18th St., N.Y.C.	Prior to 4/26/33

Denomination	Date of Discovery	Discovered at
24-$10*	4/29/33	Federal Reserve Bank Liberty & Nassau Sts. N.Y.C.
26-$10*	5/1/33	Federal Reserve Bank N.Y.C.
50-$10*	5/2/33	Federal Reserve Bank N.Y.C.
296-$10* 1-$20*	5/2/33	Federal Reserve Bank N.Y.C.
10*	5/8/33	Federal Reserve Bank N.Y.C.
10*	5/9/33	Federal Reserve Bank N.Y.C.
10*	6/7/33	Chase National Bank, 7th Ave. & 41st St., N.Y.C.
10*	6/10/33	Federal Reserve Bank New York City
10*	6/13/33	Federal Reserve Bank New York City

Traced to	Date rec'd at Place Traced to
Chemical National Bk. Cortlandt St. & Broadway, N.Y.C.	About 4/27/33
Chemical National Bk. Cortlandt St. & Broadway, N.Y.C.	Between 4/27/33 4/29/33
Manufacturers Trust Co. 149 Broadway, N.Y.C.	Between 4/27/33 4/29/33
Exchanged at Federal Reserve Bank by "J.J. Faulkner, 537 West 149th St., N.Y.C."	5/1/33
Corn Exchange Bank, 86th St. & Lexington Ave. N.Y.C.	Prior to 5/3/33
Bank of Manhattan Co. Union Sq. & 16 St. N.Y.C.	5/3/33 5/4/33
Albrecht & Co., 1373 Broadway, N.Y.C.	6/6/33
Irving Trust Co., East Fordham Road and Marion Ave., Bronx, NYC	Prior to 6/9/33
Nat'l Central Bank of Cherry Valley, N.Y.	About 2/10/33

Denomination	Date of Discovery	Discovered at
10*	6/18/33	Federal Reserve Bank New York City
5	11/20/33	First National Bank 2 Wall St., N.Y.C.
5	11/24/33	Corn Exchange Bk, Penna, Station branch 33rd St. and 7th Ave. N.Y.C.
5	11/27/33	Corn Exchange Bk, & Tr. Co., 7th Ave. and 14th St., N.Y.C.
5	12/7/33	Corn Exchange Bk and Tr. Co., 525-Bdway N.Y.C.
5	12/18/33	Corn Exchange Bk. & Tr. Co., 7th Ave. And 14th St. N.Y.C.
10*	12/27/33	Federal Reserve Bank of N.Y.C.

FBI FILES ON THE LINDBERGH BABY KIDNAPPING

Traced to	Date rec'd at Place Traced to
James A. Hearn & Sons, drygoods, 20 West 14th St., N.Y.C.	Prior to 5/29/33
Public Nat'l Bank Ave. "C" and 2nd St., N.Y.C.	Prior to 10/33
Pennsylvania RR, 34th St. and 7th Ave., N.Y.C.	About 11/
Sheridan Square Theatre 7th Ave. and 8th St. N.Y.C. (unknown man)	11/
Banco di Napoli Trust Co. 526 Broadway, N.Y.C. (Unknown Italian)	12/
Gasoline Distributors of NY, Inc. Gas station at 153 7th Ave., N.Y.C.	12/ or
Bank of NY & Trust Co., Wall & William Streets, N.Y.C. or Chartered Bank of India, Australia and China, N.Y.C.	About 12/

Denomination	Date of Discovery	Discovered at
10*	1/5/34	Federal Reserve Bank of N.Y.C.
10*	1/5/34	Federal Reserve Bank of N.Y.C.
10*	1/6/34	Federal Reserve Bank, N.Y.C.
10*	1/16/34	Federal Reserve Bank, N.Y.C.
10*	1/19/34	Federal Reserve Bank, N.Y.C.
5	2/1/34	Corn Ex. Bk. & Tr. Co., 42nd St. and 8th Ave. NYC

NOTE: Gold certificates are designated by an asterisk (*).

Traced to	Date rec'd at Place Traced to
Chase Nat'l Bank Harlem Market branch, N.Y.C.	Between 12/ 12/
Corn Ex. Bk. & Tr. Co., Fordham Road and Decatur Ave., Bronx, N.Y.C.	Prior to 12/
U.S. Postoffice, Williamsbridge Branch, White Plains Road & Gun Hill Road, Bronx, N.Y.C.	About 12/29/33
Bank of Manhattan Co., Williamsbridge Branch, West St. and White Plains Road, Bronx, N.Y.C.	Between 1/9/34 and 11/11/34
Bronx County Trust Co. 149th St. and 3rd Ave., N.Y.C.	Between 12/28/33 and 1/17/34
Globe Coat and Apron Supply Co., 526 W. 48th St., N.Y.C. (Joseph Frederick Faulkner, employees, Cafeteria, DePinna Clothing store, 52nd St. and 5th Ave. N.Y.C.)	1/31/34

Thomas Fensch

SUMMARY

Total Amount of Ransom Money Paid $50,000.00

    $10,000 in $5.00 bills
    15,000 in 10.00 bills
    25,000 in 20.00 bills
    $50,000

Amount Discovered To Date   4,390.00

    $ 80 in $5.00 bills
    4,170 in 10.00 bills
    140 in 20.00 bills
    $4,390

Balance Outstanding $45,610.00

Total Number of Bills in Ransom Payment   4,750

    2000—$5.00 bills
    1500—10.00 bills
    1250—20.00 bills
    4750

Number of Bills Discovered to Date   449

    28—$5.00 bills
    417—10.00 bills
    4—20.00 bills
    449

Balance Outstanding 4,301

Total Amount of Gold Certificates in Ransom Payment $35,000.00

$15,000 in $10 bills
20,000 in 20 bills
$35,000

Amount of Gold Certificates Discovered to Date
4,190.00
$4,170 in $10 bills
20 in 20 bills
$4,190

Balance Outstanding $30,810.00

Total Number of Gold Certificates in Ransom Payment
2,500

1500—$10 bills
1000—20 bills
2500

Number of Gold Certificates Discovered to Date   418

417—$10 bills
1—20 bill
418

                            Balance Outstanding 2,082

SUMMARY REPORT

In Re

Unknown Subjects

Kidnaping and Murder of Charles A. Lindbergh, Jr. (N.Y. File 62-3057)

SUBJECTS AND SUSPECTS

Unknown Person No. 1—"Man with ladder"
Unknown Person No. 2—"John" (received ransom)
Unknown Person No. 3—Suspect "lookout" at Woodlawn Cemetery
Unknown Person No. 4—Suspect "lookout" at St. Raymonds Cemetery
Unknown Person No. 5—alias "J. J. Faulkner", 537 West 149th Street" (passed $2980 ransom gold certificates)
Al Capone
Purple Gang

Finn Hendrik Johnson alias "Red" Johnson
Peter J. Berritella, et al
Enrico Gerardi, et al
Jack Bennet, et al
John Gorch and Walter Gray
Gerald Ducholz
John J. Baumeister
Arthur Barry
Louis V. Cummings
Nich DeAugustine, et al
Sam Goldberg alias "Sam the Gas Man"
Harry Moyers, et al
William Patrick "Squawk" Reilly, et al
Reo Verne Sankey, et al
Garrett Schenck
Charles W. Sellick, et al
Waslov Simek
Dean Preston Sutherland, with aliases
Unknown Suspect (Isadoro Ubaldi, informant)
J. Floyd Williams, et al

- o -

Thomas Fensch

SUBJECTS AND SUSPECTS

UNKNOWN PERSON NO. 1
(Man with Ladder Near Lindbergh Home)

As set out in detail in this report under "Questionable Automobiles and Persons Observed", Sebastian B. Lupica at about 6: P.M., March 1, 1932, while driving to his home near Hopewell, and soon after passing the private road leading to the Lindbergh house, observed a Dodge Sedan approaching him. Both cars topped near each other but Lupica drove by first. He saw inside the Dodge "several ladders". Later upon examining the sectional ladder found near the Lindbergh house, and which apparently was used by the kidnapers, Lupica stated it resembled the ones he saw in the Dodge Sedan. For purpose of convenient reference, at this point, Lupica's description of the man in the Dodge is quoted herewith:

"I am satisfied that the driver of it was a stranger to me. I noticed that he had a thin face and long features; however, this impression may have been caused by the shadows. He had on a dark hat and a dark overcoat; I do not remember the color more definitely but I could say that neither the hat nor the overcoat were, for example, brown or gray. I do not remember whether the driver wore gloves but I am sure he did not wear glasses and that he did not have a mustache or beard. He as not a boy or a young man, but fully mature, and I would guess his age as between 35 and 40 years, although this is purely a guess. I can say, however, that he look considerably older than a college student usually looks. His complexion must have been about medium or average. I would say that he looked like a native (an American) as opposed to a foreigner, I do not remember the color of his eyes. He appeared to be cleanly dressed and after the manner of a resident in the city. He did not impress me as looking 'tough'. He did not speak or nod to me and I did not notice anything unusual about his manner. I saw nothing to indicate that he was excited or anything except matter of fact. He made no attempt to hide his face. I do not think I would recognize him if were to see him again."

Lupica further stated, however, that he might be able to tell by looking at a photograph or an individual whether or not that person resembled the driver of the car.

For further particulars regarding the Dodge Sedan, the ladders, and the circumstances under which they were observed by Lupica, etc., reference should be made to the above mentioned section of this report entitled "Questionable Automobiles And Persons Observed".

It is further noted at this point that, as also set out in the above mentioned section, Mrs. Henry Wendling, who lived in a farmhouse on the Zion-Wertsville Road, possibly saw the same car as Lupica, and according to newspaper accounts she described it as he did, and said she had seen it between 5: and 6: o'clock on March 1st, at which time it was bound west and would have entered the Hopewell-Wertsville Road, where Lupica was bound, later. Apparently, however, she was unable to describe the man in the car, and the information available does not indicate whether she saw a ladder in the car.

This man appearing to be the first person observed, to whom definite suspicion could be attached with regard to the actual kidnaping, and is indicated as Unknown Person No. 1.

UNKNOWN PERSON #2
"John" (received ransom)

The above mentioned person is the only one of those

implicated in this Kidnaping, Murder and Extortion, who has voluntarily disclosed himself as so involved. He is the man who personally contacted Dr. J. F. Condon on two separate occasions, the first at Woodlawn Cemetery March 12, 1932, and the second at St. Raymond Cemetery April 2, 1932. On the first occasion he verbally negotiated with Condon for the ransom and return of the kidnaped Lindbergh baby. On the second occasion he received the $50,000.00 in ransom money and furnished Condon with the "receipt" containing the bogus information relative to the whereabouts of the baby.

Dr. Condon's description of "John" and taxi driver Joseph Perrone's description of the man who handed him the fifth ransom note to be delivered to Dr. Condon indicate that they may be identical. Condon's and Perrone's descriptions follow:

	Description by Condon	Description by Perrone
Name:	"John"	Unknown
Age:	30 to 32	35
Height:	5'8" to 5'10"	About 5'9"
Weight:	158 to 165 lbs.	180 lbs.
Build:	Well, and similar to "middle weight boxer".	Erect and of good build; Appeared muscular.
Hair:	Medium chestnut approaching a dirty blond or sandy.	Dark blond.
Eyes:	Bluish-gray—wide-Almond shaped—resembled those of a Chinaman or Japanese. Did not wear glasses.	Blue.
Complexion:	Fair, no blemishes.	
Facial Features:	Hatched face	Full face,

appearance: straight nose; prominent forehead; eyebrows medium heavy and in a straight line across forehead; clean shaven; prominent and high cheek bones running down to almost a pointed chin	good looking Clean shaven. Eyebrows heavy and same color as hair.
Teeth: Fair and regular; no gold or fillings noticed.	Unnoticed
Scars: None apparent. No tattoos visible.	No marks or scars apparent.
Ears: Unusually large.	Did not notice whether ears were large, small or peculiar.
Hands: Calloused; not noticed if any jewelry worn.	
Neck: Average medium slender, not short and fat.	
Shoulders: Inclined to droop but fairly straight; not quite a military carriage.	
Peculiarities: Could run fast and use hands with dexterity. Had unusually large muscular or fleshy development on inside thumb of left hand; did not wear gloves.	Appeared to be of a nervous type.
Occupation: Mariner, carpenter or painter.	Believed carpenter or mechanic.
Marital Status: Stated to be married.	
Residence: Stated Boston, Mass.	
Criminal Record: Unknown.	

<u>Color:</u> White.
<u>Nationality:</u> Said to be Scadinavian or German   German or Scandinavian.
<u>Handwriting:</u> None, other than ransom notes possibly written by this person.
<u>Speech:</u> Spoke with foreign accent; broken but fair English, presumably Scandinavian or possibly German; used expressions "Smack me <u>out</u>"; "Did you <u>got</u> our letter"; pronounced the word "perfect" as "perfet", the word "Colonel" as "kennel", and the word "five" as "fife".   Had German or Scandinavian accent, sounded more like German pronounced the word "where" as "vare".
<u>Shoe:</u> Size not determined; Color or style unknown.
<u>Feet:</u> Normal: did not walk lame.
<u>Clothing:</u> Gray trousers and black suit; coat heavier than alpaca but not as heavy as broadcloth; regular Spring overcoat worn loose, light in fabric, dark in color; one button used on overcoat; wore dark grayish brown fedora hat pulled well down over forehead.   Fairly well dressed; wore a brown soft hat and brown overcoat; did not notice whether gloves were worn; soft hat which fitted nearly straight on head and pinched in front.

UNKNOWN PERSON NO. 3
(Suspected "Lookout" at Woodlawn Cemetery)

As previously stated, Dr. John F. Condon on March 12, 1932 received the fifth ransom note directing him to secure another note (sixth) containing further instructions, which would be found at the unoccupied frankfurter stand located on Jerome Avenue, Bronx, N. Y., one hundred feet from the last subway station.

Dr. Condon proceeded to the frankfurter stand in the automobile owned and operated by Al Reich, ex-prizefighter and close friend of Dr. Condon, who has frequently been referred to as "Condon's bodyguard". After Dr. Condon secured the sixth ransom note he proceeded to the southwestern entrance of Woodlawn Cemetery at Jerome Avenue. He looked around for a moment but saw no one with the exception of a man then walking slowly past. Dr. Condon states that this man was holding a handkerchief to his face and was wearing a brown fedora hat and brown overcoat; that the man passed Dr. Condon walking in a southerly direction while he, Condon, walked north on Jerome Avenue on the sidewalk outside of Woodlawn Cemetery.

Al Reich, who remained in his automobile which had been parked opposite the frankfurter stand, also observed this man, but describes him only as a medium sized Italian. The New York Office files do not reflect that Reich has ever been interviewed for further details concerning this suspect.

It is the belief of Condon and Reich that this unknown person was in that vicinity for the purpose of observing Condon find the note and subsequently follow its directions, and to see that no police were near. It has also been suggested that this person is one who knew Dr. Condon at least by sight.

UNKNOWN PERSON NO. 4
("Suspected "Look-Out" at
St. Raymonds Cemetery)

As previously stated, the eleventh ransom note was delivered to Dr. J. F. Condon at his residence on the evening of April 2, 1932 by a taxi driver whose identity has never been ascertained. This note contained instructions to proceed to the T. A. Bergen Greenhouses, 3255 East Tremont Avenue, Bronx, New York City, and to their secure another note containing further instructions.

Dr. Condon and Colonel Lindbergh (unaccompanied by others) with Lindbergh driving, proceeded to Bergen's Greenhouses in Al Reich's automobile. Upon their arrival Condon secured the twelfth ransom note and then walked to the Whittemore Avenue entrance of St. Raymonds Cemetery, leaving Colonel Lindbergh in Reich's automobile, which was parked opposite Bergen's Greenhouses at the north side of Tremont Avenue, facing east.

Colonel Lindbergh has stated that as Condon picked up the twelfth ransom note, he (Lindbergh) observed a man pass along the sidewalk near the car. This man appeared to be interested in the car or its occupant. Colonel Lindbergh, who at the time was seated at the wheel, could not discern the features of this man as it was then approximately 8:40 P.M. and rather dark at this point. Colonel Lindbergh described this man as "a young man of average size, wearing a brown suit and a brown felt hat with snap brim pulled down in front; walks rapidly and posture very stooped." Colonel Lindbergh suggests that the stooped posture might have been natural or assumed. According to Colonel Lindbergh, this unknown man was conspicuous because of the manner in which he held a handkerchief well over his face "as if blowing his nose." He stated that the man first passed him while Dr. Condon was securing the twelfth ransom note and that upon Condon's immediate return to the Reich car, he (Lindbergh) inquired if Condon had observed this man but Condon apparently had not.

After Condon's departure with the $50,000 in ransom money, Lindbergh again observed this same unknown man pas along the sidewalk on the opposite side of the street from Lindbergh. On this occasion the man was observed to be carrying the handkerchief in his hand. When the man reached a point immediately opposite Lindbergh, he tossed the handkerchief into a vacant lot. According to Colonel Lindbergh the handkerchief has been recovered and is, with other exhibits in this case, in the possession of the New Jersey State Police.

UNKNOWN PERSON NO. 5, alias "J. J. FAULKNER 537 West 149th Street" ($2,980 ransom gold certificates), HENRY LEIPOLD, DUANE BACON, et al.

Investigation was conducted relative to the deposit containing the name of "J. J. Faulkner" and the address, "537 West 149", which was received at the Federal Reserve Bank, New York City, on May 1, from an unknown individual who surrendered $2,980.00 of the Lindbergh ransom money in gold certificates for other currency. After this exchange, the New Jersey State Police, the New York City Police, and the Intelligence Unit, and United States Treasury Department conducted an extensive investigation to determine the identity of this unknown person. More recently an investigation was instituted by the Division's New York office, relative to this phase case which has not yet been concluded. The combined efforts of the authorities have resulted in the development, to date, of the following information.

The address 537 W. 149th Street, New York City, is an apartment house known as the "Plymouth Apartments", located between Amsterdam and Broadway on the west side of Manhattan Island, in a fairly respectable apartment and boarding house district. The apartment house was erected in year 1895, and is tenanted by middle class citizens of many nationalities. The property is owned by Mr. Payne Louis Kretzmer, age 63, a German, who resides on the premises. In the year 1929 Kretzmer suffered a nervous breakdown and received treatment in a sanitarium in Englewood, N.J. eventually losing his [text garbled]. He is presently under the care of a male attendant, and his financial affairs and the management of the building are handled by his brother, Richard H. Kretzmer, who resides on the premises and by his two nephews, Arthur Bremmer of Englewood, N.J. and John Kretzmer of New York City. Bremmer is a land architect with an office in New York City; John Kretzmer is connected with Alberline Stones Company of New York City; Richard Kretzmer, age 65, and retired from business, is deaf and dumb, and consequently has been of [text garbled] value as an informant. His wife, Ella, is deceased. Payne Kretzmer is incapable of rendering assistance. Old records show that Payne Louis Kretzmer sometimes signs his name as Louis C. Kretzmer. The family name appears in various places as Kritzmer, Kritner, Keltzmer, and Kutzman.

The investigation developed that no one by the name of J. J. Faulkner lived at the Plymouth Apartments on May 1, 1933 or at any other time. A list of voters for the year 1920, all available records at the apartment house, and in the possession of various real estate brokers, and a check of city directories since the year 1900, failed to reveal that anyone bearing the name J. J. Faulkner ever lived at this apartment house. In addition there was obtained from the Post office a list of all persons who lived on the 500 block of West 149th Street. Also the mail carriers who serve the 500 block, and old tenants and employees were questioned, without results. The list of voters, of inhabitants of the 500 block, and of all tenants, past and present of the Plymouth Apartments, are in possession of the New York Office. A photostat of the list of tenants is attached hereto as Exhibit "K".

Perusal of the various lists above mentioned failed to reveal the names of any former Lindbergh or Morrow servants, laborers who were employed in building the Lindbergh home, or of any suspects in this case. An individual named Michael Cummins or Cummings occupied an apartment in the building in 1928-1928 with his wife, Mary. Although it is not believed Mary Cummins is the Marie Cummings employed as a nurse by the Lindberghs, this possibility will be determined. It is further noted that a woman by the name of Rose Rosner lived at 546 W. 159th Street and later at 530 W. 149th Street; it is not known whether she is related to Morris Rosner, but this will be determined. An individual named O'Shanghessy, initials unknown, formerly lived at 521 West 149th Street and left a removal address on 10/20/32 to 544 West 147th Street. The possibility that he is identical with O'Shaugnessy, the Morrow house man, will also be determined.

Although no one by the name of J. J. Faulkner apparently ever lived at this apartment house, it was learned that prior to the year 1920 a woman by the name of Jane Faulkner, and her daughter Jane Emily, leased Apartment 64 in this building. Available records do not indicate that any male members of the Faulkner family resided in the apartment. Mrs. Jane Faulkner (nee Jane Armstrong) died in 1923; her husband, James Faulkner, who was born in England, died many years ago. The Faulkners had a son, Harry, who died in 1917. Harry Faulkner had trouble with his wife, whose maiden name was Harriet E. Chapman. She left New York prior to her husband's death and returned to her former home in Worcester, Mass., and was reported to be unfriendly with the Faulkner family. Her handwriting does not compare with the deposit ticket or the ransom notes. Jane Emily Faulkner was employed in 1920 by S. Logan, Inc., 680 5th Avenue, New York City. Information is that the Faulkners were at one time friendly or associated with the following individuals, concerning whom nothing is known:

Theodore H. Nye, Lester Nelson, and one "Murphy." All available sources indicate that the members of the Faulkner family who resided at the Plymouth Apartments were "fine people" and bore good reputations. Apparently the family came from England. Their family physicians, who have not yet been questioned, were Dr. J. B. Thompson, who still resides at the Plymouth Apartments and Dr. Charles Hunt, of 2 East 54th Street, New York City.

Marriage records of New York City reveal that in the year 192- [text garbled] Jane Emily Faulkner married one Carl Oswin Giessler, sometimes spelled Giessler whose residence at that time was 570 West 191st Street, New York City. It appears that the couple resided in Apartment 64 of the Plymouth Apartments from 1921 to the year 1925, after which they moved from this building and took up their residence in a modest one family framehouse at 120 North Chatsworth Avenue, Larchmont, N.Y. where they have lived ever since.

In the year 1917 one Julius A. Wiegner, 57 years old, born in Germany, naturalized December 23, 1893, Cook County, Illinois, occupied Apartment 64 with his wife, Belle Wiegner, (nee Faulkner). Wiegner formerly resided at 504 East 89th Street, New York City, and was employed by the Metropolitan Opera House, 40th Street and Broadway, New York City. Belle Wiegner, 39 years of age in 1917, formerly lived at 1552 Cook Street, Denver, Colorado. Apparently the Faulkner and Wiegner families were related by marriage, and occupied Apartment 64 together for some years prior to 1920.

In the Fall of 1925 one Albin Wiegner, a relative of Julius Wiegner and a brother-in-law of Carl Iswin Giessler, rented Apartment 64 at Plymouth Apartments. He is a German, quite an elderly man, and also had been with the Metropolitan Orchestra for many years. In April, 1930 he moved out of Apartment 64 and took up his residence with the Giesslers in Larchmont. It appears that he spent some of his time at Yankee Lake, N.Y., a resort. After Wiegner moved out of Apartment 64, the apartment was vacant for several months, then, in November 1930, one William L. Griffin occupied the same until January 1933, when he moved out. The apartment has been vacant ever since. Griffin had formerly been a tenant at 564 West 149th Street; he is said to be reputable and is a life insurance agent; he is a widower, born United States, and is 52 years of age.

Investigation has shown that he was unacquainted with the tenants who previously occupied Apartment 64. On January 7, 1933 Griffin left a removal address of 225 Broadway, room 904. A Ruth Griffin, possibly the wife of a relative of the above party, on January 5, 1933, left a removal address from 537 West 149th Street to 14 West Fordham Street, City Island, N.Y.

In addition to the tenants above named, old records found at the apartment house indicate that a party by the name of Foster or Forster also lived in Apartment 64 about the year 1920, most probably as a sub-tenant or occupant of a furnished room. Nothing is known as to this individual; his name does not show upon the list of voters or the records furnished by the Post Office Department. In 1919 a William E. Haefener, born United States, lived in Apartment 64 with the Faulkner family. He was 41 years old in 1919, and was employed as Civil Engineer in the office of the Borough President, Long Island City, Queens. Haefener formerly resided at 545 W. 146th Street, New York City.

In 1920 a woman named Rose Bock, born United States, age 34 at the time, lived in Apartment 64 with the Faulkner family. She formerly lived at 545 W. 146th Street, New York City, and was employed by the American Tobacco Co., 111 5th Ave., New York City. The list of residents of the 500 block West 149th Street show a Peter and Charles Bock who lived at 508 W. 149th Street, until November 14, 1931 when they left a removal address to 522 West 160th Street. It is not known whether they are related to Rose Bock.

From information appearing on the marriage license of Carl Oswin Giessler, it appears that this party is now about 54 years of age. He was born in Prussia, Germany, his parents being Albin Giessler and Rosaline Schloffel, both deceased. The marriage to Jane Emily Faulkner was his second; his first wife, nee Johanna O'Brien, of Larchmont, is deceased. Investigation developed that Carl Oswin Giessler had two children by his first wife, Phyllis Helen and Carl Donald.

A search of the marriage records revealed that in August, 1928 the son, Carl Donald, then living with his parents at Larchmont, married one Elizabeth Marcel of Mt. Vernon, N.Y. The records show that Carl Donald Giessler was born in Palisades Park, N.J. in 1905 and that after the marriage his residence would be 7208 Hayes Ave., Jackson Heights, Long Island, N.Y. His wife's parents are recorded as Frederick Marcel and Ann Martin Marcel of 44 South 11th Ave., Mt. Vernon, N.Y. The witnesses to this marriage were Helen T. Howell and James Primrose Brown, both of 605 West 113th Street, New York City.

In June, 1929, Phyllis Helen Giessler, then living with her parents at Larchmont, N.Y. married one Henry Carl

Leipold, a landscape gardener, of Hillcrest Court, Mamaroneck, N.Y. The marriage records show that Leipold was born in Rosen Kern, Germany, October 25, 1893, his parents being Carl Leipold and Elise Heischmann, of Lincolndale, N.Y. Apparently both were born in Germany. The records further show that Phyllis Helen Giessler was a trained nurse and was born in New York City on July 20, 1903. The witnesses to this marriage were Lola McCraig, of 225 West 106th Street, New York City and Oscar Waldhauser, of 2521 31st Avenue, Astoria, L.I.N.Y. After their marriage the Leipolds lived for a while at 96 Trenton Ave., White Plains, N.Y. subsequently they moved to 70 Trenton Avenue, White Plains, and are listed in the 1935 Westchester County telephone book at the ladder address.

Investigation developed that Carl Oswin Giessler, and his son Carl Donald, had been connected for some years with the firm of Max Schling, a Seedsman, 618 Madison Ave., New York City, with a branch at 765 5th Avenue. Schling, the President of the Company, is a German, and resides at 9 Richbell Road, Scarsdale, N.Y. The police consider him above suspicion because of his reputation and financial standing. Carl Oswin Giessler is manager and treasurer of this firm and is said to possess a one-third interest in the business. The firm is an old established and reputable one and does a large volume of business in flowers, shrubbery, and seeds. The investigation brought out that the firm has been selling seeds to the Woodlawn Cemetery for a number of years, and that Carl Oswin Giessler and his son are acquainted in this cemetery which figured prominently in the ransom negotiations. Investigation further developed that Carl Donald Giessler in recent years, had been living at 157 Devonia Avenue East, Fleetwood, Mt. Vernon, N.Y. and he is so listed in the 1933 telephone directory.

The Intelligence Unit of the Treasury Department,

through an examination of income tax returns learned that for the years 1929, 1930 and 1931, Carl Donald Giessler filed returns showing his residence as 3060 Decatur Ave., Bronx, New York City. This address is an apartment house in the next block to the residence of Dr. John F. Condon, who lives at 2974 Decatur Avenue.

Further investigation developed that Carl Donald Giessler and Henry Carl Leipold were friendly with one William Krippendorf, a German rug salesman, and that Krippendorf was an acquaintance of Ralph Hacker, the architect of Fort Lee, N.J. who is Dr. Condon's son-in-law. It has been reported, but not verified, that Krippendorf at one time made his residence with the Hacker family and that Carl Donald Giessler is also acquainted with Ralph Hacker. It is pointed out that Ralph Hacker during the ransom negotiations spent considerable time around Dr. Condon's residence in the Bronx, and from the testimony of individuals who observed him Hacker was very much interested in the progress of the negotiations. It is known that Dr. Condon showed him some of the ransom letters, particularly the one containing the dimensions of the box into which the ransom money was to be placed. According to a statement made by Dr. Condon, Hacker drew up a set of plans for the construction of this box, and used dimensions supposedly more accurate than those in the ransom letter. Although Dr. Condon's telephone was not under surveillance, it was learned that numerous calls were made between his residence and the Hacker residence in Fort Lee. Ralph Hacker has a brother, Glen, who is associated in business with him, and who resides in Palisades Park, N.J. It has been previously stated that Carl Donald Giessler was born in Palisades Park, and the acquaintanceship of these various individuals may have had its origin there.

William Krippendorf is presently residing at 50 West 87th St., New York City, which is a rooming house operated by one Joe Aleksa. He has lived at this address only a short while, his prior addresses being unknown at the present writing.

A limited amount of handwriting specimens of Mr. and Mrs. Carl Oswin Giessler, Mr. and Mrs. Carl Donald Giessler, and Mr. and Mrs. Henry Carl Leipold were submitted to Dr. William Souder of the U.S. Bureau of Standards for comparison with the "J. J. Faulkner" deposit ticket and the ransom notes. Dr. Soulder gave an oral opinion that none of the writings compared with the ransom notes or deposit ticket, except that of Carl Oswin Giessler, Dr. Souder stating that in his opinion C. O. Giessler wrote the deposit ticket. Later, however, Dr. Souder suggested that it would be desirable to secure more specimens of Giessler's handwriting and to submit also the exhibits to other experts for their opinion. Specimens of Carl Oswin Giessler's handwriting were also submitted to Handwriting Expert Albert D. Osborn who expressed an opinion that the writing was similar to that on the "Faulkner" deposit ticket, however, that there was too small an amount of writing on the deposit ticket to use as a basis for a thorough examination.

Specimens of the handwriting of William Krippendorf and of Ralph and Glen Hacker have not yet been obtained. It is the intention of the New York Division Office to obtain handwriting specimens of these individuals and their associates, and at an early date to interview Ralph Hacker who has never, so far as is known, been interviewed in connection with this case.

After the development of the above facts and the decision by the handwriting experts, the investigation of the activities of Carl Oswin Giessler, his relatives and associates, was continued. In June, 1933, the Giesslers, father and son, were placed under surveillance by the New York Police. In addition, the business telephone of Max Schling, 618 Madison Ave., was placed under surveillance. It was learned that the Giessler family were reputable people, led normal lives, were comfortably situated financially, and that Carl O. and Carl D. Giessler paid close attention to business. On numerous occasions these individuals would go across the street from their place of business to Scharafft's Grill, 625 Madison Ave., for lunch. It is stated that to date no ransom bills have turned up at this restaurant. In view of the apparent character of the Giesslers it was decided to question them. They were brought to New York Police Headquarters in July, 1933, and interrogated by Colonel Schwarzkopf and Lieutenant Keaton of the New Jersey State Police, and Captain Oliver and Inspector Lyons of the New York City Police Department. At a later date Mrs. Carl Oswin Giessler and Henry Carl Leipold were also thoroughly questioned by Inspector Lyons; Captain Oliver; Lieutenant Keaton, and Special Agent Frank Wilson of the Intelligence Unit. Carl Oswin and Carl D. Giessler were also questioned on a second occasion by Special Agent Frank Wilson. All of these individuals answered the questions put to them in a very satisfactory manner, accounted for their activities on various important dates, and manifested a desire to cooperate and satisfactorily explain all matters of importance. During the interrogation of these parties, additional specimens of their handwriting were obtained. Carl Oswin Giessler furnished a three page letter written by him two years ago. The new handwriting specimens were submitted to Dr. Wilmer Souder who then gave an opinion that neither Carl Oswin Giessler, nor the others mentioned just above, wrote the "J.J. Faulkner" deposit ticket.

The only suspicious activity on the part of any of these individuals at this time was a rather hurried trip which Mrs. Henry Carl Leipold (Phyllis Helen Giessler) took to Canada about June 1933; on this occasion she reserved a berth under the name of "McCall." She was placed under surveillance on this trip but nothing of a suspicious nature was developed. It was found that Mrs. Leipold visited a McCall family at Cateau Junction, 50 miles from Montreal, for about two weeks. The McCall family were found to be very wealthy, and one of the daughters was a nurse who took her training with Mrs. Leipold at St. Luke's Hospital, Amsterdam Avenue and 113th St., New York City. Through arrangements with the United States Customs Mrs. Leipold's luggage was thoroughly examined without results. Whether this trip has a significance in this case is not known. It was made after Carl Oswin Giessler learned that the police were investigating his activities.

In July, 1933, Albin Wiegner, brother-in-law of Carl Oswin Giessler, was questioned at Yankee Lake, N.Y. by Lieutenant Arthur Keaton and Agent Wilson, and specimens of his handwriting were obtained, but nothing of value developed.

On Sunday, August 20, 1933, Henry Carl Leipold committed suicide at Arthursburg, Dutchess County, N.Y. by shooting himself in the head with a .22 calibre rifle. The suicide was approximately a month after Leipold was questioned in connection with this case. Mrs. Carl Oswin Giessler reported it to the New York Police the following day and stated that since Leipold was questioned at Police Headquarters he had been acting queerly and imagined that he as being followed, and that his telephone was "tapped". He informed his wife that in his opinion he was called to Police Headquarters on a subterfuge; that the authorities did not really wish to question him about the Lindbergh case, but were planning to deport him to Germany because he had been intimate with another man's wife a few years before he came to the United States in 1923. It appears that Leipold had been talking to his wife about committing suicide but she did not take him seriously and did not consider that he was so mentally unbalanced as to do so.

The police, according to the report of Special Agent Frank J. Wilson, had, prior to Leipold's suicide eliminated him and the Giesslers as suspects in this case, but after the suicide they decided to make some further check of Leipold's activities it being felt that he might have some direct or indirect knowledge relating to the case. A thorough search of his home at White Plains was unproductive. It is stated that his attorney, Mr. J. Krieger of White Plains, N.Y. is cooperating with the police in this connection. To date, however, it appears that nothing further has developed to indicate that Leipold had any connection with the case. During the investigation the New York Police made arrangements to have the taxidriver, Joseph Perrone, view the Giesslers and Leipold; however he was unable to identify any one of them as the individual who gave him the ransom note in the upper Bronx. Dr. Condon was not asked to view them, and was kept in ignorance of this angle of the case.

Investigation was conducted by the New York Police into the personnel of Max Schling, Inc. It was thought that some employees, having a knowledge of the Giessler or Faulkner families, might have written the "J.J. Faulkner" deposit ticket. Handwriting specimens of various employees, past and present, were obtained and submitted to Sergeant Wm. Murphy, New York Police Handwriting Expert, but no similarities were found.

Following is a list of the employees whose handwriting was examined:

Tom Longman (now in England)
Dave Adams, Plainfield, N.J.
David Plat, c/o Fight Floral Co., New York City
Richard Fitzells, c/o Palmer Seed Co., St. Louis
Charles Deinman, 47 Hillcrest Ave., Larchmont, N.Y.
George Babich, 215 West 23rd St., New York City (said to

have moved to Pennsylvania.)
George Maas or Mass (deceased)
James Magnavito, 122-33rd St., Brooklyn.

Relative to the employee, George Mass or Maas, it was learned that on April 1, 1932 this individual was found dead, slumped over the wheel of his 1931 model Buick Sedan in the private garage located in the rear of his residence, 1050 East 31st Street, Brooklyn, N. Y. When the body of Mass was found, the motor of his car was running and it appeared that death had been accidentally caused by carbon monoxide gas. The medical examiner, however, reported the case as a possible suicide. Mass was 47 years of age, born in the United States, unmarried and made his home at the above address with his two sisters, Sophie, a dressmaker, and Louise, who is married to one William Bartlett. He had been employed by Max Schling about four years as an outside man, and prior to that was with Peter Henderson, Inc., Seedsmen, 35 Cortlandt St., New York City. George Mass has a cousin by the same name who resides in Mt. Vernon, N.Y.

Investigation developed that Jane Emily Faulkner, prior to her marriage to Carl Oswin Giessler, was employed as an accountant and cashier by the Thomas Advertising Company of New York City. Relative to this employment, the report of Special Agent Frank Wilson indicates that Miss Faulkner, in the course of her duties, reported to her superiors the unauthorized withdrawal of some of the firm's funds from the cash drawer by one of the executives, a Mr. Homer A. Boushey. As a result of Miss Faulkner's disclosure Boushey was discharged, and knew Miss Faulkner was the cause of his dismissal. Subsequently Boushey moved to Los Angeles, Calif., where he resided for several years, but was in New York City at the Fraternity Clubs Hotel, 22 East 38th St., during parts of February, March and April, 1932.

According to the hotel records, Boushey checked out on April 3, 1932, which was the day after the ransom money was paid. Boushey was required to surrender his room at the above hotel and his effects were held because of nonpayment of rent. His photo was exhibited to Dr. Condon who failed to identify it; likewise his handwriting, from the hotel register, was submitted to Dr. Souder of the Bureau of Standards who failed to connect it with the ransom notes or the deposit ticket. Information is that Boushey was at one time General Manager of the Spoor-Thompson Machine Company, 1333 Argyle St., Chicago. About the year 1919 he apparently made his residence at the Pennsylvania Hotel, New York City, at which time he gave business addresses of 680 Fifty Avenue and Room 508, 110 West 40th St., New York City. George R. Spoor of the above machine company was given as a reference. Boushey has not been located since the kidnaping occurred and there is no indication as to his present whereabouts. It is believed that the circumstances warrant a complete check of his activities.

Mrs. Carl Oswin Giessler turned over to Special Agent Frank Wilson a guest book used in her home for years, containing numerous signatures. The book was submitted to Dr. Souder for comparison with the ransom notes and deposit ticket, but no similarities were found. One of the signatures in the book was that of: "P. A. Finh, Buddhist and Fingerprint Expert, December 16, 1911." Mrs. Giessler knew this individual but slightly and had not seen or heard of him for fifteen years. She states he was employed by a concern attempting to interest New York banks in the use of fingerprints for the purpose of identification of depositors. He had previously been in England and India. On the page with his signature, Finh wrote a few lines in a language which is probably Arabic. He also placed a single fingerprint impression on the page. The New York Police contemplate a check on Finh's activities.

With further reference to the Giesslers, it is stated that during the investigation of this family at Larchmont, N.Y. the officers found a cancelled check drawn by Carl Oswin Giessler, payable to one Max Halpern of 25 Alamada St., Mt. Vernon, N.Y. This matter is mentioned because of the fact that a $5 ransom bill turned up on June 30, 1932 at the Mt. Vernon Postoffice and indications were that the bill might have been received from Max Halpern. This individual was investigated by the police and apparently cleared of suspicion, the incident being looked upon as a suspicious circumstance relative to the Giesslers rather than to Halpern.

Payne L. Kratzner, the owner of the Plymouth Apartments, received treatment in a sanitarium at Englewood, N.J. in 1929. Some of his attendants came from that vicinity. The present attendant, one Messinger, has been with Kretzmer since the fall of 1932, and is looked upon with some suspicion by Richard Kretzmer, but to date a check of his activities has not been made. Apparently the attendant Messinger is not related to the David Messinger family of 1245-Elder Ave., the Bronx, who were accused by a discharged employee of having possession of the Lindbergh baby. From May, 1929 to the Fall of 1932, an attendant named Howard Arndt, of German extraction, was with Kretzmer. Arndt was hired by Kretzmer's nephews who handle the employment of all attendants. During his employment, Arndt lived at 537 West 149th Street; when he left, in October, 1932, he gave a removal address of 141 Windsor St., Reading, Pa. Arndt was the subject of considerable investigation by the New Jersey State Police, and the Intelligence Unit of the Treasury Department and was found to have a rather poor record. The investigation developed Arndt was divorced from his wife, who was remarried to a Chester Wittmer, residing at 512 Beaver St., Lancaster, Pa. This woman was interviewed by an agent of the Intelligence Unit and stated she as married to Arndt in 1918 whom they both resided in Reading, Pa. Shortly after the marriage Arndt was drafted into the army and was sent to Fort Thomas, Ky. with a medical detachment but remained in the Service only a short time as the Armistice was signed. Subsequently, both Arndt and his wife obtained positions as nurses in the Cedar Grove Hospital, Essex County, New Jersey; then at the Ludlum Sanitarium, Gladwyn, Pa. During the latter employment, Mrs. Arndt decided to leave her husband because of his "eccentric characteristics." He was a mental case, to some extent, according to his wife, and it appears he received treatment at the Ludlum Sanitarium where he was placed in a padded cell. After he had improved to some extent his wife went back to live with him and they again obtained positions at the Cedar Grove Hospital in New Jersey where they stayed for one year after which Mrs. Arndt left her husband again, this time for good. Mrs. Arndt gave an opinion that Howard Arndt would do anything for money and described him as a mere pervert and a clever maniac. She states that when their daughter was nine years of age, he attacked her, with the result that the daughter has been under a doctor's care ever since. At one time (date not known), the Arndts lived in Verona, Essex County, N.J. and while there, Howard Arndt, in an effort to get some easy money brought suit for $50,000 against one Ray Appleman, a casual acquaintance, for alienation of affections. The suit, however, was never brought to trial.

The former Mrs. Arndt advised that the following were acquaintances or friends of Arndt:

Superintendent of the State Hospital, name unknown, Trenton, N.J.; a Dr. Centre, formerly superintendent of the Woodbine Hospital, Woodbine, N.J. (now deceased); Bill Carter,

Woodbine, N.J. who several times warned Mrs. Arndt about her husband, stating he was a dangerous individual.

Mrs. Wittmer has had no communication from her former husband for a long time and it does not appear that she furnished specimens of his handwriting. She heard recently that he had re-married, and that he had called on former friends of theirs, names not given, in a large expensive make of car, accompanied by a liveried chauffeur. She states this is unusual as during their married life they possessed very little money, and were hard pressed to meet their obligations. Mrs. Wittmer furnished the agent who conducted the interview a group photo of Howard Arndt, herself and daughter, and Bill Carter. This photo is in possession of the Intelligence Unit, and will be obtained by the New York Division Office in connection with the complete check which will be made into Howard Arndt's activities. It does not appear that he has been questioned as yet. Interview will be had with the nephews of Payne Kretzmer relative to Arndt and other attendants who have been employed at various times.

The New York Police in their investigation of the apartment house at 537 West 149th Street, found on the dumbwaiter shafts in the basement of the apartment, a number of old name cards; among those was a card bearing the name of "Faulkner." This card was in full view of the various superintendents who have worked at the apartment, inasmuch as the superintendents spend considerable time in the basement, one of their duties being to dispose of refuse placed on the dumbwaiters. During the Winter months, a fireman was usually employed at the apartment, and the Faulkner card would likewise have been observed by him. The card in question is now in the possession of Captain Oliver of the New York Police Department. Inquiry will be made to determine what initials, if any, appear on same.

There were exhibited to Richard Kretzmer all photographs in the Lindbergh file of the New York Division office, including a large number recently furnished from the Division's modus operandi file on extortionists and kidnapers. Mr. Kretzmer failed to identify any of these photographs except that of Duane Bacon, one of the former superintendents of the building who is considered later.

Investigation was conducted by the New Jersey State Police, the New York Police, and the Intelligence Unit, and more recently instituted by the Division's New York office, into the activities and connections of all employees, past and present, of the apartment house, 537 West 149th Street. From available records it was learned that the following have been the superintendents of this apartment:

Name	Born	Period of Employment	Present or last known address
John L. Peterson	Sweden	1917; again in 1929	Deceased
Chas. Balson	U. S.	1918	Unknown
Frederick Becker or Boeker	Germany (?)	1929-30	Apt. 1B; 1275 Bobscobe Ave., Bronx.
Eugene Beaver	?	April 1930 to 1/31/31	14 W. 84 or 600 W. 146th New York City
Duane William Bacon	U. S.	4/1/31 to 4/15/32 Discharged	3444 Knox Pl. Bronx

| Wm. Bender | Sweden | 4/25/32 to date | 537 W. 149th St. N.Y.C. |

Following are the names of other employees of this apartment house, and periods of employment, present addresses, etc. developed to date:

Joe Malsey (or Mayslo), fireman, from Fall of 1931 to 5/7/32; present address 180-2nd Ave., New York City, or 139 West 82nd St., New York City.

Millard Nash (colored), elevator boy, since 1930; present address, 416 West 146th St., New York City.

Nelson Marks, (colored), elevator boy, from 1931 to date; present address, unknown.

Shirley James (colored), elevator boy, from 1929 to 1930; present address, 568 West 149th St., New York City.

William P. Schimpf, plumber, did contract work at apartment for years; business address, 497 West 145th St., New York City.

Keogh (initials unknown)—electrician; does contract work at apartment; business address 497 West 145th St., New York City.

John J. McKale, has done odd contract work at apartment; business address, 497 W. 145th Street, New York City.

The names of the above listed employees, and the names of all tenants past and present were checked against the records of the New York Police Department, with the result that the only individual found to have a criminal record was the former superintendent, Duane William Bacon, who had worked at the apartment under the alias of Duane Baker from 4/1/31 to 4/15/32, when he was discharged for dishonesty, inefficiency, and borrowing money from tenants. His criminal record is as follows:

1915 Arrested Hackensack, N.J., charge, grand larceny (auto) 13 months Rahway, N.J. Reformatory.

1917 Arrested New York, N.Y. Grand Larcey (auto); Blackwell's Island.

1921 Larceny charge pending at Union City, N.J.

1922 Arrested New York City as fugitive from Boston, Mass.

1923 Arrested Boston, Mass.—charge, grand larceny; placed on probation; violated parole.

1923 Arrested New York City as fugitive for violation of parole at Boston; escaped.

1925 Arrested New York City, as fugitive; returned to Boston; sentenced 5 years, Mass. Reformatory; paroled 8/22/27.

1927 Arrested New York City, grand larceny, no disposition.

It was learned that Bacon, while superintendent of the apartment house, conducted gambling games in the basement on frequent occasions. The names of the individuals who attended these games are not known. It does not appear that Bacon was acquainted with the Faulkner family or any of their relatives as the Faulkners were out of the building long before Bacon became superintendent. However, the old card on the dumb-waiter shaft in the basement bearing the name of "Faulkner" was within his full view, and that of his friends, as well as other employees. Mr. Richard Kretzmer, brother of the apartment house owner, states "Bacon stole everything he could get his hands on," and was always broke and borrowed money from tenants without paying them back. Bacon had been recommended for employment by one Arthur C. Jones of 600 West 146th Street, who for many years was rental agent for the Plymouth Apartments. It is alleged that Bacon, although married, brought numerous women to the apartment house. He did not own an automobile but had a close friend named Steward, living across the street at 544 West 149th, who owned a small sedan. Bacon's other close friends were Edward Serry of 435 West 125th Street, who also owns a car; Joe Mayslo, 139 West 82nd Street who is now unfriendly with Bacon because of money matters; and the following individuals who have an office at 497 West 145th Street; Alex Manis (carpenter); Wm. P. Schimpf (plumber); James Bradley (mason and plasterer); Koogh, (electrician) and John J. McKale. The last mentioned individuals, said to be reputable, have not yet been interviewed. According to information furnished by employees of the apartment house, Bacon made frequent telephone calls to New Jersey during the entire year of his employment. The Intelligence Unit is in possession of a list of toll calls made from the apartment house, covering a period of several years, and same will be obtained for use in this investigation. Bacon had a cousin, name unknown, who frequently visited him, remaining overnight; this cousin had a car and was allegedly from New Jersey. Bacon had made statements that he formerly worked superintendent in various apartment houses in Englewood and Jersey City, N. J. which points he was supposed to be visiting frequently. His exact whereabouts March 1, 1932 and April 2, 1932, are unknown, although the payroll records show he received full pay through March—1932 up to April 15, 1932. There are indications, however, that Bacon absented himself from the apartment house on number of occasions in the Spring of 1932, on which occasions he had the color elevator boys work for him, often several days at a time. These boys have been unable so far to associate thee occasions with any particular dates.

Bacon was said to be a good carpenter, when he left the apartment he allegedly stole some tools, small bits, and some lumber. The tools do not include a chisel similar to that found on the Lindbergh estate, nor was the lumber like that used in the construction of the ladder.

On April 15, 1932, Bacon borrowed $25 from Richard Kretzmer which might indicate he did not have a part of the ransom money. Kretzmer remembers that Bacon pleaded with him for this loan, claiming his wife was very ill. On the other hand rumors have recently come to the attention of the New York Division Office to the effect that Bacon had $5,200 on deposit in some New York bank. It appears that Bacon when he was discharged had the following funds:

$25 loan from Richard Kretzmer; $76 in rent money, embezzled; $100 salary paid him on April 1, 1932; and possibly a few dollars salary covering the period April 1st to 10th, 1932.

After leaving the Plymouth Apartments, Bacon allegedly went to live in New Jersey for a while after which he lived in Astoria, L. I., then in the Bronx at 34 Convent Place. At the latter address Bacon paid a month's rent in advance, remained only four days, and then disappeared.

He had two Prudential Life Insurance policies which were followed to lapse; the last payment was made on March 20, 1933.

He was finally located by the New York Police, on November 13, 1933 residing in an apartment house at 3444 Knox Place, corner Mosholu Parkway, the Bronx, which is only a few blocks from St. Raymond's Cemetery, and a block from the corner of Gunhill Road and Knox Place where the taxi driver, Joseph Perrone, received one of the ransom notes. Neither Dr. Condon nor Joseph Perrone, however, were able to identify Bacon, and his handwriting was found to be dissimilar to the ransom notes and Faulkner's deposit ticket, by Expert Albert D. Osborn and the Division laboratory.

Bacon was questioned at Police Headquarters by Captain Oliver and Lieutenant Finn of the New York City Police Department. At this time he was not known to have a long criminal record, and when asked whether he had a record denied the fact, stating only that he had been in jail a few times for minor offenses. The interrogation failed to develop anything which would link on to this case. His alibi as to his whereabouts on March 1, 1932 and subsequent dates is not known at this time; however, the New York Police are furnishing the New York Office with copies of their reports covering the investigation and interrogation of Bacon.

The New York Police subsequently learned of Bacon's long record and again brought him in for questioning but without further results. The investigation as to him is still active with the New York Police.

Bacon is married and has one minor child; his wife is of German extraction. Allegedly he was very friendly with a woman, name unknown, who formerly resided at 150th Street and Amsterdam Ave., New York City but who disappeared when Bacon was discharged from the Plymouth Apartments.

Bacon was born in New York City on December 23, 1896; police records list him as a citizen of New Jersey. On October 23, 1920 he married Anna McGrath at Boston, Mass.; she died a year later. Nothing is known concerning his second wife. His father is deceased; his mother, Emily Beringer Main, has remarried and presently resides at 642—39th St., Union City, N. J. care of E. B. Hufnagel. He has the following additional relatives;

Phillip Main (stepfather)
Mrs. Louis Piazza, 577 Park Ave., West New York, N. J. (sister)
Mary Bacon (with mother)—sister
Harry Bacon—chauffeur, West New York, N. J. (brother)
Elmer Bacon—Marine Foreman, 612 West 53rd St., N. Y. C. (brother)
Frank Beringer—soap manufacturer, 309—14th St., West New York, N. J. (uncle).

Bacon had no military service; he is known to have been employed as follows:

Armour and Co., 52 West 14th Street, New York City as chauffeur, in 1924. (Charles Henry Ellerson, Morrow chauffeur, worked here in 1923).
Hudson County Bus Co., Jersey City, N. J., 1925.
Board of Education, Municipal Building, New York City, as bus driver in 1921.
Superintendent of Apartment House at 442—West 160th Street, New York City, about 1930 or 1931 (not confirmed).

It has been learned recently from the New York Police that Bacon, about January 15, 1934, disappeared from his most recent address, on Knox Place, taking with him the rents he had collected from various tenants. His present whereabouts is unknown. Bacon is described as follows:

Age 37; born New York City; December 23, 1896; height 5'9:; weight 160 pounds; build, well built; eyes, blue; hair, dark blonde; smooth shaven; wears horn-rimmed eyeglasses at times; peculiarities, thin face, thick lips, peculiar eyes, set deep; sunken jaws, heavy eyebrows; pigeon toed; nationality, American of German descent.

As of possible significance, it is pointed out that Bacon has been using crutches for the past several months, claiming that he is suffering from rheumatism. There also are indications that he injured his foot, possibly in the year 1932, as a number of people have observed him limping. Individuals who knew Bacon when he was superintendent of the apartment house at 537 West 149th Street stated that he had nothing the matter with his foot at that time and had no semblance of a limp. This point is being mentioned because of the fact that the ladder, found at the scene of the crime, had apparently collapsed, possibly injuring the kidnaper.

Included in the list of residents of the 500 block West 149th Street, obtained from the Post office Department, was the name of S. N. Bacon, 500 W. 149th Street. This individual in April, 1933, left a removal address for 287 Logan Ave., the Bronx. It is not known at the present writing whether he is related to Duane Bacon.

The following rental agents and real estate companies have been connected with the Plymouth Apartments in the past 15 years:

Arthur C. Jones,
Louis Carreau & Co;
D. Wood, Charles A. Dubois, Inc.;

Maurice Stempler, Charles A. Dubois, Inc.;
K. T. Tucker, Louis Carreau & Company;
Mr. Jaegler, Louis Carreau & Company;
Miss E. M. Walsh, Louis Carreau & Company (since 1916)
Irving Trust Company (since October 1932)

As of possible significance in connection with the J. J. Faulkner phase of this case, it is stated on March 2, 1932, the New York Police found a stolen Buick Sedan abandoned in front of a residence at 515 West 149th, a few doors from 537 West 149th. The car had been stolen in Lakewood, N. J. a few weeks prior to the kidnaping. On it, when recovered, was found a set of New York license plates which had been stolen in Yonkers, N. Y. on January 20, 1932. The police investigation failed to connect this car with the kidnaping but did not prove that the car was not used in the kidnaping. The various individuals questioned at the Plymouth Apartments knew nothing about this car. Complete details concerning the matter are set forth in another section of this report.

On December 31, 1933, an individual by the name of John H. Faulkner had an accident at the corner of Gunhill Road and Bronx River Parkway, Bronx, New York City. Faulkner was driving a 1930 Chevrolet Sedan, bearing 1933, New York License plates 3V4636. The other party to the accident was one Thomas Barr of 46 Park Place, New Rochelle, N. Y. In view of his name, investigation was conducted by the New York Police to determine whether John H. Faulkner had a possible connection with the "J. J. Faulkner" angle of this case. Police investigation developed that Faulkner was being treated at the Fordham hospital for a broken leg and was in a rather serious condition. From the information furnished on his admittance card and from the motor vehicle records, it was learned that

Faulkner was born in the Bronx and is an electrician by occupation; 33 years of age, and has resided for the last four years with his wife, Freida, at 59 Parkway North, Yonkers, N. Y. His parents were given as James Faulkner and Agnes Armstrong. In connection with the parents of this individual, attention is directed to the fact that Jane Emily Faulkner, former resident of 537 West 149th Street, had parents by the names of James Faulkner and Jane Armstrong. It appears possible that John H. Faulkner and Jane Emily Faulkner are related. An examination of John H. Faulkner's personal effects at the hospital, revealed nothing of any particular value to this investigation. He had in his possession a picture of a New York City patrolman, No. 15332, of the 14th Precinct, name not given. On the back of the picture was written, A. T. Dohman, 1754 Zerega Ave., Bronx. He also had in his possession membership card, year 1923, of the Weona Yacht and Canoe Club, 203rd Street and Hudson River, New York City, and a Knights of Columbus ring. The patrolman above referred to is listed in the Chief Clerk's office of the Police Department as Theodore J. Voneschen, 1616 Melville St., Bronx.

In addition to the Chevrolet car which John H. Faulkner was driving at the time of the accident, Motor Vehicle records show that he is also the owner of a 1930 Whippet Sedan, bearing New York 1933 License 3V 4635. Faulkner has 1933-334 operator's license 3699209. The officer who attended the scene of the accident was Patrolman John Ivers of the 57th Precinct.

The Fordham Hospital admittance card written by Faulkner is in the possession of the New York Police.

With further reference to the J. J. Faulkner angle of this case, it has come to the attention of the New York Division Office that a woman by the name of Mrs. James F. Boyle nee Helen Faulkner, and her husband, in the year 1909, were involved in the Billy Whitla kidnaping case at

Pittsburgh, Pa. Billy Whitla, an eight-year old boy, was kidnaped from a school room in a method similar to the method of operation employed in the Peggy McMath kidnaping case, Harwichport, Mass. The kidnapers of Billy Whitla resorted to methods in connection with the ransom negotiations somewhat similar to those used by the kidnapers of the Lindbergh baby. The following is a quotation from one of the letters showing the similarity: "We have Billy and he is safe and well. We want $10,000 in currency. You must not report Billy's absence to the police if you want to see him alive again. If you accept our terms so indicate through an advertisement in the personal columns of the Cleveland Press. . .worded like this 'A.A.A. will do as requested. J.P.W.' . . ." Billy Whitla's father, James P. Whitla, at the time was a prominent lawyer in either Philadelphia or Pittsburgh and Sharon, Pa. His boy was returned to him alive at Cleveland, Ohio after the payment of the ransom. Subsequently, the kidnapers, Mr. and Mrs. James F. Boyle, were apprehended and convicted. Helen Faulkner was the daughter of a Chicago fireman. She was sentenced to twenty-five years in the penitentiary and $5,000 fine, but according to information, was paroled after serving a few years. Her husband was a plumber, who had a previous criminal record, and he was given a life sentence. Boyle had apparently lived all his life in Sharon, Pa. It is believed that Helen Faulkner is presently residing at 1264 Elmdale St., Chicago, as Mrs. Helen McDermott. For obvious reasons, the Chicago and Pittsburgh offices have been requested to conduct investigation to determine the activities and whereabouts of Helen Faulkner during the year 1932.

On February 1, 1934 a $5 ransom bill was discovered at the Corn Exchange Bank and Trust Co., 42nd Street and 8th Avenue, New York City, and subsequently traced to one Joseph Frederick Faulkner. Investigation to date which is fully set out in the Ransom Money section of this report has not established that Joseph Frederick Faulkner is connected with or related to the Faulkners of 537 West 149th Street.

As of further possible significance in connection with this phase of the case, it is pointed out that suspect John Gorch under the alias of Theodore Sydorak, in December, 1931, and again between March 6, and 20, 1932 lived in a rooming house at 504 West 149th Street. Recent photos of Gorch, his sweetheart Evelyn Klimasefska, and his chief associate, Walter Nevack, were exhibited to various employees at the Plymouth Apartments, who stated they had never seen them around the apartment house. Similarly, the employees knew of no one connected with the building who had friends at Gorch's boarding house.

The landlady and her family at the latter place knew of no one in the house who was acquainted at the Plymouth Apartments. Gorch is fully treated in the section of the report entitled: "Subjects and Suspects."

As of possible significance it is pointed out that Dr. J. F. Condon has never, at any time, during his long discourses on this case with Special Agent J. J. Manning, made mention of the Faulkners, Giesslers, Leipolds, or Krippendorf. Although it is possible Dr. Condon does not know of this phase of the case, it appears probable that he would have learned of some through his son-in-law, Ralph Hacker.

AL CAPONE, TORRIO, NASH, BAILEY, BERRY, CONROY, ET AL

In view of the wide spread publicity concerning Capone's offer to organize and direct a search by the underworld for the Lindbergh baby, and the numerous allegations that the kidnaping was planned for the sole purpose of enabling Capone to obtain a pardon or other favor in return for discovering the baby, a brief history of Capone, as contained in the files of the New York Office, is set out herewith.

Capone was originally sponsored in Chicago by one Jim Colosimo who, before he became a leader in the underworld, was a street sweeper in Chicago on the near south side, and later became interested in ward politics. With his first wife he started operating a bawdy house. He quickly became powerful in local politics and started operating additional houses of prostitution as well as gambling houses. In the period immediately preceding the World War, members of the Mafia, or some similar Italian criminal organization in Chicago began a program of exacting tribute from Colosimo, thus forcing Colosimo to build up an organization of his own in order to protect his multiplying operations. Colosimo called upon the Five Points Gang in New York, reputed to be one of the toughest gangs in the country at that time, for one of their young leaders to assist him. John Torrio was sent to Chicago in response to this request arriving in Chicago before the United States entered the war. He immediately took a strong hold on the organization's gang activities particularly on the south side. He operated with Colosimo in this connection until finally he worked himself well up in Colosimo's confidence and was, in fact, attending to a large portion of the business. He then began to figure that someone else should be in charge of the strongarm side of the business and in consequence, imported among others, Alphonse Capone from New York for this purpose. Al Capone began his career as a bartender on the Bowery and was also a member of the Five Points Gang. Prior to his departure from New York he was viewed by the police as but a minor hoodlum. Shortly after Capone's arrival Colosimo was killed in his restaurant. It was suspected that Torrio, desiring sole power had Colosimo "put on the spot". Thereafter Torrio assumed the gang leadership in Chicago. During this period, Capone himself was building up a strong organization in the same field although apparently operating in close harmony with Torrio. Capone first got into the organized racket in a small way and by 1923 reached the point where he was able to pay $4,500 for an automobile: in 1924 he with associates operated three gambling places in a suburb of Cicero from which point his criminal operations expanded and his power increased.

In 1925, Torrio was arrested on a charge of violating the National Prohibition Act in connection with the Sieben Brewery case. Numerous persons were in the brewery at the time of the raid, among them Dean O'Banion, reputed leader of the gang activities on the north side. Many defendants were indicted in this case on May 27, 1924, and on January 17, 1925 after withdrawing his plea of not guilty, Torrio plead guilty and was sentenced to nine months in jail and $5,000 fine, being finally committed on February 9, 1925. Some time before this, however, Dean O'Banion was murdered in a florist shop which he operated in Chicago with one Schofield; George "Bugs" Moran, a notorious north side Chicago gangster and a lieutenant of O'Banion trailed Torrio to the north side with one Schemer Drucci, and Moran and Drucci wounded Torrio. Torrio refused to identify them although Moran in Torrio's presence admitted that he had shot him and said that he would have finished him if such action would not have injured Torrio's wife. After recovering from his wound, Torrio served the sentence mentioned above and then departed for Brooklyn, N. Y. where he has resided since that time except for possible brief visits to Chicago. A difference of opinion is reported among informed persons as to whether Capone and Torrio were friendly at the time Torrio left Chicago. It is indicated, however, that Torrio left Chicago at Capone's suggestion; was still a business partner of Capone and banked considerable funds for the Capone syndicate. While operating in Chicago, Torrio carried on general criminal activities but was particularly associated with the operation of houses of prostitution and also some gambling in the vicinity of Burnham, Ill. and Hammond, Indiana.

About 1927 a feud developed between a gang headed by Hymie Weiss and Capone' organization. A number of men were associated with Capone including O'Banion; Merle; Lolardo, and Lombardo, all of whom were widely notorious and all of whom were murdered in gang wars. It is said that Hymie Weiss would have nothing to do with prostitution and for that reason scorned the Capone crowd because they were engaged in prostitution, particularly Ralph Capone, Al's brother. Hymie Weiss organized a raid on the Capone headquarters in the Hawthorne Hotel and blasted it with machine gun fire. Later when Weiss was on trial and with his attorney had just left the criminal courts building, he was killed and his attorney was wounded by machine gun fire coming from across the street from the court house. This was said to have practically ended all organized gang opposition to Capone in Chicago.

Subsequently, in October 1931, Al Capone was convicted in Federal Court, Chicago, for evading income taxes and was sentenced to eleven years imprisonment. Ralph Capone had previously been convicted and sentenced for the same offense.

On March 9, 1932, the New York Daily Mirror published a story that "Al Capone was seeking is release from the eleven year penitentiary term in exchange for the kidnaped Lindbergh baby", further stating that "a representative of Colonel Lindbergh conferred on March 8th with the emissary from Capone." Further that "it was certified that Capone was the direct source of the order carried to New York racket powers that Salvatore Spitale and Irving Bitz seek appointment as agents between the underworld and Colonel Charles A. Lindbergh." The newspaper further stated that Capone is said to have underwritten any and all expenses incurred by Spitale and Bitz including payment to the original kidnapers of any ransom monies they expected to recover. That according to the terms said to have been formulated in behalf of Capone, Lindbergh was not to pay any ransom but would request Capone's release as the price of his child's recovery. That the induction of Al Capone's name into the situation is said to have come to Lindbergh's ears as early as Saturday, March 5, 1932, when a delegation of Chicago police officials attended the conference at Trenton, N. J. called by Governor Moore.

On March 11, 1932, the New York American announced that Capone had been interviewed by Arthur Brisbane, Editorial Director of the Hearst Newspapers and that Capone had stated he would do anything in his power to get the baby back and that he could do as much as anyone alive; that he knew a lot of people who might be valuable in finding the child; that there was nothing he could do behind the bars but he was pretty sure there would be if he could get out for a while, further that he would be willing to post bond up to $200,000 for his release. At this time Capone had been in jail for four months pending his appeal from the eleven year penitentiary sentence for failure to pay income taxes.

On March 12, 1932, the New York Daily News published a story that although Capone was still reiterating his request that he be released from jail under $200,000 bond to trail the kidnapers, Attorney General Mitchell said that the offer had not been put before the Department of Justice. The article further stated that an airplane was standing by at Newark Airport to carry Max Silverman, New York bondsman, to Chicago with "more than $200,000 in bonds" which he said he would post for the release of Capone; that Silverman said he had been commissioned to take the bonds to Chicago but declined to say who commissioned him.

Early on the morning of March 12, 1932, Morris Rosner, Salvatore Spitale and Irving Bitz, as related in more detail in the section of this report entitled "Morris Rosner, et al", conferred with Colonel Lindbergh, Colonel Breckinridge and Robert Thayer relative to their approaching Al Capone in Chicago, stating that Capone's power was so great that he would surely find the child if he once started to put his force into action and that he would also upon finding the child furnish necessary ransom money to secure its release, but in return would demand a favor with reference to the eleven year sentence which is now against him. The information on file in this office does not indicate, however, that Rosner, Spitale or Bitz had been in communication with Capone or spoke with any authority on his behalf.

On March 16, 1932, an attorney named Leahy, Washington, D. C. communicated with the Director of this Division, relative to Capone and suggested that possibly Major Lamphier, a friend and associate of Colonel Lindbergh, should be ready with the money at a later date in order to fly by plane to the place where the baby would be designated as being left. Mr. Leahy informed that he listened in on the telephone while the lawyer who first contacted him as to Capone was talking with some lawyer in Chicago, and the one in Chicago said that there was no prospect of anything being done for the "big boy", indicating that they wanted something done for Capone. The lawyer talking from Chicago mentioned that the child had a cold at first but was then all right and would be returned in due time. Mr. Leahy indicated in his conversation that he believed possibly that the child would be returned by Tuesday of that week. It was indicated that the attorney they were dealing with in Chicago was a reputable member of the Bar; that the contact was identified as apparently coming directly from Capone as it was the same lawyer who had endeavored to arrange with Mr. Leahy to represent Capone in his appeal to the higher courts in connection with his income tax case. The New York Office file indicates that nothing further developed from this contact of Mr. Leahy's.

On March 17, 1932, Mr. James M. Phelan, attorney-at-law associated with Colonel Breckinridge, 25 Broadway, advised that a prominent attorney, Walter Gordon Merritt, 165 Broadway, New York City, had introduced to him, Mr. Edwin H. Cassels, who indicated that he had important information in connection with the kidnaping of the Lindbergh baby. Mr. Cassels was the former law partner of United States District Judge Wilkerson of Chicago who tried the Capone income tax case, and is presently associated with the firm of Cassels, Potter & Bentley, The Rookery, Chicago, Ill. Mr. Cassels stated in substance that a short time previously, an undercover inquiry was made by him of a client who was supposed to have underworld connections but did not state what the developments were, if any, from this inquiry. He indicated that he was interested in obtaining some consideration from Al Capone.

Later a message was received from Mr. Cassels by Mr. Thayer through Mr. Merritt to the effect that Dave Fleischer, one of the leaders of the Detroit Purple Gang, left there on the 28th or 29th of February and was probably then in Newark, N. J. and later he was further advised through this same channel that Abe Burnstein was supposed to have left Detroit with Fleischer. On March 29, 1932, Mr. Cassels was again in New York, and at the suggestion of Mr. Thayer was interviewed by Special Agent in Charge Connelley, at which time he repeated the information previously furnished by him and indicated that he had two contact men who were working on this matter, one in Chicago and one in Detroit, and that he would communicate any further information to this office. However, no further information was received from this source.

On March 18, 1932, counsel for Al Capone filed a petition for re-hearing by the Circuit Court of Appeals, of his conviction for evading income taxes. Three weeks previously the Appeals Court upheld the conviction but Capone's counsel declared that it had ignored the principal questions in the appeal.

On or about March 21, 1932, Mr. Julius Barnes of the United States Chamber of Commerce telephoned the secretary of the President of the United States, advising that an attorney from Chicago by the name of Siegelman or Singleman, who claimed to represent Capone, had requested him to go to the President for the necessary action to have Capone released from jail for at least forty-eight hours during which time Capone would be able to restore the child. They were advised that it would be best to leave this situation alone and Mr. Barnes was requested to advise this party, Singleman or similar name, to advise the party he was contacting that if they had anything to do with this in the future they should communicate with the Department of Justice.

Colonel Breckinridge, legal adviser to Colonel Lindbergh, was approached by Val O'Farrell, private detective of New York City, apparently acting as an emissary in behalf of Al Capone, and advised that bail for Capone could be obtained up to $1,000,000 if necessary.

On March 23, 1932, the New York Times published an article relative to the "mysterious entrance into the search, of H. Wallace Caldwell . . . of Chicago, former President of the Board of Education, Chicago, and a friend of former Mayor William Hale Thompson" stating that for nearly a week Caldwell had been busying himself in Chicago, Washington, Trenton, and Hopewell, following a lead. The newspapers connected Caldwell's activity with Capone's offer to organize a search for the baby. It appears that nothing further developed as a result of Mr. Caldwell's activity.

On or about March 10, 1932, information was received at Washington, D. C. by the Division, to the effect that on February 11, 1932 John Torrio, a reputed gangster of Chicago and henchman of Al Capone stopped at the Washington Hotel, Washington, D. C., as John Torrence and registered from 195-33 Hillside Avenue, Hollis, Long Island; that while at Washington he conferred with Peter Granata who at the time was serving as a Congressman but who has since been unseated; that the day following this conference Granata left for Chicago where it was reported that he had called upon Capone. He returned to Washington immediately and then proceeded to New York. Further that the persons furnishing this information to the Division were of the opinion that Torrio had been acting for Capone and possibly engineered the Lindbergh kidnaping. Investigation developed that Torrio had been living at the Hollis address for a considerable period of time and received mail addressed to him there as John Torrence, and on March 9, 1932 filed a removal notice at the postoffice giving his new address as 1577 East 18th Street, Brooklyn, N. Y. Informant stated that Torrio was absent from the Hollis address most of the time and the place was occupied by two women, one about 75 years of ago and the other, about 35 years old. Investigation further developed that the house at 1577 East 18th Street, Brooklyn, N. Y. is occupied by the same two women, and that mail is received there addressed to John Torrio; John Torrence and George B. Jacobs, also to a Mrs. Caputo. The records of the Bureau of Criminal Identification, New York Police Department, disclose that John Torrio as John Langley at Chicago, Ill. on January 17, 195 upon conviction of violation of the National Prohibition Act was sentenced to nine months at the DuPage County Jail, fined $5,000 by Judge Cliffe and on February 9, 1925 the commitment was changed to the Lake County Jail and subject was discharged October 19, 1925.

John Torrio was interviewed in the New York Office with reference to another matter on October 13, 1933 and stated that during the investigation of the Lindbergh kidnaping matter by members of the Intelligence Unit of the Treasury Department, he had been questioned on several occasions at great length in connection with is failure to report his income tax at which time the kidnaping of the Lindbergh baby was similarly discussed. Torrio stated that he had expressed his opinion to the Intelligence Unit agents that the Lindbergh baby was not kidnaped for ransom and added that he had told them at that time that the baby was kidnaped and subsequently murdered by a person who had a grouch against Lindbergh and it was purely a case of personal vengeance. Further that the underworld had nothing to do with it. Torrio also stated that two special agents of the Intelligence Unit informed him that they had actually witnessed the payment of the ransom money in New York City by Dr. Condon. Torrio pointed out that sooner or later those in possession of the Lindbergh ransom money will be caught, stating that they have to "unload the dough some time." He further said that Al Capone was "grand-standing" when he announced from his detention quarters in Chicago that if liberated he could solve the case. He characterized this as "pure bunk."

The foregoing part of this section indicates the extent of the publicity relative to Capone's offer to assist in the search, in return for a consideration,—and of the negotiations allegedly in his behalf. In the part which follows, are set out allegations received from widespread sources charging that members of Capone's organization planed and perpetrated the crime. Such of these allegations are as capable of being investigated will receive the further attention of this office.

On March 7, 1932, a prisoner in the United States Penitentiary, Atlanta, Ga. Serving a twenty-five year sentence prepared a statement for the Secret Service which was subsequently referred to the Division. In this statement he alleged that Al Capone was in back of the kidnaping and that it had been planned and perpetrated by Francis Keating; Tommy Holden and others for the purpose of securing the release of Capone, in return for locating the victim of the kidnaping.

This prisoner was subsequently interviewed at his request by one of the Division's Special Agents in Charge. He stated that prior to his entering the penitentiary he was in the absolute confidence of both Ralph and Al Capone, and had since his incarceration been in close touch with the gang; that after Ralph Capone arrived at Leavenworth Penitentiary they discussed the prosecution of Al Capone then pending and were rather satisfied that he would receive a sentence that would be affirmed by the higher court and that it was intended that the gang should engineer a move which would "show up" all of the law enforcement agencies of the United States. Ralph Capone stated that the move would be to kidnap someone of National prominence in or around Chicago or some nationally known official of the United States Government. In fact it was stated that Ralph Capone had under consideration a son of the then Attorney General Mitchell and that the kidnaping was not to be for a monetary reward but solely for the purpose of creating a situation wherein the public would be so incensed over the fact that law enforcement agencies could not solve the kidnaping or locate the kidnaped person that at an appropriate time, ostensibly to render the people of the country a service, Al Capone would step into the picture and without asking for a reward, offer his services to the relatives of the kidnaped person and to the United States and that if he was successful in having his services accepted would promptly locate and cause the return of the kidnaped person.

This prisoner stated that in none of the discussions had with Ralph Capone was the Lindbergh baby ever mentioned. That it was his understanding that the subject of the kidnaping would be some adult, nationally known. That shortly after the time of these considerations Ralph Capone was suddenly transferred to McNeil and the prisoner has not recently had any contact with Ralph.

It was stated that this prisoner is not what is known as the "snitching" type; that he is regarded as a "big shot" among the prisoners and he specifically requested that his name be not mentioned in connection with any investigation which might follow as a result of his disclosures. Although helpless to cooperate in any way he volunteered to do whatever might be possible for him to do and the only suggestion made was that transfers might be arranged so as to again bring him into contact with Ralph Capone. This information was transmitted to the New Jersey State Police and there were no further developments in this connection.

A few days after the kidnaping occurred, the Intelligence Unit of the Treasury Department as informed through a confidential source that Alphonse Capone, who was then in the Cook County Jail, had sent out word to members of his gang to locate Bob Conroy, a former associate of the gang; that Capone had recently learned that Bob Conroy was planning to "pull" a big job in the east that would shock the country and that Capone suspected the job referred to might be the Lindbergh kidnaping. Conroy was wanted for murder of a police officer in Toledo, Ohio, during the robbery of the Western Union Telegraph Company but he had evaded capture for several years. The efforts of Capone's friends to locate Conroy were unsuccessful. This information regarding Conroy was at once conveyed to the

New Jersey State Police and also the New York City Police Department. It was found that early in 1932, Conroy had been at Miami, Florida, with a blond woman posing as his wife and that they left that state in February. In August 1932, the New York City newspapers reported that a couple had been found dead in an apartment at 200 West 102nd Street near Broadway. That they were known as Robert and Rosemary Sanborn; that they had been dead about forty-eight hours before discovered; that the police and called it a murder and suicide, the man having shot the woman and then shot himself and that a counterfeiting plant was found in their apartment. Through fingerprints taken from the body of the dead man it was established that he was Bob Conroy and the dead woman was a blond who was with him in Florida in the early part of the year. They had been living in the apartment since June 1, 1932. Search of their apartment and trunks revealed several specimens of the writing of each, which were submitted to the Bureau of Standards for comparison with the ransom notes but the writing was not found to be similar. A few days after news of the death of Robert and Rosemary Sanborn was published in the New York City papers, an anonymous communication, signed "221", was received by the Commissioner of Police of New York City, as follows:

"Check activities of Robert and Rosemary Sanborn in Lindbergh case. Keep quiet until convinced."

The letter was typewritten and bore cancellation stamp indicating that it was mailed in a branch of the New York Post Office near Wall Street. Interviews with other tenants in the apartment and in speakeasies frequented by Conroy developed no information of value. A sticker was found on one of their trunks indicating that it had been shipped from Washington, D. C. on March 2, 1932 and that after their arrival in New York they lived for a few days at some hotel on West 100th Street. Conroy had occupied a small loft on West 21st Street, New York City. They lived very poorly and he had tried to borrow a small sum of money from a bartender in a speakeasy; between January 13, and March 3, 1932 they proceeded from Florida to Washington, D. C. and lived at the Hamilton Hotel and Blackstone Hotel when they checked out of the latter and shipped a trunk by express to New York City. Some counterfeit currency was found in their apartment and it was taken by the United States Secret Service who also destroyed the printing press found in the apartment. In one of his trunks was found a small undeveloped film which upon being developed and enlarged was seen to be a kodak picture of the blond companion of Conroy and a dog taken in Potomac Park, Washington, D. C. This picture is in the possession of the New Jersey State Police, Trenton. This picture and a picture of Conroy were shown to Dr. Condon, to employees of the Lindbergh home, and to persons in the vicinity of Hopewell, who had seen suspicious people in the vicinity previous to the kidnaping.

A person in Chicago, close to the Capone organization, reported that Conroy's death in New York was known in Chicago by some of that organization on the day before news of his death was published in that city and the gang alleged that Conroy had been killed by some of his enemies. Conroy and the woman had made many enemies as they had worked the "badger" game on many prominent business men, and Conroy is alleged to have been involved in the St. Valentine Day massacre at Chicago when seven of the "Bugs" Moran gang were killed by a gang that never was identified.

The Conroy angle will be kept in mind in the future investigation of this case as it may develop that persons under suspicion may have had some connection with

Conroy or Rosemary. The correct name of Rosemary was not ascertained. Her body was unclaimed and was given a pauper's burial by the City of New York. The body of Conroy was not claimed by relatives, and a suitable burial was given by the United States Government as he was a World War veteran. Photostatic copies of photographs of Conroy and Rosemary are on file in the New York Office of the Division.

On March 10, 1932, Robert Baird alias Harry Mack alias Sam Black was interviewed by an agent of the Division in connection with another matter and stated that about three or four weeks before the interview when he was confined in the Essex County Jail at Sanwich, Ontario, his adjoining cell mate was one Harold Fontaine. Fontaine advised that $20,000 would be raised by his, Fontaine's friends by April 1st in order to secure proper defense counsel for Fontaine; that in order to raise this sum of money a big coup was going to be pulled in the east. Baird presumed that this information was forwarded to Fontaine by Keating, Holden or Nash who were then escaped prisoners from the Leavenworth Penitentiary.

Baird further stated that on March 3, 1932, Fontaine was visited at the County Jail by either his sister or sister-in-law; that the first thing she told him was that Lindbergh's child had been kidnaped and that she made this remark in a laughing manner. Fontaine then asked "Was there any accident?"

On September 22, 1932 when Baird was being held in the County Jail at Lawrence, Kan. As a witness he was again interviewed by an agent of the Division and stated that when he was confined in jail with Harold Fontaine, in Canada, Fontaine mentioned to him that one Bill Bailey who is known around Herron and Canton, Ill, was involved in the kidnaping of the Lindbergh baby. Baird further stated that Fontaine told him that Bailey was involved in kidnaping charges some years ago in California where the police had a record of him.

Fontaine was later confined in the United States Penitentiary at Atlanta, Ga. On a twenty year sentence imposed December 9, 1932 upon conviction on a charge of assault with intent to murder T. B. White, warden of the United States Penitentiary at Leavenworth, Kan. On December 11, 1932 when several prisoners effected their escape by means of firearms. Fontaine then a discharged prisoner, and Frank Nash, Thomas Holden and Francis Keating, escapees from the Leavenworth Prison, smuggled into that institution the contraband ammunition used by the convicts when effecting the break of December 11, 1931. While in jail together at Sandwich, Ontario, Fontaine freely discussed with Baird his implication together with Nash, Holden and Keating in the prison break. Baird later testified to this effect in the subsequent removal proceedings and trial of Fontaine.

Holden and Keating were apprehended at Kansas City, Mo. in July 1932, and each is now confined in the Federal Penitentiary at Leavenworth, Kansas on a twenty-five year sentence for mail train robbery. Harvey Bailey was arrested with them and was given a life sentence for bank robbery, in the State Penitentiary at Lansing, Kansas. From where he with others escaped on May 30, 1933. On June 17, 1933, at Kansas City, Mo. while enroute to the U. S. Penitentiary, Leavenworth, Kan., Nash and several of his guards, including Special Agent Raymond J. Caffrey of the Division, were fired upon and killed. Harvey Bailey, who was at large at this time was charged with being a party to the murder. He was subsequently convicted and given a life sentence in the Urschel kidnaping case.

Another informant, John J. Pawelczyk, later in this section alleges that Nash told him that he and Harvey Bailey, and others, perpetrated the Lindbergh kidnaping and murder. This informant alleges that Bailey killed Nash or had him killed for fear that he might talk in this connection as a basis for bargaining for consideration.

Upon being further interviewed, Baird elaborated on the information which he asserted he received from Fontaine regarding the Lindbergh case stating that Fontaine also included Holden and Keating as well as an Italian known as "Johnny the Wop"; "Curley" Erickson of Detroit, Michigan; one Conroy and his feminine criminal associate, "Rose" of New York City, as possible suspects. The last two named were mentioned as criminals who operated the extortion and shake-down game in a big way, and were alleged to have blackmailed a wealthy Chicago man of $25,000 or $50,000 and that Al Capone had interceded by requesting a reduction in the demand; however, that Conroy had refused and had defied Capone. Conroy was also alleged by Fontaine to have committed a murder on the Pacific Coast and to be engaged "in a big way" in the circulation of counterfeit money, much of which originated from an Italian named Corosi at an unnamed place in the State of New Jersey. It appears that Conroy and "Rose" mentioned by Fontaine are Conroy and "Rosemary" previously mentioned in this section. Fontaine also mentioned an Italian named Decey and his associate in the shake-down game, called Helen Goldberg or Goldstein, both of Fort Lee, N. J. Fontaine particularly mentioned that Bill Bailey, Nash, Holden, Keating, Conroy and Erickson might have been involved in the Lindbergh kidnaping. Baird later alleged that the reported murder and suicide of Rosemary Sanborn and Conroy at New York City about August 1, 1932, was erroneous in that the two of them had been killed at the instigation of Chicago gangsters either friends or relatives of Al Capone. Subsequent investigation developed that Bill Bailey apparently was not in the United States either at the time of the Leavenworth Prison break or the Lindbergh kidnaping.

On April 2, 1933, Arthur L. Hitner then under indictment in Buffalo, N. Y. in connection with a bank case, and understood to be a confidence man, contacted former Assistant Attorney General John Marshall and later contacted Mrs. Greathouse, Assistant United States Attorney, who is a relative of Mrs. Lindbergh, stating that he was in possession of information establishing the Lindbergh kidnaping was perpetrated by Harry Fleischer, Abe and Benny Wagner and others on behalf of Al Capone.

As set out in other parts of this report, this same person subsequently injected himself into the John Hughes Curtis, et al angle of the investigation, apparently with fraudulent intent, and since that time he has appeared in Albany, N. Y.; Los Angeles, Calif.; and Green Bay, Wis., repeating his story with variations in attempting to interest attorneys and others therein, claiming that the corpse which was found on May 13th was not the body of the Lindbergh baby, that the child is still alive and being held for ransom at a later date.

Further details regarding Hitner and his stories are set out in the sub-section entitled with his name in section "Frauds and Hoaxes".

Under date of May 13, 1932. An informant signing as "B.I." wrote a letter to Mr. Frank Burke, Secret Service, Treasury Department, Washington, D. C. making various allegations with reference to Harry Fleischer and other members of the Purple Gang and other criminals in connection with the Lindbergh kidnaping, stating that Al Capone was also interested in the matter. This information is set out in more detail in section "Subjects and Suspects—Purple Gang, Harry Fleischer, et al."

On July 2, 1932, the American Consul at Palermo, Italy, transmitted a dispatch advising that Francesco Furnari of Santa Maria de Licodia had reported that he had received a letter from Margaret Finn from Chicago, concerning the kidnaping of the Lindbergh baby, and stating that her friends, Goldstein and Antonio Gatto known as "Tony the Cat" would call upon him; that Goldstein and Gatto later met him in Catonia where they asked that he remember they were in Catonia on March 1st although he did not see them until April 17th; that Gatto later informed him concerning the kidnaping and murder as follows:

Al Capone's brother had arranged for the baby to be kidnaped, and Goldstein, Gatto and Margaret Finn were detailed to carry out the job. These orders were given through Frank Nitti alias "The Enforcer"; Nitti fearing that the government might accede to the request that Capone be freed in order that the child be located, gave orders that Capone's brother's orders that the child be kidnaped be carried out, but that the child be killed immediately so that he could not be exhibited to interested parties, and Al Capone's temporary release would not then be granted. Furnari further stated that Gatto stated that both he and Goldstein were instructed to leave the country; that Gatto was somewhere in Italy and Goldstein is somewhere in France. That he does not know their exact addresses but sees Gatto from time to time; that Margaret Finn is still living in the United States. Furnari claims that Goldstein killed the baby and that this is known to Frank Nitti and Al Capone's brother though Capone's brother did not plan or intend that the baby should be killed. Investigation developed that one Louis Gatto was still in the United States and has been since and before March 1, 1932. Margaret Finn and the Goldstein mentioned have not been located.

In August 1933, Henry R. Westcott, Jr. Chaplain, United States Army, Fort Clayton, Canal Zone, transmitted to the Department, information furnished by Oral E. Rathbun, a soldier then stationed at that post alleging in substance that one Joe MacKenzie of Lansing, Michigan, was working for John Torrio and tried to get him, Rathbun, to join his gang in a racket, shortly before the Lindbergh kidnaping. Rathbun enlisted in the army to hide from the members of the gang, and further alleged that Torrio had engineered the kidnaping and that the Lindbergh child had been held in New York, N. Y. by a Mrs. Brewster who had lived in the vicinity of 4745 Greenwood Avenue, Chicago, where one Margaret, a sweetheart of MacKenzie had lived. Further, that he had identified Mrs. Brewster by a newspaper photograph as Mrs. Fern Sankey. He further stated that Torrio's gang now has its headquarters in Cicero, Ill.

Investigation at Lansing, Michigan failed to confirm that Joe MacKenzie, who has a local police record, was connected with Torrio or any Chicago gangsters. Rathbun's former employer at Lansing, a restaurant proprietor, stated that he had discharged Rathbun after satisfying himself that Rathbun was stealing from the cash register. This former employer further stated that he understood Rathbun had become involved in a difficulty with a local girl and had to leave town. The Mrs. Brewster referred to by Rathbun was located and identified as a Mrs. Burnstein at 550 Briar Place, Chicago, and while it was noted that she born some slight resemblance to the photograph of Mrs. Fern Sankey, it was obvious that she was not the same person.

There was referred to the Division, in September 1933, a communication prepared by one John J. Pawelczyk, reciting that he had copyrighted a radio puzzle in September 1931 in connection with which he had also copyrighted a symbol very similar to that used on the Lindbergh ransom notes. The Division's laboratory examination in this connection indicated the Pawelczyk's writing was dissimilar to that on the ransom notes and that while the design was not identical it was the same general design as the symbol used on the ransom notes.

Pawelczyk was interviewed by a Special Agent of the Division on October 10, 1933 in the Illinois State Penitentiary, Joliet, Ill. where Pawelczyk is serving a sentence of from one to fourteen years on a charge of manslaughter, growing out of a killing which occurred in April 1933 at Chicago, and which Pawelczyk described as a drunken brawl.

Pawelczyk further stated that in 1931 while serving a five year sentence in Leavenworth Penitentiary on a charge of counterfeiting, he designed a radio puzzle consisting in part of a design which was his idea of radio dials. This design was composed of two circles which met and two smaller circular spots at about the center of the circles and a long oblique spot in the center of the space formed by the merging of the two circles.

That while serving time in Leavenworth he worked in the shoe factory on the fourth floor, operating a shriving machine; while there he became intimately acquainted with the notorious Frank Nash who worked in the shoe factory with him. He explained this radio puzzle to Nash, who discussed with him various questions in regard to other games and puzzles which Pawelczyk was interested in creating. Nash was also interested in the design in question and on a number of occasions drew the design on the all in back of the shriving machine. Pawelczyk believes this sketch could still be found on the rear wall in the shoe factory on the fourth floor of the Leavenworth Penitentiary.

That Pawelczyk further stated that he paid little attention to the Lindbergh case but that one day a man showed him the design on the Lindbergh ransom note as it appeared in some detective story magazine, and when he examined it he saw that it was the design which he had copyrighted in September 1931.

That in January 1933 after leaving the Penitentiary he frequented a saloon at 217 South Kedzie Avenue, Chicago, operated by Mike Ryan alias Mickey Dale alias Mickey

Barron who had served two terms in the Joliet Penitentiary; that while he was in this saloon Frank Nash came in and greeted him. Pawelczyk states that Nash was wearing a chestnut wig but he does not believe that he had on glasses or a moustache. That he asked Nash right out why Nash had used his design on the ransom notes. Nash told him not to say anything about it and that he would tell him more about it another time.

That about two weeks later he again saw Nash in the same saloon and had a long talk with him. Nash admitted that he had placed this symbol on the Lindbergh ransom notes. Nash told him that the actual kidnapers of the Lindbergh baby were Harvey Bailey, Frank Nash and one Bob Berry. That Berry is supposed to have committed suicide some time ago and used the alias of Berry, Bobby Davis, Bobby Sandstron, Bob Harris and others. That Barry is from Detroit and has been wanted for murder in that vicinity and should be well known to the Detroit police. He did not know whether Berry was a member of the Purple Gang in Detroit; that Nash stated the real instigator of the kidnaping was John Torrio, a former notorious Chicago gangster, now living in Brooklyn, N. Y.; that the real purpose of the crime was the liberation of Al Capone from the Federal Penitentiary at Atlanta, Ga.; that the idea of Torrio was to have the Lindbergh baby kidnaped and brought to Brooklyn, N. Y. where it would be held pending the release of Capone from the penitentiary for the purpose of finding the baby; that Capone would then find the child and would of course, have a strong case of clemency because of his activity; that the ransom phase was carried out to assist in hiding the real intent of the kidnaping.

Pawelczyk further stated that he had discussed kidnapings with Nash when he was in the penitentiary, and Nash had always told him that if a kidnaping was to take place it was very foolish to keep the victim alive or to release the victim after obtaining the ransom money, since the victim could then give information which might assist in the capture of the kidnapers; that Nash had always said it was a better policy to kill the victim as soon after the kidnaping as was possible, secrete the body, and use the clothing and other personal articles of the victim as a means to collecting the ransom payment.

Pawelczyk stated that Nash told him Torrio had apparently secured the services of Harvey Bailey to engineer the crime, and Bailey in turn secured Nash and Berry; that Bailey told Nash and Berry that the idea was to kidnap one of the Kresge girls in Detroit. When these parties arrived in Detroit, however, Bailey told them they had a job to pull in the east and carried them to New Jersey for the kidnaping.

Pawelczyk said that Nash did not mention the details of the kidnaping, except to say that they took the child, but he understood from Nash that the place had been watched for some time before the crime was pulled, and details had been worked out by these parties before the commission of the crime; that it probably was Frank Nash who killed the child shortly after taking it from its home, being convinced that it would be impossible to safely take it any distance; that Nash told him the child was killed and was buried in the underbrush after which the ransom negotiations were carried on; that Nash did not say he had prepared the ransom notes but did say he had used the design created by Pawelczyk. He did not explain why he used this design except to say that he was aware of its origin at the time he used it, and indicated that one of the reasons for its use was the fact that he knew the originator was then in the penitentiary.

That Nash further told him Berry was the actual emissary of the gang in collecting the ransom money from Dr. Condon; that this money was turned over by Berry to

Harvey Bailey who in turn carried it to John Torrio who is supposed to have paid $50,000 in good money for the marked bills; that Bailey then cleared out of New York and did not pay either Nash or Berry. Pawelczyk stated that he believed Bailey was in fact the leader of the gang which robbed banks, etc., and that Nash while a determined criminal was not the principal figure in the gang; that Nash did not explain to him why he did not attempt any reprisals against Bailey for taking the money or did not attempt to secure some funds from Torrio, but said he was telling Pawelczyk all these facts so they would be known. Further that Nash claimed he had not seen Bailey since March 1932 when the baby was kidnaped.

Pawelczyk further stated that Nash had connections all over the country with various gangs, as most of the other notorious criminals had. He indicated that he would not have told this story had not Nash been killed. That it was his opinion Nash was deliberately killed in Kansas City and that it was not an attempt to deliver him. He based his opinion upon the story told him by Nash and said he believed, that although the gang as a whole may have thought that the attempt to get Nash was to deliver him, the real purpose was to make sure that Nash did not tell his story concerning this case and that Bailey had arranged for either himself or some of the gunmen to make sure that Nash was killed before he reached the penitentiary.

Pawelczyk further stated that he did not wish to have his name revealed in connection with this matter but was interested in possible clemency and in any reward that might be offered.

Pawelczyk's criminal record in the Chicago Police Department indicates that he has been convicted of various crimes and sentenced on at least seven occasions since 1909 and has been returned several times for violation of parole.

The handwriting of Harvey Bailey was compared with the ransom letters, and was found by Albert D. Osborn, examiner of questioned documents, New York City, to have no similarity thereto.

PURPLE GANG—HARRY FLEISHER, et al

Because of the widespread publicity relating to the Purple Gang and Harry Fleisher, et al, in connection with this case, a brief outline of its history and organization as contained in the files of this office is set out herewith.

From the time of its inception in 1926, the Purple Gang in Detroit, Michigan, has always been identified with kidnaping, as well as with the alcohol and beer rackets. Following the disintegration of the gang in 1930 due to the encroachments of the so-called "Jewish Navy" organization of rum runners, the members of the Purple Gang dispersed; some who came to the East have frequently been suspected in connection with sensational kidnapings in the Metropolitan area of New York City.

Two of its members, Samuel Handel alias Louis Green alias "Lefty" Hanlen, and Harry I. Fleish alias Henry Fink alias Harry Fleisher were arrested in New York City on February 4, 1930 and held for extradition to Connecticut on a charge of complicity in the kidnaping on January 28, 1930, of Max Price, wealthy real estate man in Hartford, Conn. However, they were dismissed on the strength of alibi testimony to the effect that both were in Detroit, Michigan at the time of this kidnaping. Both have extensive police and criminal records and Harry Fleisher is generally known as one of the outstanding members of the Purple Gang.

Subsequently the Purple Gang was again mentioned in connection with the gangster shooting of "Chicago Frankie" Marlo in New York City in February, 1931. Marlo was reported to have come to New York to "declare himself in" on the fruits of several kidnapings executed by the Purple Gang.

Three of the alleged leaders of the Purple Gang were convicted and received life sentences for the murder of three rival gangsters in the Collingwood Apartment, Detroit, Michigan, in September, 1931. These three members of the Purple Gang were Ray Burnstein, Harry Keywell, and Irving Millberg. Harry Fleish, commonly known as Harry Fleisher alias Henry Fink, another leader of the Purple Gang, was alleged to have participated in this murder but escaped and remained a fugitive until June 9, 1932 when he voluntarily surrendered to the Detroit Police.

At the time of the Lindbergh kidnaping, the known leaders of the Purple Gang were Abe Burnstein, alias Bernstein; Joe Burnstein; Charles Leiter; Abe Axler; Sam Axler; Joe Miller; Henry Fletcher and Harry Fleisher, the last named being the only one wanted at that time by the Detroit Police. Photographs of these men are on file in the New York office. In addition to these there were known to the Detroit Police at about this time forty-four alleged members of the Purple Gang whose names follow:

Name	Detroit Police Department No.
Frank Klayman	17535
Fred Smith	24775
Zizzie Selbin (killed 10/26/29)	32548
Henry Miller	29277
Donald Goldblatt	—
George Harris	—
Arthur Kelley	—
Harry Wein	—

Chas. Stein	—
Jack Cohen	—
Joles Joffe	29663
George Cordell	18602
Abe Miller	30730
Abie Zussman	24051
Abe Kaminski	26157
Issie Kaminski	29286
Erwin Shapiro	24151
Sam Bernstein	28205
Issie Bernstein	31571
Louis Fleishcher	30083
Willie Laks	31946
Sam Davis	27718
Sam Goldforb	24243
Harry Shoor	10278
Ben Marcus	4780
Louis Gellerman	25710
Alfred Russel	24587
Louis Orthman	32562
Jack Redfern	32560
John Wolf	32561
James Powell	—
Louis Rapport	32613
Sam Potasink	—
Jack Levites	32563
Maurice Raider	10320
Joe Lieberoff	33780
Joe Sascer	33771
Zigie Selbin	33770
Sam Purple	11663
Jacob Willman	29505
Hymie Altman	28453
Abe Olenick	41273
Edw. Shaw	30452

On March 4, 1932 the newspapers generally announced that the Purple Gang was being sought by the New Jersey State Police in connection with the kidnaping of the Lindbergh baby but gave no particulars. On March 5, 1932, Fred A. Ingle, who claimed to be associated with the Purple Gang as an electrician but not as a member thereof, informed the Detroit Office of the Division that Joe Burnstein, Abe Burnstein and Izzie Bernstein had been in New York for the past two weeks and that Bernard Schwartz and Harry Sutton, Purple Gang lieutenants, had proceeded to New York about six weeks before; that he had overheard conversations between members of the gang indicating that Schwartz and Sutton left Detroit about the time of the kidnaping, ostensibly, to join Lefty Hanlen who had been in the East for about two years, stating that Hanlen was the New York representative of the Purples; further he had learned that the Lindbergh baby had been kidnaped for the purpose of releasing Al Capone and that the Purple Gang was a direct representative of Capone in the kidnaping plot.

During this period, Harry Fleisher was the subject of much publicity, his pictures appearing in the newspapers and it being indicated that he was sought by the New Jersey State Police for questioning as to what he knew of the Lindbergh kidnaping case.

On March 14, 1932 the New York Daily Mirror published a headline "Purple Gang Holds Baby", and stated that direct negotiations were in progress between Spitale, Bitz and the Purple Gang for the delivery of the baby for the ransom of $250,000 which had been placed in escrow in New York City. This newspaper indicated that the Burnstein Brothers of the Purple Gang were in critical need of a large sum of money to retain legal defense for members of the gang then held in the Detroit Jail pending appeals from life sentences in connection with the above mentioned Collingwood massacre.

On March 17, 1932 Mr. Edwin H. Cassels, attorney-at-law, Chicago, Ill. apparently interested in obtaining some consideration for Al Capone, contacted Mr. James M. Phelan, attorney associated with Colonel Breckinridge, legal adviser to Colonel Lindbergh, and advised that he had learned through informants that one Dave Fleisher, head of the Detroit Kidnaping organization, "left Detroit on the 28th or 29th of February and was probably then in Newark." Later, on March 29, 1932, Mr. Cassels advised that he had been advised through his informant that it was understood Fleisher would be joined by Abe Burnstein; that later Burnstein had returned to Detroit and was reported to have again gone to New York to contact Fleisher.

On March 24, 1932 the editor of the Island News, Patchogue, L. I. N. Y. telegraphically advised Colonel Henry Breckinridge that Harry Fleisher who was wanted for questioning was identified as one of five men searched by a Patchogue policeman for guns and as suspicious characters on the day after the kidnaping; that they had been driven to Patchogue in Checker Cab, New York License #046-363, chauffeured by one Charles Gigglio of 1965-52nd Street, Brooklyn. No information is available in the New York files of this office as to further developments in this connection.

On March 24, 1932 the New York Daily News and other newspapers announced that Abie Wagner, a notorious East Side New York gangster was being sought for questioning by the New Jersey State Police in conjunction with Harry Fleisher. Abie Wagner was said to be a New York agent of the Purple Gang and to have been seen in central New Jersey shortly before the kidnaping. He has an extensive criminal record, including arrests in New York and Detroit, used many aliases, and is wanted for homicide by the New York City Police Department.

Mr. Dudley Field Malone, attorney-at-law, New York City,

informed officers of the Michigan State Police that he was approached by a representative of the New York Daily Mirror and asked if he would be willing to act as intermediary in the Lindbergh Kidnaping case; that he at first refused on account of his law practice and professional standing but replied that he would be willing to do anything in his power to assure the safe return of the Lindbergh child. He ascertained that he was very much embarrassed when the Mirror published in headlines the story that he would be willing to act as go-between in this case. He received several anonymous communications through the mail and by telephone and spent practically all of his time for five or six weeks trying to communicate with the kidnapers and had spent about $4800 of his own money in trying to bring the case to a successful conclusion. That one James W. Dooley, an ex-convict, contacted him through the New York Daily Mirror and claimed that he cold get in contact with the kidnapers if certain things could be arranged through the governor of the state of Michigan, namely, to release the three men, Ray Burnstein; Harry Keywell and Irving Millberg, members of the Purple Gang, being held in Michigan State Prison at Marquette, who were convicted and given life sentences for the Collingwood massacre. Further, that Dooley claimed he would make the arrangements with the governor of Michigan through another man and the only part that he, Mr. Malone, would take in the matter would be to receive the child. That the negotiator would be Doherty, a "Michigan politician"; further that at Dooley's request, he Malone, proceeded to Montreal and met Dooley and Harry Sitner at the Ritz Carlton Hotel, and it is his, Malone's belief that the kidnaping plot originated at the United States Penitentiary at Leavenworth, Kansas, while William Fleisher (brother of Harry Fleisher), J. W. Dooley and Harry Sitner were confined in that institution.

The report of the Michigan State Police in this connection states that on April 1, 1932 one Doherty appeared at the Governor's Office in Lansing and stated he believed that he was in contact with certain persons who could furnish information regarding the Lindbergh kidnaping. He was referred by the Governor to Pardon and Parole Commissioner Ray O. Brundage, and Deputy Commissioner Fred G. Armstrong, of the State Police. He stated that one James W. Dooley informed the New York Daily Mirror in substance the same as he stated to Mr. Malone as related in the preceding paragraph. He further stated that Dooley would come to Lansing if he would not be arrested to which Deputy Commissioner Armstrong agreed.

That on April 2, 1932 Dooley came to Lansing and did not interview any officials but talked with Mr. Doherty. He then proceeded to Toronto, Ont. And Montreal and was kept under continuous surveillance by detectives of the Michigan State Police who in cooperation with the Canadian authorities tapped the wires and recorded numerous telephone conversations in which Dooley engaged, a copy of which record is one file in the New York Office.

On April 7, 1932 that Michigan Detectives met Mr. Malone at the home of Sir Henry Thornton, President of the Canadian National Railways. Mr. Malone informed them that he had talked with Dooley and had demanded a showdown from him. On April 9th the detectives were informed that Mr. Malone had given up the case and had returned to New York.

Further, in this connection, a communication signed "B. D." dated Troy, N. Y. May 13, 1932 was addressed to Mr. Frank Burke, Treasury Department, Washington, D. C. and by him referred to this Division. The writer stated that on January 9, two days before he, "B.D.", left Leavenworth, Louis Fleisher, brother of Harry, came to him and asked if he was going to New York to which he replied affirmatively. Louis then requested him to meet Harry in Newark, N. J. and introduce him to Owney Madden and Bill Duffy as Harry "had something good in New Jersey." That during this conversation Louis asked "B.D." if he knew where the Morrows lived and if the Lindberghs lived with them. "B.D." stated he stopped in Kansas City, Chicago, and Washington on the way home, then the matter broke, and he immediately got in touch with Leavenworth through Harry Sitner who had some underground routes. That Harry wrote him he would be home March 20th and to meet him in New York as he had a message for him from Louis. He met Harry Sitner in New York and Sitner told him he was to meet Harry Fleisher in Montreal and that he had a message to Colonel Lindbergh; that he advised Sitner it would be impossible to see the colonel and suggested that he tell the story to Dudley Field Malone; that they went to Briarcliff Lodge and met Malone who in turn suggested that they allow the New York Mirror to assist in any contacts to be made; that Sitner went to Montreal and met Harry Fleisher who gave him some instructions and name the conditions on which the baby would be returned; that Sitner wanted him to go to Montreal to see Harry, and not knowing where to reach him he called George Clark, city editor of the Mirror. Clark informed "B.D." as to this and at the same time started his staffwriter named Mefford for Montreal. That he left for Montreal and on his arrival, found the managing editor of the Mirror and Mr. Mefford and Dudley Field alone with Mrs. Malone at the Ritz Carlton; that Sitner informed them of Fleisher's terms and the managing editor of the Mirror started a man to see Governor Bruckner of Michigan and that the Governor expressed a desire to see him, "B. D."; that he kept Fleisher informed of what was going on and that the Mirror secured the services of Gar Wood's plane and pilot to carry him to Michigan to see the Governor; that without telling anyone, Malone got into communication with Major Murphy and requested him to work on Governor Bruckner but the Governor saw Murphy's political possibilities and backed up on Murphy; that someone brought in the Michigan police and Malone brought Sir Henry Thornton into play and he in turn brought in the Canadian Minister of Justice, whereupon Fleisher "got leery" and moved to Quebec.

That Bill Duffy, Owney Madden, "Big Frenchy" and others held a number of conferences and Owney advised Breckinridge not to pay the money; that they knew Fleisher had "the package" because he was able to state various character marks which he relayed to Owney who had Breckinridge verify them; further, that they knew two mobs were interested, Frank Nitti and Charlie Genna for Capone; and Fleisher and Abe Wagner for the Purple Gang.

Further, that Breckinridge saw the fellow Condon paid the money to; that he knew those notes could not be faked and that the mob had protected themselves from others getting in. That Fleisher was only interested in "spinning" his pals and that Nitti and Genna wanted the money.

With reference to the communication signed by "B. D." it was stated by Lieutenant Frank Holland of the Detroit Police Department that the person who wrote the letter had a very complete knowledge of this particular angle of the Lindbergh case. The contents and initials of the communication were not divulged to Lieutenant Holland but he stated during the conversation that one William Dougherty, a former convict at Leavenworth, had made known to certain authorities information which he had in his possession which was alleged to be authentic, concerning the Lindbergh kidnaping and the activities of the Purple Gang. Lieutenant and Holland, during the interview, practically went over the same information as that set out in the anonymous letter signed "B. D." received by Frank Burke. He stated that Dougherty following his release from

Leavenworth was employed by the New York Mirror and that the trip to Michigan was for the purpose of discussing the matter with Governor Bruckner in an attempt to secure the release of the three convicted members of the Purple Gang, as above set out. It was Lieutenant Holland's theory, based on what he claimed to be authentic information secured during his inquiry, that the Purple Gang including Burnstein was merely trying to "chisel it."

It has further been stated in this connection that Abe Burnstein has exhibited much interest in his brother Ray's confinement at Marquette and it is at least possible that he wold go through with the Lindbergh kidnaping for two reasons: (1) to obtain a large ransom and (2) to release his brother and the other two members. As previously related, unconfirmed reports were received to the effect that Burnstein was in New York City, and possibly at the Piccadilly Hotel, which hotel was controlled by Irving Waxler, alias Waxey Gordon, at about the same time the kidnaping took place. It has also been found through investigation that Abe Burnstein was in El Paso, Texas during the first part of April, 1932; where, as Omar Borck, he was at the Hotel Paso del Norte on April 8, 1932 which was at the same time that Gaston B. Means was at this hotel. It was further ascertained through the local police department that a telegram was received from the Investigation Bureau of the Los Angeles District Attorney's office dated April 18, 1932 advising that A. Burnstein was in the custody of the Los Angeles Police and requesting advice as to whether he was wanted by the Detroit Police.

In September of 1931 Sergeant Michael E. Flanigan, of Detroit Homicide Squad, Detroit Police Department, proceeded to New York City for the purpose of attempting to locate and apprehend Fleisher. During his stay in New York he learned that Abe Burnstein was staying at the Piccadilly Hotel. His investigation developed that on September 2, 1931 Abe Burnstein sent a telegram reading as follows:

"Mr. Johnny Condon
701 York St.
Newport, Kentucky

Received wire I may have proposition down in Frisco. Am waiting for the party to come here that leaves there today and flying here looks good to me the party coming in is to O.K. it my best to the family A. Burnstein Room 1007"

Another wire, date unknown, was forwarded to the same addressed, reading as follows:

"Did you write me or have someone else write me a letter on the twentieth. Cannot recognize writing Abe"

Investigation in Newport, Kentucky; Cincinnati, Ohio and Detroit, Michigan, developed that the Johnny Condon who was the addressee of the above quoted telegrams was George Murphy alias John Murphy alias Condon, Detroit, Michigan Police No. 27241. Investigation did not develop that this Condon was any way related to Dr. John F. (Jafsie) Condon, nor in any other way connected with the Lindbergh kidnaping and murder.

As a result of information furnished the New York Police Department by the Division, detectives of the Police Department observed A. Burnstein enter the Hotel Astor, New York City on March 26, 1932. He used a house telephone but efforts to ascertain to whom he talked were unsuccessful. Following his telephone conversation he left the hotel, entered a Packard car, and proceed to #2375 Valentine Ave., the Bronx and after leaving there the detectives lost him in congested traffic. It was learned through a check of the license plates of the Packard car by the New York Police that they were issued to one Cunningham, a salesman of Great Neck, L. I. who had moved and whose whereabouts was unknown. It was further reported that the detectives had observed Leiter and Miller, alleged members of the Purple gang, at the Astor Hotel during the time when Burnstein was there.

On April 9, 1932 A. L. Hitner, whose activities are set out in sub-section entitled with his name, telephoned former Assistant Attorney General John Marshall by long distance stating that he had a telegram from an informant to the effect that Fleisher and Wagner of the Purple Gang, Detroit, had recently left Toronto and had gone to Detroit. That they were stopping at the Book Cadil Hotel, one of them registering under the name of White.

Under date of May 6, 1932 the Deputy Prohibition Administrator at Detroit, Michigan advised that he had been informed that Sam Leiter residing at 17604 Monica Ave., Detroit, Michigan, recently returned from a trip to Texas; that prior to this trip he had declared his intention of going to Texas as entering in the liquor business with Harry Fleisher and Henry Shoor.

Investigation developed that on March 16th and 19th respectively, 1932, two telegrams signed "Mary" were sent to Sam Leiter of the Meyers Products Co., at Detroit, Michigan, a subsidiary of the Purple Gang at San Antonio, Texas on April 13th and 15th respectively, two telegrams were sent to Sam Leiter, Detroit, from San Antonio, signed "Harry." The contents of these telegrams appear to be personal and mention is made of quotations on cars, the plant, oil barrels, etc. Mary is the wife of Sam Leiter who is said to be a very close associate of Harry Fleisher.

Early in June, 1932 information was received by the Detroit office of the Division that Harry Fleisher probably was in Detroit.

As previously stated, Fleisher voluntarily surrendered to the Police Department at Detroit on the morning of June 9, 1932 to answer to a charge of murder in connection with the previously mentioned Collingwood massacre, possibly feeling secure in believing that the evidence available would be insufficient to convict him.

Immediately following his arrest, Fleisher was interrogated at police headquarters by Special Agents of the Division to his movements since the Lindbergh kidnaping. He apparently had been thoroughly coached by his counsel and carefully avoided answering definite questions. He advised, however, that Phil Fleisher of Canton, who was alleged to be his brother, was not related and was unknown to him. He stated that he was born in Detroit; was 29 years of age; that his father, Louis Fleish resides at 2688 Cortland St., Detroit; that he has a brother, Sammy, but does not know his present address but probably residing in Detroit, and a sister, Betty, residing with his father. Another brother, Louis, is at present confined in the United States Penitentiary, Leavenworth, serving a ten year sentence on a conviction for theft from interstate shipment. It was learned that Harry Fleisher married one Harriet F. Stocker in January, 1931, and she is at present living with her parents at 593 Hague St., Detroit. Fleisher was subsequently questioned by representatives of the New Jersey State Police and the Newark, N. J. Police Department but no information tending to link him to the Lindbergh case was obtained.

FINN HENRIK JOHNSON
Known as HENRY "RED" JOHNSON

Johnson, while not employed in the Morrow or Lindbergh homes, was a frequent visitor at the servants' quarters of both, being the sweetheart of Betty Gow and an intimate friend of Mr. and Mrs. Johannes Junge, (The latter a Morrow servant). He therefore was undoubtedly acquainted with the routine of both families.

Johnson is a native of Mass, Norway; born November 28, 1905. He arrived in the United States during March 1927 as a fireman aboard the S.S. "Topdalsfjord". He jumped ship upon arrival in Brooklyn and has not returned to Europe prior to his arrest as a suspect in the instant kidnaping.

Johnson's first known employment after his arrival in the United States was as a sailor aboard the yacht of Alfred P. Sloan, Jr., during the period from May 1927 to October 1927. Immediately thereafter he visited Mr. and Mrs. Arthur Johnson (uncle and aunt) at their residence in Marlboro, Maine and remained with them until December 1927. He then visited at the home of his brother, John Johnson, 67 Foley Street, West Hartford, Conn., where he remained until January 1928 and then proceeded to New York City, secured employment with the Interborough Subway, and roomed at the residence of the Carpenter family, Simpson St., Bronx, New York City, and later secured employment aboard the yacht owned by Arthur Levine. He continued in Levine's employ until August 1928 leaving to take a position aboard the yacht of Mr. Leroy Frost of Nyack, N. J. He continued in the employ of Frost until October 1928 at which time he was laid off. Shortly thereafter he secured a position on the yacht "ibie" owned by the Christy (or Christie) family of Hastings-on-the-Hudson, N. Y., and accompanied this yacht to Savannah, Ga. Where he left the yacht December 24, 1928 and returned to New York. Upon his return to New York he took up his residence with a family named Thompson at 5323 8th Avenue, Brooklyn, N. Y. where he remained until May 1929. During this period and under date of February 15, 1929 he secured a position board "The Flying Mist", the yacht of

McKnight Mitchell, and continued in Mitchell's employ until November 15, 1929. During the ensuing winter he secured odd jobs and was next steadily employed by Thomas W. LaMont aboard the latter's yacht "Reynard" from April to October 1930. Upon being laid off in October 1930 he took up his residence with his brother, Fred Johnson, at 6922 Seventh Avenue, Brooklyn, N. Y. and during the ensuing winter secured employment as an oil worker for the Norton Company, at 53rd Street and East River, New York City. Johnson was reemployed aboard the "Reynard", the LaMont yacht, during the spring of 1931, and continued in LaMont's service until the last of October 1931, at which time the "Reynard" was laid up for drydocking. Johnson expected to be reemployed by LaMont during March 1932. The New York Office files do not reflect the nature of John's employment during the winter of 1932 prior to the kidnaping though it is reflected that during this period he resided at 41 James Street, Englewood, N. J., a rooming house operated by Mrs. W. T. Sherman. He was still residing at this address at the time of his arrest. Johnson is reported to have previously resided at the residence of Mr. and Mrs. Johannes Junge, 96 Eagle Street, Englewood, N. J. He occasionally played pool with one Heime Hattu, who also roomed at 41 James Street, at a pool room near Dean and Van Brunt Streets, Englewood, N. J.

At the time of the kidnaping and for a period of approximately four months immediately prior thereto, Johnson was the accepted sweetheart of Betty Gow. He visited her frequently at the Morrow residence and on at least three occasions was with her at the Hopewell residence of the Lindberghs. The first occasion he visited Hopewell was with Betty Gow prior to the completion of the Lindbergh residence. He next visited Betty Gow at Hopewell, under date of January 1, 1932, and again visited her at said address a few weeks prior to the kidnaping.

Johnson and Betty Gow were out together in Johnson's automobile (a green Chrysler Coupe, N. Y. 1932 license 3U 9680), February 28, 1932. They rode around, had dinner, and returned to the Morrow residence where they played cards with several of the Morrow servants.

Johnson again dated with Betty Gow, February 29, 1932, visiting her at the Morrow residence and with her and other of the Morrow servants again played cards. Upon leaving, Johnson arranged to see Betty Gow the following evening.

Subsequently to Betty Gow's receipt of Mrs. Lindbergh's telephone call instructing her to proceed to Hopewell, Betty called Johnson at his residence and upon ascertaining that he was not at home, requested that his landlady, Mrs. Sherman, have him call her at the Morrow residence upon his arrival. Johnson did not call her prior to her departure which was sometime between 2: and 3: P.M. March 1, 1932. The files at this office do not reflect the exact time Johnson called the Morrow residence and was advised of Betty Gow's whereabouts and that the Lindberghs intended remaining at Hopewell, the night of March 1, 1932. It is known, however, that Johnson received the above information sometime prior to 8:30 P.M., March 1, 1952, as he is quoted as having stated that he waited until that hour before telephoning to Betty Gow at Hopewell in order to take advantage of the cheaper rates. At 8:30 P.M., March 1, 1932, Johnson at Englewood placed a telephone call to Betty Gow at Hopewell. He talked with her from approximately 8;35 to 8:40 P.M. and then took Mr. and Mrs. Johannes Junge riding in his automobile. The exact hour of Johnson's return to his residence is not reflected in the files; however, his landlady, Mrs. Sherman, is quoted as stating that he was in his room for a few hours late the night of March 1, 1932 and that he left at an extremely early hour the morning of March 2, 1932 enroute Hartford, Conn.

After arriving at Hartford, Conn., Johnson visited at the home of his brother, John Johnson, 67 Foley Street, West Hartford, Conn. He was arrested at this address on March 4, 1932 and brought to the office of County Attorney Hugh M. Alcorn, where he was subjected to intensive questioning relative to his movements prior and subsequent to the kidnaping. Stenographic notes of this examination were made and transcribed, one copy being retained by County Attorney Alcorn and one furnished the New Jersey State Police. Mr. Alcorn has advised that he is unable to locate his copy. However, efforts are being made to secure it or a new transcript for the files of this office.

Johnson was released to the Newark, N. J. Police, March 6, 1932, and later to the Jersey City, N. J. Police. Under date of April 11, 1932 he was turned over to the United States Immigration authorities as a violator of the Immigration Laws—"Illegal Entry". He was subsequently deported.

PETER J. BERRITELLA AND MARY CIRRITO

On Sunday, March 6, 1932, when Morris Rosner and Robert Thayer were answering telephones at the Lindbergh home, a telegram was received addressed to Colonel Lindbergh as follows:

"Communicate with me at once regarding your boy's whereabouts; for further particulars telephone Harlem 7-1147 (signed) Rev. Berritella."

The sender of this telegram was later found to be Reverend Peter J. Berritella of 164 West 127th Street, New York City. When Rosner was shown the telegram, he communicated with Berritella via telephone and asked him to come right down to Hopewell. Berritella was instructed to take a train to Princeton Junction where he would be met by a representative of Colonel Lindbergh. About two o'clock in the afternoon, a message was received from him advising that he was in Princeton. Colonel Breckinridge and Morris Rosner went to Princeton and met Berritella and a Miss Mary Cirrito of 335 Willis Avenue, New York City, who was with him. Berritella explained that he was a spiritualist minister, and that Miss Cirrito was a "medium" and expressed a wish to be taken to the Lindbergh home where Mary Cirrito could sit in the nursery from which the baby had been taken. They were told by Colonel Breckinridge that on account of the physical condition of Mrs. Lindbergh, they could not be taken to the house, and he took them to a hotel room in Princeton. Mary asked that she be seated in the same position as if she were in the baby's room facing north. Berritella opened the séance by reading a chapter of the bible which emphasized that one cannot serve two masters—"must love the one and hate the other, or cleave to one and despise the other." He repeated the Lord's prayer and made some motions to place Mary in an alleged trance, which to Colonel Breckinridge, appeared to be "spiritualistic nonsense," but he and Rosner affected to fall entirely into the spirit of the occasion.

Mary claimed to be a "medium" for the soul of her departed husband, Michael Joseph. She stated that there was "too much police and too much publicity in the case;" that the baby was in an unpainted house four and a half miles northeast of the Lindbergh home; (according to information recently furnished this office by Colonel Breckinridge, she stated four and a half miles "northwest" of the Lindbergh home. However, it is noted that more than two months later the baby's body was found about four and a half miles southeast of the Lindbergh home) and that the baby was in a room with the windows high up looking out to the sun; that the occupants of the house were armed; that it would be mistake to approach them as the baby would be killed and the occupants would resist. She stated that near the Lindbergh house was a tree which was broken off (Colonel Breckinridge states that there was such a tree in the rear of the house). Mary asked "if the light had broken through" and whether Colonel Lindbergh had received any message from the kidnapers, and she was told no message had been received.

Colonel Breckinridge directed his efforts toward letting the two fatigue themselves with the "spiritualistic nonsense" and to get down to business if they had any. The spiritualistic language died out considerably and their conversation became more matter of fact. Although a letter had been received at Hopewell on March 4, 1932 from the kidnapers, Colonel Breckinridge denied the receipt of any message. He asked Mary when some word might be received and she said "two weeks." He replied "Two weeks will be too late. There are two things of no use, one is to return a live baby to a dead mother and the other to send back the dead baby to a live mother." She exclaimed "Jesus Christ, we are innocent people. We know nothing about the baby and can only tell you what the spirits tell us." Colonel Breckinridge suggested that she had better have the spirits hurry up and she said "We can't give orders to the spirits, but we might pray and when we pray hard enough the light may break through." He asked her when, and she said "Perhaps by next Saturday," to which Colonel Breckinridge replied that that would be too late as the mother might be dead.

Berritella stated that he too sometimes had received messages from spirits and that he would try, making some unexplained motions. The seance ended by an emphatic request from Colonel Breckinridge for quick action.

At one point in the seance, Colonel Breckinridge was told that he was wasting his time at the Lindbergh home in Hopewell, and that he should be at his office every morning at nine o'clock, to which he replied that that was pretty early, but they stated he had "better be there."

After the seance, Colonel Breckinridge took them to the railroad station at Princeton, N. J. Berritella asked if their railroad tickets were good at that station, explaining that he had arrived at the station at Princeton Junction, a few miles from Princeton. Col. Breckinridge told them that the tickets were good only from Princeton Junction. Berritella stated "they bought us round trip tickets from Princeton Junction." Colonel Breckinridge agreed to pay the small additional amount for the fare from Princeton to Princeton Junction and Berritella declined saying that material things meant nothing; that the spirit meant everything and he gain repeated "they bought us round trip tickets to the Junction."

On the next day, March 7, 1932, a letter was mailed in New York addressed to Colonel Breckinridge at his office, 25 Broadway, enclosing a communication for Colonel Lindbergh. This letter has been identified as one of the letters from the kidnapers, being in the same handwriting and bearing the same secret symbols as the ransom note left in the nursery when the baby was stolen. His letter was in substance a repetition of the letter mailed by the kidnapers from Brooklyn, New York and received by Colonel Lindbergh at Hopewell on March 4, 1932. In addition, the letter received at the office of Colonel Breckinridge contained a statement of possible significance in relation to Colonel Breckinridge's statement to Berritella that no message had been received, namely, that they knew the police were interfering with the private mail of Colonel Lindbergh and that their letter to Colonel Lindbergh from Brooklyn had been intercepted.

The report of Special Agent Frank J. Wilson, Intelligence Unit, Treasury Department, dated November 11, 1933, reflects that about the middle of April, 1932, investigation was conducted to ascertain the character and reputation of Berritella, his activities and his associates, as it was then suspected that he might have been sent to Princeton on March 6, 1932 by the persons involved in the crime, and it was desired that the real purpose of his visit be determined. The services of three underworld characters, Owney Madden, Salvatore Spitale and Irving Bitz, were used to get information concerning Berritella and Mary, and when Owney Madden talked to them the only statement he secured was that the spirits had prompted them to go to Hopewell. After Madden, Spitale and Bitz had failed in their efforts, Colonel Breckinridge discussed the matter with Special Agents Wilson and Madden of the Intelligence Unit, Treasury Department, and it was considered as a clue of importance. It is understood that Berritella was subsequently questioned by representatives of the New York Police Department, who had checked up on his activities but that he convinced them he had no connection with the case.

According to Agent Wilson's report, it was found that Peter J. Berritella conducted a shoe repair shop at Union City, N. J. for several years previous to taking up his residence in New York City, which was about 1929. He bore a good reputation in Union City, according to discreet inquiries made at the Post Office and other points. He took over the place at 165 East 127th Street, New York City, referred to as his church, about 1931. It is a very small store in an old tenement building in a section of Harlem inhabited by Italians and colored people. He bought the furniture in the store at that time from Mr. J. Hummell, who had conducted the place for a few years and who moved to his former home at Schuylkill Haven, Pa. Hummel died in Schuylkill

Haven early in 1932. In securing a telephone contract for the telephone in the store or church, Berritella was given a reduced rate because of being a minister. The credit files of the telephone company indicated that he was ordained at Newark, New Jersey in December, 1931.

For about one year, Mary Cirrito held herself out as a medium operating from the second floor of 335 Willis Avenue, Bronx, New York City. She gave up this place about July 1, 1932, at which time she married Berritella. The marriage was performed at City Hall, New York City, and they lived together at 324 East 114th Street. Mary Cirrito is related to Vincent Valentine, contractor, residing at 1361 Findley Avenue, Bronx.

Berritella has a brother who lives in Yonkers, where he conducts a retail grocery store. He also has another brother, John, who, he told a friend, was a taxicab driver and he is now living at 166 Manhattan Avenue, Brooklyn, New York. However, inspection failed to disclose his name. A savings bank account of Berritella was located (name of bank not given in Agent Wilson's report) which was opened on March 7, 1932, the day after he visited Hopewell, with a deposit of $35. He made a few later deposits averaging $25, but the largest balance found was about $250.

On October 5, 1933, Lieutenant Keaton of the New Jersey State Police and Special Agent Wilson interviewed Hans Eugene Waldenmaier, (address not given) at the office of the Intelligence Unit, New York City, it having been developed that Waldenmaier was acquainted with Berritella, but was not then friendly to him or his wife. Waldenmaier stated that Berritella or his wife had recently made some small investments in stock through Wertheim & Company and that Berritella has a brother who is a taxi driver. Berritella receives his income from patrons who visit his church for readings and also by practice as a divine power healer. He treats patients at the church and at their homes.

He is fifty years old, born in Italy; his father's name was Bernard, and his mother's name was Josephine. He is about 5'7" tall and weighs about 160 pounds. He does not own or operate an automobile.

Specimens of the writing of Berritella and Mary Cirrito were secured and submitted to the Bureau of Standards.

In view of the possibility of some connection with the foregoing, it is noted that on March 21, 1933, Mr. Al Dunlap, publisher of the "Detective," exhibited to Special Agent in Charge Purvis of the Chicago office, a portion of a letter referring to the Lindbergh kidnaping and extortion case, which he had received from the magazine "Startling Detective Adventures," 529 South 7th Street, Minneapolis, Minn., reading as follows:

". . . There were no gangsters in it. Two men and several women all of them 'spicks', still dwelling in the Spanish-Negro section of Harlem. Harlem, incidentally is where most of the ransom money has been found.

The principals in the case have been up all night for the past three nights with Secret Service men, who finally found one of the women who talked. Some of the original suspects freed were in on it, as was the one suicide.

If the father doesn't interfere this time, the Government will send them all to jail."

ENRICO GERARDI with aliases and JOSEPH MARAN

The report of Special Agent Frank J. Wilson, Intelligence Unit, Treasury Department, dated November 11, 1933, indicates that he in cooperation with the New Jersey State Police, conducted investigation relative to Enrico Gerardi, alias Joe, alias Frank Jerome; his demented wife, and his stepson, Charles Maran.

The body of the Lindbergh baby was found within a few hundred feet of the small house owned by Charles Schopfel near Hopewell and when this individual was located and questioned he informed Agent Wilson that he rented his house in the summer of 1931 to Charles Maran of 1231 Walton Avenue, New York City, who for a few months occupied the house with his mother, who was demented, and his step-father, an Italian, named "Joe", who, it was later developed, was Enrico Gerardi. The Gerardis were located at Ridgefield Park, New Jersey, and although the report of Wilson does not give the address, it appears probable that they were then living at the address given in the newspaper reports. Ridgefield Park is situated about five miles from the Morrow home in Englewood where the Lindbergh family was residing when Maran and the others took up their residence at Ridgefield Park. Wilson's report shows that the three moved to a small farm near Rockland, Me. In the summer of 1931, which point is not far distant from North Haven, Maine, where the Lindbergh baby spent the summer of 1931. Agent Wilson states in his report that Maran and Gerardi had no gainful employment in September, 1932 and it is noted by the press reports that they likewise have no gainful employment at the present time. Agent Wilson further reports that after investigation of the activities of these individuals nothing was developed to establish their connection with the kidnaping.

The various New York newspapers on January 10, 1934, published articles concerning the arrest at Ridgefield Park, New Jersey, of Joseph Gerardi alias Cerardi and his alleged housekeeper, Mary Griffin alias Mary Griffin Wilson, age 35, said to have been with Gerardi about four months. These individuals were arrested by the Hackensack, N.J. police on January 9, 1934, charged with false imprisonment, allegedly having held Gerardi's wife a prisoner in a small room for approximately two years.

The New York Times on January 10, 1934 stated that Gerardi lived near Hopewell, N.J. about two years ago in a small house near the spot where the corpse of the Lindbergh baby was found. According to the report, Gerardi was questioned by the New Jersey police and later released, apparently cleared of suspicion. The reports indicate this individual lived at Hopewell under the name of Gerardi and that his present residence address is 585 Teaneck Road, Ridgefield Park, N.J. According to the newspaper reports, the arrests were caused by Mrs. Gerardi's sister, Mrs. Lottie Regenstrief, 1161 Shakespeare Avenue, the Bronx, New York City. Mrs. Gerardi was found locked in a small room at the Ridgefield Park address and was entirely nude and weighed only fifty pounds. Her physical condition was reported as serious and she was said to be completely out of her mind. The woman is being treated by Dr. Galady, County physician at the Bergen Pines County Hospital. Mrs. Regenstrief informed reports that her sister was well educated and could speak numerous languages, including German, and that she was divorced ten years ago from a New York lawyer named Joseph Maran, and had a son by him who is now 22 years of age. The son Charles Maran is supposed to be living in New York. News reports stated that Gerardi had a safety deposit box in a New York bank. However, when opened by the police nothing was found in it.

The Ridgefield Park address consisted of a four room apartment above a stable on a piece of property known as the old Barnes Estate. According to newspapers, neighbors saw Gerardi and his wife move into this address about two years ago, at which time Mrs. Gerardi appeared to be in good health. Mrs. Regenstrief allegedly informed the police that Gerardi threatened to "bump her off" if she told anyone of the fact that Mrs. Gerardi was locked up in the room. Mrs. Regenstrief also informed the police that Gerardi insured his wife's life for $10,000 a number of years ago. One newspaper article states that the housekeeper's maiden name was Mary Griffin and her marriage name Wilson. From available information Gerardi is 34 years of age, was formerly a middleweight fighter and had used the following names: Enrico Gerardi; Joseph Gerardi; Joseph Cerardi; Enrico Gerardi; Joseph Geradi; Carmelli Cerardi; Carmelli Gerardi and Frank Jerome. This individual's occupation is given by one newspaper as "bootblack" although the housekeeper informed police she did not know her employer's occupation and as far as she knew he had no way of earning a living. The police are presently endeavoring to locate Charles Maran for questioning in connection with the false imprisonment charge. Photographs of the housekeeper and Gerardi are contained in a clipping from the Jersey Journal, January 11, 1934 in the New York file.

It is noted that Gerardi and his associates lived near the Lindberghs on three different occasions, and in three different localities. Apparently they have no gainful employment, and, further, they lived at one time close to the spot where the baby's body was found. Also, Gerardi and Maran apparently are natives of the Bronx, New York City, where the ransom negotiations in the Lindbergh case were carried on. Mrs. Gerardi's sister, Mrs. Lottie Regenstrief, and the war veteran, Charles Schopfel, who owned the small house near where the body was found, maybe fruitful sources of information regarding the activities of these individuals. The New York office is not in possession of the address of Charles Schopfel, the same not having been given in Agent Wilson's report.

It is noted further that one of the former tenants of the Plymouth Apartments, 537 West 149th Street, New York City, was named W. L. Griffin, and may possibly be related to Gerardi's housekeeper, Mary Griffin. Also, one Elizabeth Maran formerly lived at 504 West 149th Street from where she moved on November 10, 1931 to 217 East 86th Street, New York City.

The New York Division office was advised by Corporal Horn of the New Jersey State Police that his organization did not look upon Gerardi, et al as suspects in this case.

JACK BENNET or BENNETT
alias JEROME MEYERS;
ROBERT BENNET or BENNETT
alias BOBBY BURNS BENNET;
ROBERT HUDSON or HUTCHINS.

On May 16, 1932, an individual by the name of A. Bosman, who gave his residence address as 69 West 55th Street, New York City, called at the New York Division Office, stating he had a solution to the Lindbergh kidnaping. Bosman claimed that he had been employed by a bootlegger named Jack Bennet alias Jerome Meyers, and several of his brothers, for the period January 1, 1932 to February 12, 1932, and that the Bennet brothers had an office at 70 West 46th Street, New York City, where they operated their alcohol business under the guise of a real estate corporation. According to the informant, Jack Bennet lived on Bliss Street, Long Island. Bosman further stated that a young man from Tulsa, Okla. Named Robert Hutchins was "one of the gang". Bosman further claimed that on Robert Hutchins was "one of the gang". Bosman further claimed that on January 15, 1932, Jack Bennet alias Meyers requested him to make a ladder to consist of three sections of seven foot each. However, that he did not construct the ladder, but made a drawing from which it might be made. Bosman stated he did not know whether the ladder was ever constructed. Bosman stated that in the early part of

February, 1932, he heard Hutchins and Jack Bennet speak of "Jafsie", and also heard Bennet tell Hutchins that he was to drive the car with the baby. Bosman further advised that he left the employ of the Bennet brothers about the middle of February, 1932, due to the fact that he feared arrest for violation of the Prohibition Law.

Under date of October 9, 1933, one John Damann (true name Henry Logemann), a prisoner at the United States Northeastern Penitentiary, Lewisburg, Pennsylvania, made a signed statement corroborating information which had previously been submitted by Gaston B. Means, his fellow prisoner, to the effect that Wellington Henderson, Max Hassell, max Greenburg and James Feldman were involved in the Lindbergh kidnaping. (See section of this report dealing with Gaston B. Means and Norman T. Whitaker). In addition to mentioning these four individuals, who have been frequently named as the guilty parties by Gaston B. Means, Damann named a number of other individuals who he claimed were involved in the Lindbergh kidnaping. These individuals had not, at anytime previous, been mentioned by Gaston means. The information concerning them quoted from Damann's statement it as follows:

"Besides Max Hassel and Wellington Henderson as one of his (Hassel's) close associates engineering the kidnaping, there were two or three other of his associates in on the matter, whose names I will give if and when it becomes necessary. Also in on the kidnaping were two brothers Jack and Robert B. Bennet and the Bennet Brothers had worked with them, two Narcotic users and who had worked for them regularly, as well as in this kidnaping (the names of the two Narcotic users have escaped my memory but I will recall them later). Also the Bennet Brothers used a man by the name of Robert Hudson from Tulsa, Oklahoma, who worked for them and Dr. Condon's nephew, as I remember the relationship, (if not nephew then a close relative) and this nephew also worked with the Bennet Brothers regularly. The Bennet Brothers are American Jews. All of this above information and following information Max Hassel gave me just shortly before he was shot to death on April 12th, 1933, in the Elizabeth-Cartaret-Hotel, Elizabeth, new Jersey.

Jack and Robert B. Bennet had a basement rented under a real estate corporation name, at 72 West 46 Street, New York City, prior to, up to and after March 1st, 1932 for wholesale whiskey distribution. Also they had a furnished apartment from 1929 or during 1929, possibly later, at 69 West 55th Street, New York City, under the name of Jack Bennet. Max Hassel was their source of supply of whiskey in big quantity purchases, which they in turn distributed to purchasers in smaller quantities.

In January, 1932, Jack and Robert B. Bennet rented a place from a Bohemian family just off Sound View Ave., East Bronx near College Point, New York City, for a whiskey cutting plant.

It was Dr. Condon's nephew or near relative, who worked for the Bennet Brothers, who suggested to Dr. Condon that he insert an advertisement in the 'Personal Column' of the Bronx Newspaper offering his services as an intermediary for the safe return of the Lindbergh child with the possibility that he might get a reply and because of the nephew's or near relative's influence over Dr. Condon, the doctor fell for it and did insert the advertisement. Through this nephew or near relative's connection, at all times while the number of days of negotiations were going on for the return of the child, the nephew was able to keep the kidnapers advised of the progress Dr. Condon was making with Col. Lindbergh and his attorney Col. Breckinridge, regardless of the fact that the nephew or near relative knew that the child had met with an accidental death on March 10th, 1932. However, Dr. Condon was at all times sincere in all he did and believed he was accomplishing what all the world was attempting to accomplish, the safe return of the child."

It will be noted that the Bennet Brothers mentioned by Damann are undoubtedly identical with those mentioned by A. Bosman on May 16, 1932.

On December 1, 1933, Damann was interviewed at the U.S. Northeastern Penitentiary, by a Division Special Agent, relative to his statement. Damann advised that his true name was Henry Logemann, and that he was born in Hamburg, Germany, on February 14, 1884; all of his relatives having remained there when he came to the United States in 1901. He stated that he started a career as a pugilist in New York City about 1912, and fought under then name of Dutch Logan; that about 1926, after abandoning his ring career, he became a carpenter. Damann admitted he had been arrested many times for disorderly conduct due to excessive drinking habits. He is serving a two year sentence at the U.S. Northeastern Penitentiary for counterfeiting, convicted in the District of New Jersey. Damann stated that he was personally acquainted with Al Reich, the former pugilist who is generally known as Dr. Condon's bodyguard, and that in his opinion Reich, together with one Like Stuart, was involved in a Postoffice robbery in 1929 at Isbury Park N.J. According to Damann shortly after coming to the penitentiary he became acquainted with Gaston B. Means, who induced him to make the statement generally corroborating previous statements made by Means; that the purpose of the whole thing was to assist Means in securing a new trial. Damann recanted his entire statement of October 9, 1933, stating that every word in the statement with the exception of the lines referring to the Bennet brothers and Dr. Condon's alleged nephew or relative, was supplied by Means and written by the latter. Damann stated that there are in fact such persons as Jack and Robert Bennet and an individual known as Hudson from Tulsa, Okla.

Damann explained the insertion of the Bennet brothers in his statement, by informing that during the frequent periods Means discussed his case with him, he (Means) mentioned the names of Jack and Robert B. Bennet. Damann claimed he was surprised to learn that Means knew these men, and questioned him regarding them, until satisfied that Means actually was acquainted with them. As a result of their conversations, stated Damann, Means apparently decided to include the Bennet brothers in his statement.

Damann accounted for his own acquaintanceship with the Bennet brothers by explaining that in 1928-29 he was convicted of larceny and served a one year sentence at Welfare Island, New York City, under his true name. Incarcerated with him at that time were two characters known as "Lefty" and Charlie Neary. Damann, Neary and "Lefty" were released about the same time in 1929. Shortly thereafter they visited the combination speakeasy and restaurant known as O'Leary's, on 48th Street, west of Broadway, New York City, where "Lefty" introduced Damann to the Bennet brothers who were then hanging out at O'Leary's; and at the same time "Lefty" introduced him to a man known only as "Gus", who was believed by Damann to be a nephew or relative of Dr. John F. Condon. Although Damann has met "Gus" on several occasions at O'Leary's place, he does not remember his last name, nor does he know whether "Gus" is in fact the correct first name of this individual. Damann stated that Charlie Neary is presently serving a life term in the New Jersey State Penitentiary at Trenton, for a postoffice robbery in 1930. That the last time he saw "Gus" was in Bennet's place, 72 West 46th Street, New York City.

With reference to the individual, Robert Hudson, of Tulsa,

Okla., Damann stated that he once saw him in Bennet's place, but can furnish no adequate description of him. Damann furnished detailed descriptions of the Bennet brothers, "Lefty" and "Gus", which are set out below.

During the interview of Damann, he admitted that he had been "proposed" as bartender for a speakeasy to be opened by the Bennet brothers about January 1932; however, that due to salary differences, he was not hired.

There appears to be some possibility that Damann and the informant A. Bowman are identical, it being noted that both were connected with the Bennet brothers about the same time, and that they furnish almost identical information concerning these brothers, as well as Hutchins or Hudson.

Investigation by the Oklahoma City Division Office developed that there was an individual by the name of Robert Hudson, age 19, of Tulsa, Okla., and that he had a criminal record for carrying concealed weapons, and attempted burglary. The records of the Tulsa Police Department reflect that this Hudson was incarcerated at U.S. Detention Headquarters, New York City, on April 25, 1932, crime, maintaining a nuisance; fined $75. His photograph was forwarded to the New York Office and will be exhibited to Damann to determine if he is the Robert Hudson in question.

Following are descriptions of Jack and Robert B. Bennet or Bennett, "Lefty", "Gus" (alleged relative of Condon), all furnished by Damann, and a description of the Robert Hudson secured from the Tulsa, Okla. Police.

Name: Jack Bennet, or Bennett.
Age: 32—35 years
Height: 5'10"
Weight: 170 lbs.
Hair: Dark brown, wavy.

Eyes:	Brown.
Complexion:	Fair
Marital status:	Believed to be married.
Residences:	72 West 46th Street and 69 West 55th Street, New York City.
Occupation:	Bootlegger.
Build:	Muscular, wide shoulders. Wears snappy clothing and soft felt hats. Speaks good English; no accent
Eyeglasses:	Does not wear glasses.
Scars and Marks:	Has no scars visible on his hands or face.
Teeth:	No gold in teeth observed.
Name:	Robert B. Bennet or Bennett.
Age:	30—32 years
Height:	5'8"
Weight:	165 lbs.
Eyes:	Brown
Hair:	Dark brown, straight.
Complexion:	Fair. Good looking.
Build:	Light and thin. Round shouldered.
Eyeglasses:	None.
Dress:	Dresses well, conservative clothing, soft felt hats.
Scars and Marks:	None apparent.
Teeth:	No gold in teeth observed.
Residence:	72 West 46th Street and 69 West 55th Street, New York City
Occupation:	Bootlegger.
Name:	"Lefty" (male individual; last name unknown)
Age:	36—27
Height:	5'7"

Weight:	150—155 lbs.
Complexion:	Dark
Nationality:	American born of Italian extraction.
Marital status:	believed to be single.

Name:	"Gus"—last name unknown. (Alleged nephew or relative of Dr. John F. Condon)
Age:	30—35 years.
Height:	5'9"—10"
Weight:	150—155 lbs.
Hair:	Brunette, straight.
Nationality:	Believed born at New York City of English parents.
Eyes:	Color not known.
Occupation:	Booze racketeer employed by Jack and Robert B. Bennet.
Complexion:	Fair. Good looking.
Dress:	Expensive clothes. Continuously wears a diamond tie pin, horseshoe shaped with two larger stones in center. Also claimed to wear two large diamond rings on left hand. Suits mostly double-breasted.
Hands:	normal size, smooth, not calloused.
Mustache:	Wears small mustache at times.
Scars, etc.:	None apparent.
Eyeglasses:	None.
	Uses good English; no accent. Steady, not nervous. Seems to have plenty of money. Does not know where he does banking.

Name:	Robert Hudson, or Hutchins.
Age:	19
Height:	5'7 3/4"

Weight:	158 pounds.
Build:	Medium.
Hair:	Medium brown.
Eyes:	Light brown.
Complexion:	Medium.
Race:	White
Nationality:	American.
Occupation:	Laborer.
Marital status:	Single.
Address:	1146 N. Sandusky, Tulsa, Okla.
Relatives:	Father—Jack Hudson, address unknown.
	Mother—Lorene Hudson, 1146 N. Sandusky, Tulsa, Okla.
Police No.	9471 P.D., Tulsa, Okla.
F.P.C.	1 U 000 12
	1 U 000 10

Criminal record:

As Robert Hudson, No. 789, arrested P.D., Sapulpa, Okla., 4/7/29, carrying concealed weapons; fined $19.50.

As Robert Hudson, No. 7766, received State Reformatory, Granite, Okla., 7/23/30, from Tulsa County; crime, attempted burglary; sentence one year.

As Walter Roberts, No. 8188, held at U.S. Detention Headquarters, New York, N.Y. 4/25/32; crime—maintaining a nuisance; fined $75.00.

As Robert Hudson, No. 9471, P.D., Tulsa, Okla., 10/5/32; vagrancy; fined $4.00 and cost.

There is a notation on the records that Robert Hudson admits he was sent to Pauls Valley Training School, Pauls Valley, Okla., on 9/17/27, as a delinquent; paroled 2/22/28.

Thomas Fensch

JOHN GORCH and WALTER GRAY
(Both with aliases)

On October 24, 1933, pursuant to the receipt by the Boston, Mass. Police Department of an anonymous letter, Detective Sergeant Tiernan and Detective William Bonner, at 19 Garrison St., Boston, Mass. arrested John Gorch and Evelyn Klimasefska, on a charge of being suspicious persons. They were both taken to Boston Police Headquarters, and on that date a warrant was issued at Boston charging Gorch with having obtained $3500 by fraud on or about March 25, 1933, from Rose Ginsburg, of Brighton, Mass. At the time of Gorch's arrest, he had on his person $585 in bills of five, ten and one hundred dollar denominations. An examination of this currency indicated that none of it had been paid as ransom in the Lindbergh case. Immediately upon the arrest of Gorch and after the New Jersey State Police had become cognizant of it, he was interviewed by a detective from that organization in connection with the Lindbergh case. It appeared that prior to the date of Gorch's arrest, he was involved in a possible impersonation case in Newark, N.J. with another man of Polish extraction, whose name at this writing is not known to this office. It is stated, however, that this unknown individual had become aggrieved, subsequent to his arrest, because of the fact that Gorch had managed to make his escape. From the Newark City Jail, where this individual was confined, he wrote an anonymous letter, which he later admitted was his, to the Boston, Mass. Police stating that: "a year ago the said John Gorch was looked for by the New York State Police in connection with the kidnaping of Lindbergh's baby, and that is why he moved to Boston.—" As a result of this letter, the Police predicated their listing of Gorch as a possible suspect in this case. Gorch, in his activities, confined chiefly to "Confidence games" in New York City and elsewhere has used the following aliases:

Steve Lucie (true name)
Steve Sederak
Theodore Sydorak
John McKay
John Mitchell
John Bernard
Steven Johnson
Otto Schmidt or Smith
Steve Jankowski
Edward Buran
John Bergman
John Gosch
John Cojewska
Nilson
John Sallie
Steve Sidelunk
Tessor

When questioned by agents of the Division at Boston on October 26, 1933, Gorch made a written statement, in which he alleged that on three different occasions while at New York City during the month of February, 1932, he heard one Walter Gray, one Mickey, one Jack and one Bennie discussing ways and means of making money by kidnaping certain persons, among whom was mentioned the Lindbergh baby. Gorch further stated that three or four days prior to the kidnaping he drove Gray to a point on the Lincoln Highway in the vicinity of Trenton, N. J. where at a restaurant Gray met several men who occupied two parked cars, one of which bore a New Jersey license plate. Gorch was unable to identify the man. In his above statement Gorch further alleged that subsequent to the kidnaping he visited Gray's real estate office in Brooklyn, N.Y. and at that time Gray appeared very nervous when his attention was invited to a newspaper on his desk containing a photograph of the Lindbergh baby and setting forth an account of the kidnaping. Gorch further alleged in this statement that prior to the kidnaping Gray was apparently broke but appeared shortly thereafter to have plenty of money. This is borne out to some extent by investigation in New York City. Gray, in his swindling activities in New York and elsewhere in the east, is known to have used the following aliases:

Walter Jgayewski (believed to be true name)
Walter G. Gray
Walter J. Gray
Walter E. Gray
Walter Novack
Walter G. Novack
Walter G. Novak
Walter Nojkowski
Walter Wajowski
Stanley Burton
S. Burton
Stanley G. Burton
Walter Janowiak
Walter Lawrence
Brown
Gabolski

While Gorch was questioned by Division agents at Boston, specimens of his handwriting were obtained and forwarded to the Division laboratories at Washington for appropriate examination. It seemed from an examination of these specimens and comparison with the Lindbergh ransom notes that Gorch could possibly have been the writer of them. Further specimens of Gorch's handwriting were requested. An examination of Gorch's handwriting was also made by Handwriting Expert Albert D. Osborn who declared in his report:

"The writing of Gorch shows characteristics of one who has learned to write in Europe, and therefore has some connection with the Lindbergh letters. However, the many differences indicate, I believe, that this similarity is merely one resulting from the foreign habits in his writing and the foreign habits in the Lindbergh writing. I do not believe there is any real connection between his writing and that in the Lindbergh Letters."

It was learned from Gorch that for a short period in the spring of 1932 he resided at 504 West 149th Street, New York City, in order to facilitate the contemplated swindle of a woman residing at said address.

Investigation at this address developed that Gorch occupied a furnished room there for two weeks in December, 1931, and also from March 6, 1931 after which he rather hurriedly left. It has been previously shown in this report that a stolen automobile was abandoned on March 2, 1932 in front of 515 West 149th Street and that an unknown person made an exchange of $2,980 of the ransom money and gave an address of 537 W. 149th street. These addresses, and that where Gorch formerly lived, are all within a few doors of each other. Investigation to date, however, has not developed a connection between any of them. It has been further noted that one Elizabeth Maran resided at the same address where Gorch lived, i.e., 504 W. 149th, up to December 1931. At the present time it is not known whether Elizabeth Maran is related to the Joseph Maran, mentioned as a suspect in the section of this report entitled: "Subjects and Suspects; Enrico Gerardi and Joseph Maran."

A thorough questioning of Evelyn Klimasefska indicated that she had no probable connection with the Lindbergh case and no information could be obtained from her which would indicate that she knew anything of Gorch's possible connection with this case. Gorch was released by Boston,

Mass. authorities on November 14, 1933 and returned to Philadelphia, Pa. to answer alleged extortion charges there. Evelyn Klimasefska, his mistress, was discharged at Boston on the same date, and placed on probation. On January 19, 1934 the case against Gorch at Philadelphia, Pa. Was nolle prossed, and he was released to the Newark, N.J. authorities for prosecution on two warrants, and he is presently held in Newark in default of bond. There are also detainers against Gorch from New York City and Ossining, N.Y.

Subsequent investigation at New York indicated that Gorch and Gray with many other associates had been perpetrating real estate swindles, with women as victims, in the east. A counterfeiting violation on the part of Gray was discovered in Brooklyn, N.Y. Considerable data concerning the activities and histories of both Gray and Gorch, together with their associates, were obtained. Safety deposit boxes of Grey and Gorch were located at the National City Bank, New York City. Upon being opened each box was found to contain nothing but empty envelopes. Inquiry likewise showed the possible existence of such persons referred to by Gorch as Mickey, Bennie and Jack, and indicated that these names might be the names of three individuals presently residing at the President Hotel, New York City. No evidence has been obtained to link any of the parties mentioned above with the Lindbergh case. Gorch lived at 504 West 149th Street from March 6 to March 20, 1932, but is unknown at 537 West 149th Street, New York City. Subsequent to the return of Gorch to the Philadelphia, Pa. authorities he was questioned by agents of this Division as well as representatives of the New Jersey State Police and New York City Police Department at which time he repudiated the statement made by him at Boston on October 26, 1933 and gave as his reason for such repudiation that his statement of October 26th was designed for no other purpose than to have the authorities place Gray under arrest since he, Gorch, suspected that the anonymous letter written to the Boston Police which furnished the basis of his arrest was the work of either Gray or his wife or both. Notwithstanding this repudiation, however, this angle of the investigation will receive further investigative attention. Gray has not yet been located for questioning and the New York and Philadelphia and Boston Division offices have been engaged in efforts to locate him. He is presently believed to be driving a 1933 Pontiac 4-door Sedan, motor number 927148, serial 809562, which he registered in New York City in June, 1933, under the name of Walter G. Novack. A "Wanted Notice" has been placed in the Division files showing he is wanted for questioning.

His handwriting was compared with the ransom notes by the Division Laboratory with the resultant opinion that "the specimen of the handwriting of Walter Gray is not sufficiently similar to the extortion letters to indicate that the handwriting in the extortion letters is his. This is so although some of the movements are similar and the forms of some of the words are very much the same."

Photographs of Gorch, Gray and Gorch's sweetheart, Evelyn Klimasefska, were exhibited to Dr. J.F. Condon who failed to identify them. Al Reich, who was present at the same time, likewise failed to identify these individuals as anyone he had ever seen.

Following is a description of Gray from records of New York Police informants:

Name	Walter Gray (true name believed to be Jgayowski).
Age	37 (in 1933)
Born	Warsaw, Poland, September 15, 1896
Height:	5'4 1/2"
Weight	196 pounds
Build	Stocky
Hair	Light brown

Eyes	Blue
Complexion	Fair
Mustache	At times wears small brown mustache
Marital status	Wife listed in City Directory as Alexandria Gray; informants advise maiden name of Gray's wife is Catherine Cloyman; now believed separated.
Eyeglasses	Usually wears glasses; sometimes smoked-glasses.
Occupation	Real Estate confidence man and alleged partner of Bruno Tomaszowski, 618-4th Ave., Brooklyn.
Scars	Small linear scar on left side of nose; face pock marked
Nationality	Polish; speaks Polish well and a smattering of German and Ukrainian.
Race	White
Address	Last known address, 752 West End Ave., New York City (Paris Hotel)
Peculiarities	Always wiping eyes with handkerchief. No vision in left eye; poor vision in right eye.
War service	Allegedly served in the United States Army in France during World War and reported receiving compensation from Government.

Allegedly part owner with individual named Thomas Deren, in hotel at Acra, N. Y.

Criminal record as obtained from the records of the New York Police Department (N.Y. Police No. B-116948—5th precinct).

1917 As Walter Wajkowski, Cleveland, O. Larceny; on 6/20/17 State Reformatory at Mansfield #9429.
1921 As Walter Gray, Pittsburgh, Penna. Larceny; on 2/8/21 three years State Penitentiary, Pittsburgh, Pa. #11142.

9/12/33   As Walter Novack, Manhattan, Grand Larceny; jumped bail; Det. Shibroski, PP Squad.
8/12/33   As Walter Novack, Manhattan, Grand Larceny; Dets. Mitchell and Shibroski, PP Squad. Jumped bail.

Wanted by Det. Mitchell, PP Squad for bail forfeiture; complaint #454, 9th precinct, 8/17/33.

Photograph   On file, N.Y. Division Office
Handwriting specimen   On file, N.Y. Division Office

Following is a description of John Gorch, from records of the Boston Police Department:

Name	John Gorch—aliases: Steve Luciw; Nelson; Steven Johnson; John Sallie; Steven Sidelnunk.
Age	38
Height	5'8 1/4"
Weight	204 pounds
Build	Stout
Hair	Chestnut
Eyes	Brown
Complexion	Light
Residence	19 Garrison St., Boston
Occupation	Wrestler and real estate operator
Marital status	Single
Race	White
Nationality	Polish
F.P.	Forwarded Division 10/25/33 by Boston Police Department.

Handwriting specimen On file N.Y. office
Police number Boston Police Department No. 33277
Photograph   On file N.Y. office

Criminal record as obtained from the Division:

As Steven Johnson; #8613, arrested 4/18/23 by State Police, Joliet, Ill.; charge, confidence game, disposition 1 to 10 years; as John Sallie, #78950, arrested 8/20/26, received Sing Sing Prison, Ossining, N.Y.; charge, attempted C.L. 2nd degree; disposition 1 year and 3 months to 2 years and 6 months; as Steven Sidelnunk, #2484, arrested 11/29/27 by Police Department, Scranton, Pa.; charge, conspiracy to defraud; flimflam; disposition suspended sentence on payment of costs; as John Gorch #33277 arrested 10/21/33 by Police Department, Boston, Mass. charge S.P., robbery and extortion.

The following notation appears on above record: Magistrates Court 1916, D.C.; discharged (as appearing on print #78950, Sing Sing Prison, Ossining, N.Y.).

Following are descriptions of Mickey, Jack and Benny, furnished by Gorch:

Name	Benny	Jack
Age	28	30
Height	5'4"	5'9"
Weight	205 pounds	165-170 pounds
Build	Stout	Well built
Complexion	Light	Light
Hair	Black	Black
Eyes	Brown	Big brown eyes
Mustache/beard	Smooth shaven	Smooth shaven
Eyeglasses	No	No
	Rough talker	Prominent nose
Nationality	Jewish	Jewish
Appearance:	Jewish	Speaks good English dresses well

Name	Mickey
Age	32
Height	5'9"
Weight	225
Build	Stout
Complexion	Olive
Hair	Brown
Eyes	Brown
Mustache/beard	Smooth shaven
Eyeglasses	No
Nationality	Italian
Appearance	Looks and talks like an Italian.

GERALD BUCCHOLZ, WITH ALIASES

On November 16, 1933, an individual who gave his name as Gerald Buccholz appeared at the branch of the Corn Exchange Bank Trust Company, located at 29th Street and Fourth Avenue, New York City, and informed the manager that he desired to open an account, and upon the account being accepted he made an initial deposit of $2,000 in cash comprised of $50 and $100 bills. When filling out his signature card in the presence of the manager, Buccholz gave his residence address as 3021 Briggs Ave., Bronx, New York City, and remarked "Everybody knows where this address is because it is right in back of Dr. Condon's house, the 'Jafsie' of the Lindbergh case." Buccholz gave a business address of 55 West 42nd Street, New York City. The manager of the bank recalled that Buccholz hedged at the time of opening his account as to his first name and left the impression that he uses the names of Gerald and Samuel Buccholz. After Buccholz deposited the $2,000 he put his hand in his pocket stating, simultaneously that he had some $5 bill she would like to deposit, but on second thought stated "No, I will keep these for my personal use."

The manager of the bank further recollected that Buccholz was introduced at the bank on the date in question by one David Romyn, who has an account at the bank, and is said to be a close associate and friend of Dr. Lee Buerger of 275 Central Park West, New York City. Dr. Buerger is a well known and wealthy physician in New York and he also had an account at the bank. The manager of the bank further advised that Dr. Buerger has had Mrs. David Romyn (nee Annetta Kobb) in his employ for quite some time. It was the belief of the manager that Mr. and Mrs. David Romyn make their residence with Dr. Buerger at 275 Central Park West. The manager of the bank suspected Buccholz as a whiskey cutter or bootlegger, possibly in partnership with Romyn in the operation of a chain of liquor stores throughout Greater New York. In view of this suspicion and the statements of Buccholz with regard to Dr. Condon, the manager formed the opinion that Buccholz might have had some connection with the Lindbergh case, and consequently, on December 7, 1933, reported the matter to a Division Special Agent who was at the bank checking up on a $5 Lindbergh ransom bill which had been discovered, which bill, however, was not traced to any of the individuals above mentioned.

A photograph of one Louis Buckhouse alias Buccholz, New York City Police Department No. B-46043 was exhibited to Manager Burch of the Corn Exchange Bank, who stated that same resembled the Gerald Buccholz who opened the account but he could not be positive of his identification.

In view of the suspicious circumstances surrounding Buccholz, Manager Burch decided to watch his account and also those of David Romyn and Dr. Buerger. In going through the cancelled vouchers at the bank, Manager Burch came across a check dated November 21, 1933 drawn by dr. Buerger in the amount of $15 payable to one William Faulkner. The check bore the endorsement of William

Faulkner and also of Carl C. Christiansen, 4157 Edenhurst St., Los Angeles, Calif.

The cancellation stamp on the check indicated that it had been cashed at the Glendale, California branch of the Bank of America. Manager Burch advised that Dr. Leo Buerger during the year 1930 left New York City, and established offices in the Wilshire Medical Building, Los Angeles. Investigation by the New York Police and the New York Division Office has not developed to date that William Faulkner had any connection with the Faulkner family who formerly resided at 537 West 149th Street, New York City, or that he was associated with Gerald Buccholz. Investigation was conducted by the Los Angeles Division Office, which developed that William Faulkner was a commercial gardener; born in Ireland, and had spent the last ten or twelve years in Los Angeles. People who knew William Faulkner stated that he was honest and industrious, although not well educated, and that apparently at the present time he has a very profitable landscape gardening business. The owner of the house occupied by William Faulkner and his wife was positive that Faulkner had not been away from Los Angeles, on any extended trips, between July 18, 1932 and September, 1933, and apparently, therefore, he could have had no connection with the exchange of the $2,980 in gold certificates on May 1, 1933, at which time the name of J. J. Faulkner was given on the deposit ticket. Further investigation by the Los Angeles Division Office developed that William Faulkner was employed as a gardener on the estate of Dr. Leo Buerger, Hollywood, Calif. Since November 1, 1933 and that the $15 check referred to by Manager Burch was in payment for services. Apparently William Faulkner had never been in New York.

The address telephone directory of New York City and the Bronx, lists a Gerald Buccholz, with an unpublished telephone, at 3021 Briggs Ave., the address given by Gerald Buccholz at the Corn Exchange Bank. The Briggs Avenue address is between East 202nd Street and Mosholu Parkway, Bronx, in the neighborhood of Dr. Condon's residence. The address telephone directory also lists a Samuel Buccholz with an unpublished telephone at 55 East 42nd Street, which is the business address given by Gerald Buccholz. The directory does not give the occupation or business of this individual. It appears fairly definite, however, that Samuel Buccholz of the latter address and Gerald Buccholz of the Briggs Avenue address are identical, it being noted that the party who opened the bank account at the Corn Exchange Bank stated he was known both as Gerald and Samuel Buccholz.

Inquiry at the address 55 West 42nd Street, New York City, which is a large office building, many of the tenants of which are said to be racketeers and gangsters, revealed that neither Gerald nor Samuel Buccholz was listed in the building directory. Inquiry developed, however, that the office of Buccholz was Room 922. On the door of this office appears the following "Benjamin Meyer—Attorney-at-Law". The telephone directory lists Meyer under the name and address given with listed telephone. Through the New York Telephone Company it was ascertained that Samuel Buccholz also has a telephone listed for the above office, however, that same was unpublished.

Inquiry at the offices of the real estate company which owns the office building in question revealed that an individual by the name of Gerald Buckholtz leased Room 922 on May 1, 1933; the only reference given by Buckholtz was Simon Manges, 14 East 42nd Street, New York City. The real estate company's records contain no information concerning Buckholtz except that he is in the insurance business. The company's records contain absolutely no information concerning the "Benjamin Meyer, Attorney-at-

Law", whose name appears on the door of the office leased by Buckholtz. Information was received by the New York office to the effect that Buccholz was engaged in liquor activities and possibly was associated with a number of well known gamblers and racketeers of New York. However, this information has not been checked as to reliability.

Investigation as to Buccholz and the other individuals mentioned herein is still pending, the identity of Benjamin Meyer not yet having been determined.

The following is a description of Gerald Buccholz with aliases, furnished by Manager Burch of the Corn Exchange Bank:

Age	43 to 45
Height	5'10"
Weight	160 pounds
Complexion	Sallow; clean shaven.
Eyeglasses	Wears glasses
Nationality	Possibly Jewish
Eyes	Dark brown
Hair	Dark and straight.

JOHN J. BAUMEISTER

Under date of May 25, 1932 information was furnished the New York Division office by the U. S. Narcotic Bureau of New York City, to the effect it was the belief of Narcotic Agent William Mellon, that one John J. Baumeister, bearing the following aliases, John Clifford, Bauweister, John Carey, John Baumeister, John Lambert, Frank Lane and John Dawson, may be the "John" referred to by Dr. J. F. Condon as participating in the ransom negotiations.

According to Mellon, Baumeister attended a New York City grammar school where Dr. John F. Condon was principal. He lived near Dr. Condon at one time and some of his relatives are believed to be presently residing in Condon's neighborhood. According to Mellon, Baumeister shortly after the kidnaping was taken into custody and questioned by the New York City police and apparently established an alibi.

Mellon further stated that Baumeister is of German parentage and is said to speak that language; that he is well acquainted in the upper Bronx where the ransom negotiations took place, and formerly drove a taxicab in that vicinity. Baumeister has a long record including arrests for extortion, larceny, assault and robbery, receiving stolen goods, impersonating a Federal officer, dope peddling and forgery. According to Mellon, Baumeister several years ago was involved with a gang distributing dope in northern New Jersey, particularly in Newark and Jersey City; was also engaged in rum-running operations between New York and Canada, and has been associated with a number of well known New York gangsters including the late Jack "Legs" Diamond.

Baumeister, together with Max Kramer alias Max Feld; Morton Rothstein alias Alexander Rothstein; and Spiro Williams alias Spiro Galtis or Coltis alias William Spiro, were under investigation by the New York Division office in the year 1929 for impersonating Federal officers (New York File 47-549). Baumeister had represented himself as a Chief Inspector of Customs. His associates named above all had long records.

In many of his illicit operations, Baumeister, according to Mellon, was closely associated with one Mortimer Free, who formerly operated a private detective agency at 29th Street and Fifth Avenue, New York City, and who is now residing in Brooklyn. Baumeister about two weeks before the kidnaping, informed a Narcotic agent that his family was living on Decatur Avenue, in the Bronx. He is reported to be separated from his wife, who is presently unfriendly toward him.

Baumeister is also said to number among his acquaintances the party, Milton Gaglio (Dr. Condon's friend), who entered into the picture in connection with the ransom negotiations.

Handwriting specimens of Baumeister are being obtained by the Narcotic Bureau for comparison with the ransom notes; data are also being obtained relative to the extortion arrest of Baumeister, to determine his method of operation. Efforts are being made to obtain a recent photograph of this individual which will be shown to Dr. Condon and Perrone. The latter has already examined New York Police photograph (B-15871) of Baumeister and was not able to identify it as that of the person who on March 12, 1932 handed him a letter to be delivered to Dr. J. F. Condon. However, Mellon states that this picture is a very poor likeness of Baumeister's present appearance.

Baumeister is described as follows:

Age:	47
Height:	5'10"
Weight:	150-160
Build:	Medium
Hair:	Dark Chestnut
Eyes:	Brown; deep sunk and "hypnotic"
Complexion:	Sallow
	Smooth Shaven
	No Eyeglasses
American citizen of German parentage	
Race:	White
Occupation:	Claims to be salesman; was formerly truck driver in upper Bronx.
Relatives:	Wife and daughter (age 21) now residing on Briggs Avenue, Bronx (near Dr. Condon's residence).

Has mother-in-law, Mrs. Gleckner, who formerly resided at 3029 Briggs Avenue, corner of 202nd St. Bronx.

Addresses: Last known—718 West 177th St. or 618 West 177 St.

308 West 72nd St. (in 1929)

331 West 36th St., all New York City

ARTHUR BARRY

The New York Office file relative to the possible participation this person in the Lindbergh baby kidnaping consists entirely of clippings from daily newspapers published after the arrest of Barry, on 10/22/32, a farmhouse on R.F.D. #1, near Newton, Orange Mountains, N.J.

Barry, reputed as one of America's premier jewel thieves, escaped from the New York State Prison at Auburn, N.Y. during a riot of the inmates July, 1929. Shortly after his escape he hid out in New York for approximately one year and then moved to Newark, N.J. residing there until July, 1931 at which time, using the name of James Tomer, he moved to a farmhouse occupied by one Otto Reuter, Barry having contacted Reuter (according to the latter) answering an advertisement Reuter had inserted in a New Jersey newspaper, offering room and board at $2 weekly, for the sake of companionship. Reuter at the time was the only occupant of his farmhouse.

During his residence with Reuter, Barry sold rubber squeejees for cleaning windows, and each day, according to Reuter, Barry in a small automobile, owned by Reuter, would canvass the surrounding country, selling these items out of his vehicle at various households.

Barry's arrest was effected by Newark, N.J. detectives after an informant advised of having overheard Barry plotting the kidnaping of the same of Jesse L. Livermore (from whose home Barry had previously stolen jewels valued at

$100,000); of the Lindbergh baby; of the infant son of Gene Tunney of Julia Hodgson, 14 year old adopted daughter of Babe Ruth. Barry, according to the informant, was also heard to remark that "Lindbergh took him out on newspaper headlines and that it would be a great joke if he (Lindbergh) put him, (Barry) back in the headlines again." Subsequently, this was all denied by Barry.

According to newspaper reports, Barry usually used a collapsible [garbled] in the robberies effected by him. He is also reported to have occasionally resorted to the use of Ethyl Chloride, an odorless anesthetic, to silence dogs that might be loose around the home he intended to rob and is reported to have used this method in silencing the dogs at the estate of Percy [garbled—could be Rockefeller] One of the places, he robbed. Barry is also reported to have habitually covered his feet with old stockings from which the tops had been cut and he is also said to be slightly lame. In this connection it will be recalled that footprints found at the Lindbergh estate were reported to have been heavier on the outer edges and made by someone with stocking coverings over the shoes. [garbled. Probably: He] being lame and having been known to wear stocking coverings over his shoes is the option was advanced that the footprints in question may have been made by him.

Opposed to all this conjecture is the statement of Otto Reuter to the effect that Barry was in the Reuter farmhouse the entire evening and night of March 1st, 1932.

According to the press dispatches, Barry was to be faced by Dr. J. J. "Jafsie" Condon, his footprints were to be compared with those found under the Lindbergh baby nursery window and he was to be questioned relative to the statements attributed to him by the Newark Police informant.

The New York office files do not contain any further information relative to the Barry investigation, however, it is common knowledge that the New Jersey State Police apparently were unable to connect Barry with the Lindbergh baby kidnaping and that shortly after his arrest he was turned over to the New York State authorities who returned him to the New York State Prison where he is still confined.

LEWIS V. CUMMINGS with aliases

Information was furnished the New York Division Office in November 1933, that one Lewis V. Cummings with the following aliases, Albert V. Kennedy, Young M. Cummings, Louis Cummings, Henderson, Hambley and Anderson, characterized as a "soldier of fortune", had been engaged in activities and made remarks indicating that he might be involved in the Lindbergh kidnaping. This suspect, who is said to be of Scandinavian extraction and who fits the description of "John" to whom the ransom money was paid, as a seaman has travelled extensively over the world, particularly in Mexico, South America, Australia, South Africa and China. In the Winter of 1931-32 he allegedly made remarks to the effect that he contemplated entering the kidnaping "racket", mentioning Colonel Lindbergh, among others, as a prospective victim.

Cummings worked at the New Jersey State Village for Epileptics at Skillman, N.J., three miles from Hopewell, in 1922, and has worked in various other institutions of a similar nature in the upper Bronx and Westchester County, N.Y. as well as in Connecticut and New Jersey. According to an informant, whose information has not as yet been thoroughly checked, Cummings was studying symbolism and the construction of ladders in a New York public library, prior to the kidnaping. The suspect is apparently familiar with the Bronx and New York City, and with the New England coast. His presence in New York when the crime occurred has been verified. Cummings is known to be a clever penman and to have served time for forgery. According to his own statements, he is wanted in a foreign country for murder. He was born in the United States, and is said to possess a speaking knowledge of several languages. During the Spring of 1932, Cummings apparently spent some time in an unknown locality in New Jersey, possibly in the company of one Sidney Friedlander of Inwood, Long Island.

In the latter part of March 1932, Cummings left in the custody of a friend in New York City, a number of sealed letters addressed to several of his intimate associates with instructions that if he failed to return at the expiration of six weeks, the letters should be mailed. Cummings claimed he was going on a "dangerous mission" and might be killed. The friend with whom the letters were left, becoming suspicious, steamed them open and made copies of the contents. The following quotation from one letter is an example of the tenor of all of them:

New York City, April 27, 1932.
"Dear Sid:
When you get this letter I will have kicked off. Verification will come through the War Department when they pay you the insurance or bonus . . . Better not make any inquiries of the coroner as it might lead to embarrassing inquiry by thick-skulled officialdom."

Cummings returned about a week after leaving the above letters and they were returned to him.

Cummings' closest associated were the following: Earl Orrington of Brooklyn, N.Y.; Earl Reeves of Ridgewood, N.J.; Friedlander previously mentioned, and Sidney Maranov, who had an office at 55 West 42nd Street, New York City, until the time 1933, at which office Cummings spent most of his time. Cummings was also quite friendly with a woman by the name of Miriam Surdez alias Mrs. Marjorie Chase, who appears to be from Morocco, North Africa. Cummings frequented literary clubs and the company of writers and authors, who apparently tolerated him because of his knowledge of foreign countries and his many experiences. He was regarded by many people who knew him as being unsound mentally in some respects, and is known to have been under observation at one time as a mental case.

Photograph of Cummings was exhibited to Dr. Condon, who stated it bore a resemblance to the individual "John" to whom he paid the ransom money and that he would like to see Cummings in person. Numerous handwriting specimens of this suspect were examined by the Division laboratory and by Albert D. Osborn, and found to bear no similarity to either the ransom notes or the "Faulkner" deposit ticket.

There is information in the New York Office files to the effect that one T. Herbert Elder of Roslyn, Pa., while scouting around the Lindbergh estate and the place where the baby's body was found, picked up a white linen handkerchief, apparently home made, bearing the initials "L.C.". Elder claims he found this handkerchief in the bushes near Mt. Rose Highway, several hundred feet from where the baby's body was found. The handkerchief was found by Elder about July 1, 1932, and is presently being examined by the Division laboratory to determine whether certain stain appearing on it are blood stains. An effort will be made to determine, if possible, whether the above handkerchief was the property of Lewis V. Cummings.

Cummings has been described by former associates as follows:

Age: 33 years
Height: About 6'
Weight: 170 lbs.

Build: Rather slender, but powerful in appearance.
Hair: Light brown.
Eyes: Piercing blue eyes; one eye slightly crossed.
Facial features: High forehead; high cheek bones.
Mustache: At times has a small brown mustache.
Scars and Marks: Has a number of long scars very noticeable from gun shot wounds, on back and front of one hand, believed to be the right; Thumb on same hand is half normal size.
Occupation: Cummings served in the U.S. Army during the war, after which he has apparently followed the sea, and worked in various insane asylums.

It does not appear that Lewis V. Cummings is related to Marie Cummings, former Lindbergh nurse. Likewise, there is no indication that Lewis V. Cummings is related or in any way connected with Frank Cummings with aliases, who was at one time a suspect in this case. These persons are of entirely different descriptions and come from different sections of the country; investigation has exonerated Frank Cummings and his associate, Theodore Wedark.

<u>NICK DeAUGUSTINA.</u>
<u>LARRY VANDETTI.</u>
<u>CARLO VALENTINE.</u>
<u>JOHN DELANEY</u>
<u>JOHN ROSS (or RUSSO).</u>

Under date of August 3, 1933, the Director advised the New York Office that The Attorney General had been informed by Lieutenant-Governor M. William Bray, of New York State, that Charles W. Lynch, reporter, City News

Branch of The Associated Press, possessed new information in this case. It developed that the information in question related to the participation of the above mentioned suspects in this kidnaping and extortion as communicated to Lynch by one Jon Wellen alias Jack King alias John J. Clifford alias Jack Roberts, true name Emil Wellenreiter, an ex-police informant. According to Wellen, during February 1932, while he was operating a garage at 152nd Street and Park Avenue, New York City, known as the Park Central Garage, he was approached by John Delaney, Larry Vandetti, Carlo Valentine and Nick DeAugustina, described by him as cohorts of John Ross (or Russo), (alleged leader of a gang of Italian thugs and racketeers operating in and from New York City), with the proposition that he participate in a kidnaping being planned by them as they desired him (Wellen) to act as the driver of the automobile to be used by the kidnapers. According to Wellen he at first indicated a willingness to join them but upon learning that their intended victim was Colonel Charles A. Lindbergh, he desired to withdraw but the gang refused to permit him to do so. Wellen states that during the latter part of February 1932 he accompanied members of this gang on several trips to Somerville, Princeton, Blawenburg, Rocky Hill (where they had lunch or dinner at a roadhouse), and Harlingen, N.J, for the purpose of familiarizing himself with the roads in said vicinity and to permit the gang to locate a hide-out. Wellen claimed that on one of these trips they stopped in East Orange, N.J., at a place, with the owner of which the other members of the gang appeared to be well acquainted. He professed to be able to pick out the above mentioned places.

Wellen stated that he participated in several conferences with the above named suspects (excepting Russo) in the office of the Park Central Garage and that one Sammy Ordino (whose brother, according to Wellen, was electrocuted in the New York State Prison) would know of these meetings as he was present on at least one occasion and served these men at the garage; that on this occasion there were also present two girls known to Wellen only as Dot and Kate, as well as a man named McCullen, addresses unknown to Wellen. Wellen further stated that after the departure of the above named members of the Ross gang, he informed Ordino that he, Wellen would have to pretend to "go along with the gang", and prevailed upon Ordino to steal a "Buick Master Six" automobile for him; that Ordino did steal this automobile, and turned it over to him during the first week in February 1932; that this theft was pursuant to instructions received from the Ross gang, that he, Wellen, got another automobile for their use.

Wellen claimed that he subsequently determined not to participate in this kidnaping, and took from his garage a Chrysler Imperial Eighty Roadster, the property of one Nick Hangemelli, which was stored at the garage, and secretly drove this automobile to Urlton, N.Y. where he was arrested the following Sunday by Sergeant Wheeler of the New York State Police charged with auto theft. Wellen stated that he was subsequently returned to New York City, entered a plea of guilty to this charge and was sentenced to serve six months in the Bronx County Jail; that he completed his sentence and was released July 16, 1932. Wellen states that it was while serving this sentence that he heard of the kidnaping of the Lindbergh baby and immediately knew that the Ross (Russo) gang "pulled this job". Wellen claims that while at the Bronx County Jail he was visited by one Brett, a young Italian friend of Mangemelli; that Brett informed him that Delaney had sent instructions that he, Wellen, was to keep his mouth shut or he would "get the business". Wellen claims that on several subsequent occasions he was similarly admonished.

Wellen asserted that if he were furnished with new

clothing, sufficient funds, an automobile to be registered in his own name, and authority from the Department of Justice to conduct his own investigation, he would be able to locate and renew his contacts with the above mentioned suspects, intimating that in this way he believed he could secure confessions or admissions or evidence to prove the participation of these suspects in the kidnaping of Charles A. Lindbergh, Jr.

To date Wellen's story has not been completely checked. However, at their request, Wellen accompanied officers of the New Jersey State Police over the New Jersey State routes he claimed to have driven with the Ross (Russo) gang, and during the course of this tour it was found that Wellen was unable to point out any of the places visited or persons contacted.

Descriptions of Vandetti, Valentine and DeAugustina were secured from Wellen, and the records of the Identification Division of the New York City Police Department checked for the purpose of determining if any of the suspects mentioned by Wellen were listed therein. This check developed criminal records for Carlo Valentine, Larry Venditto and Nicholas D'Agostine as the only persons bearing names at all similar to those furnished by Wellen as listed in said records. It is noted the descriptions of the three above mentioned suspects furnished by Wellen differ considerably from the descriptions of the similarly named criminals furnished by the New York Police Department, as follows:

	<u>Carlo Valentino as described in New York City Police records</u>	<u>Carlo Valentine as described by Wellen</u>
Age:	30	25 to 30
Height:	5'4 1/2"	5'9"

Weight:	125 lbs.	175 lbs.
Build:	Medium	
Hair:	Chestnut	Black.
Eyes:	Hazel	
Complexion:	Medium	Dark
Nativity:	New York City.	
Residence:	2384 Hoffman St., Bronx, N.Y.	

Police No. NYC Police #B-76897.
Criminal record: Arrested New York City 10/16/29—assault and robbery.
F.P.C.

<u>1   Aa</u>
<u>17 U 9</u>

	Larry Venditto as described in New York City Police records.	Larry Vandetti as described by Wellen.
Age:	27	25 to 30
Height:	5'3"	6'
Weight:	131 lbs. (1929)	180 lbs.
Complexion:	Medium	Dark
Hair:	Dark chestnut	Black
Eyes:	Brown	
Build:	Medium	
Scars:	Large mole on left cheek	No marks or scars apparent.
Residence:	4122 Digby Ave., Bronx, N.Y.	
Police No.	NYC Police #76896.	

Criminal record: Arrested NYC 10/16/29—assault and robbery.
F.P.C. None secured.

Thomas Fensch

<u>Nicholas D'Agostino as
Described in New York
City Police records.</u>

Age:	19	Wellen was unable
Height:	5'9 1/2"	to describe
Weight:	142 lbs.	Nick DeAugustino,
Hair:	Dark chestnut	John Delaney or
Eyes:	Brown	John Ross (Russo)
Complexion:	Sallow	
Occupation:	Cook	
Nativity:	Corono, L.I.	
Residence:	3875 Third Ave., New York City.	
Police No.	NYC Police #100817.	

Criminal Record: Arrested NYC 2/9/32—robbery
F.P.C. <u>32   IO   MO</u>
<u>32   OI   II</u>

 Wellen was permitted to examine photographs in the rogues' gallery, but was unable to pick therefrom a likeness of any of the above mentioned suspects. He was then shown the New York Police photographs of Carlo Valentino, Larry Venditto and Nicholas D'Agostino, all of whom it will be observed reside in the Bronx, N.Y. (as does Wellen), and whose names are practically identical with the names accorded the suspects by Wellen, but after having studied these photographs carefully, Wellen stated that same did not resemble in any detail any of the members of the Ross (Russo) gang who visited his garage at 152nd Street and Park Avenue, New York City.

 At the Bronx County Jail, the visitors book covering the period during which Wellen was confined therein, was examined and reflected that with the exception of John Pinniano, 1326 Gillespie Avenue, Bronx, and Joseph Mangemi (probably the Mangemelli referred to by Wellen),

635 Morris Avenue, Bronx, who visited him February 18th and 20th respectively, Wellen's only visitors were his wife, Carrie Wellen and his sister Rose Lupson (Mrs. Carrie Wellen giving her address as 2178 Arthur Ave., Bronx).

The criminal record of Wellen as obtained from the New York Police Department reflects that Wellen's career started in 1915; that he has been arrested on eight different occasions charged variously with; September 1, 1915 abduction; sentenced Sing Sing, 1 year and six months to 5 years and eight months; January 21, 1919, burglary, dismissed; February 18, 1919, impersonating an officer, sentenced to New York County Jail; November 24, 1919, grand larceny, discharged; July 27, 1921 at Boston, charge bogus officer, no disposition; January 16, 1926 as fugitive from Norristown, Pa., no disposition; May 9, 1929 seduction, acquitted; February 17, 1932, grand larceny, six months Bronx County Jail.

SAMUEL GOLDBERG alias SAM THE GAS MAN Alias SAM GOLD alias SAM GORDON alias SAM KLINE alias SAM HARRIS alias SAM DAVIS

Goldberg, a resident of Philadelphia, Pa., maintains a home for his wife and two daughters, Sylvia and Violet, and one son Barney, in the vicinity of 52nd Street and Pine Street. He is a well known bootlegger and rum-runner, reputed to be the head of one of the principal organizations of that nature operated off the New Jersey and Virginia coasts. Until recently he operated several boats, the two principal ones being the "Sylvia" and the "Violet", named after his two daughters. Both of these boats were built for him by the ship yard at Norfolk, Va. Then operated by John Hughes Curtis, with whom Goldberg is reputed to have been intimately associated.

During July and August 1933, Goldberg was incarcerated in the Duval County Jail, Jacksonville, Fla., in the absence of bond in the sum of $100,000 awaiting trial on an indictment charging conspiracy to violate the National Prohibition Act. At that time there were two other indictments pending against him, one at Norfolk, Va. And the other at Baltimore, Md., both charging conspiracy to violate the National Prohibition Act.

Goldberg in 1933 is described as 36 years, 5'11 1/2", 190 lbs., short body, long legs, long arms, big hands, long nose, light brown sandy hair, light complexion, smooth shaven, excellent teeth, eyeglasses with silver frame and temples. Description furnished by Bureau of Prohibition.

Goldberg was first brought to the attention of this Division in the instant matter, as a result of a letter to the Director dated April 18, 1933 from S. P. Hanson, 433 West Oak Avenue, Wildwood, N.J. It was subsequently developed that Hanson, some time previously, had been employed by Goldberg as a pilot for one of the latter's rum-running vessels. Hanson's letter was to the effect that he possessed information relative to Goldberg's connection with the Lindbergh kidnaping. Singularly enough while the investigation of this complaint was in progress and prior to being called upon to run out leads in its territory, the Jacksonville Office received a complaint alleging participation by Goldberg in the instant kidnaping. Apparently this latter complaint was entirely unrelated to the complaint of Hanson.

Hansen's information was to the effect that under date of October 28, 1932, while passing the Reading terminal station in Philadelphia, he met one "Will", other name unknown, who had been in Goldberg's employ during the period of Hansen's employment by Goldberg; that upon inquiring of Will as to the, then, whereabouts of Goldberg, he was informed by Will that Goldberg had plenty of money with which to hide out and evade arrest as he (Goldberg) "was in on the Lindbergh kidnaping and was the man to whom "Jafsie" (John F. Condon) passed the money over the fence".

Investigation at Philadelphia, and inquiry of George Gordon, alleged former chauffeur for Goldberg, failed to identify anyone, employed or associated with Goldberg, as bearing the name or sobriquet of "Will"; however, it was ascertained that Hanson on March 8, 1931 "was taken for a ride" by Goldberg and Gordon, was badly beaten and shot, and left for dead by them, and consequently is very bitter toward Goldberg.

The information referred to as having been received at the Jacksonville Office, was furnished by one Walter Hayes, then a cell-mate of Goldberg in the Duval County Prison at Jacksonville, Fla. Hayes entered a plea of guilty to violation of the National Motor Vehicle Theft Act, July 20, 1933, and was sentenced to serve eighteen months in the U.S. Penitentiary at Atlanta. He subsequently volunteered information to Special Agent R.A. Alt to the effect that while occupying the cell with Goldberg, the latter, who according to Hayes could neither read nor write, had Hayes and another prisoner, one Howard T. Conn (subsequently returned to Washington, D.C. on perjury charges), write his letters and read his mail. Hayes stated that in addition to letters to and from his family, Goldberg corresponded with one Helen Walsh, Plaza Hotel, New York City, and with a woman in New York designated only as "Chippy", who was addressed c/o Helen Walsh; that in one letter to "Chippy", Goldberg cautioned her to instruct "John" to remain in the West End until further instructions were received from him, and subsequently intimated to Hayes that he (Goldberg) wanted "John" to remain in hiding because a Department of Justice agent (Prohibition Agent) had recently questioned him (Goldberg) relative to the Lindbergh kidnaping. Hayes also stated that on one occasion Goldberg informed him that at one time he "got plenty of money over the fence" which to Hayes indicated that Goldberg might have been the man to whom John F. Condon paid the ransom money.

With reference to the reliability of Hayes, Special Agent Alt advised that when originally questioned relative to the auto theft for which he was sentenced, Hayes lied constantly with reference to the violation, his past life and other matters, but that before arraignment he retracted all these statements and told the truth in every instance.

Goldberg was subsequently interviewed in the Duval County Jail, Jacksonville, Fla., and positively denied any knowledge of the Lindbergh kidnaping and murder.

Recently the Philadelphia Office conducted further investigation with a view to determining the identity of the "Will" referred to by Hansen, and of the "John" referred to by Hayes; also of other known associates of Goldberg, and as a result furnished the New York Office with photographs of Samuel Goldberg with aliases; Edward H. Doe alias "John"; George Wallace alias "John"; William Rapp alias "Ganns"; Louis Brodsky; Harry Mankin; David Goldman; Harry Miller alias Morris Vernekoff alias Murray Werner alias Murray Trusdale and Sam Vernekoff alias Torisdale. These photographs were displayed to John F. Condon and pronounced by him not to contain a likeness of "John".

Goldberg is reputed to be a braggart and one inclined to attract attention to himself by fanciful stories of his exploits. Informant Hansen is frankly bitter against Goldberg. No information is listed regarding the acumen or credulity of Informant Hayes. He is known to have lied freely when it suited his purpose.

HARRY MEYERS; MURRAY MOLL; ISRAEL ALDERMAN; MOE SIDWAY

During September, 1933, an informant, name unknown to the New York office, advised a Special Agent of the Division at Chicago, that through a confidential source he had learned that the Lindbergh baby had been kidnaped by Harry Meyers, a hoodlum of Kansas City, No. and Murray Moll alias Murray Miller of St. Louis. He stated that Harry Meyers was killed about six weeks previously and that Moll was murdered in New York City about three or four months before; that the man who murdered Moll was supposed to be one "Chink" Sheren, a narcotic peddler on a large scale, in New York City, and a pal of the underworld character known as "Ziggie" also a killer, who is well known in New York. This confidential informant also stated that the Lindbergh ransom money had been handled by Israel Alderman alias "Jew Willie" and Moe Sidway, both of St. Louis. These two men were reported to have made several trips to Armenia or Belgium to "get rid of the Lindbergh cash." The informant also stated that "Jew Willie" was recently arrested by Federal Narcotic agents at a summer resort sixty miles north of Minnesota, which resort is operated by one Dr. Goodrich, who is supposed to be well known to the Minneapolis police.

The same informant under date of October 8, 1933 wrote a letter to the Chicago office of the Division, further advising that Alderman was formerly bodyguard to Moe Sidway; that this pair made a trip to Belgium and Armenia once each year to get dope and while in Europe "they had gotten rid of the money." Further, that there had been a tremendous war in the gang over the distribution of this ransom money. He indicated that from information supplied to him the following persons were mixed up in the Lindbergh case and that the numerous deaths noted had occurred due to the feud concerning the division of the money:

Morris Moll alias Morris Marks alias Morrey Miller of St. Louis, Mo., killed in New York City.
Leo Schneider, St. Louis, Mo. dead.
Max Greenberg, St. Louis, Mo. dead.
Gus Berger, St. Louis, Mo. dead.
Abe Goldfeder, St. Louis, Mo. dead.
Harry Franks, Kansas City, Mo., killed in Hollywood, Cal.
"Waxey" Gordon, New York City.
Charles Sherman alias "Chink", New York City
"Ziggie", New York City
"Mannie" Kessler, New York City
Tommie Weber, New York City

This letter indicated that Morris Moll, Harry Meyers and Tommie Weber were supposed to have been the kidnapers of the Lindbergh baby and that Moll dropped the baby while carrying him down the ladder; that Gus Berger, Abe Goldfeder and Charles Sherman wee the ones who obtained the ransom money; that Greenberg, Moll, Berger, Goldfeder, Schneider and Franks were all killed on account of this fight over the ransom money and that this fight was started by "Waxey" Gordon who had Max Greenberg "put on the spot."

WM. PATRICK "SQUAWK" REILLY, et al

On March 4, 1932, four telegrams were sent from New York City by way of Postal and Western Union offices, from a telephone pay station in the Pennsylvania Station in New York, which were addressed to the Director, at the Benjamin Franklin Hotel, Philadelphia, Pa. These telegrams were signed Al Dyer, who indicated that one Harry Sachs Hechheimer, an attorney with offices at 140 West 42nd Street, New York City, residence 33 West 55th Street, New York City, and William Patrick "Squawk" Reilly were implicated in the kidnaping of Charles A. Lindbergh, Jr.; that Attorney Hechheimer had received $1000 from Reilly as a down payment for being the intermediary in this matter, with the understanding that he would receive an additional 25% of the ransom money if the negotiations were successful. The original telegram mentioned above are in possession of the New York office of the Division.

Investigation established that Reilly was acquainted with an attorney named Hechheimer and also with an Al Dyer, whose true name was Albert Trepanier, and that Reilly and Dyer were on unfriendly terms over an automobile transaction. Investigation further developed that Al Dyer alias Trepanier, on March 4, 1932 was in Daytona Beach, Florida. Shortly thereafter Dyer was located by Agents of the Jacksonville Division office and interviewed with reference to the above mentioned wires addressed to the Director at the Benjamin Franklin Hotel in Philadelphia. Dyer denied being in New York City on March 4, 1932, and further denied any knowledge of the telegrams sent to the Director on that date. Dyer admitted his true name was Albert Trepanier, and denied knowledge of any one else using the alias of Al Dyer, which he assumed about eight years previously because of some rules of some automobile racing association of which he was a member. Trepanier indicated, however, that some one may have used the name Al Dyer at the direction of William P. "Squawk" Reilly. Trepanier explained that in March, 1931 with four other men, he was arrested in Atlantic City, New Jersey, charged with conspiracy to defraud. The case as to him was dismissed. At the time of his arrest he owned and was in possession of a new 1931 eight cylinder Hupmobile sedan, which the Atlantic City, New Jersey police took from him and placed in storage at the Police Garage. Subsequent to the above arrest, "Squawk" Reilly, who was unknown to Trepanier, but who was acquainted with his companions, came to Atlantic City, N.J. from New York, to assist the arrested persons. Upon Reilly's arrival in Atlantic City and after he had learned that all persons arrested were broke, he is alleged to have immediately lost interest in the case, but obtained from the Atlantic City Police Department Trepanier's Hupmobile sedan. Reilly is said to have returned with this car to New York City, although no explanations has been given as to how Reilly obtained Trepanier's car from the Atlantic City Police Department. Trepanier thereafter sought legal advice as to how he could recover his Hupmobile sedan. A short while later Trepanier met Reilly in New York City and he spoke to him about the car but could obtain no satisfaction whatsoever from Reilly. He later contacted Reilly by telephone and in this conversation Trepanier was advised that Reilly had disposed of the car by sale to an unknown person. Trepanier claimed that prior to this trouble in Atlantic City, N.J. he had never seen "Squawk" Reilly, has seen him only once since that time, but has learned that Reilly is a professional crook, having been arrested as many as 87 times without having once been convicted.

Pursuant to the above, William P. "Squawk" Reilly was interviewed at his home, 25 South Munn Street, East Orange, N.J. Reilly readily identified photographs of such parties answering the names of William Connell, New Jersey State Prison picture #14139; Charles Sheppard, New Jersey State Prison picture #14140; Matt Smith, State County, Florida, picture #08388; and Alfred Dyer, Montreal, Canada #29076, as being parties known to him and individuals involved in a race track shake-down at Atlantic City, N.J., all of whom had been arrested in May, 1931 at Atlantic

City, in connection with the race track case in which Dyer was released. It appears that Connell and Sheppard were released in that case and Matt Smith on March 28, 1932, at least, was still a fugitive from justice. Reilly indicated to Agents of the New York office that his sole interest in the above parties was in the arranging of the bond for them, and that in connection with the arranging of such bond he had exhibited Trepanier's Hupmobile sedan, which he later sold to obtain the moneys advanced by him for the purpose of obtaining Trepanier's bond. "Squawk" Reilly admitted being acquainted with Attorney Hechheimer due to the fact that Hechheimer had appeared to represent the above mentioned persons when they were arrested in Atlantic City. Reilly claimed he had no direct or intimate association with Hechheimer and characterized him as being a "little crazy."

Under date of January 23, 1934, William P. "Squawk" Reilly, Jack Costa, George Kent and Terry Catina were arrested at Toms River, N.J. charged with attempting to bribe one of the Jury Panel, called in connection with he trial of the case entitled United States vs. Nicholas Delmore—Obstruction of Justice.

Following is Reilly's description obtained from the Irvington, N. J. Police Department:

Name :	William Patrick "Squawk" Reilly
Age :	40
Address:	194 West End Avenue, New York City
Race :	White
Complexion:	Medium
Height:	5'7-1/2"
Build :	Stocky
Hair :	Black
Beard :	Medium
Eyes :	Blue

Irvington Police No.: 1073
Fingerprints : <u>1 Roo 10</u>
                1 Roo 9
Born :   Baltimore, Maryland
Occupation: Salesman
              Scar on top of head.

Following is Dyer's description obtained from the Atlantic City, N.J. Police Department:

Name :   Alfred Dyer, Atlantic City, N. J. Police No. 7818
Race :   White
Height: 5'10-1/2"
Weight: 181 pounds.
Build :   Medium
Hair :   Brown
Eyes :   Brown
Age :   31
Occupation: Salesman
Fingerprint Classification: <u>1 RE 4</u>
                             1 T 4

Following is a description of Harry Hechheimer:

Age: 48 years
Height: 5'9:
Weight: 145 lbs.
Build: Very thin

Sharp features very pronounced; prominent hook nose; tortoise shell glasses; always carries a walking cane, reported to have a sword encased therein which is necessary because of his activities.

Born: United States

Admitted to practice law in the State of New York on May 11, 1916 on motion from the State of Maryland.

REO VERNE SANKEY alias VERN SANKEY

Subsequent to the public designation of Sankey as one of the kidnapers of Charles Boettcher, 2nd, he was frequently referred to in the newspapers as a suspect in the Lindbergh kidnaping. The New Jersey State Police, the New York City Police, and the Division's New York Office, have received no information that would indicate Sankey or his associates had any connection with the Lindbergh kidnaping. Likewise no information has been received by these various agencies that Sankey or his associates were in the vicinity of New York City on March 1, 1932, or at any other time. A thorough review of the New York Division Office file relative to Sankey and Gordon Alcorn developed no information that Sankey was ever in the City of New York; State of New Jersey, or in the eastern section of the United States. The file shows that Alcorn was in the territory of the New York Division Office on but two occasions during 1927, when he visited his brother Harold at Syracuse, N.Y., remained a few months, and worked as an engine wiper for the New York Central Railroad. During 1931, he is reported to have again visited at Syracuse. The tactics used by Sankey in the kidnaping cases in which he was involved apparently differ from those pursued in the Lindbergh case. Nevertheless, a considerable quantity of his handwriting was examined by Handwriting Expert Albert D. Osborn of New York City, who reported that same bore no resemblance to the Lindbergh ransom notes.

Sankey's photographs and that of his chief associate, Gordon Francis Alcorn, alias Gordon Alcorn, alias Gordon Elkhorn, alias Gordon Best, were exhibited to Dr. John F.

Condon, who stated that same bore no resemblance to the individual "John" to whom he paid the ransom money in the Lindbergh case. It is stated, however, that the photographs of Sankey and Alcorn exhibited to Dr. Condon were rather poor specimens, and better photographs, when obtained, will be exhibited to Dr. Condon and the taxicab driver, Perrone.

A number of unreliable informants have communicated with the Division, alleging that Sankey is implicated in the Lindbergh case, but upon investigation, their information was proved unfounded. One of these was Oral E. Rathbun, a soldier, who has furnished alleged information on many important kidnaping cases. Investigation of his statements proved them untrue, and indicated that much of his information was gleaned from newspaper reports.

Michael F. Kinkaid, Prosecuting Attorney, Ramsey County, St. Pa. Minn., after visiting the ranch of Sankey at Gann Valley, S.D. in the Fall of 1933, advised newspaper reporters that he found on the ranch, complete newspaper and magazine accounts of the Lindbergh kidnaping as well as a file containing information as to the earnings of Babe Ruth and Jack Dempsey. The information given to the press by Kindkaid appears to be the basis for most of the newspaper articles connecting Sankey with the Lindbergh case.

Sankey was the Chief conspirator in the kidnapings of Charles Boettcher, Jr. of Denver, Colo. On February 12, 1933, which resulted in his indictment on March 29, 1933 together with Alcorn; Boettcher was released on March 1, 1933 after the payment of $60,000 ransom. Haskell Bohn of St. Paul was kidnaped on June 30, 1932 and released after payment of $12,000 ransom. Mrs. Vern Sankey was acquitted in the Bohn case but is being held for trial in the Boettcher case. Apparently Sankey's associate in the Boettcher case were Gordon Alcorn, Carl Pearce, Elvina Ruth Kohler, Mrs. Sankey and Arthur Youngsberg. One

Ray Robinson associated with Sankey in the Bohn case, was convicted and is serving a twenty-five year sentence.

Sankey was arrested at Chicago, Ill. on January 31, 1934, and Alcorn was arrested in the same city on February 1, 1934. Both were thoroughly questioned regarding the Lindbergh case but steadfastly denied participation in same, although they admitted their guilt in the Boettcher and Bohn kidnapings. Sums of money found in possession of these individuals were found not be part of the Lindbergh ransom money.

On February 8, 1934, Sankey committed suicide in his cell at Sioux Falls, South Dakota, where he was awaiting prosecution on the indictment charging him with kidnaping Boettcher.

On February 9, 1934, Gordon Alcorn pleaded guilty in Federal Court at Sioux Falls, South Dakota, in the Boettcher case, and on the same date was sentenced to life imprisonment in the United States Penitentiary at Leavenworth, Kansas.

Mrs. Sankey, in default of bond, is being held in jail at Sioux Falls, awaiting trial in the Boettcher case.

Sankey was 42 years of age: 5'7" in height; weight 170 lbs.; heavy build; ruddy complexion; blue eyes; light brown hair; bald in front; has three small moles left side of chin and one small scar on back of one hand. He was an employee of the Grand Trunk Pacific Railroad of Montreal, Canada, from 1911 to March 1931, when he took a leave of absence to enter the United States and visit relatives, but never returned. Apparently most of his activities have been in the Dakotas, in Chicago, St. Paul, Minneapolis and Denver.

Alcorn is 27 years of age, 6' tall, 170 lbs., slender build, sallow complexion, blue eyes, dark brown wavy hair, a Canadian, and a railroad fireman.

According to W.F. Shroeder of the State Identification

Bureau, Lincoln, Nebraska, Sankey's present wife, Mrs. Fern Sankey, was the first wife of Vernon C. Miller, subject of the Kanmo case.

Neither Sankey nor Alcorn has a criminal record of any consequence, other than in the aforementioned kidnaping cases.

GARRETT SCHENCK

Schenck, who lived at Bedminster, New Jersey, and who had peddled fish in the vicinity of Hopewell, on June 10, 1932 was abducted by Private Detective John J. Devine and Ray Cummings of Johnstown, Pa. and transported via Devine's automobile to DuBois, Pa. where he was held incommunicado for approximately seventy-six days as a suspect in the Lindbergh case. This matter was investigated by Clearfield County, Pa. authorities, Pennsylvania State Troopers and Special Agents of the Division of Investigation. Their investigation developed no basis for suspecting that Schenck was involved in the Lindbergh kidnaping. Schenck preferred charges against the men involved in his abduction, and on September 7, 1932 informations were filed, and Justice of the Peace warrants issued at Clearfield, Pa. against Devine, Cummings and their confederates, Charles Horner and Edward Benshaw of Johnstown, Avery Conners and Frank Shugarts of DuBois, Paul Corp of Johnstown, Russel Love, DuBois Chief of Police, and Reuben Rakeshaw of DuBois, the first two being charged with kidnaping and the remainder with being accessories, and all of them being charged with conspiracy. Information is not available in the files of this office as to the disposition of these charges. It is noted that although Schenck was kidnaped and taken from one state to another, there was no violation of the Federal Kidnaping Law since no ransom was demanded.

CHARLES W. SELLICK (Suspect)
RUDOLPH DeBAROFF (Suspect)

Charles W. Sellick, an aviator, formerly of Atlantic Highlands, N. J., but more recently a resident of Daytona Beach, Fla., and one Rudolph DeBaroff, alias Captain Barras, alias Captain Rudolph M. Baraff, alias Count Rudolph DeM. De Baraf, for a time, were viewed as suspects. Considerable investigation was conducted by agents of the Bureau of Narcotics and later by this Division. The former during February and March, 1932, maintained telephone surveillance over Sellick and DeBaroff at Daytona Beach, due to their association with Willie Haer and Nick Costa of Savannah, Ga., outstanding dope and liquor runners in the Southeastern part of the United States. This surveillance indicated that they perhaps were engaged in smuggling drugs, planning a revolution in Central America or possibly were involved in the Lindbergh kidnaping, the last because Sellick was said to have been in New Jersey at about that time.

Investigation developed that Sellick, recently engaged in rum running and other smuggling, had discontinued such activities during March, 1932, and was then preparing to leave for Ambasmundes Tegucigalpa, Honduras, S. A., with DeBaroff for the purpose of establishing air transport or mail lines in Honduras. The investigation eliminated Sellick and DeBaroff as suspects and was discontinued at Daytona, April 1, 1932 after the Bureau of Internal Revenue and seized Sellick's plane and hangar and the Immigration Inspectors started checking on the citizenship status of DeBaroff, which government activity apparently frustrated the Central American plans of Sellick and DeBaroff.

Photograph of Sellick is in possession of the New York Division Office.

Descriptions of Sellick and DeBaroff, as furnished by Narcotic Agent G. T. Sheegog:

Name	Charles W. Sellick
Age	45 years
Height	5' 10" to 6'
Weight	200 pounds
Hair	Blonde—grey at temples
Eyes	Brown
Build	Rough—rugged
Complexion	Red—coarse

Left shoulder sags; swings arms when walking.
Marital status married; wife, Jeanette Schuman, residing at 3512 Bowman St., East Lake, Phila., Pa.

Name	Rudolph DeBaroff; aliases; Captain Barras; Captain Rudolph M. Baraff; Count Rudolph DeM. De Baraf.
Age	30—35 years
Height	5'5"
Hair	Light brown
Complexion	Fair

Brown mole, size of small finger nail left cheek near mouth. Speaks English correctly but with decided accent; possibly affected; stylish dresser; bearing, cocky; struts.

WASLOV (VACLOV) SIMEK

Information was secured by the Intelligence Unit of the Treasury Department through an informant at Detroit that one Waslov Simek might be implicated in the instant case. Simek had been arrested at Detroit, Mich. On March 25, 1924, on a charge of attempted extortion in connection with a threat to kidnap the baby of Edsel Ford. Upon a plea of guilty to extortion Simek was sentenced to serve one to two years in the Michigan State Reformatory. Simek admitted that prior to the above sentence he had also served five years on a larceny charge (place not shown). After completing his sentence at the Michigan State Reformatory, Simek was deported by this government from the port of New York, on April 29, 1925, to Czecho-Slovakia, of which country he was a citizen. Simek had left his native country in October 1923. It is reported that his wife, Maria, and his father, Anthony, are both living in Czecho-Slovakia, and that he has an uncle, Jan Kontocky alias Skoltycki, residing in the United States at Chicago, Ill. It was established by the Intelligence Unit that Simek secretly left Czecho-Slovakia because of an arson charge against him, after his deportation there from the United States. Subsequently he went to Russia where he became involved in trouble with that government. The investigation by the Intelligence Unit further reflects that Simek spent time in India, South America, and finally settled in Santo Domingo. In the latter country he was employed by a public service corporation for about a year previous to the kidnaping, and required to make daily reports as to the readings of certain instruments. According to the investigation conducted by the Intelligence Unit, the records of the corporation establish that Simek was in Santo Domingo in the employ of the corporation on the date the Lindbergh kidnaping occurred.

A photograph of Simek, mixed in with a number of other photographs, was exhibited to Dr. Condon, by the Intelligence Unit. Dr. Condon picked out the picture of Simek from the group and said "Boys, you are hot, I want to see that man". However, Condon did not definitely state that Simek was the man "John" to whom he paid the ransom money.

At the time of Simek's arrest on March 25, 1924, his description was as follows:

Born   Dec. 25, 1897 in Czecho-Slovakia.
Height   5'4"

Weight	123 lbs
Build	Medium slender
Eyes	Grey-blue
Hair	Brown
Complexion	Sallow
Marks	White raised mole outer corner right ? Horizontal scar left part of chin.

It is noted that this description does not agree with the description of "John" furnished by Dr. Condon. A considerable time after the exhibition of Simek's photograph to Dr. Condon by the Intelligence Unit, another photograph of this suspect was exhibited to Dr. Condon by a Special Agent of the Division, and Condon stated that it bore no resemblance to "John".

There is no indication in the report of Special Agent Frank Will of the Intelligence Unit or in the Division files that handwriting specimens of Simek were compared with the Ransom notes. It is the intention of the New York Division Office to obtain handwriting specimens and to make a further check of Simek's activities.

DEAN PRESTON SUTHERLAND, alias EDWIN LYELL EARL, alias EDWARD L. HARLE, alias ROBERT FARNSWORTH.

In April, 1933 information indicating that Dr. Dean Preston Sutherland, formerly of Indianapolis, Ind. Possibly had some connection with the Lindbergh kidnaping case, was furnished by Mr. Robert St. Pierre, Indianapolis, Ind. and referred to the Division. Investigation developed that Mr. St. Pierre first became acquainted with Sutherland early in 1930 while the latter was employed in a garage in Indianapolis. Sutherland claimed to have served with the Canadian Forces in Siberia during the World War; to have been shell shocked. He claimed personal acquaintance with a Colonel Morrow, who was in command of the American Regiment in Siberia and also claimed acquaintanceship with Colonel Charles A. Lindbergh, stating that he had met him at Kelly Field, Texas, and also that he had been invited by the late Dwight Morrow to visit the Morrow family in Mexico City while Mr. Morrow as Ambassador.

Mr. St. Pierre further informed that he had a child who in 1930 was about 2-1/2 years old and was unable to walk or talk. Sutherland often visited his home and stated that he firmly believed all children who indicated the slightest degree of being abnormal should be "hit in the head with a hammer" asserting that is what he would do if he had such a child; that Sutherland apparently did not like young children, although he seemed very fond of dogs. He claimed to have been educated in the study of medicine at the University of Pennsylvania and that his mother was residing in France; appeared to be well bred and spoke German, French and Russian and exhibited several war medals. Mr. St. Pierre stated that he had heard from some forgotten source that Sutherland stated he had been confined in the State Insane Asylum at Mattewan, New York, for a short period.

Mr. St. Pierre stated that about September 18, 1930 his wife received a letter through the mail which was typewritten and bore the typed signature "XY 2" and about two days alter received a second letter bearing the same signature, receiving a third one a few weeks later and on December 21, 930 receiving the fourth and last letter; that in all of these letters the writer threatened to kidnap St. Pierre's daughter unless $500 was paid. Shortly thereafter Sutherland left Indianapolis supposedly for Hollywood, California.

Further, that about February 28th or 29th, 1932, at about 8:30 A.M., he received a long distance telephone call from either Camden or Trenton, N. J. inquiring if he would accept a collect call from Dr. Sutherland; that he accepted the call and Sutherland requested a loan of $40 stating he needed it immediately; that an emergency had arisen; however, Mr. St. Pierre declined to send the money to him. Upon reading of the Lindbergh kidnaping case a day or two later, Mr. St. Pierre forwarded the four extortion letters which he believed to have been written by Sutherland with complete information to the New Jersey State Police and they subsequently advised that they had been unable to connect Sutherland with the case.

Investigation developed no record of a long distance call mentioned by Mr. St. Pierre; that there was no record of Dr. Sutherland ever having been confined in the New York State Asylum for Insane at Mattewan, New York; no report of English Oval cigarette stubs, which brand Sutherland smoked incessantly, having been found at scene of crime; that Sutherland was unknown to Colonel Lindbergh and his family and that Colonel Charles H. Morrow, who commanded the 28th United States Infantry in Siberia, had never heard of anyone named Dean P. Sutherland, but had, however, met one Edward Earle, who was later identified as Sutherland, for the first time at Deportation Proceedings held at Washington, D. C. in April, 1922 on the deportation of Gregory Semendoff. At those proceedings Earle testified he resided at St. Paul, Minn. And enlisted in the Canadian Army in Canada in August, 1914, served in the Royal Engineers of the English Army in Siberia in 1918, and was discharged April 20, 1920. Colonel Morrow had not seen or heard from Earle and knows nothing of his whereabouts since said hearings.

The record of the testimony of Edward L. Earle on April 13, 1922, shows that he was 20 years old; born at Winchester, England; resided at St. Paul, Minn.; joined the British Army August 9, 1913; served until April 20, 1920; went to

Siberia from Petrograd, Russia with the British Railway Engineers and served in that territory from March 1917 to 1920.

This subject's criminal record as shown in the Division's file #14816 as follows:

November 5, 1915, as Edwin Earl, #4293, received New Jersey Reformatory from Monmouth County; crime, false pretenses; sentence indefinite.

July 30, 1917, as Edwin Lyell Earl, #11037, received United States D.B. Fort Leavenworth, Kansas, crime A.W.O.L., obtaining money under false pretenses; sentence, one year.

March 6, 1925, as Dean Preston Southerland, #14816, arrested Police Department, Toledo, Ohio, charge suspicious person, 30 days and costs.

March 25, 1925, as Robert Farnsworth, #A40734, received Auburn Prison, Auburn, N. Y. as parole violator from Sing Sing prison; crime grand larceny, 2nd degree; sentence one year and three months to two years and six months.

His description as furnished by St. Pierre and others follows:

Name :	Dr. Dean P. Sutherland with aliases
Age :	38 to 40 years
Height:	5'8-1/2"
Weight:	175 lbs.
Build :	Stocky
Hair :	Black, short cropped, curly; closely shaved in back and around ears
Eyes :	Gray or blue; squinty; far apart
Complexion:	Medium dark
Teeth :	Good, even, some gold inlays
Nativity:	Probably not American born
Education:	Well educated, evidently for the medi-

cal profession; speaks Russian, German and French; alleged to have been instructor of Bridge

Clean shaven; heavy beard

Scars & Marks: Irregular scar right elbow; right arm squeaks when raised and lowered rapidly

Peculiarities: Round head; intellectual broad forehead; thick lips, speaks with deep, soft voice; smokes incessantly English Oval cigarettes; takes only two puffs of each cigarette and then discards same; always wears gloves; does not wear a hat; fond of dogs; dislikes children; is subject to fainting spells, alleged to be caused as a result of gas and shell shock.

Military record: Claims to have been Captain in Canadian Army during World War and in the Diplomatic Service in Australia; claims to be an aviator; possesses four military medals.

Various persons in Indianapolis, Ind. Readily identified the Auburn Prison photograph of Robert Farnsworth with aliases, as being the Dr. Dean P. Sutherland in question. A number of anonymous notes which were believed to have been written by Sutherland in Los Angeles some years ago were submitted to Albert D. Osborn, Examiner of Questioned Documents, New York City, for comparison of the handwriting with that in the Lindbergh ransom notes. After examination and comparison Mr. Osborn was of the opinion that the handwriting in these notes is entirely dissimilar to that appearing in the Lindbergh notes.

ISIDORO UBALDI (Informant)

Early in March, 1932, a letter dated 3/12/32 was received by United States District Judge G. A. Carpenter at

Chicago. This letter, signed "Isidoro Ubaldi" was to the effect that the writer possed knowledge of the kidnapers of the Lindbergh baby and of the whereabouts of the latter.

Investigation at Hartford and Waterbury, Conn. Established that Isidoro Ubaldi was arrested 8/14/30 while employed at the Scoville Manufacturing Company plant, Waterbury, Conn.—charge—violation of Immigration Laws (illegal entry); that at an immigration hearing 3/30/30 Ubaldi stated that he had been born at Sconno. Italy, 4/3/76; that he entered the U.S.A. during 1924 entering illegally from Canada; that his wife, Rosa, and seven children were still residing in Sconno, Italy. It was further ascertained that Ubaldi was released on bond in the sum of $500 furnished by the American Surety Company pending final arrangements for his deportation and thereafter failed to appear at the date designated; that his bond was forfeited and he is presently wanted by the Immigration Authorities.

Considerable investigation at Chicago was unsuccessful in determining Ubaldi's whereabouts and to date he has not been located or interviewed. Handwriting in the letter signed "Isidoro Ubaldi" was examined by A. D. Osborn, Handwriting Expert, New York City, who advised that same was entirely differing from the handwriting of the ransom letters.

<u>J. FLOYD WILLIAMS</u>
<u>OSIASE MILLAIRE</u>
<u>EARL TANNEHILL</u>
<u>STANISLAUS GRAPCWSKI</u>
<u>JOSEPH HUGO BECKER</u>
<u>MAX HUHNERT</u>

As a result of the statement made by Fred J. Tomkins, a Red Carmody, then Prisoner No. 36579, United States Penitentiary, Leave Kansas, to one Leo F. Reardon, ex-convict and retold by the latter to J. North, Jr. of the Fort Worth, Texas, Star Telegram, considerable investigation was conducted relative to suspects Grabowski and Williams and Becker.

As related by Carmody, the above named convicts prior to charge from Leavenworth, discussed kidnaping in general with Carmody. Grabowski also known as Heinie Grabowski, and Max Kuhnert, in particular, discussed the possibilities of kidnaping the Lindbergh baby. Williams discussed the general possibilities of the kidnaping racket with Grabowski and Kuhnert.

Carmody designated Heinie Grabowski and Williams as the kidnapers of the Lindbergh baby, and advised that Williams was presently in Australia and Grabowski in Germany. He designated Joseph Hugo Becker as the person who planned the Lindbergh kidnaping in Leavenworth Penitentiary in the fall of 1931 and stated that Becker wrote the ransom notes. He further designated Grabowski as the man to whom Dr. J. F. Condon paid the $50,000 ransom.

Investigation to date has developed that Williams is at present residing in San Angelo, Texas and has not been reported to have displayed any evidence of improved financial standing since the date of the payment of the ransom. Investigation indicates that he was apparently absent from San Angelo from Christmas, 1931 to March 16, 1932, but that known associates do not include any of the above named suspects.

Sample of Williams' handwriting has been pronounced by A. D. Osborn to be entirely dissimilar to the handwriting on the ransom note.

A specimen of handwriting alleged by W. W. Williams, a self-styled "Handwriting Expert" of Portland, Oregon, to be that of Mrs. J. Williams, and to resemble the handwriting of the Lindbergh ransom letter was submitted to Albert D. Osborn for comparison. Mr. Osborn is emphatic in reporting that the "Mrs. J. Floyd Williams" specimen compares unfavorable with the ransom letter.

Investigation also developed that Joseph Hugo Becker is at present confined in the United States Penitentiary at Leavenworth, Kansas, awaiting sentence for having escaped from Fort Riley, Kan. 6-28-31; Becker was returned to Leavenworth, from escape 6-25-32 and claims to have resided at Grass Lake, Illinois continuously from July 3, or 4, 1931 to date of arrest, June, 1932. Becker's alibi is still to be checked by the Chicago office.

Though all the other suspects mentioned by Carmody actually have served time at Leavenworth Penitentiary, there is no record there of Grabowski. This fact plus Carmody's statement relative to the present whereabouts of Grabowski and Williams, and the intimation that he could contact them in the countries where they are residing and secure confessions from them if dispatched to said countries, creates doubt as to the truth of Carmody's statement, however, Carmody will be reinterviewed and further details as to the true identity of Grabowski secured.

Handwriting specimens of Millaire, Tannerhill, Becker and Kuhnert have been referred to Albert D. Osborn for comparison with the handwriting on the ransom notes.

Photographs of all the above mentioned suspects with the exception of Grabowski have been displayed to Dr. J. F. Condon who stated none resembled "John" of the ransom negotiations.

DESCRIPTIONS:

Name Jay Floyd Williams, aliases: T. G. Robinson; Cash C. Crawford; John Frank Williams; J. F. Williams; Frank Williams; Jack W. Williams; Fred William Davis; Herman Purvis.

Age   58
Height   5'9 1/2"
Weight   161 pounds
Build   Medium stout
Eyes   Azure
Hair   Dark chestnut
Complexion   Medium fair
Marks and scars   Mole 2 1/2" above left elbow,
                rear; Chlo. Sqr. Of 1/2 at 1" left frt.
                Elbow; scar obl. Of 1/2 at 1/4 above
                left wrist, rear scar obl. Of 1/2 on 1st
                joint left thumb rear.
F.P.E. 32 100
        32 IMI
Photograph   N. Y. Office File
Specimen of handwriting   N. Y. Office File
Criminal Record:

    As John F. Williams, #——, Arkansas St. P. Little Rock, Ark. From Waldron, Ark.; crime—larceny, August 7, 1898; sentence, 4 years. Released by pardon May, 1899. Inquiry by U. S. P. of Arkansas St. P. disclosed that Arkansas had no record of this suspect.

    As John F. Williams, #2666, received U. S. Penitentiary, LK, from Muskogee, Oklahoma, crime—burglary and larceny, 5 years; released 1/4/06.

    As J. F. Williams, 9425, received Washington State Penitentiary from Snohomish County, crime—Arson 1st degree; sentence—5 to 10 years, Paroled May 8, 1922.

    As Jay Floyd Williams, #5282, received U. S. Penitentiary, McNeil Island, Washington, from Portland, Oregon; crime—using mails to defraud. Sentence, 5 years. Escaped August 10, 1926; returned to prison December 27, 1928. Out of prison 870 days. Loss of all good time.

Name	Osiase Joseph Noel Millaire; aliases: Osiase Miller, alias Asias Miller.
Age	42
Height	5'8 1/2"
Weight	162 pounds
Build	Medium Muscular
Complexion	Sallow
Hair	Black
Eyes	Chestnut, dark
Nativity	Ottawa, Ontario, Canada
Relative	Mrs. D. Frichette, relationship not stated, Hull, Quebec.

Specimen of handwriting   N. Y. Office file
F.P.C. (9) 9 R 14
       17 Aa 13
Photograph   N. Y. Office file

Criminal Record

As Osiase Miller, #4630, received St. Vincent DePaul Penitentiary, Canada; crime—shop breaking and theft; sentence 3 years; discharged May 13, 1908.

As Asias Miller, #F-96 (G) 90, received Kingston Penitentiary, Canada; crime—theft from person; sentence 1-5 years; paroled June 10, 1913; date of discharge from parole not given.

As Osiase Miller, #2948, arrested Detroit, Michigan, September 20, 1930; charge—violation Immigration Act; released to U. S. Authorities

Name	Earl Tannehill; aliases: Jack Evans; Jesse Hale.
Age	27
Height	5'11 1/2"
Weight	183 pounds
Build	Muscular

Eyes   Azure
Complexion   Medium
Hair   Chestnut blond
Marks and scars   Pit scar above root of nose
Photograph   Attached for New York office
Specimen of handwriting   Attached for New York office
F.P.C.   (10) 1 R 15
         1 aR 12

Criminal record:
    As Earl Tannehill, received Osage County Jail, Pawhuska, Okla. 1924, 30 days violation National Prohibition Act; released by expiration.
    As Earl Tannehill, arrested P. D. Dept., Bartlesville, Okla. Speeding—fined $7.50; released.
    As Jake Clark, arrested Muskogee, Oklahoma; charge—investigation; released.
    As Earl S. Tannehill, #4019, arrested Tulsa, Okla., crime—violation N.P.A., received U.S.I.R., Chillicothe, O. July 17, 1929; sentence 2 years.
    Taken from United States Penitentiary, Leavenworth, Kan. March 14, 1930, on a writ of Ad Prosequendum to Pocatello, Idaho. Returned to prison March 19, 1930.

Name   Joseph Hugo Becker
Age   36
Height   5'10 3/4"
Weight   157 pounds
Build   Medium Muscular
Hair   Black mixed with gray
Eyes   Light olive
Complexion   Medium light
Nativity   Hungary
Color   White
Marks and scars   Faint scar of 1/2 vertical on right

jaw. By personal observation it was noted Becker does not have a tatoo on either of his legs.

Photograph   N. Y. office file
Specimen of handwriting   N. Y. file
Occupation   Artist
F.P.C. (18) 2 U00
        6 U00

Criminal Record
    No previous record on file and he denies previous record.
    Speech   Talks with foreign accent (personal observation)

Name   Max Kuhnert
Age   42
Height   5'8 1/2"
Weight   203 pounds
Build   Stout
Hair   Black
Eyes   Azure slate
Complexion   Medium
Occupation   Farmer
Color   White

Marks and scars: Tatoo nude woman standing on ball left forearm ant.; Flesh growth at left and right elbow. Scar irregular at 2" at right wrist ant.

Photograph   N.Y. office file
Specimen of handwriting   N.Y. office file
F.P.C. (27) 13 R 0
        32 W 0 23

Criminal record   No previous record on file.

    The description of Stanislaus Grabowski has not been obtained.

SUMMARY REPORT

In Re

Unknown Subjects

Kidnaping and Murder of Charles A. Lindbergh, Jr. (N.Y. File 62-3057).

FRAUDS, HOAXES and UNFOUNDED INFORMATION

-oO-

John Hughes Curtis, et al
Arthur L. Hitner
Gaston B. Means, et al
James Oscar Farrell alias Jack Farrell
Miss Betty Jane Guthrie, re
R.F.D. Lemon, with aliases

FRAUDS, HOAXES & UNFOUNDED INFORMATION

JOHN HUGHES CURTIS, et al

Shortly after the kidnaping, a formerly wealthy and rather prominent shipbuilder of Norfolk, Va., John Hughes Curtis, advised the press that he had knowledge as to the identity of the kidnapers, and offered his services as an intermediary. His overtures were at first ignored by the Lindberghs because they felt that through Dr. Condon they were in touch with the real kidnapers, and because Curtis furnished no proof of his alleged contact.

After the payment of the ransom money, by Dr. Condon, or April 2, 1932, Curtis continued his activity in the case, in association with Dean H. Dobson-Peacock, an Episcopal Clergyman, Rector of Christ Church, Norfolk, Va., and Rear Admiral Guy H. Burrage, retired, of Norfolk. On one occasion, Reverend Dobson-Peacock journeyed to New York City and contacted Arthur L. Hitner, a confidence man, previously mentioned in this report. Hitner apparently was merely an intermeddler in this phase of the case and had no direct connection with the matter. When Dr. Condon failed in his efforts to bring about the return of the child, the Lindberghs turned to Curtis who tried to persuade Lindbergh to deposit $25,000 in a Norfolk bank, not to be paid to the kidnapers, however, until the baby was returned. Curtis claimed he had seen the $50,000 paid by Dr. Condon, that the baby was being held on a boat at sea, and that he, Curtis, was in communication with the kidnapers by wireless. Curtis turned over to Lindbergh various decoded wireless messages allegedly received from the kidnapers, whose leader was identified by Curtis as one "Dyanmite", the others he designed as "Hilda", "John", and one Maurice Truesdale. For nineteen days up to May 12,

1932, the date the baby's body was found, Colonel Lindbergh and Curtis were at sea on the yacht "Marcon" owned by Colonel Charles Consolvo, a friend of Curtis, trying to make contact with the kidnapers.

Some credence was given to the story of Curtis because he was known to be friendly with various rum-runners operating in the vicinity of Norfolk, among these being Jesse E. Foster of Irvington, N. J. and Sam "The Gas Man" Goldberg of Philadelphia, Pa. Curtis built several "rum" boats for the latter individual who is mentioned in detail under "Subjects and Suspects".

An investigation after the finding of the body, revealed that the story of Curtis was untrue, and on May 17, 1932 he confessed that his entire story was a figment of his imagination and was concocted for the sole purpose of selling it to the newspapers. Both Curtis and the police investigation absolved Admiral Burrae of any complicity in the fraud, although there was some question as to the possible guilty knowledge on the part of Reverend Dobson-Peacock. The various rum-runners acquainted with Curtis were cleared of suspicion by the New Jersey State Police.

Curtis was convicted on July 2, 1932 on a charge of giving false information to the authorities, and on July 11, 1932 was sentenced to serve one year in the New Jersey State Prison and to pay a fine of $1,000; he was released before serving his full sentence.

ARTHUR L. HITNER with aliases

On April 2, 1932, Arthur L. Hitner, an alleged confidence man, under indictment at Buffalo, N.Y. for violation of the National Bank Act, conferring at Washington, D.C. with former Assistant Attorney General John Marshall and Assistant United States Attorney, Mrs. Rebekah Greathouse, said to be distantly related to Mrs. Charles A. Lindbergh, and stated that while installing electric light plants he had come in contact with members of the Purple, Capone, and "Legs" Diamond gangs, and that he knew the baby had been stolen and taken to a place in the Catskill Mountains and later brought to New York City.

Hitner was later interviewed at the New York Office of the Division and alleged that he is certain that the Lindbergh baby was kidnaped by Harry Fleisher and Abe Wagner, members of the Purple Gang, whom he had seen at Catskill, N.Y. in Jack (Legs) Diamond's hangout on February 29, 1932 at which time he overheard their conversation to the effect that they were going to pull off a job in New Jersey where the use of a ladder would be necessary. Further, that this conversation took place at the Smith House in Catskill, N.Y. operated by one Joe Burnstein. That the men in question returned to Catskill the following Monday night in an old Dodge Sedan. That on the morning of March 2nd, at Syracuse, N.Y., he and his wife observed the headline in the papers regarding the disappearance of the Lindbergh baby, and immediately associated the parties previously mentioned with the kidnaping; that he telephoned Burnstein relative to a check and that this Burnstein informed him that if he would go to 5006 West 22nd Street, Cicero, Ill. he could make $5,000; that he proceeded to that address and by devious means and circumstances, which he related, obtained the money and proceeded to Chicago where he was instructed to go to Washington, D.C. and to see certain high ranking government officials in connection with Al Capone's turning over the baby for certain considerations, which commission he attempted to carry out but was unsuccessful.

On April 13, 1932, Hitner telephoned the New York Office and indicated he had been in Brooklyn, N.Y. all the previous night and had information as to three parties who previously had no money but now were in possession of ample means, and he believed same consisted of all new bills. He was instructed to communicate such information to the New Jersey State Police, it having been noted that he had previously been in communication with Colonel Lindbergh and Colonel Schwarzkopf.

On April 21, 1932, Hitner at New York City, telephoned Dean H. Dobson-Peacock of Norfolk, Va., who at that time was associated with John Hughes Curtis and Admiral Guy Barrage in connection with Curtis' alleged negotiations with the kidnapers. Hitner instructed Reverend Dobson-Peacock to come to New York immediately in connection with the restoration of the Lindbergh baby. Reverend Dobson-Peacock came to New York and met Hitner as requested. With much mysterious by-play Hitner attempted to intimidate Dobson-Peacock, trying to elicit the information he had concerning the kidnapers; Hitner later attempted to convince Peacock that he could locate the baby but that Peacock would have to raise a certain amount of money. Later both Rev. Peacock and Hitner talked to Mrs. Greathouse at Washington on the telephone, informing her that the baby would be delivered to her in the near future. Several other persons were associated with Hitner during these proceedings, and Rev. Peacock later tentatively identified a photograph of Gaston B. Means as one of the persons whom he met with Hitner.

Under date of May 7, 1932, Hitner using the name "Markle" addressed a letter to Mrs. Evelyn Walsh McLean, Washington, D.C., requesting her to answer certain specified questions regarding her association and dealings with Means, and referred her to Mr. John Marshall or Mrs. Rebekah Greathouse as to his identity. Mr. Marshall advised that at the time Hitner was in Washington he was out of funds and Mr. Marshall endorsed a $75. Draft for Hitner and subsequently had to make it good. Hitner gave Mr. Marshall as security some apparently worthless gold mining stock.

On May 25, and 26, 1932, Hitner introduced one Joseph Mass alias Lorraine, a convict on parole, to an agent of the Division, in an undercover manner. Hitner and Mass made numerous allegations as to their knowledge of concerted activities of John F. Condon, Peacock and Gaston B. Means. Later, however, in a signed statement Lorraine advised that this information was fabricated by Hitner and that he had carried on the fraud at the suggestion of Hitner.

In June 1933, Hitner contacted William C. Merchant, attorney-at-law, and informed him in great detail that the kidnapers of the Lindbergh baby were Harry Fleisher, Dutch Wagner and Norman Hill, and two unknown parties; that Norman Hill, known as "Hilly" was Hitner's chauffeur and drove Hitner's Chrysler automobile from Saugerties, N.Y. to use in the kidnaping on the night the child was taken; further that the body identified as that of the Lindbergh baby was one taken from a Westchester County cemetery, and that the Lindbergh baby is still alive, and that he, Hitner, is aware of its whereabouts. Mr. Merchant apparently intends to develop Hitner's story and stated that he has offered it to the Hearst newspapers for $50,000 of which he was to get 40% and Hitner 60%.

In December 1933, Hitner contacted Mr. James H. McGillan, attorney-at-law, Green Bay, Wisconsin, and also informed him in much detail that on the night of the kidnaping he had loaned his car at Catskill, N.Y. to Dutch Wagner and Harry Fletcher of Detroit, who were associated with Waxey Gordon in the liquor business; that these two men left the Smith House, Catskill, N. Y. on that night with his chauffeur, Norman Hill. Hitner claimed that later he had returned to New York "with some special deputies from the Department of Justice" and cooperated with some operative whose name he did not state, and that subsequently Waxey Gordon and Dutch Schultz had threatened to shoot him.

It appears that Hitner also attempted to work a confidence game on Mr. McGillan in connection with $75,000 in securities which he alleged he had in a safe deposit box in Toronto, Canada. Hitner asserted that the Lindbergh baby was alive; that he knew its location. Late in December, 1933, he left Green Bay for the purpose of procuring the child in the vicinity of New York City, and on December 23, 1933, McGillan received a telephone call from Hitner at El Paso, Texas, claiming that he had the child with a nurse and also the ransom money; on December 31, 1933, Hitner again called from Los Angeles, California, where he drew at least two drafts without authorization, on the Northern Trust Company, Green Bay, Wisconsin, of which Mr. McGillan was president, which drafts were not honored.

Hitner's criminal record, Division No. 378227, is set out herein, inasmuch as he is a fugitive and it is possible that he may appear in various parts of the country, attempting to use his story of the Lindbergh kidnaping for fraudulent purposes:

As Arthur S. Hitner, #36068, arrested P.D., Philadelphia, Pa., June 7, 1917, charge—false pretenses and larceny. Discharged on first charge; held for Lock Haven, Pa. on second charge.

As Arthur Linderman Hitner, #K-1207, arrested by State Police, Sidney, N.Y., April 15, 1932, charge—grand larceny, 2nd degree; charges withdrawn-Disch.

As Arthur L. Hitner #L-378 arrested by State Police, Sidney, N.Y. January 29, 1932, charge—fugitive from justice and grand larceny 2nd degree; held for extradition on first charge; discharged on second charge.

As Arthur Hitner, #5184, arrested P.D., Miami, Fla., June 22, 1932; charge—fraud; ordered out of town—hours.

As Arthur L. Hitner, #—, arrested Sheriff's office, Warrenton, Va., Oct. 3, 1932; charge—bad checks.

As Arthur Linderman Hitner, #42108, arrested P.D., Washington, D.C., Oct. 13, 1932; charge—false pretenses; 90 days District of Columbia Reformatory at Occoquan, Va. On two charges of false pretenses, sentences to run consecutively.

As Arthur L. Hitner, #5223-33, A. and J., Washington, D.C., Oct. 14, 1932; charge—false pretenses (3 cases), fugitive; 60 days on each of first three charges, to run consecutively. rel. to U.S. Marshal for return to Albany, N.Y., May 6, 1933 on charge of conspiracy, 37 P.C.

As William Wightman, #1025/33, arrested P.D., Toronto, Ontario, Canada, August 26, 1933, charge—fraud at Burlington, Ontario, Canada; disposition, ret.

The following notations also appear on record:

Wanted at Buffalo, N.Y. as bond defaulter on national Banking Act indictment by U.S. Marshal. Notified 10/7/32.

As Arthur L. Hitner, arrested 2/17/32, P.D., New York, N.Y.; bad check; 2/23/32, dismissed.

As Arthur L. Hitner, indicted at Rochester, N.Y. violation of National Bank Act; did not appear at trial; nolle entered 10/19/32.

WANTED: As Arthur L. Hitner (poss. ident.) 7/21/33, released on bail from County Jail, Malone, N.Y., charge, conspiracy; failed to appear. Notify Sheriff's Office, Malone, N.Y.

Description of Hitner as furnished by Mr. McGillan follows:

Age:	About 50
Height:	5'10"
Weight:	185 lbs.
Build:	Medium.

Hair:	Dyed jet black, apparently gray.
Eyes:	Uncertain color—believed bluish gray.
Complexion:	Medium.
Scars:	Cut scar between eyes extending to forehead and on one side of nose. Bullet wound in arm—which arm unknown.
Occupation:	Cosmetic chemist—bootlegger.
Marital status:	Married.
Race:	White.
Nationality:	American.

GASTON B. MEANS and NORMAN T. WHITAKER
Alias "THE FOX" alias NEIL WILLIAMS

Mrs. Evelyn Walsh McLean of Washington, D.C., about March 4, 1932, conceived the idea that she could be of possible assistance to Colonel Lindbergh in procuring the return of his child. In this connection she thought of Gaston B. Means as an individual who might establish the necessary underworld contacts. Mrs. McLean was acquainted with Means because of the fact that during the Harding administration he had performed certain investigative work for her husband. Mrs. McLean located Means at his Chevy Chase, Maryland home, and requested that he get in touch with her, which he did the evening of March 4, 1932. Mrs. McLean stated her reasons for desire to see him, and he at once told her he was quite positive he could establish contact with the kidnapers, because a few weeks before he had met a friend of his in a New York speakeasy, who approached him with reference to "pulling off a big kidnaping." Means informed Mrs. McLean that he refused to participate in the contemplated kidnaping and that since the disappearance of the Lindbergh child, he had concluded that this friend and the latter's associates were the kidnapers. On the following day Means reported back to Mrs. McLean that he had "made contact" with the people who had the baby, and requested that Mrs. McLean obtain Colonel Lindbergh's permission for him to work on the case privately. Means also requested that Mrs. McLean arrange for a Catholic priest to cooperate as the kidnapers desired to deliver the child to a priest when the appropriate time arrived. Later, Mrs. McLean put Means in contact with Captain E.S. Land, United States Navy, a cousin of Colonel Lindbergh, with Father J. Francis Hurney, a Catholic Priest of Washington, D.C., Colonel Robert E. Guggenheim of New York, and Robert F. Fleming of Washington, D.C., to whom Means narrated a story that he had become acquainted with one of the kidnapers of the Lindbergh baby while he, Means, and this kidnaper known as "The Fox" were serving time in Atlanta Penitentiary. Means did not go into particulars nor produce any proof that he was in touch with the real kidnapers. As the result of a conference with the above individuals, it was agreed that Mrs. McLean should furnish the necessary funds to effect the baby's return. Subsequently, Colonel Lindbergh gave his approval of Mrs. McLean's plans, without knowledge, however, that Means was her informant.

On March 6, 1932, Means informed Mrs. McLean that the kidnapers had doubled their original ransom demand of $50,000 and requested Mrs. McLean to procure $100,000 cash in unmarked bills. Mrs. McLean obtained this money as instructed by Means and delivered the same to him on March 7, 1932 in her Washington, D. C. home in the presence of Reverend F. J. Hurney. No record was made of the serial numbers of the bills. Means stated he would give the money to the kidnapers, who would return the baby directly to Mrs. McLean on a future date not specified.

Means kept Mrs. McLean waiting at her Washington

residence and also at Fairview, her country home near Washington, from March 6 to March 18, 1932, daily expecting delivery of the child to her. He offered, from time to time, various excuses for the delay, stating that the kidnapers were having difficulty in "getting through the heavy police ring drawn around the baby." Because of this difficulty, Mrs. McLean suggested that delivery be made at her summer home in Aiken, South Carolina, and Means acquiesced in this plan. On March 18, 1932 he requested $4000 additional funds for expenses of the kidnapers, and this sum was given to him by Mrs. McLean.

Mrs. McLean and her retinue of servants arrived at Aiken, South Carolina on March 20, 1932. Subsequently, on March 22nd Means and "The Fox", later identified as Norman Whitaker, arrived at Aiken where Means introduced "The Fox" to Mrs. McLean as a representative of the kidnapers. "The Fox" informed Mrs. McLean that the baby was well and happy and would be delivered at Aiken no later than March 23, 1932. As on previous occasions, nothing happened, and Means made further excuses for the delay.

During the period of the above "negotiations" Means and his relatives expended for personal purchases in the neighborhood of $1,000, in nearly every instance tendering a $\underline{\$100}$ bill.

After several days' absence from Aiken, during which time Mrs. McLean was patiently waiting for delivery of the baby, Means returned and explained that rival gangs were attempting to take the baby from "his crowd," resulting in delay.

On April 1, 1932, Means advised Mrs. McLean that "The Fox" had "broken through the lines with the baby" and was on his way to El Paso, Texas, where he could deliver the baby safely and get across the border into Mexico. Means and Miss Elizabeth Nelson, McLean nurse, proceeded to El Paso to receive the baby. Prior to their departure, Mrs. McLean gave Means $1000 cash as expense money for the trip. The two arrived at El Paso on April 4, 1932, where Means apparently devoted his entire time to drinking bouts with various friends. Pursuant to Means' request, Mrs. McLean proceeded to El Paso to receive the baby, arriving on April 7, 1932. Upon arrival, she was informed by Means that the baby was not well and was suffering from diarrhea. During her stay in El Paso, Mrs. McLean was again approached by "The Fox" who made excuses for the delay. After a few days, Mrs. McLean tired of the delay and returned to Washington, D.C. but before leaving gave Means an additional sum of $1200, which was to be used in shadowing "The Fox" to prevent a double-cross. Means also informed Mrs. McLean at this time that he was arranging to place in escrow the $50,000 ransom money paid by Dr. Condon in New York City. After Mrs. McLean's departure Means collected an additional sum of $200. from the nurse, Miss Nelson. On April 9, 1932, Means and "The Fox" departed for Chicago leaving Miss Nelson in El Paso to receive the baby which they informed her would be delivered on April 11, 1932.

On April 13, 1932, Means appeared at Mrs. McLean's Washington, D.C. home and proposed that she raise $35,000 in "good money" which would be given to the kidnapers in exchange for $49,000 of the $50,000 marked money paid to them by Dr. Condon. Mrs. McLean made an attempt to raise the $35,000 but was stopped by her attorneys.

On April 17, 1932, Mrs. McLean requested that Means return her $100,000 and he informed her that it was at his brother's place in Concord, North Carolina, and that he would proceed there immediately and procure it. On April 21, 1932, not having heard from Means for several days, Mrs. McLean had Father Hurney call at the Means' home near Washington, D.C. to find out what he had done about the money. Means appeared to be surprised when Father Hurney asked him about the money and stated that he had actually proceeded to Concord, picked up the money, and was on his way back to Washington, when he was stopped on the highway near Alexandria, Virginia, by an unknown man who said he represented Mrs. McLean, gave the proper code number, and demanded the money. Means further informed that inasmuch as this man claimed to be Mrs. McLean's representative and knew the code, he gave him the money.

The whole matter was referred to the Division of Investigation by Mrs. McLean's attorneys on May 3, 1932, and on the following day a complaint was filed before a United States Commissioner at Washington, D.C. charging Means with larceny after trust, of $100,000 from Mrs. McLean. He was arrested on May 5, 1932, and subsequently indicted for larceny after trust and embezzlement in connection with the sums of $100,000 and $4000 obtained by him from Mrs. McLean. Means was convicted on June 13, 1932, without taking the witness stand or offering any defense whatsoever. On June 15th he was sentenced to serve fifteen years in the United States Northeastern Penitentiary at Lewisburg, Pa. "The Fox", Norman T. Whitaker, was arrested at New York City on June 27, 1932 and in May, 1933 he and Means were tried jointly at Washington, D. C. under an indictment charging conspiracy to defraud Mrs. McLean of $35,000. Both were convicted and sentenced on May 26, 1933 to serve two years each in a Federal penitentiary.

As a defense in the trial of himself and Whitaker in May, 1933, Means took the witness stand and testified that he had seen the Lindbergh baby at Aiken, South Carolina, on March 8, 1932 (in later statements he does not so claim) and that he knew the identity of the kidnapers. He identified them as Wellington Henderson, head of the Communist Third Internationale in this country (officials of the Communist Party have stated that no such person was ever connected with their organization); one Irving Fenton, whom he claimed to have met in the Atlanta Penitentiary; Max Hassell, and Max Greenberg, the latter two being well known liquor operators. Means testified further that the ransom money paid in the Lindbergh case by Dr. Condon was in the safety deposit box of Max Hassel in the Elizabethport Banking Company at Elizabeth, N.J. together with the $100,000 given to him by Mrs. McLean. Means further testified that Whitaker was an innocent party to the whole transaction, and knew nothing as to the identity of the kidnapers.

He further testified that he had information that the baby found dead near Hopewell was not the real Lindbergh baby but a "plant;" that the real baby was alive in Juarez, Mexico. Whitaker did not take the witness stand; he had orally admitted, however, after his arrest, that "he was an accomplice of Means and that the whole affair was manufactured by Means."

On May 13, 1933 the contents of the safety deposit box of Max Hassell at the Elizabethport Banking Company, Elizabeth, N. J. were examined by Agents of the New York Division office (the box had previously been opened on April 23, 1933). It was found to contain currency totalling $214,500, in denominations of $50, $100, $300, $1000, and $5000 bills, practically all of them unused bills. As previously shown in this report, the $50,000 ransom money paid by Dr. Condon consisted of $5, $10 and $20 bills. It is obvious, therefore, that the ransom money was not included in the funds found in the safety deposit box, and that Means' statement in this regard is untrue. Means had also claimed that the $100,000 given to him by Mrs. McLean was in this safety deposit box, and this statement was also found to be untrue inasmuch as the money given to him by Mrs. McLean was composed of $90,000 in $20 bills and $10,000 in $100 bills, all of which was old money. A thorough examination of all papers found in the safety deposit box failed to show any connection between Max Hassell and the Lindbergh kidnaping or anything which would indicate that Hassell was holding money for Means, Mrs. McLean, Colonel Lindbergh, or any of the principals in the case.

After the arrest of Means, a whole year had elapsed during which period he came forward with no information regarding the instant case other than his testimony at the trials as above indicated. On April 12, 1933 Max Hassell and Max Greenberg, well known liquor operators associated with Irving Wexler, better known as Waxey Gordon, had been shot and killed at the Elizabeth-Carteret Hotel, their headquarters, Elizabeth, N.J. It was shortly after this murder, widely published in the newspapers, that Means and Whitaker were tried in connection with the $35,000 fraud, and Means seized his opportunity to lay the crime at the feet of two dead men. By letter dated May 25, 1933, addressed to his attorney, B. Mercer Hartman, Washington, D.C. Means repeated the story told at his trial that the two men who were directly responsible for the kidnaping were Max Hassell and Max Greenberg. Means alleged that these two individuals planned the whole thing and executed it through their agents, James Feldman alias Irving Fenton, and Wellington Henderson, and that Mrs. McLean's $100,000 had been given to Max Hassell by Feldman. Means alleged that Hassell placed this money, together with the $50,000 paid by Dr. Condon, in a safety deposit box at the Elizabethport Banking Company, Elizabeth, N.J. In addition to the publicity concerning the shooting of Hassell and Greenberg, there was also considerable publicity, prior to Means' statement and testimony, concerning the safety deposit box in question.

Means claimed that he mentioned Hassell and

Greenberg to his attorney, Mr. Hartman, prior to the death of these individuals and that he had informed Hartman that Mrs. McLean's $100,000 was invested in Hassell's whiskey syndicate. After receipt of the letter from Means containing the above information, Hartman executed an affidavit tending to corroborate the information furnished by Means. The affidavit states that Hassell and Greenberg were mentioned by Means as the persons behind the kidnaping prior to April 12, 1933 the date of the murder. Hartman also alleged in this affidavit that an individual who claimed to be Hassell contacted him several times prior to April 12, 1933. In another affidavit Hartman alleged that he had been visited in Means' behalf by an individual who identified himself as James Feldman.

Under date of May 27, 1953 Gaston Means wrote another letter to his attorney, Hartman, elaborating on the first letter, and stating that the baby was killed from a fall. He went on to state that Mrs. McLean's $100,000 was to have been returned to her on May 15, 1932, but that he (Means) was arrested prior to that date and consequently he was unable to get the money. Means indicates that he, nevertheless, made arrangements at a later date to have Hassell or one of his agents return the money to Mrs. McLean; however, about the time the money was to be turned over, Hassell was murdered. As corroboration for his statements in this regard, Means attached the affidavit of a fellow prisoner at the United States Northeastern Penitentiary, one John Damann alias Henry Logemann, who alleged in his affidavit that he had known Hassell and Means for a long time and that several days before the murder, Hassell told him that the money he had in his safety deposit box at the Elizazbethport Banking Company belonged to Charles A. Lindbergh, Mrs. McLean and Gaston means, and was to have been returned to Means on May 15, 1932; however, that the arrest of Means prevented this.

Logemann was interviewed at the United States Northeastern Penitentiary by a Division Special Agent, at which time he recanted the affidavit in question and stated that the affidavit and statement were in reality written by Gaston Means at whose solicitation Logemann signed them. Logemann stated that Means wanted to use the statements in connection with an appeal he was taking on his conviction, and promised to pay him (Logemann) $50,000 cash if he would testify to the contents of the statements at a new trial Means anticipated would be granted him by the Court of Appeals. Logemann further stated that he told Means he was a personal friend of Waxey Gordon and served as a body guard to Max Hassell and Max Greenberg, and that as a result of the information furnished by him (Logemann) and some newspaper articles, Means prepared various statements and affidavits. Logemann further stated that Means had revealed to him that he knows no such individuals as Wellington Henderson and James Feldman, these names being purely imaginary on his part. Logemann further stated that after his release the scheme was for him to get in touch with Afton Means, a brother of Gaston, after which the two of them would proceed to the spot in North Carolina where McLean's $100,000 is said to be buried intact. Logemann further advised that during their conversations, Means frequently told him about two brothers named Jack and Robert Bennett, who operate a speakeasy in New York City; that Means decided to mention these individuals, as well as one Robert Hudson of Tulsa, Oklahoma, in his statement. According to Logemann, the last named individuals actually do exist.

Summarizing the various statements, affidavits and letters which have emanated from Gaston means, it appears that he names the following individuals as being involved in the Lindbergh kidnaping:

Wellington Henderson with aliases: John Henderson, William Walton, James Henderson, Henry Wellington, Henderson Wellington, John Alexander, John Cowen. Characterized by Means as the "brains behind the crime" and with Max Hassell "engineered the kidnaping."

James Feldman alias Irving Fenton—characterized as an agent for Max Hassell and Henderson.

Max Hassell alias Mendel Cassell—"brains behind kidnaping"; engineered whole thing.

Max Greenberg—partner of Hassell; helped engineer crime.

Robert Hudson—the actual kidnaper.

Jack and Bobby Burns Bennet (brothers)—Employers of Robert Hudson and also involved.

Violet Sharpe—Maid in Morrow home; furnished "inside information to her friend, Wellington Henderson.

Mike Keller—part not described.

Ah unidentified man—said to have been an employee or caretaker at the Lindbergh home, Hopewell, allegedly furnished inside information to Robert Hudson.

A nephew or relative of Dr. Condon—Through virtue of his relationship to Dr. Condon obtained "inside information" as to negotiations, etc. and kept the other informed. Alleged to make headquarters with Bennet brothers.

A number of other individuals—names of some known personally to Gaston means; names of others not known.

Elizabeth-Carteret Hotel, Elizabeth, N.J.—allegedly kidnapers headquarters.

The files of the Division reflect the following criminal records of Gaston B. Means and Norman T. Whitaker in addition to the instant matter:

Gaston B. Means as #20103 received at the U.S. Penitentiary Atlanta, Georgia, May 22, 1925, from the Southern District of New York, Crime—Conspiracy and Violation of the National Prohibition Act; sentence 2 years, $10,000 fine.

The records of the Department show that Means, together with Elmer Jarnecke, was convicted in the Southern District of New York on July 1, 1924 for Conspiracy to Violate the National Prohibition Act in connection with withdrawal of liquor on fraudulent permits, and sentenced July 2, 1924 to serve two years in the Penitentiary at Atlanta and to pay a fine of $10,000.

The Department records further show that on January 30, 1925, Means and James D. Felder were convicted in the Southern District of New York for Conspiracy to Bribe a Federal Officer, Means being sentenced to serve two years in the Atlanta Penitentiary and to pay a fine of $10,000, said imprisonment to run consecutively to the two years imposed in the previous case.

It also should be borne in mind that Means was tried and acquitted of murder of Maude King in North Carolina about twelve years ago. In addition, he was charged in 1932 with disorderly conduct at Bethesda, Maryland, in connection with a drunken brawl between himself and his wife at their Chevy Chase home; also, on May 12, 193 he was arrested by Traffic Officer H. H. Hartman at 14th and F Streets, N. W. for assault committed on Lee Somers, reporter for the Washington Times, and imprisoned at #1 Precinct Station. Here he was charged in Docket Entry #437 with disorderly conduct, in Docket #2156 with assault on Lee Somers, and in Docket #2157 with being drunk. He deposited $65.00 collateral on these charges for his appearance in Police Court on the morning of May 13th at 9:30 A.M. He failed to appear and the collateral was forfeited.

Norman Whitaker, #21164, received U. S. Penitentiary, Leavenworth, Kansas, May10, 1924, from Los Angeles, California, crime Dyer Act; sentence 2 years.

As Norman P. Whitaker, #2173, arrested St. Petersburg Florida, P. D., December 17, 1929, charge investigation; pending.

As Norman F. Whitaker, #133, arrested Pleasantville, N.J., December 4, 1930, charge malicious fraud; disposition not given.

Whitaker also received a three year sentence in Federal Court, Florida, in 1933 for violation of the National Motor Vehicle Theft Act. This conviction he appealed to the Supreme Court, which court however affirmed the conviction on October 9, 1933.

Further reference to Damann alias Logemann, the Bennet brothers and Robert Hudson is made in the section of this report entitled "Subjects and Suspects."

JAMES OSCAR FARRELL alias HARRY DAVIS

Under date of July 20, 1932 Mr. Joseph B. Connolly, General Manager of the King Feature syndicate, and affiliated with the Hearst newspapers referred to this office two reporters who had recently received information from one James Oscar Farrell, an ex-convict, to the effect that he possessed knowledge concerning the identity of the perpetrators of the instant kidnaping, and that he (Farrell) had a part therein.

James Oscar Farrell was interviewed by then Special Agent J.J. Manning, of the New York office. Farrell at that time resided with his wife and three children at 315 East75th Street, New York City. His personal history as developed by this interview and subsequent investigation established that he was born at Philadelphia, Pa. October 5, 1886; that he married while residing in that section of the country, subsequently divorced his wife and migrated to the Pacific Coast. While there he enlisted in the United States Army under the name of Harry Davis, and during the course of the latter service, spent several years in the Philippines. While in the Philippines, Farrell hoaxed the Secret Service there into paying him a salary for several months while they investigated allegations made by Farrell re Narcotic Law violations by prominent officials, subsequently proved unfounded. Farrell returned from the Philippines to San Francisco, March 19, 1934 and shortly thereafter deserted from the army. He was arrested at San Francisco, Calif. June 12, 19134; charge, robbery; sentence, six years San Quentin Prison, California; paroled October 10, 1917 and discharged from parole a year later. Prior to his arrest on the robbery charge Farrell was connected with the Connecticut State Board of Pharmacy as a Narcotic undercover informant. Farrell has been a Narcotic addict for many years. At the present time he claims to have cured himself of this addiction but this statement is seriously questioned by agents who have interviewed him.

At the time of his first interview, Farrell stated that he, together with one Billy Burke alias Hughie Hughes, a former cell mate at San Quentin Prison, California; Kitty Murphy, a paramour of Burke; one Farrington, alias Morgan Wellington; Hoppy Joe DeLong; Swede Henderson alias Swede Anderson; Patty McGuire; Louise Dubois and Pauline Dubois; Violet Sharpe; Elizabeth Morrow and Ollie Whateley, participated in the kidnaping of Charles A. Lindbergh, Jr. and subsequent extortion of $50,000 from Charles A. Lindbergh, Sr.

Farrell stated that the actual kidnaping was perpetuated by Billy Burke; Hoppy DeLong and the two Dubois sisters, Louise and Pauline while, he, Farrell, waited in an automobile on a nearby road; that the kidnaped baby was brought to this automobile and that he, with the kidnapers and the baby, drove to Phila., Pa. and thence to Becket, Mass. where they secreted themselves in a bungalow at

Camp Graylock; Farrell further stated that he was the unknown man who handed Dr. J. F. Condon the ransom letter designating point ransom was to be paid.

Under date of December 22, 1933 Farrell was reinterviewed by former Special Agent J.J. Manning and Special Agent E. Sandberg of the New York office at which time Farrell admitted that the story related to Agent Manning during interview set out in Agent Manning's report, 8/7/33, was untrue in every respect, stating that the reason he told this untruthful story on that occasion was that he was taking a dope cure and was in a very nervous condition, and that certain unnamed individuals had persuaded him to tell this story. In a subsequent conversation with Special Agent T. H. Sisk he also repudiated his first statement.

Farrell subsequently wrote to Mrs. Evelyn Walsh McLean at Washington, D.C. advising her that he was in possession of information concerning the identity of the kidnapers and the present whereabouts of the Lindbergh baby, claiming that the latter was still alive, his obvious purpose being to swindle Mrs. McLean which is indicated by a conversation had by Farrell with Special Agent T. H. Sisk wherein he inquired as to whether he was guilty of extortion for accepting money from Mrs. McLean. He managed to interest Mrs. McLean in this story and was invited by her to come to Washington, D.C. and communicate the information in his possession to Division Director J. Edgar Hoover. Farrell demurred to the proposed interview with Mr. Hoover but on January 13, 1934 he visited Mrs. McLean at Washington, D.C. (A verbatim report of this interview was secured). On October 19, 1934 he furnished the Division and Mrs. McLean with a statement very similar in outline to the statement previously made by him to Manning. However, in this latter statement Farrell lists those participating in the kidnaping as Billy Burke; John Barbu; Kitty

Murphy and Catherine Morrissey assisted by Olly Whateley and Violet Sharpe. In the latter statement Farrell claims that he was not with the others at the time of the actual kidnaping.

The recent statement also differs from the statement furnished Manning in that Farrell now states that he cut the hair of Charles A. Lindbergh, Jr. at Camp Graylock, near Becket, Mass. seven days after the kidnaping, whereas, in his original statement he claimed he cut the hair of Charles A. Lindbergh, Jr. at the bawdy house operated by one "Big Mama" near 1320 Green St., Philadelphia, under date of March 2, 1932. In the recent statement, Farrell claims that under date of April 3, 1932 he personally handed Dr. John F. Condon the note instructing Condon where and how to deliver the ransom money. This is obviously untrue inasmuch as it has been definitely established that the eleventh ransom note from the kidnapers was delivered to Dr. Condon at his home by an unidentified taxi driver and that this note instructed Condon to proceed to Bergen's Greenhouse where the twelfth ransom note would be found under a stone. It was this later note that contained directions as to the place where the ransom money was to be believed to the representative of the kidnapers.

Other misrepresentations and questionable statements have been made to Mrs. McLean by Farrell, (1) That the baby is still alive whereas the body found near Mt. Rose, N.J. has been positively identified by Colonel C. A. Lindbergh and Betty Gow as being the body of C. A. Lindbergh, Jr.; (2) That Billy Burke occupied the same cell with Farrell at San Quentin Prison, California, whereas prison records do not reflect Burke ever incarcerated at said prison; and (3) That the edges of the ransom note paper were perforated whereas in fact they were not. Other representations by Farrell are presently under investigation.

Farrell is described by Division Agents who have interviewed him as being

Age	49 years
Height	5'6"
Weight	135 pounds
Build	Slight
Hair	Darn brown, grey at temples
Eyes	Blue (very shifty)
Complexion	Ruddy
Eyeglasses	Worn occasionally
Scars	1/2" scar lower center of forehead
Marks	Tattoo Butterfly left wrist

MISS BETTY JANE GUTHRIE (Informant)
(Re: Reginald Fontaine DeMere Lemon
with aliases)

On November 16, 1933, Miss Betty Jane Guthrie of 1272 Tabor Court, Brooklyn, N.Y., was interviewed at the Division with reference to information she desired to impart relative to the Lindbergh case.

Miss Guthrie advised that she is convinced that one R.F.D. Lemon or LeMon, Vice President of the Lava Cap Gold Mining Corp., "was connected with the kidnaping of Charles Augustus Lindbergh, Jr." and "was the brains behind this kidnaping and extortion." It developed that Miss Guthrie was at one time employed by Lemon as his secretary; later was associated with him in the sale of gold mine securities, and presently is affiliated with a group of stockholders engaged in combating Lemon's control of the Lava Cap Gold Mining Corporation.

Miss Guthrie gave the following reasons for suspecting Lemon:

1—Immediately prior to the kidnaping and payment of ransom, Lemon was in desperate need of $50,000, whereas at present he exhibits many evidences of prosperity, maintaining two apartments, one for his wife and family and another for his paramour.

2—During the early part of February, 1932, Lemon pretended to leave New York for Grass Valley, Calif. When, as a matter of fact, he remained in the vicinity of New York until some time in March, 1932; that though reported to be in California, she observed Lemon in a telephone booth at Grand Central Station, New York, on the morning of March 2, 1932; that Lemon was in New York from March 18, 1932, through the greater part of April, 1932; that on April 4, 1932 she observed Lemon standing under the Bronx River Parkway Bridge at a point between Tuckahoe and Crestwood, New York. Miss Guthrie attaches significance to this inasmuch as newspapers reported that Dr. J. F. Condon contacted a woman representative of the kidnap gang at Tuckahoe, New York, during the ransom negotiations.

3—Lemon had been acting suspiciously since the kidnaping and is believed to have a safe deposit box in a New York bank. Miss Guthrie intimates that the ransom money is secreted in this safe deposit box.

4—Lemon is the type of man capable of committing such a crime, possessing unusual intelligence and being absolutely ruthless and without scruples. It appears that he was indicted for mail fraud in Arkansas in the year 1906, but was never brought to trial.

5—Lemon had a number of cardboard boxes in his desk, and Miss Guthrie believes that from these he may have obtained the idea of having the ransom money placed in a box.

6—That letter of introduction possessed by him purporting to have been signed by Governor Ralph and Secretary of State Jordan, both of California, were actually forgeries, and were obtained by him to establish an alibi as to his whereabouts on March 1, 1932.

Miss Guthrie suggested that Reginald Fontaine DeMere Lemon had been assisted in the kidnaping and extortion by his son, Reginald ?? and the latter's intimate, one Vincent Jordan. She believes that Lemon was the actual kidnaper.

Miss Guthrie furnished the New York Office with specimens of handwriting of Mr. and Mrs. Reginald Fontaine DeMere Lemon and of Virginia Wakeley, alleged paramour of Lemon. These specimens were examined at Division's Laboratory, and the report of said examination states definitely that "none of these handwriting specimens is identical with that on the Lindbergh extortion letter."

Miss Guthrie via telephone and in person has communicated with New York Office on numerous occasions inquiring as to the progress of investigation concerning Lemon's participation in this kidnaping, offering suggestions relative to leads to be developed, stressing the necessity determining if Lemon, his family or associates, have a safe deposit box in any of the New York banks. In this latter connection, Miss Guthrie previously advised that it is the intention of her attorney, Nickerson attach Lemon's safe deposit box, if located, in connection with a civil suit and judgment.

On several occasions, Miss Guthrie called the New York Office and a? that Lemon was bout to make deposits at the Chase National Bank, to the [text garbled] it of the Lava Cap Gold Mining Corporation and that he probably was using account to dispose of the Lindbergh ransom bills. Inquiry at the Chase National Bank established that the various deposits were made up entirely of a [text garbled]

During various interviews, Miss Guthrie has advised Division Agents she is in daily fear of bodily harm from

Reginald Fontaine DeMere Lemon; the latter has frequently threatened to throw acid in her face and otherwise "get her"; that he has followed her on numerous occasions and that he determined to harm her in order to avenge himself on her because of the trouble she caused him in opposing his control of the Lava Cap Gold Mining Corporation. She stated that the police do not possess sufficient intellect to 'get [garbled] in the Lindbergh case, that "the thing is too big for them", which is what has referred her information to the government.

During the numerous interviews with Miss Guthrie, she has asserted both Reginald Fontaine DeMere Lemon and his son were the perpetrators of "Collings murder"; that young Lemon has recently engaged in hold-ups in York City and that she believes the elder Lemon is in possession of $60,000 of the money paid to secure the release of Edward G. Bremer. In connection with this latter statement, Miss Guthrie claims that she is not prepared to present to state how she links Lemon to the Bremer case, advising that in opinion, it was up to this Division to find out in what way Lemon is implicated in this particular case. Miss Guthrie also advised that she believes Lemon is presently planning another kidnaping, to be a sort of sequel to the Lindbergh case. She suggests that the Division keep Lemon under constant surveillance in connection with his kidnaping activities.

It has been ascertained that Miss Guthrie has communicated her suspicion of Lemon as the perpetrator of the Lindbergh kidnaping to the New Jersey Police; New York City Police; James M. Phelan, law partner of Colonel Henry Breckinridge, attorney for Colonel Lindbergh; to the District Attorney of York County, Manhattan, New York, and to Mr. Robert W. Whooley, a Washington D.C. attorney, who she states is a close personal friend of Attorney General Homer S. Cummings. She stated that she expects to see

Colonel Henry Breckinridge shortly about Lemon for the purpose of ascertaining "certain facts about the kidnaping. She has also stated that she has an entrée to Mrs. Franklin D. Roosevelt, and contemplates putting before her the facts showing Lemon's implication in the Lindbergh case. Recently, Miss Guthrie signified her intention of reporting Lemon to the Federal Securities Corporation, U.S. Internal Revenue Bureau, and the Postoffice Department, for income evasion and mail fraud. Representatives of the above mentioned police departments and Mr. Phelan advised that after listening to Miss Guthrie's story they viewed her as a "crank informant" and made no effort to investigate her claims.

On one occasion during Lemon's absence from his apartment, Miss Guthrie persuaded detectives of the New York Police Department to search his trunks for Lindbergh ransom money. However, no such money was discovered. She has also suggested that the New York Division Office make arrangements to open the safe of one of Lemon's business associates, stating that the Lindbergh ransom money may be in it.

Investigation by the San Francisco Division Office has established that R.F.D. Lemon of New York City registered at the National Hotel, Navada City, California, February 22, 1932 and checked out on February 28, 1932; that he registered at the Stewart Hotel, San Francisco, Calif., February 29, 1932 and checked out March 1, 1932; that he reregistered at the National Hotel, Nevada City, California, March 2, 1932 and checked out March 4, 1932. The records of the St. Francis Hotel, San Francisco, Calif., reflect that Lemon registered in March 14, 1932 and out March 15, 1932. Photostatic copies of the register of the National Hotel, Nevada City, California, for February 22, and March 2, 1932 contain the registration of R.F.D. Lemon, New York City. The Division Laboratory is being furnished these photostats and requested to advise if the registrations referred to are in the handwriting of Lemon.

The San Francisco Office also established that the letters of introduction from Frank O. Jordan, Secretary of the State of California, and from Governor Ralph of California, in possession of Lemon, were authentic and not forgeries as alleged by Miss Guthrie.

On February 14, 1934, Miss Guthrie appeared at the New York Division Office and stated that she is taking a business trip to the Pacific Coast shortly, in connection with the Lava Cap Gold Mining Corporation, an that while there she expects to obtain further information showing Lemon's guilt in the Lindbergh case and will report it to the San Francisco Division Office.

Description of Reginald Fontaine DeMere Lemon, alias LeMon alias DeMere, alias Fontaine, alias Abbott, alias Wakeley:

Age:	62; appears younger.
Height:	5'11-1/2"
Weight:	190 lbs.
Build:	Powerful.
Hair:	Black, tinged with gray.
Eyes:	Green, very round.
Complexion:	Medium, smooth shaven
Peculiarities:	Very broad shouldered; distinctive crows feet around eyes; shaggy black eyebrows; deep furrows radiating from lower nose through cheeks.
Marks & Scars:	1-1/2" scar left side of chin. 1/2" scar over left eyebrow.
Eyeglasses:	Wears eyeglasses when reading.
Race:	White.
Nationality:	American; born U.S.
Marital status:	Married; 2 children—Reginald Dean, 28

years; Irene E., 34 years.

Occupation: Vice president and director, Lava Cap Gold Mining Corp.

Photograph: In possession of New York Office.

Criminal Record: Indicted 1/26/07, U.S. District Court, Fort Smith, Ark., charge—accepting deposits after knowledge of insolvency in connection with failure of Southern Bank & Trust Co.; convicted 7/2/07; sentenced to 17 months U.S. Penitentiary, Leavenworth, and assessed fine of $500. Appealed and granted new trial 11/25/08; subsequently continued; never retried.

Name: Reginald Dean Lemon
Age: 28 years; born U.S.
Height: 5'8"
Weight: 130 lbs.
Build: Slender
Hair: Curly, brown.
Eyes: Blue
Complexion: Fair.
Nationality: American.
Eyeglasses: None.
Occupation: None.
Residence: Apt. 2F, 644 Riverside Drive, New York City.
Criminal Record: Unknown.

THE FBI FILES:

The Kidnaping and Murder of Charles A. Lindbergh Jr.

Index

Alderman, Israel, 469-470
Associated Press, 161, 204-205, 460

Banks, Septimus, 132
Barry, Arthur, 343, 454-456
Baumeister, John, 343, 451-454
Bay, Wm., 257
Beattie, Mary, 116
Bennett, Jack, 343, 429-437
Bernstein, Abe, 385, 412-413
Berritella, Rev. Peter, 38, 86, 197-198, 343, 419-425
Bitz, Irving, 37, 41-42, 85, 188-189, 190, 196-198, 200, 202, 204- 208, 252-253, 382-384, 423
Brandt, John, 147
Breckinridge, Col. Henry, 35-38, 40, 42, 45, 50, 56, 79, 86, 88- 89, 92, 148, 153, 190-197, 220-221, 224-227, 235- 237, 240- 245, 250, 255, 25
Bremer, Arthur, 352
Breslin, Edward F., 217, 263
Brisbane, Arthur, 352
Bronx Home News, The, 43-44, 46-53, 87-90, 209, 215, 217-219, 227, 235-236, 238-243, 250, 253, 263, 269, 271-272
Buccholz, Gerald, 447-451
Burrage, Adm. Guy, 46, 498
Bush, Oscar, 83, 147

Capone, Al, 38-39, 41, 43, 45, 47, 66, 86, 193, 200, 202, 203, 207, 379-390, 395-397, 400, 406-407, 411, 497
Capone, Ralph, 38-39, 382, 389-390, 397
Cassels, Edwin H., 45, 385
Cirrito, Rev. Mary, 38, 86, 197-198, 419-425
Coleman, Gregory, 243
Colosimo, Jim, 380
Condon, Dr. John ("Jafsie"), 39-48, 50-53, 55-56, 87-93,

109, 163, 201, 204, 209-276, 278, 346, 349-351, 358, 362, 364, 373, 388, 392, 411, 431, 433, 447-448, 450-451, 453, 455, 458, 468, 482-483, 495-496, 515-516
Condon, John, 211
Condon, Joseph, 211
Condon, Lawrence, 211
Condon, Myra, 211, 254
Cummings, Louis, 343, 456-459
Cummins, Marie, 101, 110-112, 353, 459
Curtis, John Hughes, 46, 51, 55, 59, 86, 91, 396, 465

DeAugestine, Nick, 343, 459-464
Delaney, John, 459
Devine, Det. J.J., 58
Diamond, Jack "Legs," 189, 192, 452, 497
Dobson-Peacock, Rev. H., 46, 54
Donovan, Col. Wm. J., 35, 191-192, 194, 223

Ellerson, Henry, 32, 79, 108, 132-135

Farrell, James, 513
Fleisher, Harry, 45, 47-49, 51, 58, 270, 396, 403, 406, 411-412, 414-415, 497
Finn, J.J., 255-256, 272, 275, 285-286, 373
Fitzgerald, James, 271
Ford, Edsel, 480
Fort Worth Star-Telegram, The, 488

Gaglio, Milton, 56, 87, 92, 211, 223-224, 227, 243, 245, 263-264, 268-270, 272-276, 453
Geraldi, Enrico, 343, 425-429
Goldberg, sam, 343, 465-468
Gorch, John, 343, 379, 438-447
Gordon, Waxey, 192, 499, 508

Gow, Betty, 32-36, 38, 48, 55, 74, 76, 79-83, 90, 92, 101-102, 105, 109, 117, 153, 227, 415, 417-418
Gray, Walter, 343, 438-447
Grimes-Greame, Mrs. R., 116, 137-139
Guthrie, Betty Jane, 517-523

Hearst newspapers, 383, 499
Hitner, Arthur, 51, 54, 69-70, 396, 414, 496-502
Hognall, Dabiel, 273-274
Hoover, J. Edgar, 191, 515
Horn, William, 148-149
Hughes, Flora, 116

Irey, Elmer, 250, 261
Island News, The, 407

Jersey Journal, The, 190
Johnson, Henry "Red," 33, 35-37, 47, 53, 82, 107-109, 231-232, 343, 415-419
Junge, Mrs. Johannes, 116, 135-136, 416-417

Kelly, Frank, 76
Keaton, Lt. Arthur, 117-119, 213
Kesselman, Abraham, 204

Leebove, Isiah, 204
Lindbergh, Anne Morrow, 32, 34, 74, 76, 79, 81-82, 85, 96, 98-99, 101, 107-108, 111, 117, 141, 153, 195, 198, 211, 220, 233, 396, 418, 496
Lindbergh, Col. Charles, 32-34, 36-37, 39-40, 42-43, 50-52, 55, 74-76, 78-82, 84-88, 90-92, 96, 98-99, 101, 103-107, 110, 141, 153, 191, 194-198, 200-205, 208-211, 218, 220-226, 2228, 233, 238, 242-250, 254, 257-261, 263-264, 279, 286, 350-351, 382-384, 386-388, 409, 460, 482, 498

Lindbergh, Charles Jr. (infant), 32-34, 54-55, 74, 78-79, 81-82, 92, 96, 98, 101-102, 107-108, 149-153, 209-210, 233, 262, 455
Logemann, Henry, 430, 432-434, 509-510
Lupica, Sebastian, 155-163, 344

Madden, Owney, 36, 40, 47, 190, 192, 194, 196-200, 204-205, 207, 410-411, 423
Malone, Dudley F., 36, 195-196, 407-409
Manning, J.J., 149, 225, 253, 255, 256, 261, 379, 515
Marshall, Jlohn, 396, 414
McLean, Mrs. E.W., 39, 54, 58-59, 65, 86, 498. 502-515
Means, Gaston, 37, 39, 54, 58-59, 65, 86, 412, 430, 432, 499, 502- 513
Millaire, Osiase, 487-491
Mitchell, Charles H., 150, 152
Moore, Gov. A. Harry, 26, 37, 204, 280, 383
Morrow, Constance, 114
Morrow, Dwight, 35-36, 84, 102, 114, 136-138
Morrow, Dwight Jr., 114-115
Morrow, Elizabeth, 114, 116
Morrow, Mrs. Dwight, 137

Nash, Frank, 399-402, 411
Nathan, Harold, 26, 117-118
New York American, The, 43-45, 48-49, 51-52, 87-89, 90, 201-202, 221-222, 227, 235-236, 238-242, 250, 253, 383
New York Daily Mirror, The, 200, 206, 406, 408-410, 412
New York Daily News, The, 47, 119, 203-204, 207, 383, 407
New York Times, The, 386, 427
Nitti, Frank, 397

O'Bannion, Dean, 381-382

O'Brien, James, 267-268, 271
Osborn, Albert D., 176, 183-185, 475, 487-489
Osborn Albert S., 176, 177-183, 373, 403

Peremi, Frank, 254-255
Perrone, Jos., 56, 92, 228, 266-273, 275, 346, 373
Phelan, James W., 220-221, 385, 407

Reich, Al, 42, 47, 56, 212, 228-229, 231, 235, 239-240, 246, 250, 256-257, 263, 349-350, 432, 443
Reilly, Wm. Patrick, 343, 470-475
Rosenhain, Max, 56, 87, 92, 211, 216-219, 223-224, 227, 243, 262- 265, 272-273
Rosner, Morris, 35-38, 40, 42, 43, 85, 188, 190-208, 221, 252, 353, 384, 419, 420
Rothstein, Arnold, 286

Sankey, Reo, 343, 475-478
Saunders, John, 16, 136
Schrenck, Garrett, 343, 478
schultz, Dutch, 499
Schwartzkopf, H. Norman, 24, 26, 36, 84, 189-191, 195, 203, 205, 280, 286, 498
Sellick, Charles, 343, 479-480
Sharpe, Edna, 52, 131-132, 139
Sharpe, Violet, 33, 52, 58, 79, 85, 93, 116-117, 130
Sheetz, Betty, 80, 101, 110
Sidway, Moe, 469-470
Simek, Waslov, 343, 480-482
Silverman, Max, 383
Spitale, Salvartore, 37, 41-42, 85, 188-190, 193-194, 196, 197-198, 200, 202-207, 252-253, 382-384, 423
Springer, Arthur, 35, 84, 116, 136-137
Stein, Elbridge, 176, 185-186
Sutherland, Dean, 343, 482-486

Tannehill, Earl, 487-492
Thayer, Robert, 35-36, 40, 42-43, 190-199, 201-206, 223, 384-385, 419
Thompson, Douglas G., 35, 84
Torrio, John, 380-382, 387-388, 400-401
"True Story of Jafsie's Effort to Locate Stolen Lindbergh Baby, The," 53
True Story of the Lindbergh Kidnapping, The, 147
Tunney, Gene, 455

Ubaldi, Isidoro, 486-487
United Press, 204

Valente, Louis, A., 208
Valentine, Carlo, 459-463
Vandetti, Larry, 459-463

Wagner, Abie, 47-48, 396, 407, 411, 497\
Wagner, Benny, 396
Washington Times, The, 512
Watson, Victor, 201-202
Walsh, Harry W., 117, 213
Warden, Dr. Carl, 29
Weiss, Hymie, 382
Whately, Ollie, 33, 75, 78-80, 82, 101-104, 109
Whately, Phoebe, 33, 75, 78-80, 82, 101, 103-105
Whitaker, Norman, 59, 65
Williamson, Charles E., 34, 75, 146
Williams, J. Flody, 343, 487-490
Winterhalter, Charles, 217
Wilson, Frank J., 25, 57, 68, 213, 423, 429-430
Wolfe, Harry, 34, 75, 146, 190-191

Zapulsky, Andrew, 271-1272, 274

H. Norman Schwartzkopf, Superintendant of the New Jersey State Police, which handled the kidnapping investigation. His son, General "Stormin' Norman" Schwartzkopf, was known to a later generation as the leader of the Allied Forces in the 1991 Gulf War with Iraq.

The Lindbergh mansion, oustide Hopewell, New Jersey, at the time of the baby kidnapping.

The handmade ladder leading to the second floor room of the Lindbergh baby.

Wood expert Arthur Koehler, who traced the wood used in the ladder. He discovered that the wood originally came from the Dorn Lumber Mill in McCormick, South Carolina and was eventually traced to the National Lumber and Millword Company in the Bronx (Berg pp. 296-297), which was the closest lumberyard to the home of Bruno Richard Hauptmann. Koehler sent letters to 1,600 lumber yards regarding the source of the wood before narrowing his search to the National Lumber and Millwork Company.

Remains of the Lindbergh baby subsquently found in a hand-made shallow grave near the Lindbergh mansion.

THE FBI FILES:

The Arrest of Bruno Richard Hauptmann

Changed: Richard Hauptmann alias Richard Hauptmann alias Richard Hoffman alias Karl Pellimeier

PESONAL AND CONFIDENTIAL

$10.00 ransom gold certificates, #A-75873174-A, discovered August 20, 1934, at Federal Reserve Bank, New York City, and traced to Bank of Sicily & Trust Company. This was first ransom gold certificate discovered since February 13, 1934, and when checked against original list of serial numbers of gold certificates paid as ransom indicated portion of ransom gold certificates being passed one at a time. All banks in New York City and vicinity were immediately contacted individually and requested to concentrate on check of gold certificates for ransom money. This resulted in the notification of the New York Division office by neighborhood banks of the discovery of nine ransom gold certificates. In addition to this the Federal Reserve Bank notified this office of the discovery of four ransom gold certificates. Investigation in several instances succeeded in securing a fairly accurate description of the person passing bills, indicating but one person engaged in this operation and the localities in which he was operating as Yorkville and the Fordham section of Bronx, N. Y. in conjunction with New York City and New Jersey State Police, teams of agents, troopers and detectives patrolled these sections in an effort to apprehend person described as passing ransom money. While plant still in progress and under date of September 18, 19834, Corn Exchange Bank, 135th Street and Park Avenue, notified New York Division office of receipt of $10.00 ransom gold certificate #A-73976634-A. Investigation conducted by representatives of three agencies cooperating in the investigation traced bill to Warner-Quinlan Oil station, East 127th Street and Lexington Avenue, and manager advised of receipt from man subsequently identified as Bruno Richard Hauptmann. Residence of Hauptmann, 1279 East 222nd Street, kept under surveillance from afternoon of September 18th to

8:55 A.M., September 19th. Hauptmann apprehended 9:15 A.M., September 19, 1934, en route Yorkville. $20.0 ransom gold certificate, #A-35517877-A, found in his possession. Residence of Hauptmann and safe deposit box at Central Savings Bank searched, and Hauptmann brought to Police Headquarters and there photographed, fingerprinted, questioned and booked and further search of his residence and garage ordered.

REFERENCES: Report of Special Agent L. G. Turrou, New York, 8/22/34.
Report of Special Agent W. F. Seery, New York, 8/28/34.
Report of Special Agent W. F. Seery, New York, 8/28/34.
Report of Special Agent T. H. Sisk, New York, 8/29/34.
Report of Special Agent W. F. Seery, New York, 8/30/34.
Report of Special Agent W. F. Seery, New York, 8/30/34.
Report of Special Agent W. F. Seery, New York, 9/1/34.
Report of Special Agent W. F. Seery, New York, 9/6/34.
Report of Special Agent W. F. Seery, New York, 9/7/34.
Report of Special Agent W. F. Seery, New York, 9/8/34.
Report of Special Agent W. F. Seery, New York, 9/8/34.
Report of Special Agent W. F. Seery, New York, 9/14/34.
Report of Special Agent W. F. Seery, New York, 9/14/34.
Report of Special Agent W. F. Seery, New York, 9/14/34.
Report of Special Agent W. F. Seery, New York, 9/18/34.
Report of Special Agent W. F. Seery, New York, 9/18/34.

DETAILS: AT NEW YORK CITY.

This is a joint report prepared by Special Agents W. F. Seery and T. H. Sisk, covering the arrest of subject Hauptmann and the events leading to same.

On August 20, 1934, the Federal Reserve Bank of New York discovered $10.00 Lindbergh ransom bill, gold certificate, #A-75873174-A, and reported the discovery of same to the New York Division office and the New York Police Department. Inasmuch as Special Agent W. F. Seery, who has been assigned to the investigation of all ransom money discovered in this case, was busy on another matter, the writer instructed Special Agent L. G. Turrou to proceed with the investigation of the ransom bill in question. The discovery of the bill was reported by the writer to Lieutenant Arthur Keaten of the New Jersey State Police, who assigned Sergeant E. A. Haussling to accompany Agent Turrou on the investigation. The New York Police Department did not participate in the investigation of this particular ransom bill, inasmuch as Acting Lieutenant James Finn, the only officer from that Department assigned to the case, had been on vacation since July 29, 1934, it being also noted that he returned from his vacation on September 6, 1934. The investigation of the above mentioned ransom bill was unproductive of any information of value except that it had been received at the Bank of Sicily Trust Company, 196 First Avenue, New York (near East 12th Street) from an unknown person, during the period from June 20, 1934 to the date it was deposited, August 17, 1934, at the Federal Reserve Bank. A copy of the report covering the investigation of this bill was delivered to Sergeant William Grafenecker, New York Police, who had been designated to receive any information concerning the Lindbergh case during the absence of Acting Lieutenant Finn.

The significant feature in connection with the discovery of the above referred to ransom bill was the fact that it was the first ransom gold certificate discovered since February 13, 1934. A further significant fact was developed as a result of a check of the serial numbers of all ransom bills discovered against the original list of the serial numbers of ransom bills prepared by the employees of

J. P. Morgan & Company, at the time the ransom money was assembled. The results of this analysis, as set forth in the report of Special Agent W. F. Seery, August 28, 1934, reflected that of the last eight $10.00 gold certificates discovered, seven of which were listed in the Summary Report, and the eighth the above referred to bill traced to the Bank of Sicily Trust Company, seven are set out on page four of the original listing by Morgan & Company in the same sequence in which they were discovered, indicating almost beyond question that the person passing the ransom money was passing the gold certificates one at a time and still had in his possession a large part of the gold certificates paid as ransom.

On August 28, 1934, the Federal Reserve Bank of New York discovered two more $10.00 Lindbergh ransom gold certificates, bearing serial nos. A-73697975-A and A-17385388-A. These bills were reported to the New York Division office and the New York Police Department. The New York office notified the New Jersey State Police as to the discovery of these bills and the subsequent investigation as to same was conducted by Special Agent W. F. Seery and Corporal William Horn of the New Jersey State Police. A representative of the New York Police did not participate in the investigation for the reasons already stated. However, upon completion of the investigation, reports were transmitted to Sergeant Grafenecker so that the New York Police would be kept advised at all times as to developments in the case.

The first mentioned gold certificate was traced to the branch of the National City Bank located at 123 East 86th Street, near Lexington Avenue. The officials at the bank were unable to furnish any information concerning the identity of the person from whom this bill was received, except that it had been received at the bank on or about August 23, 1934.

The investigation with reference to the second bill developed that it had been received at the Bank of the Manhattan Company branch located at 424 East Tremont Avenue, (between Webster and Park Avenue), among the receipts of August 23, 1934.

As a result of the investigation of the two bills in question and the other $10.00 gold certificate mentioned in previous paragraphs of this report, it was obvious that the neighborhood and branch banks were making no effort to detect Lindbergh ransom money and that the only financial institution in New York making a real effort to detect the ransom money was the Federal Reserve Bank of New York. Although the Federal Reserve Bank had in the spring of 1934 put on eighteen additional clerks to assist those already engaged in searching all deposits for ransom bills, it became apparent that the Federal Reserve Bank was valuable only as a catch-all and that after a bill reached this institution it was almost impossible to trace it beyond the bank making the deposit at the Federal Reserve. With this condition existing, there was no opportunity to procure a description of or gain any information as to the identity of the person or persons passing the ransom money.

The bank situation was further unsatisfactory in that the bank tellers found it impossible to check $5.00 bills, due to the large number of this denomination in circulation in the New York area. Contact with various banking institutions over a period of months by Agents assigned to the Lindbergh investigation had quite conclusively shown that the impossibility of checking $5.00 bills had been used by the tellers as an excuse for not checking money of any denomination in the search for Lindbergh ransom bills. Likewise it had become evident that it was impossible to trace $5.00 bills even when they were discovered by the banks.

In view of the above situation, it was decided to concentrate on the search for the gold certificates making up the ransom money, there being greater possibilities in tracing gold because of the comparative scarcity of this type of money, resulting from the President's gold proclamation in the spring of 1933.

In view of the above situation, the writer decided to have the Agents assigned to the case make personal contact with all banks and the branches thereof in Greater New York and Westchester County, for the purpose of emphasizing the importance of maintaining a close lookout for gold certificates making up the ransom money, instructing the banks to disregard the $5.00 bills and concentrate on the gold alone, thus eliminating the favorite excuse used by bank tellers that it was impossible to check Lindbergh ransom money because of the large number of $5.00 bills received by them daily. In order to stimulate interest and insure the cooperation of the banks, the Agents were instructed to confidentially inform the bank officials that some of the Lindbergh ransom gold certificates had recently appeared in circulation in Greater New York.

At the time the above instructions were issued, several of the Agents assigned to the investigation were engaged in the investigation of other angles of the case in cooperation with New Jersey State Troopers. In view of this situation, the writer communicated his decision to Lieutenant Arthur Keaten of the New Jersey State Police, who concurred in the matter and suggested that some of his Troopers be assigned to work with the Agents on the bank contacts.

During the talk with Lieutenant Keaten regarding the bank contacts, this officer pointed out that the New York Police Department had since the start of the investigation assured the New Jersey State Police that all the New York banks were keeping a close lookout for Lindbergh ransom money, which statement was obviously unwarranted in view of the situation described. Lieutenant Keaten at this time suggested that the bank contacts be delayed until the return of Lieutenant Finn from his vacation, stating that he felt that the New York Police should have representation in the group making the contacts and that possibly Finn might take offense at any such drastic step during his absence; however, the writer pointed out to Lieutenant Keaten the necessity for contacting the banks immediately, in view of the indications that the person possessing the ransom money was once again passing gold certificates. It was further pointed out to Lieutenant Keaten that any delay at this time might result in the kidnaper passing a large amount of ransom money without being detected, which might prove fatal to the investigation, and therefore that the writer was having his men start on the bank contacts immediately, regardless of anyone's feelings in the matter.

On August 29, 1934, Special Agents E. Sandberg and L. G. Turrou contacted the executive vice-presidents of the larger chain banking institutions in Greater New York, as follows:

Bank of the Manhattan Company
National City Bank
Central Hanover Bank & Trust Company
Manufacturers Trust Company
Chase National Bank
Public National Bank & Trust Company
Corn Exchange Bank Trust Company

On August 30th, Special Agent E. Sandberg, unaccompanied, contacted the Brooklyn Trust Company, Irving Trust Company, First National Bank, Guaranty Trust Company of New York, Chemical Bank & Trust Company.

Thereafter, on September 1, 4, 5 and 6, 1934, Special Agent E. Sandberg contacted approximately fifty independent and smaller banking institutions throughout Greater New York.

On August 29, 30 and 31, and September 4 and 5, Special Agent W. F. Seery, accompanied by Corporal William Horn, new Jersey State Police, contacted all banking institutions having their main offices or principal branches in the Bronx, also various savings institutions in the midtown New York area.

Starting August 29, and continuing through August 30, 31, September 1, 4, 5 and 6, Special Agent H. C. Leslie, accompanied by New Jersey State Trooper Samuel Leon, contacted nineteen banks in New York City, and all banking institutions at Yonkers, Hastings, Dobbs Ferry, Greenburg, Mt. Vernon, Scarsdale, Hartsdale, Bronxville, New Rochelle, Larchmont, Mamaroneck and White Plains, with the exception of three banks at White Plains which were covered by Special Agent Austin.

On September 10 and 11, Special Agent R. M. Austin, specially assigned for the purpose, unaccompanied contacted thirty-five banking institutions scattered throughout New York City.

Starting September 13, and continuing through September 14, 15, 17, 18 and 19, a squad consisting of special Agents F. X. O'Donnell, Joseph A. Genau, R. M. Austin, and Peter J. Nolan, contacted one hundred fifty-nine banking institutions in Greater New York. A list of the banks contacted is presently in the New York Division office files pertaining to this case. The above-mentioned Agents were unaccompanied while contacting the various banks.

The writer's notes and those of the Agents who contacted the banks are in the New York file and reflect the dates on which contact was made and the name and address of the various banking institutions contacted.

In connection with the bank contacts, there was prepared at the New York office a card index system indexing the name and address of all banking institutions in Greater New York and Westchester County, the same having been prepared as an aid to the contemplated frequent contact with these banks until the desired results were obtained.

In addition to the personal contact had with the managers of the various banking institutions, arrangements were made by the Agents with the executive vice-presidents of the large chain banking institutions to immediately notify by letter the managers of each of their branches throughout Greater New York, instructing them to make diligent search of all gold money received for the purpose of determining whether any of it was Lindbergh ransom money and if so to notify immediately the New York Division office. As a result of these arrangements the following letter, which was sent out by the main office of the Corn Exchange bank Trust Company under date of August 29, 1934, is being quoted herewith, as it is representative of the letters sent out by the other chain banking institutions:

CORN EXHANGE BANK TRUST TCOMPANY
New York

Aug. 29, 1934

To the Manager:-

Referring to the booklet containing the numbers of all the bills paid out in connection with the Lindbergh Kidnaping Case, we have been requested by the United States Department of Justice to watch every $10. and $20. Gold Certificate which is being turned in to us, and if the number of the bill is followed by the letter "A", to immediately check the same against the numbers in this booklet before the customer leaves.

If the number of the bill corresponds with any in the booklet, ascertain from your depositor from whom received, if possible, and communicate the information directly to the Department whose telephone number is Caledonia 5-8694.

Have every teller understand the importance of this request.

Very truly yours,

DUNHAM B. SHERER
President

Photostatic copy of the above letter is attached to this report.

The above letter is of particular interest as one of the branches of the Corn Exchange Bank ultimately discovered and reported to the New York Division office a Lindbergh ransom gold certificate which brought about the apprehension of Bruno Richard Hauptmann.

The value of the above described bank contacts became immediately apparent when during the ensuing three weeks nine ransom bills, each a gold certificate, were discovered by neighborhood banks and reported directly to the New York Division office. In addition the Federal Reserve Bank reported to the New York Division office and the New York Police the discovery of two gold certificates during this period. Although separate investigative reports have been submitted covering the tracing of each of these ransom bills, the important facts developed in the investigation of each are herewith being repeated so that the Division will have a complete picture of the entire situation.

Under date of August 29, 1934, Henry J. McQuade, Manager of the Chase National Bank branch at 116th Street and Third Avenue, telephoned the New York Division office and advised the writer that a $20.00 gold certificate, serial #A-16329829-A (one of the Lindbergh ransom bills) had been discovered at the branch of the Chase National Bank located at 2011 First Avenue (corner of 104th Street) and, that the bank had detained the man who deposited the bill.

The writer, accompanied by Special Agent J. L. Geraghty, proceeded to the latter branch and was there advised by P. L. Eiler, Manager, that the bill in question was discovered by Mr. McQuade in deposit made by Angelo J. DeFelica, proprietor of a fruit and produce business at 1993 First Avenue, (near East 103rd Street). Subsequent interview with DeFelice developed that this bill had been received by him at approximately 9:30 A.M., August 29, 1934; that it was received from a man, name not known, who entered the fruit store, made a small purchase of beans (approximately $5.10), and departed. DeFelice advised there was nothing suspicious about the appearance of the man from whom the bill was received. DeFelice's description of the man from whom he received the bill was not enlightening in connection with descriptions developed during the investigation to date. The results of the above investigation were communicated to representatives of the New Jersey State Police and the New York Police Department.

Under date of August 30, 1934, G. A. Guerdan, Assistant Vice President of the National City Bank, New York City, called the New York Division office and advised that $10.00 ransom gold certificate #A-0244196 had been discovered that date at the Bronx branch of the National City Bank located at 149th Street and Courtlandt Avenue. This information was communicated to a representative of the New Jersey State Police and the investigation in connection with the bill was conducted by Special Agent L. Sandberg and Sergeant E. A. Haussling of the New Jersey State Police.

Mr. Guerdan informed Agent Sandberg and Sergeant Haussling that it had not been the habit of the bank to check up on the gold certificates received; that they merely collected them over a period of a month or more and forwarded them to the Federal Reserve Bank; that in response to this Department's request that all gold certificates of the $10.00 and $20.00 denomination be checked, he caused all certificates in his bank at the time the order was received to be checked and found this certificate among them. Mr. Guerdan advised that the bill probably was received at the bank anytime between July 2, 1934 and August 30, 1934. However, further investigation appeared to indicate that the gold certificate in question was received at the bank some time subsequent to August 6, 1934. However, all efforts to determine the source from which received were unavailing. The results of this investigation were communicated to the New York City Police Department.

Under date of September 6, 1934, H. D. Raasch, Assistant Cashier of the National Bank of Yorkville in New York, located at 207 East 86th Street, (near Third Avenue), called the New York Division office and advised that the bank had just received a Lindbergh $10.00 ransom gold certificate in a deposit made by one of the bank's regular depositors. The above information was communicated to the New Jersey State Police and Acting Lieutenant James Finn of the New York City Police Department.

Agent W. F. Seery, accompanied by Corporal William Horn of the New Jersey State Police, proceeded to the National Bank of Yorkville, where investigation developed that the $10.00 gold certificate in question bore serial #A-57232100-A; that it was discovered by Teller Frank Hoffman, 2914—23rd Road, Astoria, Long Island, in a deposit made by Raphael Boccanfuso & Company, operators of a fruit store located at 1582 Third Avenue, southeast corner of Third Avenue and East 89th Street.

Accompanied by Corporal Horn and Acting Lieutenant

Finn, Agent Seery proceeded to the Boccanfuso store and there ascertained that the bill in question had been received by clerk Salvatore Levatino (residence address 1962 Third Avenue, top floor), between one and three P.M., September 5, 1934, Levatino advising that he distinctly recalled the gold certificate as it was the only gold certificate of any kind received by him in months; that the purchaser had made a distinct impression upon him, inasmuch as it was unusual for anybody to tender a bill of such denomination for such a small purchase, which to Levatino's recollection did not exceed ten cents. Levatino described the man from whom the ransom gold certificate was received as follows:

Age	38—42 years
Height	5' 10 or 11"
Weight	150—155 lbs.
Build	Slender, athletic; described by Levatino as resembling a "track racer" or "runner". Shoulders fairly broad, square but not thick.
Hair	Extremely light brown; a shade or two under a dark blonde.
Eyes	Not recalled
Eyebrows	Not recalled
Complexion	Light
Facial features	Straight nose, with slight flare at nostrils; high cheekbones; hollow cheeks; pointed chin—not cleft, dimpled, nor protruding; lips thin, straight.
Teeth	Not recalled.
Nationality	Unknown. Possibly Irish, German or Scandinavian; not of Latin extraction.

Dress	Well dressed; linen clean; hat, light grey fedora with dark, regular width band, worn up in back and down in front.

Worn double-breasted suit of bluish-grey mixture, of the shade designated as "royal blue" (dark powder blue).

Wore white shirt with a white starched collar, four-in-hand tie of color not recalled by Levatino.

The investigation in connection with the bill described immediately above developed the first worth-while description of the passer of the gold certificate since the inauguration of this investigation. In addition to being a fairly complete description, Levatino's description of the man from whom he received the bill in question was almost identical with the description of the man described by Dr. John F. Condon as the person to whom he paid the ransom money. Levatino at the New York Division office examined the sketch of "John" prepared by James Berryman, a newspaper artist of Washington, D.C., as his conception of the man described by Dr. Condon, and advised that to the best of his recollection it was not a good likeness of the man from whom he received the $10.00 bill in question, though the chin in the sketch representing the side view of "John" was practically identical with the chin of the unknown man from whom here received the gold certificate.

On September 6, 1934, upon the return of Acting Lieutenant Finn from his vacation, the developments which occurred during his absence were made known to him in detail, and copies of all reports made during his absence which had not been furnished to Sergeant Grafenecker were handed to him. Acting Lieutenant Finn, after hearing of the developments, stated that it was his intention to see Inspector John J. Lyons at Headquarters immediately, and that the New York Police would throw out a squad of undercover men in the neighborhood of Yorkville and Harlem where it appeared the ransom bills were being passed. Acting Lieutenant Finn did not consult with the writer prior to making this statement, nor with Lieutenant Arthur Keaten of the New Jersey State Police, who was in the New York office at the time. The writer learned that Lieutenant Finn had an appointment with Inspector Lyons for 8 P.M. that evening, and accompanied by Lieutenant Arthur Keaten proceeded to headquarters and talked with Lieutenant Finn prior to his conference with Inspector Lyons, and as a result of the talk Lieutenant Finn, Lieutenant Keaten, and the writer, had a joint conference with Inspector Lyon, and it was decided that each organization would place six men, or eighteen men in all, in the neighborhood of Yorkville and Lower Harlem, between 59th Street and 86th Street, from First Avenue to Third Avenue. Acting Lieutenant Finn suggested at this conference that a larger number of men should be assigned to this duty, however it was finally decided that it would be better to have a limited number of men in the neighborhood in question for a few days, for the purpose of sizing up the situation, surveying the possibilities, and later if necessary more men could be added. It was also brought out at this conference that if too many men were suddenly thrown into the neighborhood they would be noticed by residents of the neighborhood, by the precinct police officers and others, and the publicity that might possibly result would jeopardize success of the plant.

Accordingly, on September 7 and 8, 1934, Special Agents H. C. Leslie, E. Sandberg, J. E. Saykora, L. G. Turrou, and J. L. Geraghty, and the writer, were paired off with either a New Jersey State Trooper or a New York Police Detective, the pairing being so arranged that no two men of any organization were working together. In other words, there were three teams composed of Division Special Agents and

New York Police officers, three teams composed of Division Special Agents and New Jersey State Troopers, and three teams composed of New York detectives and New Jersey State Troopers. The writer's notes, which show the names of the police officers and state troopers engaged in this plant during its continuance, are on file at the New York office.

The plant was maintained daily from 9 A.M. to 7 P.M., and those engaged on same were furnished with appropriate descriptions and were given instructions to keep a close lookout on fruit and vegetable stands, particularly corner stands, in view of the modus operandi of the person passing the money, as previously outlined.

On September 8, 1934, the Division instructed that ten additional Special Agents be assigned to the plant, in view of the obvious impossibility of the small number previously assigned to adequately cover the designated territory. Both Captain J. J. Lamb and Lieutenant Arthur Keaten of the New Jersey State Police and Inspector John J. Lyons questioned the availability of concentrating so many men in the given area, giving as a reason the danger of publicity and the fact that men who were "green" on the case might jeopardize the success of the investigation. However, these officers further stated that they likewise would place ten additional men on the plant, making a total of forty-eight men on duty in connection with the plant. The plant with the additional men was continued from September 9, 1934 to September 18, inclusive, being abandoned on the latter date for obvious reasons.

The plant was extended so that two teams of two men each were assigned to cover Fordham Road, in the vicinity of the Jacobson Brothers Exquisite Shoe Corporation store, at which a $20.00 ransom gold certificate was passed September 7, 1934. These teams, at the time of the finding of the $10.00 ransom bill containing Hauptmann's automobile license number, consisted of Detective William Wallace, New York Police Department, Detective Sergeant J. Wallace of the New Jersey State Police, Detective Chester Cronin of the New York Police Department and Trooper Dennis Dore of the New Jersey State Police.

During the operation of the plant two ransom gold certificates were discovered, and upon being traced were found to have been passed in the territory covered by the plant. However, both of these bills apparently had been passed in that neighborhood a few days prior to the institution of the surveillance in that neighborhood. Both of these bills are included in the eleven gold certificates previously mentioned.

One of these bills, $10.00 gold certificate, serial #A-76444003-A, was discovered September 11, 1934 at the Manufacturers Trust Company branch located at the corner of First Avenue and East 64th Street. The discovery of this bill was reported to the New York Division office by F. Steininger, Manager of the branch, and in turn the New York Division office advised both the New York Police and the New Jersey State Police of the discovery. Joint investigation was conducted by Special Agent W. F. Seery, Corporal William Horn, and Acting Lieutenant James Finn, and it developed that this bill was passed at the fruit store of Charles Aiello & Sons, 1596 Second Avenue (near East 83rd Street), under date of September 5, 1934, by an individual who was described by Aiello as follows:

Age	35 years
Height	5'10:
Weight	150—155 lbs.
Hair	Color unknown, not believed to be dark
Eyes	Not recalled
Complexion	Medium ruddy
Chin	Round, not square

Build	Medium slender
Nationality	Appeared to be of German extraction. Did not speak with accent. Hands not those of a laboring man. Manner quiet and assured; not nervous.
Dress	Well and neatly dressed. Wore dark fedora hat; suit of bluish mixture; color a shade lighter than navy blue. Shoes black; shirt negligee, [used in a secondary, and now out of date, dictionary definition: *easy, informal attire*—TF] with starched collar attached; the four-in-hand, extending to or slightly over belt.

Aiello advised that the bill was tendered by the above described individual in payment for a small purchase of vegetables or fruit, that the man did not enter the store but stood out on the sidewalk when making the purchase.

It will be noted that the store description and modus operandi tallied closely with that of the individual who had passed a ransom bill at the Boccanfuso store.

Under date of September 14, 1934, $20.00 ransom gold certificate #A-37994420-A was discovered at the Lincoln Savings Bank, 531 Broadway, Brooklyn, N. Y., and reported to the New York Division office by telephone by H. A. Smith, Head Teller. The New York office immediately communicated this information to representatives of the New Jersey State Police and the New York Police, and joint investigation was conducted as to same by Special Agent W. F. Seery, Corporal Horn and Lieutenant Finn. This investigation resulted in the tracing of this bill to Bloomberg's General Market, located at the corner of Second Avenue and 80th Street, New York city. Miss Ruby Altman, Cashier at this store, distinctly recalled the receipt of this bill and placed the date of its receipt as approximately 4 P.M., September 8, 1934. Her description of the man who passed same is as follows:

Age	35 years
Height	5'11"
Build	Slender
Weight	Unknown
Complexion	Light
Hair	Dark
Eyes	Not recalled
Teeth	Not recalled
Face	Long
Nationality	Appearing to be of foreign extraction, probably German, although without noticeable accent.
Dress	Dressed in shirt, trousers and shoes without hat or coat.

It will be noted that the above description, with the exception of the hair, was generally similar to the descriptions furnished at the Aiello and Boccanfuso stores. However, at the Bloomberg store the unknown individual did not stand on the sidewalk when making his purchase, but walked into the store and purchased a quantity of meat, although the store did maintain a fruit and vegetable stand on the sidewalk.

Under date of September 8, 1934, H. French, Manager of the Chase National Bank, Fordham Branch, 301 East Fordham Road, Bronx, New York, called the New York Division office and reported the discovery of a $20.00 ransom gold certificate, #A-35272048-A. This information was communicated to representatives of the New Jersey State Police and the New York Police, and joint investigation conducted by Special Agent Seery, Corporal Horn and Acting Lieutenant Finn, resulted in tracing the bill to the Exquisite Shoe Corporation, 266 East Fordham Road, where it was ascertained that the bill had been received in payment for merchandise between 6 P.M. and 11 P.M., September 7, 1934.

Check of all known sales wherein $20.00 bills had been tendered in payment developed that the names of only four of the thirteen purchasers were listed on the sales slips, nine of the sales tickets wherein $20.00 bills had been tendered being without names and addresses. The four named purchasers were all interviewed without the investigation determining the source from which the bill was received at the Exquisite Shoe Corporation.

Under date of September 15, 1934, H. E. Schneider, Manager, Corn Exchange Bank branch located at 385 East Fordham Road, Bronx, new York, communicated with the New York office and reported discovery of $10.00 ransom gold certificate #A-27063410-A. This information was immediately communicated to representatives of the New Jersey State Police and New York Police and joint investigation by Special Agent Seery, Corporal Horn and Lieutenant Finn succeeded in tracing this bill to one Max Harfenist, proprietor of a grocery store at 2323 Webster Avenue. Harfenist, however, was unable to furnish any information concerning the source from which the bill was received by him except that he believed he received it from one of his regular customers.

Under date of September 17, 1934, $10.00 ransom gold certificate #A-44293574-A was discovered at the Federal Reserve Bank, New York City, and this office and the New York Police were immediately notified. Joint investigation by Special Agent Seery, Corporal Horn and Acting Lieutenant Finn of the New York City Police, succeeded only in tracing this bill to the Manufacturers Trust Company branch at 822 East Tremont Avenue. The officials of the latter branch could furnish no information other than that the bill had been received from an unknown person during the period from August 29 to September 6, 1934.

Under date of September 18, 1934, $10.00 ransom gold certificate #A-77310232-A was discovered at the Federal Reserve Bank, New York City, and was reported to the New York Division office and to the New York City Police. Joint investigation conducted by Special Agent Seery, Corporal Horn and Acting Lieutenant Finn of the New York Police, succeeded only in tracing this bill to the Irving Trust Company, 149th Street and Third Avenue where officials advised that it was utterly impossible to determine the date of the bill's receipt at this branch or the identity of the person from whom it was received.

Under date of September 18, 1934, the New York office was informed by W. A. Fry, Jr., Manager of the Irving Trust Company branch at 149th Street and Third Avenue, that he had just discovered $10.00 ransom bill, gold certificate, serial #A-74151743-A. This information was communicated to representatives of the New Jersey State and New York Police, and joint investigation by Special Agent Seery, corporal Horn and Acting Lieutenant Finn succeeded in tracing this bill to the Wieland Bakery and Lunch Room, at 1993 Webster Avenue. Neither A. Wieland, his family, nor other employees, could furnish any information concerning the source from which this bill was received.

Under date of September 18, 1934, Mr. F. C. Dingeldien, Assistant Manager of the Corn Exchange Bank Trust Company, located at the corner of Park Avenue and 125th Street, New York City, telephoned Special Agent T. H. Sisk at the New York Division office, at 1:20 P.M. and advised that $10.00 gold certificate #A-73976634-A had been discovered a few minutes prior to the telephone call by Teller W. R. Strong. Dingeldien further stated that the bill had not been received at the bank by Teller Strong but had been received September 17, 1934 by Teller M. J. Ozmec, who had neglected to check it against the list of serial numbers of the ransom bills. However, that a few minutes before the telephone call Teller Strong, while checking a number of gold certificates accumulated in the bank, discovered that the particular bill in question was one of the Lindbergh ransom bills, and that it came from Teller Ozmec's work. Mr. Dingeldien also advised that the bill was one of the two gold certificates received on the 17th by Teller Ozmec, but Ozmec could not recall from whom he had received the two gold certificates, however that it was his recollection he had received one from a depositor, name not remembered, and the other from an unknown person who came in the bank and exchanged the bill for ten singles.

When the telephone call from Mr. Dingeldien came into the office, the writer and Lieutenant Arthur Keaten of the New Jersey State Police were in the New York Division office attending to details pertaining to the plant in the Yorkville section. The writer reported the discovery of the bill to Lieutenant Keaten and then telephoned the New York Police Department Undercover Squad in an effort to locate Special Agent Seery, who at the time was in company with Lieutenant Finn and Corporal Horn, engaged in completing investigation as to other ransom bills which had been discovered, as previously mentioned. The writer, in inquiring as to Agent Seery's whereabouts, talked to Captain John J. Lamb of the New Jersey State Police, and advised him of the discovery of an additional ransom bill, and likewise requested Captain Lamb to have Agent Seery call his office in the event he appeared at the Undercover Squad or phoned in to that office.

At 1:40 P.M. Agent Seery called the New York office and the writer advised him of the discovery of the bill in question. At the particular moment when Agent Seery telephoned and spoke to the writer, he was in the company of Acting Lieutenant Finn and Corporal Horn, who were unaware of the discovery of this particular bill, it not having been reported to the New York Police Department.

Agent Seery, Corporal Horn and Lieutenant Finn proceeded to the Corn Exchange bank, 125th Street and Park

Avenue, arriving at the latter branch about 2:45 P.M., and there interviewed Assistant Manager F. C. Dingeldien, who repeated the information he had previously communicated to the writer and turned over to the investigators of ransom bill in question, which upon examination was found to contain on the back, in the margin, the pencilled inscription "4 U 13-41" which appeared to be an automobile license number. Photograph of this bill was secured from the New York Police and is being attached to the Division copies of this report.

Myron Ozmec, Corn Exchange Bank Teller by whom this bill was received, advised that he distinctly recalled receiving two $10.00 gold certificates during the business of Monday, September 17, 1934. He was unable to recall the identity of the persons from whom the bills were received other than that one bill was received from one of possibly one hundred fifty depositors and the other received from a man whom he could not at the moment recall who tendered a bill to be exchanged for ordinary currency.

At this time Agent Seery in conversation with Assistant Manager Dingeldien ascertained that the search for Lindbergh ransom bills by the employees of the Corn Exchange Bank resulted from instructions received August 30, 1934, from Dunham B. Sherer, President, in a letter dated August 29, 1934. This letter is quoted on pages 7 and 8 of this report, and photostatic copy of same will be found attached to the Division copies of this report.

Subsequent to the apprehension of Bruno Richard Hauptmann, Special Agent F. X. O'Donnell, acting upon instructions from the writer, interviewed Assistant Manager Frederick C. Dingeldien and Teller William R. Strong, at the bank, and thanked them for their cooperation in this matter. The memorandum submitted by Special Agent O'Donnell covering this interview is set out below:

September 31, 1934.

At the Corn Exchange Bank Mount Morris Branch, 85 East 125th Street, New York, Agent interviewed Mr. Frederick C. Dingeldien, Assistant Manager, and William R. Strong, Teller, who advised that on September 18, 1934, Strong in breaking package of odd bills from collections of September 17, 1934, found the bill in question and immediately brought same to Mr. Dingeldien's desk, who at once phoned this office, in conformity with memorandum received from the main office of the company within the past few days, which instructed that in such an emergency this office should be called at once. The memorandum was not available at the time of Agent's visit and it was not deemed advisable to ask the privilege of reading it, in the absence of an offer on Mr. Dingeldien's part to produce it.

Mr. Dingeldien stated that he called no one else but this office as his instructions had mentioned only this office as a point of contact. Of course I had previously expressed appreciation along the lines suggested. I led up to the main issue by reviewing the fact that several agencies had been engaged on the case and that if he had communicated with one or more other than ourselves, we would like to get in touch with them to avoid duplication of effort.

Until its discovery by investigators, neither Ozmec nor Assistant Manager Dingeldien had noticed the license number on the back of the bill. Ozmec was requested to furnish the names and addresses of gasoline stations and garages who had made deposits at his window on September 17, 1934. After consulting his deposit tickets, Ozmec furnished the following names and addresses:

Lind & Glantz, 2481 First Avenue (garage)
Dluka Garage, Inc., 1725 Park Avenue (garage)

Warner-Quinlan Oil Company, east side of Lexington Avenue, between East 127th and 128th Streets (filling station)

The latter address being the closest to the bank, the investigators proceeded there and interviewed Walter Lyle, Manager of the filling station. After examining the bill, particularly the license number on the back of the bill, Lyle advised that this number had been placed on the bill by him at about 10 A.M., September 1, 1934, at which time a man described as being 32 years of age, 5'11", 165 lbs., light complexion, Scandinavian type, driving an automobile, make and model not recalled, purchased five gallons of special gasoline at a cost of 98¢ and tendered in payment thereof the $10.00 bill in question. Lyle stated that he had questioned the value of this bill, having in mind that at some recent date the government had recalled all gold or gold certificates; that the unknown customer had reassured him that the bill was of the value represented and was perfectly good legal tender, the man remarking, "I have a hundred more just like it". Lyle stated that being reassured by this reply he accepted the bill and made the necessary change and the man drove away, but that prior to the man's leaving the station he (Lyle) had noted the license number of the automobile driven by this man and had written same on the back of the bill. Lyle stated his reason for writing the license number on the bill was because, in spite of the man's reassurance, he (Lyle) recalled when he got to thinking over the matter that the President had issued an order calling in all gold and gold certificates and he feared the bank might refuse to accept this bill, which was a gold certificate, and he would then have to make it good to the company.

Subsequent to the arrest of Hauptmann, Lyle was reinterviewed relative to the statement attributed to him in the press to the effect that the bill had been received by him under date of September 15, 1934 whereas he had informed the investigators that the bill was received by him September 17, 1934. Lyle stated that his present recollection is that the bill was received by him September 15, 1934 instead of September 17, 1934, explaining that after reading of Hauptmann's arrest and the manner in which Hauptmann was traced, he discussed the matter with his assistant, John Lyons, and the latter refreshed his memory, recalling to him the fact that he, Lyle, had given this bill to Lyons September 15, 1934, at the time Lyons cashed his pay check, from the receipts of the station. This latter date is corroborated by Lyons, who advised that it would have been impossible or him to have deposited this bill at the Corn Exchange Bank September 17, 1934, as on that date he was absent on leave.

In view of the above, Teller Myron Ozmec was reinterviewed, but insisted that the bill was deposited with him September 17, 1934 by Lyons. At the present time it is impossible to reconcile these contradictory statements, due to the fact that Ozmec is still in the Fifth Avenue Hospital recovering from a recent operation for appendicitis and cannot be moved or questioned for any length of time.

Inquiry was made of the State Motor Vehicle License Division by telephone, Lieutenant Finn contacting the Police Department representative on regular duty at said Division, who advised him that New York 1934 license no. 4 U 13-41 had been issued to one Richard Hauptmann, 1279 East 222nd Street, for a 1931 model Dodge sedan, motor #DD-42570, serial #3513972. At this time it was also learned that Richard Hauptmann had been issued operator's license #12671161, which bears the same address, and also bears the description of Hauptmann as 35 years, born November 29, 1899, height 5'10", white, 180 lbs., eyes blue, hair blonde. Photostatic copies of the registration and operator's license are attached to the Division copies of this report.

Immediately upon securing the above information, Special Agent Seery communicated same to Special Agent T. H. Sisk, via telephone, who at the time was in the New York office with Lieutenant Arthur Keaten of the New Jersey State Police. Shortly thereafter Special Agent Sisk and Lieutenant Keaten joined Agent Seery, Corporal Horn and Acting Lieutenant Finn, and all five proceeded to the vicinity of 1279 East 222nd Street, and commenced surveillance of these premises, also determining that a Bruno Richard Hauptmann and his wife, Anna, had been residing at these premises since 1931 and that they had a small male child about a year old. It was also ascertained that Hauptmann was a carpenter, apparently unemployed, and that he kept his Dodge sedan in a garage at the side of his house. A check of the Post Office records failed to reveal any information concerning this family except that the Hauptmanns had formerly resided at 1462 Needham Avenue.

The information developed at that time concerning Hauptmann was communicated to Special Agent J. E. Seykora at the New York office, who immediately instituted an investigation to determine all possible facts and information as to this family. Also the writer instructed Special Agent Seykora to have the other Agents assigned to the case available in the event it developed Hauptmann was the individual who was passing the ransom money.

Photostatic copies of Hauptmann's automobile registration and driver's license were immediately obtained by Special Agent Seykora and forwarded to the Division Laboratory for comparison with the ransom notes. Special Agent Seykora also checked the property records and ascertained that the premises at which the Hauptmanns resided were owned by Max Rauch, and that a painter by the name of Victor Schlusser, also resided at the premises in questioned.

The Agents and officers engaged in the surveillance of 1279 East 222nd Street observed that the house was a two-story house apparently containing three families, and in a German neighborhood. The house was located at the corner of East 222nd Street and Needham Avenue, a sparsely settled section one block from the Boston Post Road. It was also observed that a dirt road which in reality was East 223rd Street cut through the rear of the premises about thirty yards from the back of the house, and that it was possible to drive a car from the Hauptmann garage through East 223rd Street.

A conference between the Agents and the officers engaged in the surveillance resulted in the agreement that if Hauptmann left his house he would be followed for the purpose of determining whether he passed any ransom money. The surveillance was maintained by the original five men from 4 P.M. to 9 P.M., at which time a Ford sedan containing New York Police Detectives William Wallace and Chester Cronin and New Jersey State Troopers Dennis Dore and Jack Wallace appeared on the scene. These men immediately started circulating around the neighborhood and around the Hauptmann residence and Special Agent Seery and the writer remonstrated with Acting Lieutenant Finn and Lieutenant Keaten, inasmuch as it had been agreed that no additional men be called to the scene for the time being. It was pointed out to Finn and Keaten that too many men circulating around such a sparsely settled neighborhood would attract attention and that if Hauptmann were actually the man passing the ransom money he would undoubtedly be apprehensive and on the lookout for officers.

Considerable argument as to this question ensued. Lieutenant Keaten stated that he had not ordered his men to the plant and that his two Troopers had merely accompanied the two New York Detectives inasmuch as they had been working with them on the Fordham Road plant. The writer finally advised Keaten and Finn that if they did not adhere to their agreement and instruct the additional men to leave that an equal number of Special Agents would be called to the scene immediately. In the meanwhile, pending the outcome of the talk with these officers, the four additional men left the premises and went downtown to dinner. At approximately 11 P.M. the four additional men again returned, not having been advised by their superiors of the agreement reached. It was then decided that they would remain there until about midnight but would not return the next day.

At about 1 A.M., September 19th, Lieutenant Keaten and Acting Lieutenant Finn both stated that in their opinion the surveillance should be discontinued until the next morning, their reason being that the precinct police officers in squad cars had stopped and questioned the officers and Agents on this detail on a number of occasions, complaints having been received at the precinct from local store-keepers and residents of the neighborhood, who feared that a stick-up was being planned. It is the writer's opinion that these complaints resulted directly from the appearance of the four men on the scene, which men frequently walked up and down past the Hauptmann residence and likewise frequently drove up and down East 222nd Street past the house. In additional Detective William Wallace and Detective Sergeant Jack Wallace walked right up alongside of the Hautpmann residence on Needham Avenue on several occasions and peered into the garage.

The writer during this surveillance was in company with Lieutenant Arthur Keaten in the writer's personally owned Ford coupe. However, when the four additional men appeared on the scene, and pending the decision as to future surveillance, Detective Chester Cronin of the New York Police was taken in the writer's car for a period of approximately an hour and a half. The writer's car was parked between East 222nd and East 223rd Street on Boston Post Road, so that if Hauptmann approached or left his house via East 222nd or East 223rd Street, he would be immediately observed. While parked in this position, which was near a house, the only one on the block, Lieutenant Keaten and Detective Cronin got out of the car and walked up on the lawn of the house in question, with the result that a woman came to the door with a dog and "sicced" the dog on the officers, resulting in considerable noise and confusion. Shortly after this incident a precinct car pulled up alongside of the writer's automobile and inquired as to what was going on, resulting in Detective Cronin exhibiting his New York Police badge to the precinct men and assuring them that everything was all right.

In the meanwhile, Special Agent Seery, Lieutenant Finn and Corporal Horn, were stationed on the Boston Post Road just south of East 222nd Street, in a position to take up the surveillance of Hauptmann in the event he left or entered his residence.

During the one and one half hours that the additional four men were at the scene, they were stationed about a block and a half or two blocks west of the Hauptmann residence on East 222nd Street, in a position to cover entry or departure from or to the west. It was stated that the squad cars from the precinct covering that neighborhood also approached the car occupied by Corporal Horn and the Ford car occupied by Detective Wallace on two occasions and inquired as to what the men were doing at that point. Acting Lieutenant Finn reassured the precinct men by exhibiting his police badge.

About 1:30 A.M., Lieutenant Keaten and Acting Lieutenant Finn both expressed the opinion that the surveillance of the residence should be discontinued until morning, in view of the activity as previously stated, and these officers, together with Corporal Horn, decided to go to their respective homes and hotels for the balance of the night and return the next morning at 7 A.M. Each of these officers, prior to leaving, stated they would not have their additional men at the scene in the morning. Under the circumstances it was deemed advisable to agree with the officers regarding the discontinuance of this surveillance. However, the writer instructed Special Agent Seery to proceed to the nearest subway station as though we were going home for the night but to immediately return and continue the surveillance. In the meanwhile the writer drove Lieutenant Keaten downtown to his hotel and then returned to the office to learn the results of the inquiries instituted by Special Agent J. E. Seykora and to confer with the men thee.

At approximately 3 A.M. the writer returned to the scene of the surveillance and continued same with Agent Seery until approximately 6:15 A.M., when Agent Seery was left in the neighborhood while the writer went downtown to pick up Lieutenant Keaten. Upon arriving at Lieutenant Keaten's hotel, this officer insisted upon having Troopers Wallace and Dore accompany him back to the neighborhood for the purpose of determining whether Lieutenant Finn had his men back on the job, he expressing the opinion that Lieutenant Finn would probably have "half the New York Police Department up there in the morning".

The writer and the Troopers in question arrived back near the Hauptmann residence about 7:15 A.M. and there contacted Agent Seery, after which another argument ensued in connection with the two troopers being present. Lieutenant Keaten promised that as soon as Acting Lieutenant Finn arrived he would have the men returned to the plant at Fordham Road.

Bout 8:15 A.M. Detective Chester Cronin arrived in the neighborhood and shortly thereafter Detective William Wallace, both of the New York Police. About 8:30 A.M. Lieutenant Finn arrived, accompanied by Corporal Horn. Immediately thereafter a conference was had with Lieutenant Finn and Lieutenant Keaten and it was agreed that the men should leave, after the writer threatened to go to a telephone booth and have a group of Special Agents come to the scene. By the time this matter was straightened out it was close to 9 A.M., and in fact at 8:55 A.M. a man answering the description of Hauptmann was observed to come down the front steps of 1279 East 222nd Street and go into the garage alongside the residence and drive out in a 1931 model Dodge sedan bearing New York license plates 4 U 13-41.

The writer was standing on the corner of East 222ndStreet and Boston Post Road talking with Lieutenant Keaten and Detective Chester Cronin was walking down the street when this man came out. When he was observed to drive down the driveway in the Dodge car, Detective Chester Cronin ran back and got in Agent's car, as did also Lieutenant Keaten.

The Dodge car was seen to turn east from the Hauptmann residence and continued to the corner of East 222nd Street and Boston Post Road, at which point the driver seemed to hesitate for a few moments and then turn south on Boston Post Road. The writer, driving his personally owned car, with Keaten and Cronin, followed the Dodge sedan, and Detective William Wallace, who was waiting for Detective Cronin, observing the writer's car pull away in pursuit of another car, followed. The car driven by Detective Wallace contained New Jersey State Troopers J. Wallace and Dennis Dore. Also Corporal Horn, driving a Buick sedan with New Jersey license plates, to which were Acting Lieutenant Finn and Agent Seery, followed along behind the other cars.

As previously stated, Hauptmann in his Dodge sedan turned south on Boston Post Road and proceeded to Pelham

Parkway, then west on Pelham Parkway to Fordham Road and Washington Avenue, thence south on Washington Avenue to East 189th Street, then west on 189th Street to Park Avenue, thence south on Park Avenue to a point in front of #4227 Park Avenue, which is between East 178th Street and East Tremont Avenue, where he was pulled to the curb by a car driven by Detective William Wallace, upon instructions from Acting Lieutenant Finn. As previously stated, it was the original intention of the officers maintaining the surveillance to follow Hauptmann with a view to detecting him in the act of passing some of the ransom money. However, the speed at which he was driving and his actions in constantly looking in his rear vision mirror convinced the officers that Hauptmann was aware of the surveillance and was attempting to elude pursuit. Hauptmann from the time he turned into Boston Post Road until he was stopped by traffic at the point in front of 4227 Park Avenue, maintained an average speed of at least forty miles an hour. During the chase the positions of the three automobiles changed. This was done with a few to deceiving Hauptmann if he was suspicious of the surveillance. At the time Hauptmann's car was stopped the car driven by Detective Wallace was in the lead, immediately behind Hauptmann's car, and was followed by the car driven by Corporal Horn, which in turn was followed by the car driven by the writer.

Upon being stopped, the officers with the exception of the drivers immediately left the automobiles and surrounded Hauptmann's car. Hauptmann was pulled out of his car by Lieutenant Arthur Keaten, Special Agent W. F. Seery, Detective Sergeant Jack Wallace and Detective Chester Cronin, and was immediately searched by Lieutenant Keaten, Acting Lieutenant Finn, and the writer. Lieutenant Keaten pulled Hauptmann's wallet out of the left back trousers pocket and took out of this wallet a $20.00 gold certificate, serial

#A-35517877-A, which was checked against the Division booklet containing the serial numbers of the ransom bills by Special Agent Seery, in the presence of Lieutenant Keaten and the writer, and found to be one of the ransom bills, appearing on page 77 of said booklet. (This number appears on page 8 of the original list prepared by J. P. Morgan & Company.) The bill was then taken inside Hauptmann's car by Agent Seery, who rechecked the bill at that time. It was then handed to Lieutenant Keaten and the latter, Acting Lieutenant Finn, and the writer placed their initials on same. Lieutenant Keaten in the presence of Agent Seery and the writer then turned this bill over to Lieutenant Finn. Photograph of this bill was secured from Acting Lieutenant Finn, and is being forwarded with the Division copies of this report.

When first pulled out of his automobile, Hauptmann was asked his name and address. He replied, "Richard Hauptmann, 1279 East 222nd Street", and while Agent Seery was checking the serial number of the $20.00 bill found in Hauptmann's possession, Hauptmann turned to the writer and said, "What is this about, what are they doing, what is it?" Keaten and the writer replied, "It's counterfeit money", and asked Hauptmann if he had purchased some gasoline at a gas station at the corner of Lexington Avenue and 127th Street a few days previous. Hauptmann replied, "Yes, Monday". Hauptmann was then asked if he had informed the attendant of the gas station that he had "a hundred more just like it" and he replied "Yes, I said that". He was asked if this statement was true and if he did have one hundred more gold certificates and he replied "Yes, at home".

Hauptmann was handcuffed to Detective Sergeant Jack Wallace and with Wallace entered the back seat of his (Hauptmann's) automobile. He was there questioned by Special Agent Seery, Sergeant Wallace, Detective Wallace,

Lieutenant Keaten and the writer, at different intervals, while the detail was awaiting the return of Acting Lieutenant Finn, who had entered a nearby garage to telephone to Police Inspector Lyons at Police Headquarters. In reply to questions Hauptmann at this time advised that he was a carpenter, not regularly employed; that he did odd jobs; that he was unable to recall the last place of his employment, but finally stated that he believed it was at the Majestic Hotel, 72nd Street and Central Park West; however, he could not remember the exact dates of his employment except that it was his last job and that it was in the spring of 1932.

Photostatic copies of the 1932, 1933 and 1934 automobile registration of Richard Hauptmann of 1279 East 222nd Street and of operator's renewal application, 1933-34, 1934-35, were secured by Special Agent H. C. Leslie and forwarded to the Division Laboratory under date of September 19, 1934. Articles found in possession of Bruno Richard Hauptmann by the writer at the time of his apprehension, consisting of

Identification card of the Liberty Mutual Insurance Company, bearing subject's name and address.
A member's card of the Minnieford Canoe Station, City Island, N. Y., bearing subject's name.
A piece of paper baring the name of Henry Uhlig, his address and telephone number, in the handwriting of subject.
Subscription form in subject's handwriting.

After the search and preliminary questioning of Hauptmann it was decided to have him accompany officers to his residence and there conduct a search in his presence. However, Acting Lieutenant Finn insisted that the combined forces await the arrival of Police Inspector John

J. Lyons. This was reluctantly agreed to by the writer after Lieutenant Keaten consented. Keaten stated that in his opinion inasmuch as the pickup was made in New York City, which is within the jurisdiction of the New York Police Department, he felt that it was proper to permit the New York Police to make the arrest and supervise the further search of Hauptmann's residence. As a result of this agreement there was a delay of an hour and a half from the time of Hauptmann's apprehension until the arrival of Inspector Lyons, during which period in order to avoid publicity Hauptmann was driven around the immediate vicinity.

Upon the arrival of Inspector Lyons, the latter, who was accompanied by a New York City detective and his chauffeur, together with the members of the three organizations named above, proceeded to the residence of Bruno Richard Hauptmann at 1279 East 222nd Street and there with the permission of Hauptmann made a hasty search of the rooms on the second floor of this address occupied by Hauptmann. A cursory inspection of the nearby private garage where Hauptmann kept the automobile was made by Inspector Lyons, Lieutenant Keaten, and the writer. This latter inspection was very brief and cursory due to the insistence of Inspector Lyons that the investigators should immediately proceed to the Central Savings Bank and there examine the safe deposit box of Hauptmann, the key to which was found during the search of Hauptmann's residence. For this reason the garage was not thoroughly searched at this time, and a police officer was left on duty at the garage and another at the residence with instructions to see that all callers were taken into custody as they arrived at Hauptmann's residence and that no one be permitted to touch anything in the garage or residence pending further investigation by the three organizations.

Shortly after the arrival of the representatives of the three organizations at the Hauptmann residence, Mrs. Bruno

Richard Hauptmann arrived with her infant son, Manfried, and the search continued with her permission. A list of the articles deemed of interest to the investigation found during this preliminary search of the Hauptmann residence, is set out in the report of Special Agent W. F. Seery, dated September 26, 1934.

During the search the writer found an empty shoe box reflecting that the shoes which had been contained therein were a pair of lady's slippers, size 7 1/2-C, and had been purchased at Jacobson Brothers Exquisite Shoe Corporation, 226 East Fordham Road. Subsequently Mrs. Hauptmann at the writer's request located the shoes and an examination disclosed that they were a pair of suede slippers. Hauptmann and Mrs. Hauptmann admitted that these shoes had been purchased at the Jacobson Brothers store under date of September 7, 1934, and Hauptmann admitted having tendered a $20.00 bill in payment of same, but denied any recollection as to whether or not the $20.00 bill so tendered was a gold certificate. By reference to report of Special Agent W. F. Seery, September 14, 1934, it will be noted that $20.00 gold certificate, serial #A-35272048-A, had been received at the Jacobson Brothers Exquisite Shoe Corporation store from an unknown purchaser during the business of September 7, 1934.

Immediately after the preliminary search of the residence of Bruno Richard Hauptmann, during which keys to the safe deposit box in the Central Savings Bank were discovered, Inspector John J. Lyons, Acting Lieutenant James Finn, Special Agent W. F. Seery, Sergeant J. Wallace and Corporal William Horn of the New Jersey State Police accompanied Hauptmann to the Central Savings Bank, where Hauptmann voluntarily opened safe deposit box #8137, which according to the bank's records had been rented by him January 10, 1933. Examination of the box developed nothing of value. No gold certificates or money of any kind was found in the box. A list of the articles contained in the safe deposit box is set out in the report of Special Agent W. F. Seery, September 27, 1934.

Hauptmann was then taken to the office of the Police Undercover Squad at 156 Greenwich Street, and was there interrogated the balance of the day of September 19, 1934 and the entire morning of September 20, 1934, by Inspector Lyons acting as questioner, submitting to Hauptmann questions suggested by Colonel H. Norman Schwarzkopf, Captain Lamb and Lieutenant Keaten, New Jersey State Police; Acting Lieutenant Finn, New York City Police; and Special Agent W. F. Seery and the writer. Separate report is being submitted covering the results of this interrogation and various investigations growing out of same, subsequently conducted.

Bruno Richard Hauptmann was photographed and fingerprinted at New York Police Headquarters, where his photograph and prints were accorded Police #B-128221. Copy of his fingerprints was forwarded the Division under date of September 20, 1934. Photograph of Hauptmann is being forwarded with the Division copies of this report.

Hauptmann is described as follows:

Age	35
Height	5'9 2/2"
Weight	180
Build	Medium
Hair	Medium chestnut
Eyes	Blue, deep set
Complexion	Fair
	Clean shaven
Teeth	Ordinary
	No marks or scars visible
	High cheekbones
	Slightly pointed chin

Peculiarities	Speaks with decided German accent
Eyeglasses	None
Residence	1279 East 222nd Street, Bronx, New York
Occupation	Carpenter
Marital status	Married—infant son
Race	White
Nationality	German
Citizenship	German
Handwriting specimen	Forwarded Division
Police no.	New York City Police #128221
Photograph	Forwarded Division
Criminal record	3/6/19—Kamenz, Germany

Charge—joint great robbery

Sentence, 2 years, 6 months imprisonment and 4 years loss of civic rights.

On joint highway robbery, 2 years 3 months prison, 2 years loss of civic rights, in addition to punishment under first charge

Source of above record—Identification Service, Berlin, Germany, via Division.

In addition to the above, Hauptmann under the name of Karl Pellmeier attempted illegal entry into the United States July 13, 1923, as a stowaway aboard the S.S. HANOVRE. He was deported July 24, 1923, aboard the S.S. SEYDLITZ.

The title of this report is being changed to include additional alias discovered during the investigation.

PENDING

ANNOTATED BIBLIOGRAPHY

Books by and about Charles Lindbergh

Ahlgren, Gregory and Monier, Stephen. *Crime of the Century: The Lindbergh Kidnaping Hoax.* Brookline Village, Ma.: Branden Publishing Co., 1993. These authors argue that Lindbergh himself killed his son and cremated the body.

Bak, Richard. *Lindbergh: Triumph and Tragedy.* Dallas: Taylor Publishing Co., 2000.

Berg, A. Scott. *Lindbergh.* New York: G.P. Putnam's, 1998. This book won a Pulitzer Prize in Biography and should be considered the definitive biography of Lindbergh.

Fisher, Jim. *The Ghosts of Hopewell: Setting the Record Straight in the Lindbergh Case.* Carbondale, Ill.: Southern Illinois University Press, 1999. Fisher is a former FBI agent who argues that the Lindbergh baby case was simply an attempt by Hauptmann to get some badly-needed money by kidnaping the baby.

Jones, Wayne D. *Murder of Justice: New Jersey's Greatest Shame.* New York: Vantage Press, 1997.

Kennedy, Ludovic Henry. *Crime of the Century: The Lindbergh Kidnaping and the Framing of Richard Hauptmann.* New York: Penguin USA, 1996. This book was first published in 1985 as *The Airman and the Carpenter.*

Lindbergh, Charles. *Autobiography of Values.* New York: Harcourt Brace Jovanovich, 1977.
———. *Of Flight and Life.* New York: Scribner's, 1948.
———. *The Spirit of St. Louis.* New York: G.P. Putnam's, 1927. Reprint edition; New York: Scribner's, 1953.
———. *The Wartime Journals of Charles A. Lindbergh.* New York: Harcourt Brace Jovanovich, 1970.
———. *We.* New York: GP. Putnams, 1927.

Luckett, Perry D. *Charles A. Lindbergh.* Westport, Ct.: Greenwood Press, 1986.

Mosley, Leonard. *Lindbergh: A Biography.* New York: Doubleday & Co., 1976.

Ross, Walter S. *Last Hero: Charles A. Lindbergh.* New York: Harper & Row, 1968.

Waller, George. *Kidnap: The Story of the Lindbergh Case.* New York: The Dial Press, 1961.

APPENDIX

The following are sample pages from the FBI Files on the Lindbergh Baby Kidnaping case.

N.Y. File 62-3057

CHRONOLOGY

Feb. 26, 1932 -- Colonel and Mrs. Lindbergh with Charles A., Jr., leave
(Friday)   Englewood, N. J. to spend week-end at new home near Hopewell.
                 Whately already there - Nurse Betty Gow left at Englewood.

Feb. 27, -- -- Lindberghs and child at Hopewell.

Feb. 28, -- -- Lindberghs and child at Hopewell.

Feb. 29, -- -- 9:00 A.M., Colonel Lindbergh leaves Hopewell and spends day
               in New York City. Sleeps this night at Englewood. Mrs.
               Lindbergh and child still at Hopewell.

March 1, -- -- 10:30 A.M., Mrs. Lindbergh extends usual week-end stay at
               Hopewell - telephones Morrow home and speaks to Violet
               Sharpe - leaves message for Nurse Betty Gow to proceed to
               Hopewell and advises family will remain at Hopewell due to
               baby's cold.

               1 to 2:00 P.M., Betty Gow arrives in Morrow car driven by
               Chauffeur Ellerson.

               5:00 P.M., Mrs. Lindbergh returns from walk. Nurse Gow
               sews flannel under shirt for baby to wear.

               6:00 P.M., Sebastian B. Lupica observes men driving 1929
               Dodge Sedan with ladders in it on highway near Lindbergh
               home.

               7:30 P.M., Colonel Lindbergh telephones home - advises on
               way from New York. Mrs. Lindbergh and Nurse Gow prepare
               baby for bed.

               8:00 P.M., Lindbergh baby asleep in nursery on second floor -
               last seen by Betty Gow. Colonel Breckinridge phones Lindbergh
               home relative to Colonel Lindbergh's absence from banquet.

13

N.Y. File 62-3057 - Chronology

March 1, 1932 -   6 to 10:00 P.M., Betty Gow in kitchen or west parlor on
(Continued)   first floor. Whatelys in kitchen on first floor.

8:30 to 11:05 P.M., Violet Sharpe, Morrow waitress, with
escort and another couple allegedly at "Peanut Grill"
roadhouse in the Oranges, N. J.

8:25 P.M., Lindbergh arrives home from New York in car
alone - telephones New York explaining absence from
New York University banquet engagement.

8:30 - 9:15 P.M., Dinner served to Lindberghs in dining
room.

8:35 P.M., Henry "Red" Johnson telephones Betty Gow -
informs her he is leaving for Hartford, Conn. and inquires
about baby's health.

9:15 to 9:30 P.M., Lindberghs in parlor next to dining room.

9:45 P.M., Colonel and Mrs. Lindbergh hear noise apparently
outside - resembling two boards striking - attribute it to
natural causes.

9:50 - 10:00 P.M., Lindbergh in library under nursery.

10:00 P.M., Betty Gow discovers baby gone - informs Lindberghs
Colonel Lindbergh finds note on window sill of nursery demanding $50,000 ransom. Lindbergh and Whately search premises and
immediate vicinity.

10-20 P.M., and shortly following, Lindbergh telephones Hopewell
Deputy Police Chief Williamson, who calls for Chief Wolfe -
they proceed to Lindbergh home - suggest notifying State Police.

Ladder and chisel apparently left by kidnapers found near house.

10:40 P.M., Lindbergh telephones New Jersey State Police
Headquarters, Trenton - State Police assume charge of case.

10:50 P.M., News teletyped to police in New Jersey and
neighboring states.

Traces of mud found on floor of nursery and footprints found
on ground under nursery window.

12:00 P.M., No fingerprints found or developed, after expert
search and examination.

New York File 62-3057

NARRATIVE

On Tuesday night, March 1, 1932, between 8 P.M. and 10 P.M., Charles Augustus Lindbergh, Jr., 20 months old son of Colonel Charles A. Lindbergh and Anne Morrow Lindbergh, was kidnaped from his nursery on the second floor of the Lindbergh home, situated on a five hundred acre estate, which is partly in Mercer County and partly in Hunterdon County, New Jersey, the residence being in the latter county and three miles north of the nearest town, Hopewell, N. J. Betty Gow, the baby's nurse since shortly after his birth, was the person who discovered the baby was missing. She immediately notified Mrs. Lindbergh, then in the bathroom, and Colonel Lindbergh, who was downstairs in the library directly beneath the nursery. He came upstairs and with Mrs. Lindbergh and Betty Gow entered the baby's room where he observed a number of small particles of mud between the windows at the southeast corner of the room and the baby's crib, which was located in the far corner of the room away from the windows. An inspection of the room and the baby's bed by his parents indicated that the bed clothes were still pinned on the bed as Betty Gow had left them when she last saw the child, about 8 P.M.

On the window sill of the east window, Colonel Lindbergh found a note in a small, plain white envelope, which was unaddressed. The window was closed and the note had been placed on the window sill inside of the nursery. The note, very crudely written, read as follows:

"Mr. Col. Lindbergh
Hopewell, N. J.

Dear Sir:

Have 50,000 $ redy 25 000 $ in 20$ bills 15 000 $ in 10$ bills and 10 000 $ in 5$ bills. After 2-4 days we will inform you were to deliver the mony.

We warn you for making anyting public or for notify the Police. The child is in gut care. Indication for all letters are singature.

Ans. L 3 holes "

45

New York File 62 J57 - **Narrative**

This note bore a peculiar symbol signature. A photostatic copy of the ransom note, as well as other ransom notes received in this case, are attached to the instant report and will show clearly the nature of the symbol in question and the crudeness of the handwriting.

After the discovery of the ransom note, which was read by Colonel Lindbergh and his butler, Ollie Whately, Colonel Lindbergh and Whately immediately ran outside of the house and searched the grounds nearby, while Mrs. Lindbergh and Mrs. Whately peered out the nursery windows and heard a faint cry apparently coming from some distance. At approximately 10:20 P.M., Colonel Lindbergh, despite the warning in the ransom note, personally telephoned Deputy Chief of Police Charles E. Williamson, of Hopewell, and the New Jersey State Police. Since Lindbergh was able to put through those calls, the telephone wires leading to the Lindbergh estate had obviously not been cut. Williamson had retired for the night and there was some delay while he dressed, and there was further delay when he stopped to pick up Chief of Police Harry Wolf of Hopewell. These two officers arrived at the Lindbergh home at approximately 10:40 P.M. At 10:50 P.M. a flash on the kidnaping was teletyped throughout the East from police headquarters, Newark, N. J. Upon looking over the scene of the crime, the Hopewell officers suggested that Colonel Lindbergh get a fingerprint expert from Trenton to examine the ransom note and the nursery for fingerprints, and accordingly, Colonel Lindbergh called the State Police at Trenton and about midnight, State Trooper Frank Kelly, a fingerprint expert, arrived and powdered the ransom note and sections of the baby's nursery, but was unable to bring out any fingerprints whatsoever. Subsequently, efforts made by other experts were also unsuccessful.

The nursery window, through which it appeared the baby had been removed, is approximately fourteen feet from the ground. Inside the nursery, against the wall and just below the window in question, was a long, low cedar chest, on top of which was a large black suitcase, and on this was a child's "Tinker toy" on wheels. Betty Gow and Mrs. Lindbergh had observed the arrangement of these articles before and after the kidnaping, and stated there was no indication they had been disturbed. A close examination failed to reveal mud particles, footprints, or fingerprints on them. Experiments conducted by the New Jersey State Police showed that it was possible to hurdle these articles in effecting an entrance through the window if a certain amount of dexterity were used. However, it appeared to be a very difficult task for anyone to go out of the window with a thirty pound baby in his arms, without disturbing the objects at the window, or leaving a muddy footprint, mud particle or other telltale evidence on the objects. The walls of the Lindber

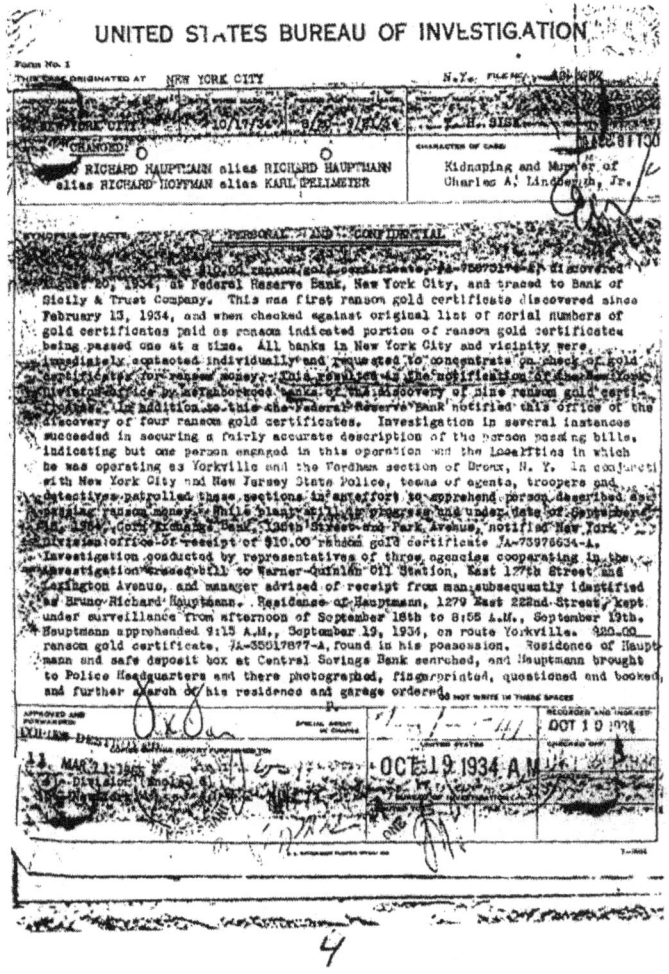

```
2-3057.
```

Criminal record Sentence, 2 years, 6 months
(continued)   imprisonment and 4 years loss
              of civic rights.

On joint highway robbery, 2
years 3 months prison, 2 years
loss of civic rights, in addition
to punishment under first charge.

Source of above record – Identification
Service, Berlin, Germany, via Division.

In addition to the above, Hauptmann under the name of
Karl Pellmeier attempted illegal entry into the United States July 13,
1923, as a stowaway aboard the S.S. HANNOVER. He was deported July 24,
1923, aboard the S.S. SEYDLITZ.

The title of this report is being changed to include
additional aliases discovered during the investigation.

PENDING

ABOUT THE EDITOR

Thomas Fensch is the editor of the Top Secret series and is the publisher of New Century Books.

He has written or edited over twenty books of nonfiction, published since 1970.

His previous books include:

Steinbeck and Covici:
    The Story of a Friendship
Conversations with John Steinbeck
Conversations with James Thurber
The Man Who Was Walter Mitty:
    The Life and Work of James Thurber
Of Sneetches and Whos and the Good Dr. Seuss:
    Essays on the Writings and Life of Theodor Geisel
The Man Who Was Dr. Seuss:
    The Life and Work of Theodor Geisel
Writing Solutions:
    Beginnings, Middles & Endings

Thomas Fensch has a Ph.D. degree from Syracuse University and lives near Houston.

www.ingramcontent.com/pod-product-compliance
Lightning Source LLC
Chambersburg PA
CBHW021912180426
43198CB00034B/125